Soccer
and
Philosophy

Popular Culture and Philosophy®
Series Editor: George A. Reisch

For full details of all **Popular Culture and Philosophy**® books, visit **www.opencourtbooks.com**.

Popular Culture and Philosophy®

Soccer and Philosophy

Beautiful Thoughts on the Beautiful Game

Edited by

TED RICHARDS

OPEN COURT
Chicago and La Salle, Illinois

To Corin—the only one I could never 'meg

Volume 51 in the series, Popular Culture and Philosophy®,
edited by George A. Reisch

Permission is acknowledged to the following: Corbis, for the
front cover picture of David Beckham, ©Reuters/CORBIS;
iStockphoto.com, for the pictures on pages 36, 160, 214, 346, and
368; Shutterstock, for the pictures on pages 5, 105, 139, 197, 251,
and 317.

**To order books from Open Court, call toll-free 1-800-815-2280,
or visit our website at www.opencourtbooks.com.**

Open Court Publishing Company is a division of Carus Publishing
Company.

Library of Congress Cataloging-in-Publication Data

Soccer and philosophy : edited by Ted Richards.
    p. cm. —(Popular culture and philosophy ; v. 51)
    Includes bibliographical references and index.
    ISBN 978-0-8126-9676-9 (trade paper : alk. paper)
    1. Soccer—Philosophy I. Richards, Ted, 1968-
    GV943.S645 2010
    796.33401—dc22

                            2010007732

Contents

SECOND EXTRA-TIME
Soccer and Society

KICKS FROM THE MARK
It's Down to Penalties

THE OFFICIALS

THE POST GAME INTERVIEW 379

It's a Simple Game, Really

TED RICHARDS

Take a ball. Move it, bounce it, run with it, keep it in the air.

Just don't use your hands.

Such a simple idea. But a surprisingly fun amusement.

Now add nine of your friends. Pass the ball back and forth. Try to control it within an enclosed area. Try to get it into a net eight yards wide by eight feet high.

Just do it without your hands.

Still simple; and a great way to pal around with your buds.

Now add ten other people, but still use just one ball. This other ten, they will try to pass the ball; they will try to get it into their own net. All the while trying everything they can to keep you and your friends from passing the ball, from getting the ball into your net.

And nobody is using their hands; at least not on the ball.

A bit more chaotic, sure, but not complicated. All you have to do is get the ball into the back of the net. Simple.

Now add two more people, a guard for each net.

And let them use their hands.

Now we have some real fun! In fact, it's so good that a few people might stop by to watch. And they too will be entranced by this simple game.

Play the game with finesse and agility, strength and speed, intelligence, foresight and style, against a few who are intent on preventing you with guile and brutish rancor, and more than a few will watch. Billions of people will be enthralled. Grown adults will weep in frustration or cry out with joy according to your fortunes. Total strangers will lean on each other in despair, or dance in exultation, depending on how you play. Children will be named after you. Captains of industry will mortgage their lives in an attempt to ride on your coattails. Cities will stop, halting in mid-breath, just to follow your exploits.

All because you can make a ball dance, in a tangle of high-speed human traffic, in the biggest venues constructed by humanity, without using your hands.

Such a simple thing, when compared to the fervor and fanaticism evoked.

This is soccer as we know it.

The fascination with soccer is remarkable not only in the strength of the passions kindled, but also in the way it transcends every human division. Social, cultural, economic, educational, national, regional, tribal, even gender—soccer's enchantment cuts across all these differences.

Not even philosophers have been immune to soccer's spell.

This is the origin of the book you now hold in your hands. I am a philosopher who loves soccer. I have spent the majority of my life either playing, coaching, refereeing, or just watching soccer. When I'm not engaged in soccer, I'm contemplating questions as universal as soccer's fascination. Questions like: What makes a thing that thing? What is the right thing to do? What makes something beautiful? Why am I part of this group? What is the best way to organize a society? Is there such a thing as luck? How can I judge things correctly? How does language convey meaning? These questions, in one form or another, have been wondered about for thousands of years, and, on the face of things, have little or nothing to do with soccer.

But these questions are human questions. They are a part of us. They don't make us who we are, so much as they arise out of our being. That is why they have continued to pique our collective curiosity, to demand our intellectual energy, urging debate in ivory towers and neighborhood pubs, for thousands of years.

Our fascination with soccer must come out of the same place. The worldwide zeal, the excitement that emanates from the boardroom to the barrio, the all-inclusive, all-embracing rapture can only be explained by a common well-spring. Soccer has become such a universally loved game (in a mere 150 or so years) because ultimately soccer is a human game like no other. Thus the study of soccer—be it historical, sociological, economic, or philosophical—is a study of humanity, in all its glory and debauchery. And there is nothing more worthy than that.

Crazy, huh? But, oh so simple.

It turns out that I'm not the only crazy one. There are lots of philosophers who are as infatuated with the game as I am; philosophers for whom the game is an integral part of who they are. And there are other (non-philosopher) fanatics who have pondered the essential questions of philosophy through the lens of soccer. There are so many out there, in fact, that I could have edited three books. But reading such a book would take too much time away from what's important (soccer!), so I've limited the book to thirty-one chapters.

As you turn through the pages, you'll see Kierkegaard and Aristotle, Plato and Nietzsche, Kant, Dewey, and Sartre. You'll also see Pelé and Maradona, Zidane and Cristiano Ronaldo, Messi, Fàbregas, and Beckenbauer. But mostly you'll see very bright and intelligent folk— people who know their philosophy—writing passionately about the game they love. And, when it comes right down to it, that's what's worth reading.

The universality of the appeal of soccer is reflected in the international team of authors: forty authors from fifteen different countries. Each with their own particular perspective on the game. As editor, I have tried to keep their language as close to the original as possible, in an attempt to preserve their unique voice. I have not selected between British or American spellings, punctuation, or the name of the game; rather I have allowed each author to use what they were most comfortable with. I don't expect this will cause undue confusion for you the reader. For whether the word is "Football" or "Calcio," "Fußball" or "Futballcipö," "Fútbol," "Fotball," "Bōōl bō," "Voetbal," or "Soccer," we all know what it is: glorious!

Because at the end of the analysis, it's a simple game, really: get the ball into the back of the net.

Just don't use you hands.

THANKS

Thanks to all the authors for the effort and joy they put into their chapters; that this project has been a unique pleasure is due in large part to them. And thanks Cuteness for encouraging me to undertake this project and for supporting me along the way.

FIRST HALF

The Nature of
the Game

1

Why Is Football So Fascinating?

PAUL HOYNINGEN-HUENE

You may be scratching your head when you read this: What? Why is football so fascinating? Isn't that about as obvious as can be?

Yes, indeed, it is. Or so it appears. Or, more precisely, so it appeared to me, until 2002.

2002?

Yes, 2002.

Remember the FIFA world cup in South Korea and Japan? My son, aged ten at the time, was really into football. So I watched many games with him, more than I would have done, had he not dragged me into watching them. Somewhat tired one evening and not especially interested in the particular game, a strange thought crossed my mind. What is so special about a ball crossing a line between two posts? Why are so many people, including me, watching it, sometimes with an incredible degree of emotional tension? Sure, the ball crossing the line means a goal being scored. But still, why cheer or bemoan a ball crossing a conventionally defined line? Is this a world-shattering event? No, it's of no more importance than a leaf dropping from some tree. It is not one of those events which we really cheer or mourn, like getting a dream job or falling in love, or like having a bad accident or losing a loved one, or the outbreak or the end of a war, be it in victory or in defeat. The emergence of strong feelings in these cases is not particularly mysterious, but in the case of the goal it is. This cannot just be a ball crossing a line: it must be more. But exactly what?

Having been a professional philosopher for a long time, I immediately realized that this is one of the rare moments of a genuine philosophical experience. It works like this: You are famiiar with a certain phenomenon. You know it, you've experienced it many times, you've

7

shared your experience with others, and it's just a common thing, nothing special. Suddenly, the being-taken-for-granted of the phenomenon cracks. Suddenly, the phenomenon, at least some aspects of it, becomes mysterious. That's the philosophical experience: something entirely self-evident loses this quality and becomes a puzzle, completely unexpectedly. If you want to find out what's going on, the first step is usually to explore the puzzlement: What exactly is it that used to be not mysterious, but is so now? What is the source of this air of mystery? And why was it not mysterious before? You try to understand as many aspects of the puzzle as possible *before* trying to resolve it. That's important because otherwise you don't realize the size and the nature of the problem, and your answers will tend to be superficial. In a second step, we work on answers to solve the puzzle: that is, gaining an understanding for which there was no need before, before the crack in the self-evidence of the phenomenon occurred. But first things first.

Football's Universality

So let's look more closely at the puzzling aspects of the fascination of football.

First, there are the spectators. Within some 150 years, football has turned from a British college peculiarity into a truly global phenomenon. Asia became part of the world football community a few decades ago, and even in the United States with its own garden variety of locally favorite sports, soccer keeps on gaining more and more followers. There is only one continent on which football is comparatively unimportant, and this is Antarctica—but many other important things are unimportant there, too! Of course, these geographical differences are closely linked to cultural differences, but as soon as football is concerned, these cultural differences apparently become more and more unimportant.

Football's universality, however, is amazing not only in geographical and cultural terms. Every society is somehow vertically structured, according to income, education, social status, power, and the like. This vertical structure (or more precisely: this set of partly overlapping vertical structures) is very important for many aspects of societal life. Just look at who enjoys the opera, who enjoys holidays on yachts, who actually enjoys driving fancy cars, who enjoys owning race horses, who enjoys large amounts of beer in smoky bars, who enjoys exerting power, and so on, and you predominantly find people from one or the other segment of the societal ladder. But when it comes to football, these differences in societal hierarchy by and large disappear: amongst football fans, there are sophisticated sensitive poets, rough blue collar workers, highly educated professors of philosophy or medicine, clerks who hardly read a newspaper let alone a book, priests having devoted their life to God, atheists of all sorts, wealthy and powerful businessmen and managers, the unemployed and poor bachelors whose only joy in life is football (and beer, perhaps), glamorous kings, princes, or movie stars, any Tom, Dick and Harry, and so on.

Another difference among human beings, extremely important in almost all other contexts, plays no role in football-mania: age (at least if you are over four or so). Kids may get as excited over football as senior citizens, and as everyone in between.

Apart from these geographical, cultural, societal and age differences that do not strongly affect football fascination, even the arguably most important difference among human beings loses influence: gender. Traditionally, of course, football was a men's sport. "Traditionally", of course, means societies that were much more male-dominated than today's Western societies. The decrease of the importance of gender differences in society also brought about an increase of female interest in football (and an equalization of smoking habits, for instance). Today the proportion of female spectators of football is between ten and twenty percent, but moving up. Although other behavioral differences among males and females have not changed (like going to the bathroom alone or together with your best friend), with respect to football the two genders are substantially approaching each other.

So, all these otherwise very important differences among human beings—geography, culture, societal status, age, and gender—are insignificant when it comes to being subject to football's fascination. There are many other things that find (almost) universal interest among human beings like food, drinks, shelter, sex, health, and so on. No big surprise, because there is a common biological basis for the universality of these interests. Football, however, is a specific cultural product of a very special and tiny segment of a very special society in a very special geographic location in a very special historical time—and it becomes universal in some 150 years. Isn't that amazing?

Football's Intense Emotions

The second amazing feature of football's fascination is the intensity of emotional excitement and its public exhibition, especially by men. This concerns both positive and negative feelings, like explosions of joy and tears of frustration and sorrow. To capture the astounding character of these events, compare them with other occasions for exposure of intense feelings. Take, for example, the behavior of a CEO, dressed in a smart double-breasted suit with a decent tie, at a stockholder meeting when announcing a five billion profit or, for that matter, a five billion loss. This is truly important, and emotionally moving, information both to him and his audience. Nonetheless, the emotions actually shown are low-key. He (yes, he, because most CEOs *are* male) will most certainly not wave his arms in the air and shout "yeah, yeah" several times before hugging his vice president whilst jumping up and down laughing. Or, in the negative case, he will most certainly not kick his lectern several times, punch the air with his fist, his red face contorted in anger, and finally turn away shouting to the ground, his fist still moving. But that's exactly what you can see when observing the manager during an important (or not so important) match. He may well be dressed exactly like the CEO, and some of them really look like CEOs (and, by the way, in top flight football they also earn as much as CEOs!) but he will still behave very differently from a CEO in doing his job. The fans behave very much in the same way. Look at the publicly displayed joy or sorrow at the end of an important game. Do you often see tears publicly running down the cheek of a fifty year old man? So the existence of very strong emotions and the apparent legitimacy of their public display is another interesting and puzzling feature of football.

Thirdly, and this makes the existence of these strong emotions and the underlying fascination of football even more mysterious, consider the incredible banality of the main subject of these emotions. It is all about whether a ball of roughly 430 grams of weight and a circumference of sixty-nine centimeters has passed through, with its full diameter, an absolutely arbitrary surface defined by goals placed on a patch of lawn. Compare this event to events like the end of World War II, the Moon landings, or the fall of the Berlin Wall. People were extremely excited about these events, and for good reason. In the case of the end of a war, for example, people's well-being and the safety of their lives depend considerably on such events so it is unsurprising that they evoke strong emotions. In addition, these are very rare or even unique events. But a ball passing through an imaginary surface of eight by twenty-four foot? This event has no intrinsic value whatsoever, and goals are scored by the dozen every weekend.

Here's an objection. There are other processes apparently missing intrinsic value that we take very seriously indeed, such as the transfer of pieces of paper that have something printed on them (like dollar bills) or putting one's signature under something written (like a contract). Again, the action itself and the material involved are exceedingly ordinary. However, these actions stand for something else, broadly speaking for the transfer of certain property rights or the binding commitment to a contract. In contrast, the achieved goal in football does not stand for something else, it is just a goal, and its only importance is its contribution to the final result of the match. The consequence of the result of the match is again a contribution to something larger of roughly the same kind, namely the table position in the respective league. And what is the consequence of a certain position in a specific league? This table position determines whether, in the next season, you are allowed to play in the same league or a better or a worse one.

So in contrast to money transfers or the signing of contracts, the results of football have consequences that are of the same nature as the actions constituting football itself and are therefore incapable of explaining what football is all about. If you don't find this easy to accept, take the following analogy. Suppose someone suggests to you that you should raise your hand three times in the space of five seconds. Your may ask in return why you would do that. The answer is that once you've fulfilled this task, you are required to again raise your hands three times in five seconds. This isn't much of an incentive, and you won't understand what the point of the whole procedure is. The same holds true for football. Success or failure in football has consequences in exactly the same area, so in order to understand the meaning of success or failure you must understand these events in themselves and not by their consequences. (I am aware of the financial consequences for the respective clubs and teams but they have only secondary significance, as I will show below.)

Fourth, the event of an achieved goal is, in itself, not only exceedingly ordinary. On top of that, the means by which it is accomplished are extremely artificial. Biologically, human beings are distinguished from other animals by characteristics such as their brain and their hands, the latter having acquired its special function from walking upright, freeing them for other uses than locomotion. One would think that human beings enjoy the use of their hands tremendously, and that in the setting of games, their hands (and brains) would play a preeminent role. But in football they don't. Instead, we are only allowed to use our clumsy feet and our, not necessarily less clumsy, heads (and other clumsy parts of the body) to move the ball in football (apart from the keeper, of course, and for throw-ins). The rules of football outlaw the use of our hands which are extraordinarily well-suited to handle objects of the size of footballs (and smaller) in a very controlled way. Why do we handicap ourselves in such an artificial way? And why are we fascinated by the outcome of these highly artificial processes? I guess that other animals watching us humans playing football are deeply irritated: these animals envy us for our extremely fine-tuned hands that are governed by a fine brain (fine in principle, anyway), and we're not really using our hands in our most cherished game?

There are other elements of artificiality in football. Just take the off-side rule. Why make the beautiful game so complicated that some people never understand the rule (it's an ugly prejudice that this mainly applies to women) and that the referees need two independently movable eyes in order to apply that rule? You're not allowed to give a little push to the opposing player who has the ball that you want of have, or to punch him a little when he annoys you, or to shout at the referee when he's made a mistake to your disadvantage. These are completely natural human behavioral traits, but in football, they are prohibited by virtue of the time-honored concept of good sportsmanship, as if they were inhuman or something! Very strange, indeed.

Re-enacting the Drama of Life

So far, I've tried to deepen your sense of puzzlement about the existing fascination of football. Now, I have to resolve the puzzlement and I will do so by suggesting a thesis. But I ought to tell you right away that in philosophy, a good thesis is never the end of the story. Instead, a good thesis in philosophy has so much content in condensed form that it needs unpacking. Knowing just the thesis is thus merely the beginning; only a discussion of the thesis makes clear what it really means. Okay, here's the thesis that explains the fascination of the beautiful game: *Football re-enacts the drama of life.*

The first thing we'll have to discuss in order to really understand the thesis is the question, what does the drama of life consist of? I'll tell you a story. Imagine that you want to bake a cake. You take your cookbook from the shelf, you identify the appropriate recipe, you check the ingredients, you go to the grocery store and buy these ingredients in the required quantities, you go home again and prepare the batter according to the recipe, you put the batter in a pan, you put the pan into the pre-heated oven for some forty-five minutes, and then you're done.

Where's the drama? There isn't any. There's no dramatic element in this story because everything went just according to plan. You had the intention to bake the cake, you had a plan to accomplish this, you carried out the plan, and this is it. It's an everyday occurrence when every-thing works according to plan; nothing surprising, nothing exciting, and nothing dramatic (unless you've never baked a cake in which case you would probably be putting your life at risk). You would never tell the story of this particular baking adventure unless you did it for educational reasons concerning baking, but certainly not to entertain a crowd by sharing something exciting of your life.

Contrast this dull baking experience with a story such as this one: you went sailing with two friends of yours, so you went to the harbor where your boat is, you brought the four six-packs that you bought beforehand with you on board. The sun was shining, but after an hour or so a heavy storm started and it was too late to return. Then, suddenly, the mast broke, one man went overboard and in trying to pull him back aboard he slipped back into the water several times. Then a ship, appar-ently on its way to rescue you, did in fact not recognize your dangerous situation and turned away again. Then it was slowly and dangerously darkening and on top of all of that, the electricity on board went down, so you couldn't switch on the light. At the very last moment—one of your friends had already started fighting with you because he thought that he could do better at the helm—a ship moved alongside and res-cued you all. This is undoubtedly a dramatic story. But what's the dif-ference between this story and the boring story about baking a cake?

The difference is that not everything worked out according to plan. There are countless possibilities why something may not work out according to our plans. It may be due to miscalculations, stupidity, inep-titude, wishful thinking and so on our side, or due to interference by others, or to unexpected circumstances of all other sorts. We know that not every attempt to realize a plan is successful because there are myri-ads of possible obstacles. So we devise different sorts of tactics and atti-tudes, and different people do so in different ways, in order to realize their plans: we do it alone or with a team, directly or rather indirectly, with brutal power or soft persuasion, in a fair or an unfair way, through hard work or through brilliant inspirations, audaciously or timidly, and so on and so on. But whatever we try to do, be it pursuing a university career, maintaining a happy relationship, raising children, staying healthy, founding a company, helping in an accident, emigrating or immigrating—in whatever way we try to achieve our goals, in these larger projects we are always dependent on circumstances that are not in our hands. Sometimes, someone achieves something that one would guess is completely out of his reach—he nevertheless succeeds. This could be said to simply be good luck. Sometimes, we're well-prepared for our task and still fail, perhaps even unfairly; bad luck. Sure, these cases exist. However, in the longer run (or statistically), you're better off the better you are equipped with the relevant abilities and capacities for your tasks. Yet, there is never a guarantee that you will succeed no matter how well-prepared you are when it comes to things that count in life. And there is fool's luck—sometimes. So it is this unavoidable mixture of our own capabilities and willful actions with good and back luck—something relevant to your actions but outside of our control—that is characteristic of most of what we do. This is what I mean by the drama of life.

Games and Real Life

It should be pretty obvious by now that football contains very similar elements. The fundamental difference is that football is a game: it's not real life in all its seriousness, but a game. What's the fundamental difference between real life and a game (like football)? Just look at the real life goals that I mentioned above: a well-paid career, a happy relationship, raising children, good health, a functioning company, a successful emigration or immigration, and so on. There is something important at stake; these things have intrinsic value in life.

In a game, however, the primary goal of the game has no intrinsic value whatsoever: a ball crossing a line or falling into a basket, accumulating the most monopoly money, achieving a certain formation of wooden pieces (in chess, say), possessing, at the end of the game, more playing cards of a certain kind than your opponent, and so on. These events are intrinsically worthless. They have meaning and worth only within the game, in the particular little universe that the game willfully creates as a contrast to real life with all its seriousness. Games are much lighter than real life.

The key to love of games is that they contain the same elements as real life, but without the burden. In games, we play life; in specific games, we play specific aspects of life. The game of football is especially rich in re-enacting the most important ingredients of life's drama. To see this, we need only analyze the rules of football with respect to their function. There is no need to explain these rules in detail, as anyone reading this book will be familiar with them. (If you want to know the fine print, go to FIFA's webpage and have a look at the seventeen "Laws of the Game".) These rules have been fairly stable for more than one hundred years, more precisely since 1898. It's no exaggeration to say that they define the game, as the rules of chess define the game of chess.

Why the Game Has Rules

There are four main functions of the rules of football. These rules:

- **guarantee equal conditions for both teams in certain respects,**

- **generate the analogies to the drama of real life,**

- **bring the drama of the game to an end, and**

- **secure the distance of the game from the seriousness of real life.**

The first function of the rules of the game is pretty obvious: equal conditions for both teams. There are the same rules for both teams, the same size of the goals, the same number of players, a change of sides after half time, a referee who is neutral, and so on. Also the separation of teams into different leagues serves this very purpose: teams of roughly the same strength should compete. Note, however, that the complete equality of the teams is never achieved. Players have different abilities, different clubs have vastly differing monetary resources (which is very important in professional football), the game is supported in different ways in different countries, and so on. The sort and the amount of equality that the rules of football provide is just the same sort of equality that can be realized in real life even under optimal conditions, say, before the law or in an educational system. The individuals bring with them differences that play out in life, these differences can never be eradicated completely, these equality generating conditions being what they are. Similarly, in football, fairness with respect to equal treatment of the teams is high, but not complete. This is already an analogy to real life.

Football is full of these analogies, especially regarding the dramatic element of life. The essence of the drama of life is the mixture of (more or less) well-planned and well-prepared intentional actions with good and bad luck. For short, I will call these two factors *"ability"* and *"chance."* Both factors play a role, but in the long run—or at least in the very long run!—ability tends to pay off. However, the chance factor may even entirely dominate a certain course of events, both in the direction of good and back luck.

The similarity to football should already be obvious, but let me develop the details of the analogy further because they are interesting and fairly subtle. The secret of the beautiful game is its variability in the mixture of the two elements. This concerns parts of a match of very different lengths: from the fraction of a second like in controlling the ball after a high cross, a few seconds like in a short dribble or a brief one-on-one, some ten or twenty seconds, such as in a well-orchestrated attack, significant fractions of an hour like in a certain strategy of defense, to the full length of the match or even of a season. (If you want to express that in a highly sophisticated fashion, you may say that football has something like a fractal structure, or self-similarity, with respect to the mixture of ability of chance: the same sort of mixture exists on very different time scales.) Ability or chance may dominate the course of events in severely unequal proportions, or they may be more or less equally mixed; everything is possible in this context.

The rules of football are designed to generate just this: an unforeseeable mixture of ability and chance, on very many different time intervals, ranging from fractions of a second to the full year (and even beyond, if you take into account that a club may be promoted or relegated as a result of the season's final outcome). So the spectators are permanently confronted with what they are familiar with from their own lives: the unforeseeable mixture of ability and chance where one or the other may dominate. Just look at the result of a match. There are "just" results and there are "unjust" results. The former when the superior team wins, the latter when the inferior team wins, and of course, both outcomes are possible. Remember those matches where the superior team continuously attacks for ninety minutes but never succeeds, and in the final minute the inferior team scores (for example, Manchester United vs. Bayern Munich, Champions League Final 1999)!

A Mixture of Ability and Chance

This mixture of ability and chance occurs throughout the game. To control a ball with your head or foot is much more complicated than with your hands; you need much more skill, and at the same time the element of chance is much bigger. The smallest imperfection of the pitch can cause a bobble that, while not changing the overall direction of the ball, can cause it to be mis-controlled if it dances the wrong way. Whether the ball jumps left or right, or deflects at all, due to that imperfection is a matter of chance. The result is that even during the shortest periods of ball control, both of the dramatic elements are present, with an unpredictable mixture of their relative strengths. Of course, some players are better at controlling the ball than others and in the long run, this pays off. But even for these players, there's no guarantee that in a particular instance they will be able to control the ball; every football fan remembers most astounding examples of extremely skilled players losing the ball—anything can happen.

This mixture is important not only in the small scale of touches, but in the large scale of whole tournaments as well. The World Cup is organized first with a group phase, as a round-robin, and then with a knockout phase. Why? The general idea behind this organization is that in the group phase, the element of ability plays a more prominent role. Of course, it doesn't when the groups are formed: here the element of chance is entirely explicit! However, once the groups are formed, the element of ability is comparatively strong because by means of every team in the group playing every other team, spectacular cases of good or bad luck can be corrected. Statistically, you can expect that the better teams will prevail. The idea is to have the best teams in the knockout phase. In this phase, however, the element if chance is willfully augmented compared to the group phase. One lucky win by an inferior team may eliminate the former World Cup winner, and there is no comeback. The element of ability does not disappear but it is somewhat weakened if you look at the fate of one particular team, both with respect to its victories and its defeats.

The presence of the element of chance is also deeply felt when it comes to objectively wrong decisions made by the referees. As every reader of this book probably knows, referees' decisions are so-called decisions of fact, rendering them definitive. However, by means of television recordings, it can sometimes be shown that the referee's decisions were wrong, and sometimes, even the match result may crucially depend on such a wrong decision (for example, Chelsea v Barcelona, Champions League semi-finals 2009). In spite of the objectively proven inaccuracy of a referee's decision, the decision will not be overturned; it is set in stone. In other words, football contains the possibility of irreversible injustice, and this possibility sometimes becomes real in the most dramatic fashion. Just think of "God's hand" which was in fact Diego Maradona's hand in a dramatic match between Argentina and England during the 1986 World Cup—and this unpunished handball was decisive. Again, you see the parallel to real life: with some bad luck, unpunished, irreversible injustice may hit you, and in the worst case, it may even destroy your life in the cruelest way. You may just be in the wrong place at the wrong time.

Chance does not consistently dominate the game of football, just as ability doesn't either. It's mostly a mixture of both, sometime one factor more dominant, sometimes the other. The thrill is that when you go to the game, you don't know what the mixture will be this time—anything (or nearly anything) can happen. As Les Ferdinand famously put it, "I was surprised, but I always say nothing surprises me in football."

In one specific way, the drama of football is superior to the drama of life—unlike life, the rules of football give the drama a definite and inevitable end. Typically, in dramatic situations in life, it is not clear when (and even whether!) the drama will end (and with what result). Sometimes it is clear that the drama has ended, for instance when a particular rescue operation succeeds—or fails to succeed and all hope is gone. On other occasions, the drama may go on and on with no end in sight, and you may even be unable to imagine what, realistically speaking, the end of the drama could consist of, short of the annihilation of everyone involved. Just think of some marriages, or of the deep and bitter conflicts between nations or between smaller political, ethnic, or religious groups which may go on for decades or even centuries. What a contrast to football: it is absolutely clear when the drama of a match will have terminated, or the drama of a season or the drama of a World Cup. You can predict the time when the drama will end almost to the minute, or you may have to add an additional thirty minutes, and then perhaps some additional time for the penalty shoot-out, but this is it. In addition, the relevant result of the drama is absolutely unambiguous; it's a ratio of two numbers with no interpretive leeway. In real life, however, ambiguity permeates many supposed conclusions of dramas in a way that you may doubt whether the drama has really ended, or whether only a new chapter of it has begun. I guess we wouldn't watch games with such devotion which were similar to real life in this respect. We watch the game, we know it will come to an end, we will know the result. The result may move us for some time to come (or not), but the game will be finished and we will be able to turn our attention to something else. What a relief!

Finally, the rules of football ensure a distance between the drama of the game and the drama of real life. The game must not become serious in the sense of the seriousness of real life; otherwise the game would negate itself. There is a variety of sanctions whose aim is to prevent this transition from game to real life. For instance, most actions that endanger the physical integrity of other players are penalized. Furthermore, the principle of equal treatment of and fairness to both teams, which the referee stands for, is particularly protected. Any attack on the referee, physical or verbal, or even protest against any of his decisions, is severely penalized.

The punishment inflicted on a player for violating the rules of the game is not a real-life sanction, but a game sanction: it makes sense and hurts only within the game. Real-life sanctions bring about a disadvantage in real life, like having to pay money or losing your freedom for a while. Game sanctions bring about a disadvantage in the game in the form of a special advantage for the other team, like a penalty for them or the sending-off of a player of your team. We may therefore say that the sanctions stay within the game. They serve a similar function as the sanctions of real life, but they remain within the game (apart from exceptional cases).

Football as Part of Real Life

You may want to voice an objection. Maybe you began to voice this objection as soon as I started on about football as a re-enactment of the drama of life. Isn't it true that football is already a part of real life? Isn't it the case that, for instance, the game sanctions also have serious consequences, like possibly losing the match, then possibly relegation to a lower league with serious financial consequences? Is the skill of a really good player not remunerated handsomely in real life? Is football not a real career? Many more aspects can be enumerated in which what is supposedly just a game is intimately intertwined with real life factors. So it looks as though my thesis, "Football re-enacts the drama of life" collapses. How can football re-enact the drama of life, if it is already a part of the drama of life—and a very important one, at that, for every true football fan.

Yes, I do see the force of the objection. Yes, in today's professional football immense financial stakes are involved, with all the serious consequences that serious money usually brings with it. Yes, an additional financial aspect consists in betting which, for quite a number of people, is of existential importance. Yes, you may even be shot for being the (supposed) cause of the defeat of your national team (as has happened more than once, for instance to the Colombian Andres Escobar after he had contributed to Colombia's elimination in the preliminary round to the 1994 World Cup by an own goal). Yes, I do not deny that being shot is very serious indeed, especially for the person who is shot. And, to add a last example, football may even contribute to genuine national uproar.

Some analysts suspect that Hungary's defeat in the finals of the 1954 World Cup (against Germany) after thirty-one consecutive victories over more than four years contributed to the national uprising against Soviet rule two years later, in 1956. (Robert Imre looks at this issue in Chapter 23.) According to these analysts, the frustration of the Hungarian population about their political system was somehow canalized and focused by the 1954 defeat of their national team after all these four happy years, and it exploded two years later.

This objection against my division of the game from real life is beside the point. All these entanglements with finances, careers, fast cars, beautiful models as spouses of well-known players, hatred against players of a losing team, and possibly even with political revolts are real. "They are real": that means that they are, indeed, part of real life, like anything else that contributes to the drama of real life. However, this entanglement is secondary. It is not what makes football a fascinating game. The entanglement is parasitic on the intrinsic fascination of the game. This parasitic dependence of real life things on the game is possible in societies in which everything that is marketable will be marketed—legally or illegally, football being no exception. To see this, just turn to the game of two boys' teams from neighboring schools or of two village clubs belonging to so low a league that you don't even know its name (unless you yourself play there—no hard feelings!). No money or any of the other values may be involved and yet, both for the players and for their fans, the same quality of fascination prevails. Thus, when moving to the higher leagues or to national competitions, it is this primary fascination that becomes the anchor point for these other things from real life that today are so strongly connected to the game. These secondary features reinforce the existing fascination of the game but they do not create it, and they should not be mistaken for the respective primary features of the game creating fascination.

Here is another, possibly somewhat surprising consequence of my analysis. Consider hooligans (or other people who are so obsessed with football that their whole life is totally organized around football—I mean spectators, not players!). Most people would probably diagnose some imbalance in these people with respect to violence, values, and what not. Given my view, there is something else in play. People like hooligans cognitively miss the difference between real life and a game; they are thus unable to place different values with differing strengths on the two different kinds of things. They are so overwhelmed by the drama of the game that they mistake it for the drama of real life, as if it were a real-life fight. And they want to be part of this real-life fight.

Here's a final question. Aren't all games and sports somehow idealized representations of real-life situations without intrinsic value? For instance, isn't a hundred-meter sprint just an idealized case of running away from a hungry bear? Again, running away from the bear gets you, if successful, a real life advantage whereas winning the sprint means just winning the sprint (apart from secondary consequences, see above). And isn't fencing just a stylized form of real sword fighting? And so on.

Yes, indeed. All these games and sports mimic aspects of the drama of life, and the mimicking processes have no intrinsic value. Football, however, is special in the simplicity of its rules that generate an incredible variety of situations such that the specific proportion of ability and chance is extremely variable and therefore unpredictable. First, look at the simplicity of the rules. If you discuss football, it's by no means clear that the better educated person will dominate the discussion. It's absolutely amazing how well-versed people with a poor educational background may be when it comes to football. The social hierarchy becomes unimportant when the subject is football: the company director may have to listen to the unskilled worker and not the other way round (if they talk to each other at all). So football is accessible to anyone; it eliminates social filters that govern so many other areas of life. And you may enjoy it at very different levels of expertise: the more you know and therefore see in a match, the more there is to enjoy—if it's a good match!

The second point to be mentioned when comparing football with other games and sports is the incredible variety of the mixture of ability and chance in a match. As contrasts, take two other, extreme cases: roulette and the solving of chess puzzles. Roulette has an extremely high percentage of chance; the solving of chess puzzles has a very low one. These percentages appear to be constant and therefore predictable in these games. In football, however, the proportion of ability and chance is highly variable. Partly as a result of this fact, there is an infinitude of possible matches that are very different in character. Have you ever noticed that the final scores of a football match are very small numbers in comparison to other games like basketball or Olympic handball? The larger the numbers of the final score, the larger the probability that the score results mostly from ability; chance is averaged out, as the statisticians call this effect. The small numbers in the final score of a football match indicate that chance plays a comparatively large role in the result: just one lucky shot may be decisive.

Not only are complete matches very different from one another, episodes within a match also may vary tremendously—or not! When watching a match, you never know what to expect: suspense or boredom, predictability or surprise, rewarded or unrewarded efforts, incredible luck or enormous misfortune, justice or injustice, elegance or brutality, cleverness or routine. Apparently everyone, if at all susceptible to football, can find something in a match, no matter whether young or old, poor or rich, doctor or laborer, from the North, the South, the West, or the East. The variability of football is so immense that one football analyst, Roland Loy, goes so far as to say that we are light-years away from an understanding of football. For any seemingly reasonable tactic or strategic rule, you'll find statistical evidence to the contrary. Nothing compares to this incredible variability and the unpredictable mixture of ability and chance in the beautiful game—apart from life itself.[1]

[1] Thanks to Nils Hoppe for substantial improvements to this chapter and Ted Richards for several elegant editorial improvements.

2

May the Best Team Win!

STEFFEN BORGE

The best team always wins and the rest is just gossip.

—JIMMY SIRREL, Notts County Manager

Sometimes in football the best team loses.

Determining who won a football match is easy. Just look at the result and you will know. Determining who the best team is, apart from looking at the result, is another question.

If we follow Sirrel's lead, and think that the result always shows which team was the best, then we'll probably not accept that there exist standards of excellence in football that go beyond the result of particular matches. We can call this *the Nominalist-view of football*, since this view, like the philosophical position of Nominalism, is that only particulars exist. Football Nominalism is that only particular matches and their results exist. Over and above particular matches and their results, there is nothing. Only gossip.

If, on the other hand, we think that it makes sense to say that the best team lost, perhaps even calling the result of a particular football match unfair, then we could appeal to some standard of excellence of athletic performance that the score does not reflect. Anyone familiar with the post-match ranting of football managers will know that it is not uncommon for them to claim their team was the best despite having lost. Some will even stare a 1–4 defeat in the eye and claim that their team was the best, like Manchester United's manager Alex Ferguson who after their 1–4 defeat to Liverpool FC in March 2009 insisted that "we were the better team."

23

One way to understand what it is for the best team to lose is to say that there is an ideal way of playing football or an ideal football team. The best team, irrespective of result, is the team that come closest to fulfilling such an ideal. We can call this *the Platonist-view of football*, since this view, like the philosophical position of Platonism, is that there are universal ideas over and above the particulars, which represent an ideal for these particulars. Football Platonism says that there's an ideal way to play football. This ideal exists, independently of particular football matches, football teams, or match results.

The Dual Nature of Football

A Platonist-view of sport in general fits well with *measurement sports*. The defining feature of measurement sports is that winning a singular competition is settled by reference to a measurement; who ran fastest, who jumped highest, who threw longest, who lifted heaviest and so on. The meritocratic standards for these types of competitions are realized by measuring numerically a physical phenomenon, like the time of running, the length of the throw and so on. Another feature of measurement sports is that the sport activity could, in principle, be done independently of other competitors.

How fast you run, how high you jump, how long you throw, how heavy you lift are not directly a result of the other competitors' performance. Indirectly, however, competitors in measurement sport competitions usually influence each other's performance. The influence, though, is not due to the mechanics of measurement sports themselves, but rather because of the psychological make up of human competitors. A human high jumper will raise the bar, both literally and competitive wise, if other high jumpers in the competition do well. This tells us something important about the nature of human motivation and its role in competitions, but not about high jumping as a measurement sport.

Some complex measurement sports like running the marathon and bicycle racing often involve a lot of tactics. Here the performance of others in the competition does influence each competitor's game plan. So there is an aspect of these latter sorts of measurement sports that involve considerations about how the other competitors behave, though there are no direct hindering actions. Examples of measurement sports are track and field, weightlifting, and archery. One can imagine an ideal way of running the hundred metres and an ideal hundred-metre competition. An ideal hundred-metre competition would be one where all the runners fulfil the Platonic ideal of running the hundred metres, and everybody won.

Football is not a measurement sport. Football is, as we all know, a game of two halves, but rarely is it noted that it is also a sport with a dual nature. Football is a *constructive-destructive sport*. The defining feature of constructive-destructive sports is that winning a singular competition is settled by reference to a conventionally decided way to count the score of the competition, or by one of the competitors being unable to continue the competition. Another essential feature of constructive-destructive sports is that the sport activity could not be done without the other competitor. How well you perform in a football match is partly a consequence of your opponent's performance. The reason for this is that constructive-destructive sports are dual in nature. The nature of a constructive-destructive sport like football is partly, on the constructive side, to aim at constructing, creating or inventing ways to score, while at the same time, on the destructive side, to aim at destroying, preventing or hindering the other team's attempts to score. This direct-hinder criterion is what sets constructive-destructive sports apart from complex measurement sports like running the marathon and bicycle racing. Other examples of constructive-destructive sports are ice hockey, lacrosse, and boxing.

What would a Platonic ideal of a football team look like? Easy. It would be a team that fulfilled the dual nature of football to perfection by scoring whenever they had the ball and never conceding any goals. Perhaps this should also be executed in a certain style. On the other hand, a Platonic ideal of the perfect football match is inconceivable. Two teams fulfilling the Platonic ideal of football could not meet. It would be metaphysically impossible for two teams to meet and simultaneously both score on every opportunity they have, while not conceding any goals. It just cannot happen. To appeal to Platonic standards of playing football as a way to understand how the best team could have lost a particular match does not make sense when the Platonic ideal of football matches is inconceivable and downright impossible.

The Variety of Playing Styles

If we give up on a Platonic ideal of football, perhaps we could say that there is, in practice, a common-sense understanding of when the better team lost, and what counts as good play, as opposed to merely winning football matches. This line of thinking immediately runs into the problem of different playing styles. Is the *catenaccio* of the great Inter Milan team of the mid-1960s closer to the ideal way of playing football than the attacking flair of the Brazil team that won the World Cup in 1970? How would you argue for a definite answer to that question without appealing to the result of particular matches? One could point out that the two styles did clash in the World Cup final in 1970 in Mexico where Brazil beat Italy 4–1. That, however, is an appeal to the result of a particular match and thus a vindication of Jimmy Sirrel's method.

This doesn't mean that we can't compare playing styles. We can talk of the virtues and vices of different playing styles with a view to winning football matches. We may also consider which playing styles best fit the players a manager has at his disposal and how well a playing style tends to fare against other types of playing styles. But an unqualified comparison of widely different playing styles with regard to the question of which is best, is harder to make sense of. Inter Milan manager José Mourinho got it right when he declined to compare teams observing that, "Chelsea were made to be English champions and Barcelona were made to be Spanish champions and the culture is completely different. This Inter is adapted to the reality of Serie A."

Moreover, Mourinho was talking about regional differences in Europe. Football being a truly international sport encompasses even a wider variety of football styles. Not only is Chelsea's playing style adapted to the English Premier League, it is also adapted to the English weather. The classical action packed English style of football with box to box action, a frantic tempo and aggressive defending goes well with the moderate temperatures in which Premiership games are played. The style, however, might have been catastrophic for a team playing a long season in temperatures akin to those in which matches in the Brazilian Série A (*Brasileirão*) take place. Temperature surely plays a role in understanding why long spells of possession, and a build up from the back with short safe passes are integral parts of the Brazilian style of football. Both elements conserve the players' energy, which is important in games played at high temperature. Is the Brazilian style of football with more possession and longer build-ups better than the more direct English style of football where there are fewer passes before attacking the goal? Yes, perhaps if you play in the *Brasileirão*, but otherwise it does not make much sense to ask, unless we have an actual match between two teams from the two different leagues to consider, in which case one can compare the two teams' players, the match venue and so on.

One might be tempted at this point to bring in aesthetic considerations or entertainment value as a way to make good on the claim that the best team can lose, but that will not do. That sort of thinking has an unfortunate tendency to mistakenly consider *shiny but shallow* teams like Brazil's national team from the 1982 World Cup as the ideal football team.

The allure of such teams is that they, at their best, display breathtaking attack football, which results in proper hammerings whenever they meet lesser teams. The shallowness of such teams is that their brilliance at the constructive side of the game is achieved by—or as a consequence of neglecting—the destructive side of the game.

Shiny but shallow teams have a tendency to be beaten out of knock-out tournaments whenever they run into the harsh reality of football in the form of a more balanced team, one with a stronger ability on the destructive side of the game and enough constructive quality to punish such teams' defensive weaknesses. One might grant that shiny but shallow teams are more entertaining than the teams they lose to, but that just shows that football is not primarily about aesthetics. Football is about winning football matches and trophies, and the biggest trophies are seldom won by teams exclusively focused on the constructive side of the game, while making light of the fact that football is also a destructive game.

Furthermore, what counts as entertaining seems partly to be in the eyes of the beholder. What is entertaining for a neutral audience might not be perceived as entertaining for a particular team's supporters and *vice versa*. The loyalty of any team should be to their own supporters. Consider my native Norway, a nation not renowned for its charming football or massive international footballing success. Still, in a period from 1990 to 1998, under the reign of manager Egil Olsen, our national team qualified for two World Cup tournaments in 1994 and 1998. In the latter tournament we even handed Brazil a rare defeat in the group stages. The team-tactic was extremely direct play utilizing a 4–5–1 formation, where the emphasis was on breakdowns, set-pieces, and the use of long-balls towards a towering mountain of a Norwegian striker, Jostein Flo, when facing an established defence.

The style won us few friends internationally. In Denmark, a country which apart from being our former colonial rulers also harbours the *illusion de grandeur* that they are the Brazilians of Scandinavia, the style was even met with contempt and ridicule. To us Norwegians, however, the style was highly entertaining, since it provided us with something we had barely experienced before—victories in matches that mattered.

Football as Fiction

One way of putting the idea that the best team can lose, is to say that the result of a particular football match was unfair. But what does fairness have to do with football?

Assuming that sometimes the best team can lose and that this is unfair, one might say that the aim of any competition—like a football match—is to measure the athletic skills specific to that sport and if the result does not properly reflect the difference in the skills of the two teams, then the match in question is flawed. Such a purely meritocratic view of football immediately runs into the problem of how to define superior skills with regard to the dual nature of football and keeping in mind differences in playing styles. But even if we suppose that we can somehow untangle those theoretical knots, the view still does not ring true.

If fairness of result with regard to some well-defined definition of the sport-specific skills involved in playing football were at the heart of football, as both a phenomenon and a sport, then one would expect that matches with unfair results would be frowned upon and not held in high esteem. But that's not what happens.

Consider the 2005 Champions Leagues Final between Liverpool FC and AC Milan. The match ended 3–3 after extra time and Liverpool won the penalty shoot-out 3–2. The match quickly entered football folklore as one of the most thrilling matches ever played, and as the greatest comeback in the history of football.

Milan, led by their star midfielder Kaká and a deadly Hernan Crespo up front, went on a rampage as Liverpool got ripped apart in the first half. Liverpool, coming into the final as underdogs, was dead and buried by halftime, being 3–0 down against the top team of a country renowned for their ability to hang on to a lead. Milan also started the second half best, until Liverpool scored in the fifty-fourth minute and then, in what Milan manager Carlo Ancelotti appropriately dubbed "six minutes of madness," scored another two in the fifty-sixth and sixtieth minutes. It took Milan some time to regain their composure, but they forced Liverpool to clear a ball off the goal line in the seventieth minute. From there on in it was once again, more or less, Milan's match. In the extra time Liverpool hung on for dear life and with one minute remaining in the match Milan striker Andriy Shevchenko forced Liverpool keeper Jerzey Dudek to pull off an amazing double-save. A vastly superior Milan had been held by Liverpool to a draw and the latter promptly went ahead and won the penalty shoot-out. Was the result fair? Absolutely not. Does it matter? Seemingly not. The match is by common consensus considered a classic, but that just shows that football is not primarily about fairness. Football is about the drama, about the tension and the emotions it provokes.

Indeed, football is fictional in character. The main fiction present in football is that winning football matches matters. But in truth it does not. That, however, does not detract from the game. On the contrary.

Consider the following analogy. We might think that it's wise in real life, and also useful as a coping mechanism, to keep our emotions under control when facing difficult times. On the other hand, we allow ourselves when watching an emotionally stirring melodrama in the movie theatre to give these emotions free reign. Similarly, football matches are one occasion where emotions can flow freely. Football is not *only a game*, it is *because it is a game* that it captivates us the way it does. This I think was what former Liverpool manager Bill Shankly was getting at when he said that "Some people believe football is a matter of life and death. I am very disappointed with that attitude. I can assure you it is much, much more important than that." And Shanks was right, because football is not a life or death question belonging to the realm of real life, it is something else. It is a special kind of fiction. We can even identify certain re-emerging universal storylines in football matches.

Football Storylines

Sometimes football matches, usually cup finals, get nick-named after players who dominated them or otherwise secured the victory for one of the teams. The 2006 FA Cup Final between Liverpool FC and West Ham United is often described as the Gerrard Final, and it would not be off the mark to suggest that the 1986 World Cup in Mexico should be known as the Maradona World Cup. Apart from identifying certain players as worthy of having their names associated with particular matches or tournaments there are also certain themes or storylines of football matches that apply universally. Here are a few of them (there are many more):

The Hammering

A hammering occurs when one team is superior to the other team in all or most aspects of the game and are able to capitalize on that superiority by winning the match by a wide margin. The most thrilling hammerings are those handed out in important games where the spectators expected the game to be close. Examples are Real Madrid's 7–3 demolition of Eintracht Frankfurt in the European Cup Final in 1960. Another is the football lesson received by Johan Cruijff's so-called Dream Team in 1994, when AC Milan outplayed FC Barcelona 4–0 in the Champions League Final.

The Escape

An escape occurs when a team having been dominated in all aspects of the game by the other team, still manages a draw or a win. The team "gets away with" a result (so to speak) against the run of play. A classic example of an escape was the 1–1 draw between England and Poland in a World Cup qualifier at Wembley in 1973. The English laid siege to the Polish half only to find that behind a packed Polish defence their goalkeeper Jan Tomaszewski was having a legendary match. On Poland's only attack of the evening, Gregorz Lato scored. It did not matter that England afterwards equalised on a penalty. The result meant that Poland had qualified for the World Cup in West Germany the following year and England was out. Another escape close to this writer's heart was Norway's 0–0 draw away against the Netherlands in a World Cup qualifier in 1993. The Dutch swept over a Norwegian team clearly out of their depth, but Norway was helped out by the woodwork three times and also by the Dutch strikers' inclination to backheel absolute sitters, instead of merely scoring them.

The Comeback

Any equaliser is, in one sense, a comeback. However, for a match to earn this title the team making the comeback must have looked deflated and beaten at one point in the match, which usually means being down by two or more goals. Examples are the already mentioned 2005 Champions League Final between Liverpool FC and AC Milan. Another is the epic 1982 World Cup semi-final between West Germany and France, where France led 3–1 early in extra time, whereupon the West German substitute Karl Heinz Rummenigge orchestrated a staggering comeback ending with a 3–3 scoreline. The West Germans won the penalty shoot out 5–4. Eusébio's Portugal also staged a comeback classic in the 1966 World Cup quarter-final when they were down 0–3 against North Korea, but ended up winning the match 5–3. Some comebacks like Liverpool's Champions League victory in 2005 also count as escapes.

The Upset

An upset is when an underdog, a team given no chance of winning by experts and others, defy those odds and win. Examples of big upsets are North Korea's 1–0 win over Italy in the group stages of the 1966 World Cup and England's 0–1 loss to the USA in the group stages of the 1950 World Cup, which was also England's first World Cup appearance ever. Upsets might also be comebacks and quite often are escapes, though they need not be. We might also talk of upsets with regard to tournaments. Greece's victory in the European Football Championship in 2004 is perhaps the biggest of them all.

The Rollercoaster

A rollercoaster is a match were the character of the match changes more than one time and where there is an oscillation between which team is favoured by the scoreline at any given point. Tournaments like Copa Libertadores (from 2005 and with the exception of the final) and Champions League (with the exception of the final) with their design of home-away matches in the knock-out rounds and with away goals counting double should the score be tied after two matches, are well designed for rollercoaster matches.

A good example from the World Cup is Italy's 3–2 victory over Brazil in the World Cup second group stage in 1982. The premise of the game was that Brazil would go through to the semi-final with a draw, while Italy needed to win. With a goal from Paulo Rossi in the fifth minute Italy were in pole position, then Brazil were back in the semi-final with an equaliser in the twelfth minute by Socrates, then Italy (25 Rossi), then Brazil (68 Falcao) and finally Italy (75 Rossi) to book their place in the semi-final.

Another rollercoaster classic was the 1970 World Cup semi-final between Italy and West Germany, which ended 4–3 to the Italians. The match came alive when West Germany forced extra time with a 1–1 equaliser three minutes into stoppage time. The thirty-minutes extra time rollercoaster resulted in five goals. First, West Germany was in the lead 2–1, then the score was 2–2, then Italy in the lead 3–2, then West Germany equalised to 3–3 and finally, nine minutes before full time, Gianni Rivera settled the score 4–3 to Italy. Another famous one was the FA Cup Final of 1989. In the all-Merseyside Derby, Liverpool FC was up 1–0 for most of the match thanks to a John Aldridge goal in the fourth minute, until the substitute for Everton Stewart McCall equalized with one minute remaining. In extra time, it went 2–1 Liverpool (Rush 95), then 2–2 (McCall 102), then 3–2 (Rush 104) for Liverpool.

The Robbery

The robbery is a close cousin to the escape. In the escape the team winning or drawing the match against the run of play, gets away with being the inferior team. In a robbery, on the other hand, the match is prized away from one of the teams due to a mistake or mistakes by the referee. One of the clearest robberies in the history of the World Cup was South Korea's 5–3 penalty shoot-out win against Spain in 2002. The match ended 0–0. Spain had two perfectly good goals disallowed—where the second one in extra time would have counted as a golden goal—together with some, at best, highly disputable off-side decisions going against Spain. No doubt Spain got robbed.

Another robbery, at least according to the supporters of AS Roma, is the case of Turone's goal (*Gol di Turone*). In a 1981 Serie A match between Juventus FC and AS Roma with the match at a 0–0 stalemate and only ten minutes remaining, Roma's Maurizio Turone headed the ball into the net behind Juventus keeper Dino Zoff. The goal was controversially disallowed. Had Roma won the match, they would have been in the driver seat of the Serie A with two matches remaining, but as it were, the *Scudetto* ended up in Turin. To this day Roma supporters will insist that they were robbed that day, which ever since has added special flavour to the clashes between the two teams.

If you look back at these storylines you'll find that I have freely used expressions like, "against the run of play," "get away with a result," "get robbed," and, "unfair result." Do I think it's possible that the best team can lose? Yes. And it happens a lot. We could not talk about football storylines like the escape unless we also admitted that in those games the best team loses. We must account for this possibility without falling back on a Platonic view of football or on some naive common-sense view that does not hold up under closer inspection. And we can account for it— with the philosophical magic of counterfactuals.

What-if Scenarios

Sometimes in football the margins between scoring a goal and a near miss are so slim that it seems reasonable to say that it could have gone either way. This is most vivid in escape-type matches. To acknowledge such slim margins in escape-type matches is to acknowledge that there can be an element of chance or luck when it comes to winning football matches. Indeed, one of the important elements of football is the real possibility of upset and escape matches.

Supporters of small teams like my own Norway always go to matches against football superpowers like Brazil hoping that today might be the day where all the margins go our way; today the ball will bounce off the post and out onto the pitch, not into the net. You never know, we tell ourselves. The world being as it is, most of time the biggest nations with the best teams win, but every once in a while, and way more often than in any other sport, the inferior underdog comes out on top. Small teams like Norway might also use playing formations and tactics which to some extent exploit the possibility of chance. The long-ball tactic is perhaps the clearest example of this. The small margins and the element of chance keep football matches more open-ended and unpredictable than all other sports. Football matches involve many contingencies and it is like life's own uncertainties have been woven into the very fabric of the football fiction. A crude version of the Nominalist-view of football *à la* Jimmy Sirrel, on the other hand, is committed to denying the element of chance or luck, and that just seems wrong.

We might, however, remain a Nominalist about football while dealing with the element of chance or luck counterfactually. Counterfactual scenarios are what-if scenarios. When we consider a what-if scenario we imagine a world which is similar to ours in all relevant respects, apart from the one what-if element we want to look into. Call that the relevant or closest possible world. This might sound dreadfully complicated, but the fact is that most football supporters freely avail themselves of counterfactual reasoning on many occasions.

Consider the case of Chelsea captain John Terry's penalty miss in the penalty shoot out against Manchester United in the 2008 Champions League final. It's not difficult to imagine a Chelsea supporter claiming that, if Terry's standing foot had not slid when he took the potentially deciding penalty, then the ball would not have bounced off the right post but ended between the posts, and Chelsea would have won the final, given that Manchester keeper Edwin Van der Sar had already gone the wrong way. This claim is counterfactual. Terry did lose his footing; he did slip while taking that fifth penalty, but what if he had not? The relevant possible world for our what-if concern is the world where Terry does not slip, while Van der Sar behaves in the same way as he did in the actual match. This is the closest possible world to ours with respect to Terry's penalty in the 2008 Champions League Final. Our imaginary Chelsea supporter is correct to point out that chance played a role in deciding that final and that they were unlucky.

Not all counterfactual scenarios are interesting or relevant when trying to figure out whether the best team lost. I might for example claim that Norway would have won the 1998 World Cup had we had the same quality players as Brazil. True as that might be, it is a rather uninteresting counterfactual claim when debating whether the best team won the 1998 World Cup. The possible world where the Norwegian national team starts with the same sort of quality players as Brazil is not a very close possible world. Questions of how well a team would have performed in some tournament had not some or many of their key players been injured are more interesting. How are we then to view particular matches counterfactually with a view to the idea that the best team can lose? We should be careful not to identify that with features of certain playing style, like, for example, arguing that the team with most possession is always the best team even if they lose. I suggest that the best way to counterfactually account for how the best team could have lost is to consider the goal scoring opportunities in a match that were not converted into goals, but which might as well have been in the back of the net. Let us call those *objective scoring opportunities.*

One will in many cases disagree on what counts as an objective scoring opportunity, but as long as we can find some clear-cut cases that everybody would agree on, then the model will work. And we can. If a shot beats the keeper, bounces off the inside of one goalpost, bobs along the goal line, bounces off the other post and lands in the arms of the beaten keeper, then that is an objective scoring opportunity. It might as well have been a goal. The defining feature of an objective scoring opportunity is that it is chancy whether the ball ends up in the net or not. We can also put this in terms of what the players can influence or what rests on their skills. A chance to score a goal is not an objective scoring opportunity if the reason for the miss is lack of skill. A footballer lacking the necessary skills to score when the opportunity comes also misses in the relevant possible worlds. It makes a difference counterfactually whether a scoring opportunity in the actual match falls to a striker who usually scores from that position or a defender who does not.

Another way of putting the idea of an objective scoring opportunity is to say that the margins are so small that they cannot be influenced by the players. Luck decides. Being lucky or unlucky is then explained counterfactually. If a team had ten objective scoring opportunities in a match, but still lost 1–0 to a team that only had one, then the best team lost because in the closest possible worlds teams that have ten objective scoring opportunities in matches against teams with only one, tend to win.

The Good Gossip

What would the late Jimmy Sirrel have thought? One can imagine him complaining that the theory I have presented opens up for all sorts of fruitless speculations about who could have won and what could have been, had only thus and such happened. "This," we can envisage Sirrel saying, "is just what I warned about." Sirrel could have further complained that I have not understood how goals define matches. There can never be a simplistic counting of objective scoring opportunities and then a calibration of this counterfactually. Imagine that a match ends 0–0, but that quite a few objective scoring opportunities have gone begging for the home team in the first half, but not the second. One cannot straightforwardly from that conclude that the home team was best and should have won, since there's no telling how the away team would have responded had they conceded a goal or two in the first half.

There are actually some counterfactual considerations that give definite answers for football matches, but they are rare. Consider again the 2002 World Cup quarter-final match between South Korea and Spain. Spain was unlucky to have Fernando Morienties's goal in the first half of extra time disallowed. We make sense of that by noting that this was such a big mistake from the linesman that we can safely say that in most of the closest possible worlds the goal would have stood. The goal would have been a golden goal, so there is no uncertainty to the conclusion that Spain was the best team and should have won. Otherwise counterfactual claims about football and which team was the best will have to be evaluated as more or less reasonable. If a team has many objective scoring opportunities just at the end of a match, but the match still ends 0–0, then it seems safe to say that they were the best team and that the result was against the run of play. In many other cases one ought to admit a certain amount of uncertainty surrounding counterfactual thinking, but is that really a problem?

My aim was to investigate how we should understand the idea that the best team can lose, but I never promised that such consideration would always be easy or that everyone would agree with each other. Far from it. The important thing is that football seems to be a sport where the element of chance is an integral part of the sport, and I have argued that that is best understood counterfactually. Counterfactual thinking is in some sense speculative. The objection that there is no telling with regard to what-if scenarios should be regarded as an observation that most counterfactual claims will to some degree be uncertain and speculative. Some highly speculative. Some beyond belief.

But that's just the beauty of it. What would the life of the football supporter be, if he was not allowed to bitch and moan about all those oh-so-near misses, the referee decisions mistakenly going against his team and all those other could-have-beens and should-have-beens? These are the themes that get the temperature going in all those barstool discussions around the world. The footballing world would be a poorer place without it. Perhaps the correct thing to say is, "The best team can lose and the rest is gossip—good gossip."[1]

---

[1] Thanks to Jan Harald Alnes, Ted Richards, Tor Ivar Hanstad, and Margrethe Bruun Vaage for their comments and critiques.

3
Nietzsche's Arsenal

DAVID KILPATRICK

Having just announced that "God is dead," Friedrich Nietzsche's mad-man asks, "What sacred games shall we have to invent?" If God gave one's life meaning, and organized religion united people with a shared system of belief, something would have to compensate for this great loss. For all the various interpretations of what Nietzsche means with his most famous or infamous words—first published in 1882 in *The Gay Science*—it is now a fact that Christianity no longer plays the most prominent guiding role in the lives of the majority of people.

Today the cathedral has been replaced by the stadium. It is through sport that communities produce a shared narrative, on the field of play where contemporary heroes are made and worshipped. Soccer, more than any other sport, is the global phenomenon that has most fully replaced religion in modern life.

Part of soccer's own guiding myth is its appeal to medieval, even ancient, origins; the Chinese *cuju*, the Japanese *kemari*, the Greek *episkyros*, the Roman *harpastrum*, the Mayan *pitz* and the mob or folk football played on the village streets in rural Britain have all been viewed as pre-decessors of the beautiful game. Efforts to link the contemporary sport to ancient forms of play through such origin myths belie the modernity of soccer and neglect its rapid global growth in the late nineteenth and early twentieth centuries.

Descending into madness on the streets of Turin in 1889, Nietzsche never had the opportunity to witness the full emergence of the modern game of soccer. The first *Laws of the Game* were only formalized in 1863 in London by the Football Association and weren't translated into German until 1891 (David Goldblatt, *The Ball Is Round*, Penguin, 2006, p. 159); the Deutscher Fussball-Bund, the sport's governing body in

Germany, was founded in 1900, the year of Nietzsche's death. Nietzsche may have seen the seeds of the sport being sown; he moved to Turin in the spring of 1888 and the first game of soccer was played there just the year before (Goldblatt, p. 152), but surely he never saw a stadium filled with thousands of fanatical supporters and could never have predicted the central role that soccer plays in the lives of millions of modern people, for whom the game has become a secular religion, an opiate of the masses far more powerful and intoxicating than traditional religions, its teams inspiring more devotion and its stars more adulation than church or saint within a century of the sport's formalization. Nietzsche's madman would not have known that the sacred game had just been invented that would fill the void left by the death of God.

Dionysus and the Team

I've often been confronted with the argument that Nietzsche wouldn't have any interest in team sports and that a true Nietzschean spirit is only to be found in individual sports, especially extreme sports. Does the quote often attributed to Ernest Hemingway, that "There are only three sports: bullfighting, motor racing, and mountaineering; all the rest are merely games," accurately convey a Nietzschean sense of athleticism? We know that Nietzsche enjoyed a bullfight in Nice (Curtis Cate, *Friedrich Nietzsche*, Overlook, 2005, p. 447), where the first auto racing venue was established in 1897. So like soccer, auto racing didn't emerge until Nietzsche had succumbed to madness. His love of mountain climbing (or at least hiking) is well documented, so we can safely contend that Nietzsche would approve of two out of those three sports and admit that there's at least a strong possibility that Nietzsche might have been an advocate or enthusiast of individual sports that involve an inherent sense of danger.

What's missing in individual sports, though, is the tension between the individual and the collective, as the player strives with his teammates who, in turn, are cheered by the team's fans against an opponent. This tension is precisely what Nietzsche explores in his first book, *The Birth of Tragedy* (found in *Basic Writings of Nietzsche*, Modern Library, 1968), with his concepts of the Apollonian and the Dionysian. The Apollonian is the principle of individuation, represented in Greek tragedy, Nietzsche claims, in the figure of the suffering hero. The Dionysian, by contrast, is the primordial unity, the ecstatic loss of individuation represented in Greek tragedy by the chorus—the many who speak as one.

Greek antiquity reached its greatest artistic achievements, Nietzsche argues, when tragedians were able to bring together these two extremes of the Apollonian and the Dionysian. Is there any more powerful expression of these two extremes of existence than when a goal is scored? The scorer celebrates his individual accomplishment with an ecstasy that takes him beyond his merely individual concerns and links him with the very source and vitality of Life itself. His teammates celebrate their collective joy, all having contributed to the permutations of play that have resulted in the goal, while the fans (present in the stadium or watching on television in pubs or living rooms around the world) share their joy—or despair if they identify with the vanquished foe.

Soccer as an Aesthetic Phenomenon

All too often, though, we see negative tactics employed in soccer where a team doesn't attempt to score so much as prevent the other team from scoring; or when they do attempt to score, it is done in a way that poses little risk—a long kick up the pitch to a waiting striker hoping to exploit a brief moment of vulnerability. While Nietzsche's appreciation for competition is clearly expressed in his essay, "Homer's Contest" (*The Portable Nietzsche*, Penguin, 1959, pp. 32–39), in which he explores the desperate drive for victory in Greek antiquity, such vulgar tactics—where style of play is sacrificed for the sake of winning at all costs—would offend Nietzsche's sensibility. And so, taking his famous ontological valuation from *The Birth of Tragedy* where he claims that "it is only as an *aesthetic phenomenon* that existence and the world are eternally *justified*" (p. 52), I would argue that, from a Nietzschean perspective, soccer can only be justified as an aesthetic phenomenon. In other words, Nietzsche would only approve of soccer when it is played artistically—in a creative, positive, and imaginative manner—with a sense of the game's potential for beauty.

Club v Country

So, if Nietzsche was a soccer fan, what team would he support?

If one is to consider possible clubs based upon the places Nietzsche lived, FC Basel, OGC Nice, or, given his love for Turin, Juventus, would all warrant consideration. The "Old Lady" certainly has the record of success that comes from a persistent will-to-power, but for one who often called himself "homeless," the randomness of location shouldn't be a determining factor. Rather, to answer the question one should seek a match between Nietzsche's philosophy and the philosophy of football that informs the play of the club. Manchester United's iconography is too closely related to the symbolism of Christianity—one who seeks to move "beyond good and evil" would never cheer for Red Devils. Barcelona's style of play certainly meets the highest aesthetic standards but the club is too closely identified with Catalan nationalism.

One would need to look solely to club football rather than making the assumption that the German thinker would support the German *Nationalmannschaft*, for Nietzsche saw nationalism as one of modernity's great blights. This is where the Nazi appropriation of Nietzsche's writings is most obviously ignorant and misguided. Although in the latter part of his first book he did call for a rebirth of German myth, ten years later in *The Gay Science* (Vintage, 1974), in the section addressed to "We Who are Homeless", Nietzsche proclaims that

> we are not nearly 'German' enough . . . to advocate nationalism and race hatred and to be able to take pleasure in the national scabies of the heart and blood poisoning that now leads the nations of Europe to delimit and barricade themselves against each other as if it were a matter of quarantine. (p. 339)

Nietzsche often called himself a "good European," and as such, could not in good conscience support a team dedicated to pursuing glory in the name of a nation-state.

In the ongoing "country v club" debate, where administrators argue that players and leagues should serve the interests of their national federation or football association, whose ultimate aim is to win international competitions like the World Cup, Nietzsche would doubtless reject such international events. The brilliance of such spectacles simply serves to worship what he calls in the first part of *Thus Spoke Zarathustra* (published in 1883) "the new idol." The state, Nietzsche claims, "is the coldest of all cold monsters. Coldly it tells lies, too; and this lie crawls out of its mouth: 'I, the state, am the people.' That is a lie!" (*The Portable Nietzsche*, p. 160). Perhaps more than any other sporting event, the World Cup fosters the identification of the fans, as the people, with the team as a nation, perpetuating the worship of this false and monstrous idol. Nietzsche would choose club over country.

From Boring to Scoring

Given the current state of the sport, one club reveals itself to be the most ideal candidate to be Nietzsche's favorite: Arsenal Football Club of north

London and the English Premier League. Having served as an artillery-man, Nietzsche might have an affinity for the cannon on the club's crest. But it is the grand style of play that Arsenal has become known for since Arsène Wenger took over as manager in the fall of 1996 that would most appeal to a Nietzschean sensibility, as well as the methods employed to attain that style.

Prior to Wenger's appointment, the club were mocked as "boring, boring Arsenal" for their grind-it-out approach, especially under manager George Graham (1986–95 seasons), when "one-nil to the Arsenal" was often the desired result. That changed quickly and radically when Wenger arrived and (while a mocking media, not a few fans and even several of the Arsenal players asked "Arsène who?") immediately set about transforming the club's culture.

As Nietzsche insists in *Twilight of the Idols*, "It is decisive for the lot of a people and of humanity that culture should begin in the right place . . . the right place is the body, the gesture, the diet, physiology; the rest follows from that" (*The Portable Nietzsche*, p. 552). Before his first match in charge, away at Blackburn, Wenger "asked the players to practise muscle-honing poses in the hotel ballroom for half an hour" (Amy Lawrence, "How Wenger Changed English Football" *Guardian Observer*, 1st October 2006). Half-hour stretching exercises were introduced both before and after sessions and plyometrics were integrated into the training regimen. Having just coached in Japan, Wenger shocked the local sports establishment with his frank criticism of the English diet, claiming in his first week of work in north London, "I think in England you eat too much sugar and meat and not enough vegetables. I lived for two years in Japan and it was the best diet I ever had. The whole way of life there is linked to health" (*Evening Standard,* 18th October 1998). So the pre-match custom of steak was replaced with raw carrots and celery, fish or chicken, mashed potato and steamed vegetables with apple pie (nothing on it) for dessert ("The Arsenal Diet," *BBC News* website, 20th May 1998). Further, the drinking culture that had long been a fixture among players was abolished.

Veteran players were initially resistant to Wenger and his methods, like then-captain Tony Adams, whose first impression was, "What does this Frenchman know about football? He wears glasses and looks more like a schoolteacher" (Alex Fynn and Kevin Whitcher, *Arsènal: The Making of a Modern Superclub*, Vision Sports, 2008, p. 47). But players like Adams quickly saw that the methods of "the Professor" paid dividends. In his first full season at the helm (1997–98), Arsenal won the league and cup double with a mix of rejuvenated veteran English players (the famous back five of keeper David Seaman, Martin Keown, Nigel Winterburn, Lee Dixon, and captain Tony Adams) and new signings from the Continent (joining the Dutch Master Dennis Bergkamp were key signings by Wenger of Patrick Vieira, Marc Overmars, and Emanuel Petit). This blend of inherited and discovered players came together quickly and proved that the training and dietary innovations would not only bring victory, but the fitness base allowed technique to flourish as the title was won with flowing and attacking football.

Wenger and his staff supervised the design of the club's new training centre in London Colney, which opened in 1999—the manager's influence reportedly extending to flatware in the dining hall—allowing the squad to train and condition in optimal conditions built to foster peak physical, mental, tactical, and technical performance. Nietzsche's Zarathustra claims that "Man is something that shall be overcome," and asks, "What have you done to overcome him?" (p. 124). In a footballing sense, by essentially creating a soccer laboratory at London Colney, Wenger is allowed to pursue a comprehensive approach to player development that cultivates a new standard, overcoming measures of peak performance to cultivate a sporting Overman [*Übermensch*].

By the time Arsenal won the double again in 2002, Wenger had essentially remade the team and was well on his way to remaking the club (and the way the game is played). Many of the veterans he had inherited either departed or assumed more limited roles, while further Wenger signings improved the standard—none more so than Thierry Henry, who languished as a winger at Juventus until Wenger converted him into the English Premier League's most lethal and poetic striker. On the morning of the celebratory parade through Islington, goalkeeper David Seaman reflected on the changes from the time Graham was manager to what was accomplished under Wenger, telling David Frost:

> Arsène's brought a new dimension to Arsenal—you know, new training facilities, new training regime, diet regime and a lot better way of playing. You know, people are enjoying how we play now and [while] we're at it, we've got rid of the boring Arsenal title. (*Breakfast with Frost*, 12th May 2002)

Boring, boring Arsenal had become scoring, scoring Arsenal.

The concept of total football is generally seen as a Dutch invention, but the Clockwork Orange national side featuring Johan Cruijff and coached by Rinus Michaels never accomplished the victory that would grant their beautiful game a state of perfection; despite the 1972 treble winning Ajax side, the legacy of total football was great for the eyes but not practical enough to win the prize. Under Wenger, Arsenal showed a commitment to a free-flowing, short-passing attacking approach that lead countless critics to praise their game as poetic, symphonic, even erotic in its beauty, achieving perfection with the 2003–04 unbeaten Premier League season, the team earning the title, "the Invincibles."

None other than legendary manager Brian Clough reluctantly celebrated Arsenal's triumph, claiming they, "caress a football the way I dreamed of caressing Marilyn Monroe" (Quoted in Flynn and Whitcher, p. 47). The team would go forty-nine league matches without facing defeat, an unprecedented run of perfection unparalleled in the modern game, made all the more remarkable given the aesthetic brilliance of their style. Here is an approach to the sport that doesn't take technique as a means to an end and rejects the utilitarian approach of playing not to lose or pursuing the merely functional or efficient means of achieving victory. Arsenal play as if winning can only be justified as an aesthetic phenomenon; the squad pursuing Wenger's vision to play in a way that seeks championships but also, like a work of art, to both entertain and instruct—or the even more noble pursuit of inducing a sense of ecstasy.

Young Guns

Having taken a team to invincibility, Wenger quickly dismantled the core of that squad, showing little or no sentiment in dealing with aging players. That lack of sentimentality may be seen in the most radical and controversial change to occur at the club in the Professor's era—the move from historic "Home of Football," Highbury, for the state-of-the-art Emirates Stadium at nearby Ashburton Grove in 2006. The new stadium (just a stone's throw away from the old) is quite literally the House that Wenger Built, with details like the shape of the locker room and the texture of the floor tile built to the manager's specifications.

Just two seasons into their new home, legends such as Vieira and Henry were notably absent from the pitch at Ashburton Grove, but the spirit of total football is celebrated as sacred there with the play of Wenger's "Young Guns," featuring the likes of Cesc Fàbregas and Robin van Persie. Despite a trophy-less run since the FA Cup of 2005, Arsenal can be relied upon to delight and inspire. As comedian Russell Brand describes:

> Arsenal move with the fluidity, grace and purpose of a couple who remain very much in love, the kind of yogic coitus that I like to think Sting and Trudie Styler have. Arsenal pass confidently from deep positions and are unencumbered by needless flair but make the functional aesthetically titillating. (Russell Brand, "Watching Arsenal, Thinking of Sting and Trudie," *Guardian Online*, 5th January 2008)

With Wenger working on essentially a third Arsenal squad, the manager seemed to be defending his principles, his philosophy of sport, in the face of mixed criticism from both fan and foe. Wenger's and Arsenal's detractors said their love for the aesthetic had eclipsed their ability to finish—ever seeking the perfect goal they would opt out of taking the easy and obvious shot. Their advocates defended Arsenal's approach, claiming like Matthew Syed that, "Arsenal's relentless and unadulterated pursuit of beauty has itself been a thing of beauty: a daring, epic and ultimately doomed journey that has taken the English game, against all expectation, into the territory of the artistic." Rather than fault the Young Guns for not yet lifting trophies, Syed insists on, "celebrating something in Wenger's team that goes far beyond success and failure; it is about saluting a philosophy . . . Wenger understands that, in this curious journey called life, there are things that matter beyond the merely functional" (Matthew Syed, "Why Arsène Wenger Should be Proud Rather than Cowed," *The Times*, 10th April 2008). It is this rejection of utility that takes Arsenal's play to the realm of the poetic.

Loathed Like the Antichrist

Such praise is far from universal. As Nick Hornby concedes in *Fever Pitch* (Penguin, 2000), "It is part of the essential Arsenal experience that they are loathed" (p. 233). Once loathed for being "boring" they are now loathed for being "foreign." There was always a touch of xenophobia to the criticisms of the Alsace-born manager, the first foreigner to lead an English team to a Championship, but as Wenger remade and remade the squad, the number of English players diminished to the point that it is common for the Arsenal to field an eleven of non-English players, leading many to criticize him for threatening to destroy the English game. Regardless of the innovations in diet and stretching that have become *de rigueur* among English football clubs, the lack of English talent fielded by Arsenal is seen by many as detrimental to the development of English talent and, therefore, the English national team.

None other than FIFA President Sepp Blatter has advocated limiting the number of foreign players fielded among any team's starting eleven, his "Six-Plus-Five" proposal—mandating a maximum of domestic players as starters for each club match—earning the support of many who want to preserve the import of national team competitions. Wenger has been an outspoken critic of Six-Plus-Five, insisting "What they want to do is artificial. I like to think that a boy can grow up anywhere in the world, and has a big passion and a big dream, and can fulfill it. We are there to allow that" (quoted in *Arsenal: The Magazine*, August 2008, p. 75). Meanwhile UEFA President Michel Platini has been especially critical, claiming, "I do not like the system of Wenger," whereby teenagers from outside England are recruited to train and play the Arsenal way (Quoted in John Ley, "Michel Platini Criticizes Arsène Wenger's Policy," *Daily Telegraph*, 31st October 2007). Bayern Munich chairman Karl-Heinz Rummenigge, echoing Platini's sentiments and citing Cesc Fàbregas leaving his native Spain for Arsenal at age fifteen as an example, argues: "Arsène Wenger signs hosts of players from France and elsewhere year-in year-out. We have to take care that this sort of child trafficking is stopped. This has taken on a different scale in the meantime; the word kidnapping is not too far off anymore" (quoted in Alan Dawson, "Bayern Chief Accuses Arsenal Boss Wenger of 'Child-Trafficking'," *Goal.com*, 29th April 2009). Such vitriolic opposition to Wenger's methods demonstrate that the loathing of Arsenal remains.

But this youth-foreign player policy would appeal to Nietzsche's sensibility, eschewing nationalism in favour of youth. Turning his back on fatherlands and motherlands, Nietzsche's Zarathustra claims, "I now love only my children's land [*Kinderland*]" (*The Portable Nietzsche*, p. 233). It's this promise of youth, identifying and developing talent regardless of passport, seeking out players who can play with creativity and verve, that inspires Arsenal's current "Young Guns" policy.

Oh to Be a Gooner

This is not to say that Nietzsche should support Arsenal just because of Wenger, though the one polyglot Professor would probably admire the other as exemplifying a "good European." It is the all-around approach that the club now personifies that would appeal to a Nietzschean sensibility. Asked at the end of the 2008–09 season to reflect upon his legacy at Arsenal, Wenger claimed that:

> There is philosophy, a style of play and a culture of how you want to play the game. We have all that. . . . What is the most important is the Club goes on and continues to improve. That for me is the biggest pride for any manager who has a positive ambition and philosophy. (Quoted in Chris Harris, "Wenger: The Season Has Not Been a Disaster," *Arsenal.com*, 22nd May 2009)

This positive example of the will-to-power, where an ambitious philosophy that looks to the future inspires a club in all facets of its organization, would surely make Nietzsche a Gooner.

Arsenal, then, based upon this club philosophy, most adhere to Nietzschean principles. Nietzsche's fascination with genius would find ample depth for consideration with the manager and players of the current and most recent Arsenal sides. These glory days hearken back to Arsenal's first glory days decades before under Herbert Chapman (from 1925 to his death in 1934)—the sport's first great manager, whose innovations like a white ball, floodlights and numbered jerseys are now taken for granted. In the 1930–31 season, Chapman was blocked by authorities from bringing an Austrian goalkeeper into the squad on the grounds that he would be taking the job of a British worker. When he found a loophole and brought in a Dutch keeper, the Football Association, Player's Union and the government agreed to ban importing non-British players (Simon Page, *Herbert Chapman: The First Great Manager,* Heroes, 2006, p. 168). Chapman is perhaps best known for having conceived the "W-M" formation and his philosophy of play is summed up with this phrase: "Spectators want a fast-moving spectacle, rapier-like attacks that have the spirit of adventure, and ever more goals" (Quoted in *Arsenal: The Magazine,* July 2009, p. 72). Such a statement can easily be mistaken as a quote from the current Arsenal manager and it encapsulates the Arsenal way of playing the beautiful game.

I hope with this to provoke debate among lovers of wisdom and lovers of soccer. The love of one can easily involve the love of the other. There are times when I'm watching Arsenal, as I've watched my club transform into a Superclub, when I can't but think of a phrase or a concept of Nietzsche's and I'm hoping this habit of mine will prove contagious. The writings of Friedrich Nietzsche lend themselves all-too-easily to misappropriation—even to catastrophic political consequences—but I believe that this way of playing with Nietzsche is true to his spirit.

Just as many have claimed posthumous camaraderie with the philosopher, so too my effort here is to take him along, as a friend, to support the club I love. Now I must confess that prior to Wenger I took great (perhaps perverse) delight in a "boring" one-nil to the Arsenal and I know that my love for the Gunners will last long beyond the Wenger era. But I have learned a greater appreciation of the beautiful game from watching this philosophy of play shape the club just as I have learned a greater appreciation of life from reading Nietzsche and aim to pass the passion to others.

4

Aristotle's Favorite Sport

MATTHEW A. KENT

"Gggggooooooooooaaaaaaaaaaaallllllll!!!!"

It's the word that every soccer fan wants to hear. It's also Aristotle's favorite word. If you had to sum up soccer in one word, and if you had to sum up Aristotle in one word, you just saw it.

That's because everything focuses on the *goal*, the *end*, the *purpose*, both in soccer and in Aristotle's philosophy. As Aristotle himself puts it, "The end is everywhere the chief thing" (*Poetics*, Chapter 6, in *The Basic Works of Aristotle*, Random House, 1941, a great collection still in print and the source of all the quotes in this chapter). Translate "end" as "goal" and you might already be past midfield in understanding why Aristotle would have been a soccer fan. No other sport, and almost no other philosopher, is quite so obsessed with that one beautiful word: GOAL!

A Bit of Pre-Game History

We soccer fans should be glad that we don't live in ancient Athens. Soccer wasn't around twenty-four centuries ago when Aristotle was a student at Plato's Academy. Whatever games Aristotle played there, soccer wasn't one of them. Whatever athletic exhibitions Aristotle attended at the royal court while tutoring the young Alexander the Great, soccer wasn't one of them. Whatever exercises Aristotle prescribed for his pupils when founding a school of his own (called the Lyceum) in direct competition with the Academy, soccer wasn't one of them.

Isn't it amazing, then, that we can find several pages' worth of evidence that soccer is Aristotle's favorite sport? You wouldn't be so surprised if you knew more about Aristotle. He was always ahead of his time. In a nation of polytheists, he concluded that there was one God, the first source of all motion. In a world consumed by consuming, he argued that the ultimate goal of human life is to practice virtue and, above all, to contemplate eternal truths about God and the universe. All of this centuries before the Greeks were converted to Christianity.

Soccer appears in Aristotle's writings just as many of those Christian ideals do: implicitly. Think of a coach who prepares a team for every possible opponent by teaching the players a wide variety of tactics. That's Aristotle in the realm of philosophy. He takes as his starting-point everyday common sense. He then tries to precisely state, classify, and organize its insights. I'm not pretending that Aristotle is absolutely perfect in his use of this method, nor that he (or anybody) could figure out everything by philosophical methods alone. But his procedure does result in a large body of general principles that we can still use today to tackle pretty much any topic in a systematic way—even topics that Aristotle himself never explicitly addressed, like soccer. So, what did Aristotle say about soccer? Nothing explicitly, but a lot implicitly!

Why Are There Shinguards?

Shinguards are a great example of this. Aristotle never heard of shinguards, but he provided a way to analyze them two thousand years ahead of time. He noticed that, even in everyday conversation, people answer the question "why?" in four basic ways, no matter what they're trying to get to the bottom of: They'll tell you about either the stuff the things are made of, the structure of that stuff, who made the things, or (most importantly) the purposes that the things have (*Physics*, Book II, Chapters 3 and 7). So, a complete answer to the question "Why are there shinguards?" would take into account:

- **the stuff that shinguards are made of—plastic, foam rubber, and Velcro. Aristotle calls this the *material cause* of shinguards.**

- **the curved, peculiar shin-fitting shape that the plastic, foam rubber, and Velcro are formed into. This is the *formal cause* of shinguards.**

- **the owners and employees at Mitre who manufactured the shinguards. They're the *efficient causes* of the shinguards.**

- **the purposes that the shinguards serve: to protect the lower leg from vicious tackles and to make lots of money for Mitre Corporation. Now we're dealing with the *final causes* of the shinguards.**

Without any one of these four kinds of causes, there'd be no shinguards.

Aristotle remarks that "all men seem to seek" these four fundamental ways of answering *why* questions, "and we cannot name any beyond these; but they seek these vaguely" (*Metaphysics*, Book V, Chapter 2). Making us more precisely aware of what we already know vaguely is part of philosophy's job (*Physics*, Book I, Chapter 1). Score one for Aristotle.

It's All about Goals

The very name *shinguard* tells us that the function of a shinguard—to guard the shin—gives it its most basic identity. Without a purpose for shinguards, the materials would not be brought together and assembled into a shin-fitting shape by the workers at the Mitre factory. The final cause thus drives the other three causes. No wonder Aristotle remarks that, "each thing is defined by its end" (*Nicomachean Ethics*, Book III, Chapter 7). The final cause—the GOAL—is the most important of the four kinds of causes.

To illustrate this, imagine a volleyball that's made out of the same materials as a soccerball. This volleyball might have the same round air-inflated structure as a soccerball. It might even be made at the same factory as a soccerball. But nobody would maintain that the volleyball and the soccerball are fundamentally the same. They have different purposes.

Now imagine two soccerballs. One is made of plastic. The other is made of leather. One is a little underinflated. The other is overinflated. One is made in the Czech Republic. The other is made in South Africa. Wouldn't you agree that they can still both be soccerballs, as long as it's clear that both balls have the primary purpose of being kicked on a soccer field? This shows that Aristotle is right on target. (I'd call it another shot on goal for Aristotle, but sometimes editors choose to pass on the puns that I kick around in my mind.) The final cause (end, purpose, function, GOAL) is the most fundamental source of a thing's identity.

Goals Are Good

Aristotle also points out that common sense uses the concept "good" for a thing that is achieving its goals (*Ethics*, Book I, Chapter 7). Good shinguards are shinguards that fulfill the purpose of shinguards—to protect the shins. A good pair of cleats is one that fulfills the purposes of cleats—to grab the soil for quick turns while padding the feet. A good goalkeeper is one who achieves his goal of keeping the ball out of the back of the net. A good team is one that achieves its goals of scoring more goals than it allows.

Sure, the examples are mine, but the concept is Aristotle's. Or, rather, the concept of "good" belongs to common sense, and all Aristotle has done is point it out a little more clearly.

Didn't I caution you earlier that Aristotle, like any good soccer fan, is really into *goals*?

The Best Sport

Soccer is not just a good sport; it's the best sport. You and I know that. Aristotle's principles lead to the same conclusion. Just apply what we said a moment ago about the concept of "good." A good sport is one that achieves the purposes of sports. The best sport, then, is the one that most fully achieves the purposes of sports.

So, what are the purposes of sports? Aristotle helps us to identify three:

- *Physical and moral discipline for the players*

The body is an important part of human nature. So is virtue, which includes the ability to subdue bodily desires when appropriate. Thus, Aristotle's ideal system of education would include several years of physical training. Teenagers' exercise should be light, but "hard exercise and strict diet" are appropriate for young men in their twenties (*Politics*, Book VIII, Chapter 4). I'm sure you can already begin to see how soccer is ideal for fulfilling this purpose of sports.

- *A healthy release of emotion for both players and spectators*

Any great sporting event is a drama. Think of the World Cup. By means of a fairly harmless game, the players imitate some form of more deadly international strife. Aristotle's comments on the purposes of theater, which is all about actors imitating various deeds, thus apply to sports too. He remarks that it is "natural for all to delight in works of imitation" (*Poetics*, Chapter 4). They teach the spectators something about human nature by showing how different types of people might handle certain imaginable situations.

So: "The poet's"—and the sporting event's—"function is to describe, not the thing that has happened, but a kind of thing that might happen" (*Poetics*, Chapter 9). By doing so, both theater and sports cause us to enter more deeply into our shared humanity. They bring to the fore and cleanse various hidden emotions in us. The triumphs and tragedies of our favorite characters and teams become, in a way, our own, just as, a friend is "another self," whose joys and sorrows we share (*Ethics*, Book VII, Chapters 4 and 9).

Experience shows that these emotional purposes found in sports are best fulfilled in a soccer stadium. What other sport creates so many followers who choose to remain standing and singing for a full ninety minutes of action? What other sport's fans regularly travel, not only within the borders of their own country, but even around the world to cheer on their teams? Evidently, nobody rejoices and suffers together quite like the players and spectators at a soccer match.

• *Recreation for both players and spectators*

Sports are supposed to be fun. They should take our minds off work. (You pro soccer players out there reading this book will interrupt me here to quibble that playing soccer *is* your work. Point conceded. Having fun playing soccer is your job. Please don't rub it in.) No matter how much physical and mental exertion it might require, a sporting event should renew our energy for our other, more serious tasks in life. As Aristotle says, "Amusement is a sort of relaxation, and we need relaxation because we cannot work continuously" (*Ethics*, Book X, Chapter 6).

Soccer achieves this goal for both players and fans. The evidence is all around us and inside us. Here's my own personal testimony. It probably resembles your own. When I need some recreation, I run a mile to the local soccer fields with my ball. Usually nobody else is around at the time of day when I arrive. So I play a mock World Cup match against myself. Up and down the field, frantically zig-zagging as if to avoid defenders on all sides, passing across the field to myself, next executing a quick turn at the top right corner of the penalty area as the clock is about to expire . . . and then, without warning, a sudden, well-aimed rocket of a shot launched off my right instep, sails over the would-be goalkeeper's outstretched left hand, and flings itself, spinning, into the back of the net with a satisfying *r-r-r-r-i-i-i-i-i-p-p-p-p-p-p-p*—YES! GGGGGOOOOOAAAAAAALLLLL!!!!!! Another victory for the underestimated Americans! Mighty Brazil falls one–nil to the U.S.A. at the hands—oops, I mean feet—of thirty-five-year-old "Mateo," the dual-threat philosopher-striker!

This kind of fun exercises my imagination as well as my legs. (Wishful thinking is apparently a form of mental relaxation for me.) Now, when you need a break from work, maybe you don't do exactly what I do, but I'm sure you find your own way of using soccer to do it. Soccer is fun to play, fun to watch, fun to talk about, and (as you're seeing right now) fun to read about. No sport is more popular worldwide, and that by itself proves that no sport is more fun. As far as recreation goes, human nature was built for soccer.

How What's the Matter with Soccer Makes It Great

There's a more complete way to explain *why* soccer is the best sport. Remember that there are four ways of answering the question "Why?"

First, there's the material cause of soccer—what "stuff" is a soccer game made of? What's the "matter" with soccer?

Think of the field, the ball, the eleven players per team, and the lone referee. Each of these physical components, in its own way, makes soccer able to fulfill the purposes of sports better than any other sport can.

A soccer field is much wider and longer than a basketball court or a hockey rink. The players are expected to cover an enormous area of turf. Yet, unlike other big-field sports (say, baseball or cricket), soccer demands almost constant running. The field's dimensions never quite allow any of the twenty-two players to feel completely removed from the action. This produces more exercise and more recreation for all of them. A player's physical exertion and mental attention are required by the game practically one hundred percent of the time.

The field, the ball, and the jerseys in soccer are also exceptionally suitable for the theatrical purposes of sports. The field is large enough to dominate a spectator's view, including peripheral vision. The vast expanse of bright green grass is pleasing to the eye. But whether you're seated in the back corner of the upper deck or next to the head of FIFA in a luxury suite overlooking midfield, you can always see what's going on. The ball is large enough to be easily visible from a distance (unlike a hockey puck). The jerseys are colorful and graceful, with different designs from time to time for variety. All of this delights the senses. Aristotle indicates that such pleasures are very natural (*Poetics*, Chapter 4).

That's why I'm sure you and Aristotle would agree with me that the 1981 movie *Victory* is, at least artistically, the best movie ever made. A film that centers upon a soccer match is bound to be exceedingly beautiful, because the stuff of soccer is beautiful!

Long Live the Ref!

Let's not forget that the referee is part of the stuff that you need for a soccer game. What's especially interesting about soccer is that there's only *one* referee. (The linesmen are just his assistants, you know.) This coincides with Aristotle's political ideals. He maintains that, in the abstract, monarchy is the best form of government (*Ethics*, Book VIII, Chapter 10).

But you need a king whose virtue far surpasses his subjects'. That situation is often lacking in monarchical societies. (When we're mad at a ref, we're convinced that it's lacking in soccer, too.) A lot also depends on national character, Aristotle adds. When we leave behind abstract considerations and consider people as they actually are, monarchy quite often turns out not to be the best form of government for a particular country.

So, Aristotle concludes, one-man rule is not suitable for every time and place. Even when and where some form of monarchy is appropriate, the king's powers usually need to be limited (*Politics*, Book III, Chapters 16–17; Book V, Chapter 11). Yet *limited* monarchy isn't the ideal form of government for all times and places either—it's just what's best for some particular nation at some particular time. Some other nation might thrive more under an aristocracy or under a more republican form of government.

What does this have to do with soccer? Well, soccer just happens to be one of those realms where *limited* monarchy is appropriate. You don't need seven people to figure out whether to award a direct free kick for a flagrant foul. You only need one. One-man rule helps soccer to preserve its status as the most continuous, uninterrupted, smooth-flowing game there is. No time-outs for a refereeing committee to discuss what really happened—the game must go on! So, we might gripe about the refs, but I think we can all agree that the fewer of them there are, the better.

To soccer's credit, the original architects of the game realized all of this. Aristotle would be proud of them for perceiving the kind of government that's most suitable to their sport. They vested all executive powers in the referee, but they limited his powers. The ref doesn't *invent* the Laws of the Game. (It just *looks* as if he does, when he ignores all the shirt-tugging, elbowing, and tripping perpetrated against your team.) The ref simply *enforces* the Laws, adapting them to the circumstances of a match as needed. And his decisions can be appealed to FIFA if he's even more incompetent than usual.

By the way, don't be too hasty to dismiss the idea of limited monarchy as out-of-date even in the political realm. Think of how presidents and prime ministers act today. A friend of mine, Edmond Micucci, makes a case that they're actually limited monarchs. Aristotle seems to think so, too. (Just take a look at the opening lines of *Politics*, Book III, Chapter 16.) Each of them is a solitary head of state, but their powers are limited by a constitution (corresponding to the Laws of the Game) and by other branches of government (corresponding to FIFA). They're essentially the referees of their countries!

The Most Virtuous Sport

Imagine twenty-two athletes wearing their uniforms as they sleep on a grassy meadow with a soccerball nearby. The material cause of soccer is present. But this isn't a soccer match. (Unless you argue that I've just described an extreme version of *catenaccio*.) The formal cause of soccer is missing.

Soccer happens when the material causes of soccer are *structured* a certain way, according to the Laws of the Game. Think of it this way: Rugby is also made of a field, a ball, players, and referees. But there's a tremendous difference between those material causes performing soccerlike activity and the same material causes performing rugbyish activity. (Aside from the usual disclaimer about what you feel the ref allows the other team to do to your team.) The rules of soccer specify the unique markings on the field, the permissible methods of controlling the ball, the length of the game, the nature of European league play or World Cup tournament play, and so on. All these factors come together as soccer's formal cause. They form a genuine soccer match out of the stuff soccer's made of. They're the internal structure of the game.

One really striking feature of a soccer game's structure is its continuity. No team sport demands a longer period of uninterrupted action than soccer. Players who want to rest can't call time-out to catch their breath. Typically, they can't even leave the game (except in youth soccer), since almost no substitutions are allowed. The clock never stops, even if the ball goes out of bounds. Yet each half lasts a *minimum* of forty-five minutes. Only the referee knows for sure exactly when time will expire. As a result, every half ends with a flurry of panicked activity as the teams strain to get one last shot on goal. Players who should be—and are—exhausted have to push themselves hard until the very second they hear the final whistle.

Aristotle would praise soccer's continuity. It's apt to make players more virtuous. Virtue is one of the two or three ideas on which Aristotle's whole theory of ethics hinges. You become more virtuous by repeatedly choosing the *right amount* of eating, drinking, joke-telling, spending, working, playing, and so on. ("The right amount" can change according to circumstances, although some acts, like adultery, are always wrong because they're always cases of "too much.") Gradually, this lifestyle tames your less reasonable desires, like your desire to eat too many sweets and not enough vegetables. Choosing the "right amount" of everything then becomes second nature (*Ethics*, Book II).

Like a penalty kick shot straight at the goalie, soccer's continuity plays right into Aristotle's hands here. (Okay, I admit it, that last pun was about as lame as the shot that it described. But I like to throw in a little humor sometimes just for kicks, to prove I'm not out of touch.) For over ninety minutes, the players are confronted with a situation that requires renewed acts of self-mastery. They occasionally have the opportunity to slow to a walk or a trot for a few seconds—only to have the circumstances of the game suddenly demand a quick sprint toward the ever-returning ball. The action really is nonstop. Not once, not twice, but hundreds of times during a match, players must again subdue their more animalistic desires for rest and ease in favor of the nobler quest for victory.

That's just what Aristotle says the virtue of courage is all about. He writes that courage "chooses or endures things because it is noble to do so, or because it is base not to do so" (*Ethics*, Book III, Chapter 7).

The Most Civilized Sport

Aristotle would also be pleased that soccer is such a civilized way to form the virtue of courage. He notes that, in physical education, "What is noble, not what is brutal, should have the first place. No wolf or other wild animal will face a really noble danger; such dangers are for the brave man" (*Politics*, Book VIII, Chapter 4). Soccer keeps the amount of raw violence to a minimum. (Well, aside from what the ref allows the other team to do to yours.) The sport still raises the amount of self-mastery to a fever pitch by the constant, constantly renewed acts of running, turning, kicking, trapping, heading, throwing, playmaking, and defending.

One more thing: Aristotle says, "Courage and endurance are required for business and philosophy for leisure, temperance and justice for both, and more especially in times of peace and leisure." Why is some method of fostering virtue *especially* needed *in times of peace and leisure?* Because usually it's war that "compels men to be just and temperate, whereas the enjoyment of good fortune and the leisure which comes with peace tend to make them insolent."

Aristotle's right. You can't deny that boot camp teaches draftees a certain amount of self-denial that couch potatoes lack. But don't assume that Aristotle is a militarist. "The legislator should direct all his military and other measures to the provision of leisure and the establishment of peace," he writes. The goal of promoting virtue in the citizens doesn't justify the violation of the virtue of international justice.

Putting together all these ideas (from *Politics*, Book VII, Chapters 14–15), what is Aristotle essentially pleading for? A way to teach citizens virtue without involving them in unnecessary wars. That's yet another reason why soccer would be his favorite sport.

Soccer won't develop every virtue in a player. It won't by itself turn a bad person into a saint. No sport can. But it's exceptionally well designed for teaching virtue to someone who is willing to learn.

The Most Equitable Sport

Cameroon is on the attack. The Indomitable Lions' left wing passes diagonally ahead of the striker at midfield. The Argentine defenders are backpedaling. Suddenly a collective gasp emerges from the crowd. Out of the corner of his eye, the Cameroonian striker sees a player clad in blue-and-white stripes lying on the ground, writhing and pounding the grass in agony. Instantly, the attacker gives up his advantage. He turns toward the sideline and kicks the ball out-of-bounds. An enemy player has severely twisted his ankle in his attempt to intercept the pass.

After the medical personnel escort the injured Argentine player off the field, the Laws of the Game award a throw-in to Argentina. One of the Argentine midfielders calmly picks up the ball . . . and purposely tosses it directly at the foot of the Cameroon striker. The action resumes where it left off. Cameroon's attack continues. Argentina has returned the advantage that Cameroon had yielded for the sake of the injured player.

Such athletic chivalry is unknown outside soccer. In other sports, opponents might help each other up after a fall. But their willingness to assist the opposition in resuming play doesn't extend to the actual situation of the ball. Only in soccer!

If Aristotle witnessed the Cameroon-Argentina scenario, he'd consider it an excellent demonstration of what he calls "equity." This virtue applies justice by making an exception to a law when needed.

Legislators, including the framers of soccer's Laws of the Game, write laws to cover what usually happens. Sometimes there's an unusual case where following the letter of the law would defeat the purpose of the law. If the legislators had seen such a situation, they'd have made an exception.

To practice equity is to interpret the obvious spirit of the law in such cases, and actually make the exception. That's a virtue—especially when dealing with peculiar cases that the lawmakers never intended to address. Of course, it's *not* actually illegal for Argentina's throw-in to help Cameroon, but it simulates an illegal act (namely, Cameroon doing the throw-in). And right now I'm just pointing out how far equity can take us. Aristotle is rightly convinced that we must value justice above legalisms when there's a conflict.

True, some laws are exceptionless. Try this sample moral law, which I'm sure Aristotle would endorse: "Don't gouge out and eat your eyeballs for fun." You can't really imagine a reasonable exception to that command. It's based on the built-in purpose of the eyeballs, which is to see, not to feed us. By its very nature, making an exception to that law would be "too much recreational human eyeball eating." The "right amount of recreational human eyeball eating" is always zero.

But not all laws are exceptionless. Nor can they be. Many of them deal with areas of life where there will always be strange exceptions to the rule.

Argentina (in my earlier example) recognizes that soccer is one of those areas of life. The Laws of the Game weren't intended to punish the gentlemanly conduct of Cameroon. Sure, the strict letter of the law gives the throw-in to Argentina. The ball did go out of bounds off a Cameroon player's foot. But Argentina ignores the privileges granted by the letter of the law. The Argentine midfielder who executes the throw-in knows that Cameroon deserves the ball. He gives what's owed. It's justice, and it's equity at the same time (*Ethics*, Book V, Chapter 10).

A Sport for All of Humanity

Soccer's rules favor finesse over mere muscle. Players must develop every body part, from head to toe—including their hands and their arms, which are necessary for doing throw-ins, for posturing so as to shield the ball while dribbling, and even just for maintaining general balance while defending or ball-handling, or while jumping for a header. (And don't forget about the goalie!) Soccer players must also use their minds. How many team sports permit less advice from the coaches during the game? The tactics are almost entirely left up to the players on the field. Soccer thus engages the whole of human nature, both physical and mental.

All this squares nicely with Aristotle's advice on exercise: "A man's constitution should be inured to labor, but not to labor which is excessive or of one sort only, such as is practiced by athletes" (*Politics*, Book VII, Chapter 16). The athletes in Aristotle's day evidently weren't soccer players! The exercise in soccer varies from head to arm to knee to foot to mind. And the fun of the game offsets the work, so that nobody can charge soccer with "excessive labor."

Aristotle would also love a sport that involves both the body and the mind because of his views about the relation between the two. He maintains that each of us is one person with two aspects. There's a physical aspect and an invisible but equally real mental aspect.

The physical aspect is your body. Unlike his teacher Plato, Aristotle thinks that your body is a genuine part of the "complete you." St. Thomas Aquinas (a thirteenth-century thinker who builds on Aristotle's insights) explains why in even simpler terms than Aristotle by using Aristotle's own principles: Your five senses operate through bodily organs. Right there you have a sign that there's more to you than your mind (Aquinas, *Summa Theologiae*, Part I, Question 75, Article 4).

Aristotle agrees with Plato that your mind is part of you, too. Your thoughts occur inside you. Yet nobody can see your thoughts under a microscope or with a surgical instrument. Ideas aren't that kind of thing. Your brain is in your skull, but your abstract ideas (like the definition of "*justice*") aren't. So, your mind is part of you and is real, but it isn't three-dimensional space-filling stuff (*On the Soul*, Books I–III).

The result? Chess wouldn't be Aristotle's favorite sport—it's too exclusively mental! Aristotle does say that something purely intellectual (namely, the contemplation of truth) is the highest human activity (*Ethics*, Book X, Chapter 7), but the unique purposes of sports—as discipline, as theater, and as recreation—mean that the most perfect *sport* and the most perfect *activity* aren't the same thing. A simple footrace wouldn't earn Aristotle's highest admiration, either. Not enough mental stimulation. Soccer alone provides a maximum of nonstop physical and mental exercise simultaneously. It's the sport that most completely addresses the whole of human nature!

Tragedy and Comedy in Soccer

We call soccer athletes "players." They're fulfilling various roles (goalie, sweeper, midfielder, and so on) in an unscripted play. We don't know whether it's a tragedy, a comedy, or something else until it's over. Aristotle would say soccer's formal cause makes it marvelous theater. And, as you know, that's one of the purposes of sports.

How can I connect Aristotle's views on theater with soccer's formal cause? Easily. Remember that continuity is one of the most unique and most important attributes of the structure of a soccer game. Aristotle thinks that continuity is one of the most important attributes of a great tragic play or work of literature, too. "The story, as an imitation of action, must represent one action, a complete whole," he states. The incidents must be "so closely connected that the transposal or withdrawal of any one of them will disjoin and dislocate the whole." So, the best kind of plot has "all the organic unity of a living creature." The worst kind presents "neither probability nor necessity in the sequence of its episodes."

These comments (*Poetics*, Chapters 8–9 and 23) reveal that Aristotle would approve of soccer as theater. At almost every moment, the location of the ball on the field has a direct connection with where it was a moment ago. Even after a foul or after the ball goes out of bounds, the referee resumes play from the location where the ball was most recently. The energy of the game flows gradually, not in quantum leaps, as the ball moves first toward one goal, then toward the other. The only disconnects occur at halftime and when a goal is scored—major and rare events!

Other sports lack this level of unity. They consist of multiple "scenes" and "acts." Basketball routinely interrupts the game for in-bounds passes and free throws, sometimes at the opposite end of the court. Baseball and cricket separate their action into unconnected segments as one player after another (and one team after another) takes a turn at hitting the ball. Hockey, besides having not one but two intermissions, often restarts play after a stoppage with a face-off far from the spot where the puck was before the stoppage. And American football is interrupted literally every few *seconds*, as soon as a ball-carrier is tackled. No sport can rival the unity of the "plot" in a soccer game.

What about the kind of plot? Aristotle seems to think tragedy is a nobler form of theater than comedy. In a tragedy, the main character is a fairly virtuous person who commits "some error of judgment." This error leads to the person's downfall. A cleansing of the audience's inner emotions of fear and pity results (*Poetics*, Chapters 4, 6, and 13).

Now think of a game where your team plays hard yet loses one-nil. A simple mistake by the sweeper in the fifty-ninth minute leads to a breakaway for the other team's hitherto hapless striker. A desperate shot emerges from the foot of the lucky opponent during his unaccustomed split-second of open field. It's his first and only goal-scoring opportunity of the day. One of your team's defenders lunges feet-first for the ball instantly as it leaves the enemy's foot. He doesn't realize that the opponent's shot is off target. The defender's foot just barely reaches the ball . . . and accidentally redirects it into the back of his own net behind the startled goalkeeper. The better team (yours, of course) falls to the underdog. One-nil. You go home, shaking your head, frustrated. One-nil.

That was truly a tragedy! Especially since Aristotle says that the most powerful tragedies are those where the main character's blunder harms his own family (*Poetics*, Chapter 14). Soccer can be quite tragic in this way. It's one of the few sports where own goals regularly occur. Relegation games, when the favorite loses, provide another instance of tragedy in some professional soccer leagues. We all want our team to win. But according to Aristotle, tragedy yields a healthy form of emotional cleansing for the spectators. Defeat succeeds as a form of theater. (Next time your team loses, console yourself with this insight from Aristotle!)

Why Aristotle Loves FIFA

The efficient causes of soccer are primarily FIFA, the team owners and organizers, and the coaches. They make games happen, and Aristotle would love the way they do it.

FIFA emblazons its praiseworthy motto "Fair Play" everywhere. Every stadium posts this reminder that soccer is supposed to uphold the virtue of justice. FIFA proves it expects gentlemanly conduct from its players and coaches. Think of the severe punishments meted out to players who provoke red cards or even a few too many yellow cards. Doesn't this concern for fair play remind you of Aristotle's emphasis on virtue? FIFA knows that fouls make for foul play, not fair play.

Coaches, team owners, and team organizers also promote virtue. They not only exhort the athletes to courage and justice but also discipline them in drills and practices. This method would earn Aristotle's approval. What especially helps us to mature morally is not so much words as discipline. Punishment and reward encourage us to perform certain kinds of actions until they become second nature. "It makes no small difference, then, whether we form habits of one kind or another from our very youth." A virtue—or a vice—will result (*Ethics*, Book I, Chapter 3; Book II, Chapter 1; and Book X, Chapter 9). Don't complain the next time your coach tells you to run laps before practice. He's helping you to become a better person!

The drills that you perform over and over again likewise imitate the way virtues are formed. Each time you do the drill, you get better at it. At the same time, as you get better at it, the drill becomes easier to repeat. It's sort of the opposite of a vicious circle. (A virtuous circle, I like to call it.) After you've mastered the drill, you get more out of the coach's verbal instructions. Suppose he says to use your instep more in passing, or to use the center rather than the top of your forehead. You know what those actions feel like, now. The coach's advice is more meaningful. You can put it to use right away, because of the habits of coordination that you've already formed.

As in soccer, so in life! The more you perform virtuous actions, the easier they become. The easier they become, the more likely you are to repeat them, and the more deeply you can understand good advice and put it to use.

The Goals of Soccer

Practically nobody wants to be alone all the time. Human nature drives us to seek the company of others. Friendships, marriages, towns, and countries are the result. Men need women, and women need men. Babies need their parents for everything. Families need other families for a fuller life of sharing each other's talents and companionship. Towns need other towns for trade and defense. The government is needed to enforce laws that punish vice and encourage virtue. Aristotle is very clear about these topics in *Ethics*, Books VIII–IX and *Politics*, Book I, Chapters 1–2.

What does all of this have to do with soccer? Well, the most basic final cause of soccer is to score goals *as a team*. Nobody wins or loses alone in soccer. (Except me, when I take my ball to the local field and pretend that I'm the U.S.A. beating Brazil.) You have to cooperate with your teammates. A brilliant header flicked toward a teammate is worthless if the teammate can't or won't receive the pass and continue the attack. A well-aimed wall pass won't succeed at getting around a defender if the teammate acting as the wall is a ball hog who won't pass back.

That means soccer, as a team sport, fulfills the social side of human nature. When you try to achieve the purposes of a soccer match—above all, victory for your team—you find yourself practicing social virtues like friendliness and generosity toward your teammates. Individual sports like golf and tennis don't present the same opportunities for on-field collaboration and shared experience.

Soccer promotes the social virtues even better than most other team sports, too. Basketball players score goals as a five-man team. Hockey players score goals as a six-man team. But soccer players perform as an eleven-man unit. Wider cooperation is developed. The defenders, midfielders, and forwards are like different families working alongside each other in the same town or country. The goalkeeper participates, too, but in a different way. Maybe we can compare him to the government since he's the one most ultimately responsible for defense. He ceaselessly watches the enemy's goal and never abandons his own, just as good rulers would do in a country. (Or you might compare him to the military, since he never leaves his post. Literally.)

Soccer brings recreation and exercise to more people because of the large number of players per team, too. And the choreography of an eleven-man unit provides a more beautiful theatrical spectacle than the teamwork of a smaller group of athletes would.

Finally, soccer's final cause emphasizes the importance of . . . the final cause (that is, a thing's purpose, the end, the *goal*). Remember how Aristotle emphasized the final cause? He connected the notion of goodness with the notion of goals. Also remember how he stated that the definition of a thing comes above all from its purpose. Well, can you imagine any sport besides soccer where goals are so important?!?!?

Zero-zero ties regularly occur, because it's so difficult to score. Soccer mirrors Aristotle's philosophical insights by the premium that it places on goals.

Extra Time

My chapter is coming to an end. I don't want to bore you with an academic-sounding conclusion summing everything up. I want to end like a soccer game, with an insane scramble to get in one last goal before time expires. The referee is looking at his watch. . . .

That reminds me of another philosophical insight from Aristotle . . . What is time, anyway? Do events (like the ticking of the second hand on the ref's watch) measure time? Or does time measure events?

Quickly, quickly! Well, let's take a look at *Physics*, Book IV, Chapter 11. Uh-oh . . . the referee is reaching for his whistle! Where's the quote?!?!? . . . WHERE'S THE QUOTE??!?!? . . . here it is!! "Time," Aristotle says, "is just this—number of motion in respect of 'before' and 'after.'" YES!! I got it in before the chapter ended! I'd continue, but you'll have to look it up yourself. The final whistle and my would-be explanation of Aristotle's definition of time are now being drowned out by ten thousand jubilant voices as the editors of this book carry me out of the stadium on their shoulders . . .

GGGGGOOOOOOOOOOOAAAAAAAAAAAALLLLLLLLL!!!![1]

---

[1] Credit for the assist on this goal goes to Ted Richards for his editorial savvy.

5
Plato and the Greatness of the Game

ANTONIS COUMOUNDOUROS

We are enthralled by feats of greatness, feats that take great skill and ability to pull off. Soccer provides us with many moments of greatness and it does so frequently. Well executed shots, tackles, headers, passes, dribbles, bicycle kicks, saves, and goals make the soccer fan's blood flow a little faster and a little hotter.

Soccer mystifies so many people because of the magnificent skills soccer players exhibit on the field. Pelé, Diego Maradona, Zinedine Zidane, Thierry Henry, Lionel Messi, Cristiano Ronaldo, to name but a few great footballers, have managed to capture our imagination through their supreme excellence. We have their posters on our walls, their pictures on our screensavers, and we wish we could be like them. Such footballers are the soccer greats. But what is soccer greatness? What is it that makes a soccer player great?

Some 2,500 years ago, Plato lived in a culture which emphasized greatness and excellence. A competitive spirit defined the ancient Greeks and they thrived through competition in athletics, poetry, politics, philosophy, and war. Plato was naturally very interested in the question of excellence in general, and in human excellence in particular, and he made several important contributions to our understanding of both. He wanted to explain what makes something the best it can be, and what makes a human an excellent or great human. While Plato was primarily interested in human greatness in moral terms, his reflections on greatness are applicable to athletic excellence. So, even though we're separated from him by over two millennia, Plato's reflections on what makes something great can illuminate our understanding of soccer.

Plato discussed greatness in three distinct ways throughout his dialogues: his theory of Forms, his view of excellence, and his understanding of the four virtues of moderation, courage, wisdom, and justice. By applying each of these three ideas to soccer we can answer the question of what makes someone a great soccer player, and increase our appreciation of the superstars of the game.

The Form of a Footballer

Plato sought to explain reality and to provide a framework for human knowledge and goodness through his theory of Forms. According to Plato's student Aristotle, Plato as a young man espoused the doctrine of Heracleitus that all things are subject to constant change (Aristotle, *Metaphysics*, 987a29–b13). For Heracleitus, nothing in reality remained the same for long. Everything moved and mixed with other things, ceasing to be what it was just a little while ago. It was Heraclitus who first said, "One cannot step into the same river twice." But it seemed to Plato that humans could know all sorts of things in definite and unchanging ways. To have knowledge in the sense that what one knows, he knows in a secure and unchanging way requires that the object of knowledge not be subject to change. If everything is constantly changing, then knowledge would be impossible, since the objects of knowledge would change. No claim about anything could hold true for long since nothing would remain a fact.

Plato ingeniously managed to conceive of a position that allowed for both change and for knowledge. Since knowledge presupposes that the objects known must be stable, particular sensible things make terrible candidates for knowledge. But since it seemed to Plato that we do know things, and that what we know cannot be the particular things we experience with our senses, we must know something else, something that must be unchanging, non-physical, and beyond the evidence of our senses. These unchanging objects of knowledge are the Forms.

Plato thought that reality has two realms: the realm of physical reality which we access through our senses and which is subject to constant change, and a realm of supersensible reality—the realm of the Forms—which we access through our thought and which is not subject to change. Thus, for Plato, knowledge of the Forms is the only knowledge possible. By making one part of reality subject to change and another not, Plato managed to have a position that allowed for change and for knowledge.

What are Forms exactly, and how do they relate to the things in the physical world that we experience with the five senses? To know that the thing in front me is a *mountain*, Plato would say that I must know the Form of mountain. To know that an action or a person is *just* I must have access to, and know, the Form of justice. I have to know what a mountain is and what justice is to be able to recognize an actual mountain and an actual act of justice, but what I know in both cases is the Form. Plato envisioned the Forms as perfect or ideal originals in which the things in my sense experience relate to by participation or imitation. These things are copies or embodiments of the Forms. A particular mountain, triangle, or human participates in the perfect Form of mountain, triangle, or human.

Plato also thought that particular things are always imprecise imitations of the Forms. They can only approximate, but never equal, the perfection of the Forms in which they participate. A particular triangle drawn on a piece of paper cannot have its angles equal 180 degrees exactly whereas the Form of triangle, being perfect, necessarily does. A particular human being will always have some flaws whereas the Form of a human being is perfect. Even great particular instances or copies of the Form, which are very close imitations of the Form, can never be as perfect as the Form itself. In this way, Plato understands greatness in relation to the perfection of the Form. One thing is greater or better than another given how closely it is an imitation or copy of the Form.

How Pelé and Maradona Imitated the Form

If Plato were alive today he would speak of soccer player Form. He would tell us that actual soccer players are more or less accurate copies of this Form depending on how good each player is at the game, and that the great soccer players are very close imitations of soccer player Form.

What is the Form of soccer player? Imagine the absolutely perfect soccer player: someone who could play all positions on the soccer field equally well and with absolute perfection, who can never fail to score, who scores a tremendous amount of goals, who always scores exceptionally beautiful goals, who can win every trophy there is to win, who never fails to tackle someone, who never gets tired, who never concedes a goal, who can dribble past anyone without fail, who runs much faster than everyone else on the field, who heads the ball successfully every single time and so on. This is the Form of soccer player, it is perfect, and it is what many actual players try to imitate; they try to be as great at the game as they can by developing and refining the necessary skills. It is also what we think of when we try to figure out whether a player should make the list of great soccer players or not. We try to match the skills of actual soccer players to the array and excellence at the skills entailed in soccer player Form.

Plato's conception of the Forms allows us to explain how one thing may be greater than another by comparing the things in question with a Form. We can already see that actual players can only approximate this ideal Form of soccer player to a higher or lower degree. Some players are clearly better than others and the better players are closer approximations of the Form. Moreover, actual players can only imitate the Form in some ways but not in others; the best forward or winger is never also the best defender or goalkeeper. Great goal-scorers don't always score beautiful goals, and in fact, many of their goals are rather mundane. Thus, actual soccer players have limitations one does not find in the Form. Still, there are some players in particular who are exceptionally close imitations of soccer player Form.

Pelé and Maradona should be at the top of anyone's hierarchy of soccer greats. Pelé was the first person to be presented as a complete soccer player worldwide and the first player to make famous the enchanting and dynamic Brazilian style of play. Soccer styles other than the Brazilian seemed rather tedious when one watched Pelé and Brazil perform their magic on the field. Regardless of nationality, most people support Brazil in the World Cup when their own national team is not a contender.

Pelé is a supreme example of a footballer who closely approximates soccer player Form in several ways: scoring, scoring beautiful goals, winning trophies, dribbling, athletic ability, stamina, heading the ball, and speed. Let's begin with goals scored: Pelé scored five goals six times, four goals thirty times, three goals ninety times and he totaled twelve hundred and eighty one goals in his career! He averaged one international goal per game, which means that it was a surprise if he did not score during a game. When he first signed for the New York Cosmos, he complained to his teammates that they should play with him more and stop constantly giving him the ball and expect him to score every time. He made scoring look so easy even his teammates thought he could do it any time. Pelé is also the only soccer player to have been a member of three winning World Cup teams. Thus, Pelé, being a great goal-scorer and an exceptional winner of trophies, managed to imitate soccer player Form faithfully in both of these ways. Being so able to score so many goals would not be possible without the requisite spectacular speed, dribbling skills, stamina, balance, and athletic ability.

Pelé is also a great imitation of soccer player Form when it comes to scoring beautiful goals. In the World Cup final of 1958 against Sweden, the eighteen-year-old Pelé fulfilled every player's dream to score in such an important game—he scored two magnificent goals. The first goal was an accurate lob over a defender followed by a spectacular volley, which smashed in the back of the net. As a member of the victorious 1970 Brazil World Cup squad (arguably the best national team of all time), Pelé scored another beautiful goal in the final against Italy, and he was involved in what are probably the most famous save and the most famous miss in World Cup history. In the game against England, Pelé's wonderful header was saved spectacularly by goalkeeper Gordon Banks (many fans consider this the save of the twentieth century).

In the semifinal against Uruguay, Pelé received a through-ball and while Uruguay's goalkeeper attempted to come off his line to intercept the ball outside the eighteen-yard box, Pelé got to the ball first and without touching it, he tricked the goalkeeper so the ball went past him. After beating the goalkeeper, he took a shot with his right foot while being off-balance and under pressure from a defender, and the ball licked the post and went out of bounds.

Both the save and the miss have come to acquire such glory largely because it was Pelé who headed the ball saved by Banks, and the one who missed the shot against Uruguay. A great soccer player, paradoxically, "infects" even his misses with greatness. People were so used to Pelé scoring goals that they felt the only way to explain his failing to do so was due to extraordinary circumstances: a great save in the first case and terrible bad luck in the second.

Diego Armando Maradona, like Pelé, is undoubtedly a soccer great in Platonic terms. Maradona deservedly shares the title of player of the twentieth century with Pelé. In Argentina's successful campaign during the 1986 World Cup, Maradona managed to score two of the most famous goals ever. He did this in a single game and led his team to a 2–1 victory against England in the semi-finals. Soccer fans have seen highlight after highlight of both goals and remember them well. The first goal, known as the "Hand of God" (*La Mano de Dios*), was a handball that initially looked like a legitimate header over goalkeeper Peter Shilton. A five foot five Maradona managed to score what seemed like a header over a six foot one Shilton.[1] The referee allowed the goal due to the tremendous speed of play and due to the fact that Maradona kept his hand very close to his head when he struck the ball. It was only upon viewing replays that it became clear that Maradona had scored by using his arm. This is an instance in which a soccer great infuses even an illegitimate goal with greatness. Maradona's speed and athletic ability

---

[1] There is something amazing about rather short players being able to score spectacular goals with headers since they are not supposed to be good at headers—for example, Lionel Messi's goal against Manchester United in the 2009 Champions League Final.

tricked our eyes and made the goal appear legitimate and beautiful, if only for a moment.

But it is the second goal in the match against England that proves without a doubt that Maradona was a great imitation of soccer player Form. Maradona received the ball on the right side of the field at the half way line, and he managed to dribble with lightning speed and agility past five English players using only his left foot, to score for a second time during that game. Most people expected him to be stopped, at least after he got past the second player, but to everyone's amazement, he kept going past three more until the ball was in the back of the net and Argentina on their way to winning the World Cup. This goal is rightly known as the "Goal of the Century." (Kirk McDermid compares these two goals further in Chapter 11.)

Maradona was a very skilled dribbler with incredible ball control, passing, and scoring ability. He would be able to draw several defenders and then dash past them very quickly in very limited spaces or provide assists to unmarked players. After practices, he often used to stand on the penalty spot and kick the ball onto the crossbar, the ball would bounce back to him, he would control it with his foot or chest, and then kick it off the crossbar again and again. (To begin to realize how good Maradona was, try this one the next time you are on the soccer field. I have seen a documentary where Zinedine Zidane admits to having a hard time doing it!) Needless to say, this is a superb example of his ball control and accuracy.

Neither Pelé nor Maradona were great players defensively and in this way they fall short of soccer player Form. But given that soccer is a game that involves a variety of positions, we could speak of the Forms of the various positions as well, which would be subsets of the more encompassing soccer player Form: forward Form, attacking midfielder Form, winger Form, central defender Form, goalkeeper Form and so on. If we consider the more narrow subset Forms, forward Form for Pelé, and attacking midfielder Form for Maradona, this justifies even more thinking of them as soccer greats. They approximate these Forms much more closely than they do soccer player Form in general.

Ooh Ronaldo, Ooh Henry, Ooh Marta, I Wanna Knoooooow How You Scored that Goal: Excellence as Ability at a Function

In conjunction with his discussion of excellence in relation to the Forms, Plato argued that excellence or virtue (*aretê*) in general is associated with ability at a function. Something is excellent when it performs its proper function well. We have seen that soccer player Form entailed a number of abilities at functions such as goal scoring, speed, ball control, and dribbling. The Form also entailed excellence at these functions. But what is a thing's proper function? Plato tells us succinctly that, "the function of each thing is what it can alone do or do best" (*Republic*, 353a). He means that the proper function of something is what something is able to do exclusively (exclusive function) or what something can do better than other things (optimal function). So to figure out a thing's excellence, we have to know its ability at a function.

If we think of the proper function of a central defender, we can see that it is largely to defend and hold the middle of the defensive line. This is the central defender's optimal function and a player is an excellent central defender when he is able to perform this function very well. Players who are good at playing in other positions may perform the function of a central defender, but such players are not very likely to perform it well. If I were in charge of picking the central defenders for a team, I would do better to pick Rio Ferdinand, Nemanja Vidic, or Carles Puyol over, say, Lionel Messi or Cristiano Ronaldo, since neither Messi nor Ronaldo can perform this function excellently or optimally. Each position on the field requires that a number of abilities and skills—such as speed, toughness, ability to head the ball well, good positioning, awareness of opponents, dribbling—be nested together in such a way so that the overall function of that position can be performed with excellence. Different positions entail different sets of abilities. Some abilities will certainly be shared by all positions, but the full set of abilities will be different for different positions. In general we wish to see players with the requisite abilities in the appropriate positions on the pitch.

Thinking of optimal function (what something can do better than other things) entails a comparison among different things that can perform the same function, and picking out the one that can perform it the best. Optimal function is really the most relevant type of function in considering soccer excellence. Given that soccer is a game in which there are many great players, a player may perform the function of his position optimally during one season, whereas in another season, even though the same player performs excellently, another player ends up performing optimally. The same is true of players performing in individual games. Furthermore, when thinking of the various positions in soccer it becomes clear that many players are so talented, that they are able to combine the functions of traditional positions into something of a new position on the field.

When we talk about the modern game and player's abilities, we cannot avoid talking about Cristiano Ronaldo. His ability and potential were recognized early on by none other than Manchester United's Sir Alex Ferguson. Ferguson brought Ronaldo to Manchester United to replace the most recognized soccer player in the world (David Beckham), and he may be the best player ever to have played for Manchester United.

Ronaldo plays as a winger or outside midfielder, the traditional function of which is to carry the ball down the right or left touchline and to assist the forwards in scoring goals. Wingers are often also very skilled in set pieces. Have you seen Ronaldo take his "Terminator" free kick lately? He takes three steps back, spreads his legs, picks his spot, steps up to the ball, takes what looks like a short swing at the ball, and then . . . Goal!

In the modern game, the outside midfielder is often allowed much more mobility and given more attacking responsibilities on the field, turning him into a midfielder who can make supporting runs and score more goals than traditional wingers. In this way, the function of the outside midfielder can be different, more mobile, and more encompassing than that of the traditional outside midfielder. Modern outside midfielders can hardly be called "wingers" any more, since they do not just play on the wing, they do not merely serve the ball, and they get involved in more goal scoring opportunities. Ronaldo's fiery pace, tremendous ball control, his capacity to perform ball tricks during a game against formidable opponents (no wonder people call him "twinkle toes"), his scoring and dribbling abilities, and his ability to explode into a forward, set him far apart from most other players of his time. These abilities also make him an excellent outside midfielder in the modern game: Ronaldo has outside midfielder excellence or greatness.

Ronaldo's goal tally and the beautiful way he scores goals are impressive by any standards and they are a testament to the fact that he is not a traditional outside midfielder. In the 2007–08 season alone, he scored forty-two goals, which included a memorable thunderous header against Chelsea in the Champions League final. He is clearly the reason why many defenders and goalkeepers have nightmares.

Thierry Henry's greatness became clear only after Arsène Wenger brought him to Arsenal. Wenger had coached a young Henry at Monaco and he was not sure whether to play him as a winger or a striker. Henry's quick pace made him look like an ideal winger, since this could cause all sorts of problems for fullbacks. After a rather silent season at Juventus in 1999 where he still played as a winger, Henry signed for Arsenal and never looked back. Wenger decided to play Henry as a striker instead of a winger, and Henry was able to bring his experience as a winger into his new role.

It is a mark of all great soccer players that they make what is tremendously difficult for mere mortals appear easy. Henry clearly performs the forward's function excellently since he can score quite easily. He often slides off to the left flank, where he looks very comfortable, to take what is essentially a winger's position. In this way he's able to perform the function of two positions during a game. This also allows him to contribute a considerable number of assists and to allow other players to impact the game. Henry is able to score, seemingly without much effort, from one-on-ones in front of the goal and this, in addition to his pace, dribbling skills, field awareness, and positioning, has turned him into a superb forward.

Henry scored a spectacular two hundred and twenty six goals for Arsenal making him the club's all-time leading scorer. While scoring so many goals is not the highest number of goals scored by a player from an English Premier League club (Dixie Dean scored 383 goals for Everton from 1925 to 1937), Henry managed to score this many goals from 1999 to 2007—a relatively short time for scoring so many goals—and to score them at this point in the history of the game when it is much more difficult to score against defenders and goalkeepers. His splendid thirty-nine goals during the 2003–04 campaign (he was the top scorer that season) contributed to capturing the Premier League trophy and to an unbeaten season for Arsenal. In 2008–09, he won the Spanish league, Spanish cup, and Champion's league treble with Barcelona, and between him, Lionel Messi, and Samuel Eto'o they scored more than ninety goals that season. No team that season could hope to compete against a goal tally that high.

Three-time FIFA Women's World Player of the Year (2006, 2007, 2008) Marta Vieira da Silva, known simply as Marta, is a formidable forward by any standards. All forwards are expected to score in every game they play, the expectation that Marta will is more realistic than in the case of other players. Her actual goal scoring proves this. Like Pele did, she averages one international goal per game. She has also scored more than twenty goals in all the seasons she has played. Her consistency in goal scoring is a testament to her excellence. She wears the legendary number ten shirt for Brazil (worn by such greats as Pelé, Zico, and Kakà) and she performs the function of the forward, which is to score goals, optimally.

Marta's excellent performances also prove that women's soccer does not lag behind men's soccer in exhibition of spectacular skills, speed, fascinating goals, and physical and mental toughness. Her second goal against USA in the 2007 Women's World Cup is a great example of her excellence. Marta was on the edge of the eighteen-yard box, facing away from goal, with a defender on her back. She received a bouncing pass, took a touch to control it, throwing the defender behind her slightly off balance, and then she flicked the ball with her heel in the air, made a quick one hundred and eighty degree turn around the defender, thus getting past her. Then, she took another touch to dribble past a second defender and then, as expected, she scored.

How Beckenbauer and Zidane Practiced the Four Cardinal Virtues

Understanding excellence in terms of exclusive or optimal function places the focus on outward aspects of people, on their results and abilities. Plato also believed that excellence corresponded with inner attributes, that the character of a person can establish excellence. In the fourth book of the *Republic*, Plato names four main virtues pertaining to human beings: wisdom, courage, moderation, and justice. Possessing these virtues makes a human a morally good and a happy human, that is, an excellent person. These four virtues came to be called the four cardinal virtues and they are internal characteristics that accompany the external exhibition of excellence.

Plato divided the human person into three parts. Each of these parts is identifiable by a particular function: the rational part whose function is thinking; the spirited part whose function is the experience of emotions; and the appetitive part whose function is the experience of appetites of the body for such things as drink, food, and sex. When each part performs its proper function well, then, as expected, each part has its proper excellence. In addition, when all the parts perform their function well, then the whole person is excellent.

The excellence of the rational part is wisdom, which is the knowledge of what is true and good for the whole person. Wisdom for Plato is essentially a thorough knowledge of the Forms. The excellence of the spirited part is courage, which is the experience of emotions in the right way in relation to fear. Courage entails fearing what one should and not fearing the things one should not. The excellence of the appetitive part is moderation, which is the control of one's appetites so as to avoid excess or deficiency. Moderation is essentially striking a balance between excess and deficiency: doing neither too much nor too little but the right amount. Finally, justice, for Plato, is the excellence of the whole person. It is present when each part of the soul is performing its proper function without interfering with the proper function of the other parts.

In order for this harmony among the parts to take place, the rational part should rule over the other two parts since it can guide the whole person according to wisdom and knowledge. Plato suggests for example, that to be courageous one needs to know what to be afraid of and what not to be afraid of, and this knowledge can guide one to courageous acts. All of these excellences need to exist together for someone to be a balanced, harmonious, and well functioning, in short a just person.

This scheme of excellence by means of virtues is applicable in areas beyond moral excellence: soccer player excellence as exhibited on the field can also be understood by the presence of the four cardinal virtues. In the previous two sections we have associated Plato's philosophy with primarily physical aspects or abilities of the game of soccer. Now we have enough tools to discuss the internal, psychological, aspects that go into being an excellent soccer player.

A successful soccer player requires each of the cardinal virtues to play a significant role both on and off the field. Off the field, players need to watch their diet, get plenty of rest, and practice and exercise the right amount; this is soccer player moderation. They need to persevere in practice and battle fatigue, yet know when not to push through an injury; this is courage. Often, practicing hard may seem difficult or entail things one is not so sure they can do and thus give rise to fear. But we can see that a player who is able to persevere is one who conquers his fear and is thus courageous. Players also need to improve their understanding of their position, of the formation their team plays, and of the game to be able to perform better on the field. This is soccer player wisdom. Balancing all these things without having one dominating the others would be the equivalent of what Plato called justice. A successful soccer player would not just seek to understand the game but not practice or exercise properly, or to exercise without understanding the game or his position very well.

A few examples will help us see how the four cardinal virtues are applicable to soccer players on the field. Franz Beckenbauer (*der Kaiser*), the legendary defender and captain of the German team in the 1970s (then West Germany), played a large part of the 1970 World Cup semifinal against Italy with a fractured clavicle after the Germans had used their two allowed substitutions. This is clearly a supreme example of courage in soccer. Germany lost the game 4–3 in extra time and the game was called the "Game of the Century." Beckenbauer was also largely responsible for shutting down Johan Cruyff and Dutch "Total Football" in the 1974 World Cup final, through very close man-to-man marking. Beyond his physical abilities as a master defender, Beckenbauer was known for his tactical awareness and decision-making on the field (his wisdom), for always being calm and collected (moderation), and for always inspiring his teammates to play harder through his own way of playing (courage). Holding all these things in a balance, which produced tremendous results on the field, would also make Beckenbauer "just" in soccer terms.

Zinedine Zidane is another player who has exhibited extraordinary ability and who has scored many breathtaking goals and provided superbly accurate assists. In the 2002 Champions League final, Zidane scored the winning goal for Real Madrid with a spectacular left volley from the top of the eighteen-yard box. Zidane also won World Player of the Year three times, a World Cup and a European Championship with France, he scored two goals in the 1998 World Cup final, and he managed to score in two World Cup finals. Zidane led great teams to many trophies due to having all four virtues during his long career, but in one famous instance in the 2006 World Cup final, the four virtues seemed absent.

What soccer fan does not remember the famous image of Zidane walking past the World Cup trophy after being sent off for head-butting Italy's Marco Materazzi? Zidane allowed his emotions to overtake him, got angry, and after losing his composure he head-butted Materazzi in the chest and was sent off. How would Plato explain this incident? In Platonic terms, Zidane was ruled by his emotions (his anger in particular) or spirited part and not his rational part. He should have been able to control his anger by having his rational part outweigh his emotions. If he were able to listen to his rational part, which was presumably telling him that responding with a violent head-butt would have bad consequences for him and his team, he would have been able to outweigh his anger and would have probably acted differently. Plato's conception of the four cardinal virtues is clearly applicable to soccer and it allows us to understand and explain both cases in which greatness is exhibited and cases in which greatness is absent.

Plato's conceptions of the Forms, excellence, and the four cardinal virtues are applicable to soccer and the several players we have considered serve as good illustrations of these ideas. Moreover, Plato's ideas allow us to understand and thereby appreciate how special the superstars of soccer and their abilities really are. Now I leave you to contemplate the Forms of soccer team, soccer manager, and soccer fan, and what excellence is for each of these.

6

Can Robots Play Soccer?

PETER STONE, MICHAEL QUINLAN,
and TODD HESTER

On July 8th, 2007 in Atlanta, Georgia, five people, including one of the authors, stepped onto a small indoor soccer field to play the first ever exhibition soccer match between humans and autonomous robots. The robots from the University of Osnabrück, which moved on wheels and were outfitted with omnidirectional cameras to allow them to see all over the field, had just won the "middle-sized league" of the annual RoboCup robot soccer competition. The experiment was repeated in 2009 on a larger field against five robots from Stuttgart, the champions from that year.

In both cases, the waist-high robots turned out to be no match for the amateur human players. The people were more mobile, better at passing, and generally able to use the field more effectively. They were able to score quickly, and by the end of the twenty minute game, they were toying with the robots, keeping control of the ball without running—only walking. (You can see for yourself at www.cs.utexas.edu/~AustinVilla/RobotsVsHumans2007.mov.) However, there was a marked improvement in the robots' play in 2009, lending some degree of credibility to the claim that, just like they have already done in chess, machines may someday overtake humans at soccer.

Building robots that will be able to overtake humans at soccer is the goal of a vibrant and continually growing scientific community of computer scientists and roboticists known as "RoboCup" or the robot soccer World Cup. The stated goal of the RoboCup initiative is to develop a team of robots that is better than the best human soccer team by the year 2050. But this goal begs a central philosophical question: Can robots play soccer?

We may be able to build robots that can run, kick a ball, head, dribble, and pass. In fact we have already built robots that can do a few of these things. But will they be able to *play* soccer, or will they only be able to *mimic* soccer?

One way to determine if robots can play soccer is to conduct a modified Turing test. Alan Turing originally proposed the following test for determining if a machine is intelligent: A human judge converses by typing in natural language at two different computer screens. At one, the judge is conversing with a person, at the other, she is conversing with a computer program. If the judge cannot tell the difference between the computer and the human, then the computer has passed the Turing test and is deemed to be intelligent. The general idea is that if a human can't tell the difference between the behavior of an intelligent being and a computer, the computer is intelligent (as far as we can tell). This idea can be easily modified to determine if robots can play soccer. In the case of soccer, if a robot team can compete with a human team, and what results is recognizable to the fans as a soccer match, then it is safe to say that robots can play soccer. This is one reason why some RoboCup participants phrase the goal of the initiative as, "to create a team of robots that is capable of beating the World Cup (human) Champion soccer team on a real, outdoor soccer field by the year 2050."

To test whether robots can play soccer, however, we don't really need such a lofty ambition. While being able to beat the World Cup Champions makes for a wonderful slogan, the difference between a world class team and a good lower-division professional team is not all that great. Consider, for example, that it is not uncommon for a League 1 team to defeat a Premier League club in the English FA Cup. To determine whether robots can play soccer, all that need be done is for them to compete against a serious human team.

To date, RoboCup competitions have always been between teams of fully autonomous robots—with no people "in the loop" via remote control or otherwise. People program the robots, but when the game is being played, the robots are entirely on their own. Detailed sets of rules govern the play in several different "leagues," including simulated robots, wheeled robots, and legged robots of various sizes. But so far, little thought has gone into developing rules that could govern matches between robots and people.

However, to have robots and humans competing on the same field will require a modification of the rules of soccer. Currently, the definitive rules—called *The Laws of the Game*, administered by the International Football Association Board (IFAB), a subcommittee of FIFA—are vague as to what constitutes a player. Under the heading "Players", the Law reads:

A match consists of two teams, each consisting of not more than eleven play-ers, one of whom is the goalkeeper. A match may not start if either team consists of fewer than seven players. (p. 15)

The tacit assumption is that the players are human. But what if they are not?

The prospect of robots playing the game forces us to consider what aspects of the rules are essential to the game of soccer, and what rules can and should be changed.

Change the Rules, Are You Kidding?

Currently, there are no size or weight limits placed on human players: all people are eligible. However the physical form of robot players must clearly be restricted in some way. Consider, for example, a "robot" that is exactly the size and shape of a goal that remains stationary on the goal line, thus guaranteeing no goals against. Surely such robots should not be allowed.

That modifications to the rules would be necessary for robots to com-pete against humans should come as no surprise. The same situation was previously addressed in the world of tournament chess. Leading up to the famous match between the computer Deep Blue and the human cham-pion Gary Kasparov, the rules of chess had to be modified to address issues such as what to do if a person makes an error carrying out the pro-gram's move, and what to do in the event of a power failure, due to the fact that the computer may lose vital information about the match.

Nor should any hue and cry about preserving the purity of the game prevent us from considering a change of the rules. Soccer is a game that is easily modifiable. It is played worldwide in many variations: indoor soccer, futsol, beach soccer, 3 versus 3, kids games with no goalies, and many others. There are different rules in friendlies versus international tournaments, and the rules have changed over the years (for example, modifying the definition of offsides, and the addition of the "pass-back" rule). But in all these variations, nobody questions whether the game is still soccer. Indeed, *The Laws of the Game* specify that modifications to the ball, goals, field size, length of play, and substitution procedure are permissible (p. 4). Arguably these allowances, written into the rules of the game as they are, add to the popularity of soccer by making it acces-sible to players in a wide range of age, skill and ability. All other modi-fications require the consent of the IFAB. Presumably, this is because other changes run the risk of violating the essence of the game. For example, few would consider it soccer if players other than the goalie were permitted to use their hands.

But changing the ball, goals, field size, time, or substitutions won't help us with our robot wall problem. If we're going to have robot versus human matches, we are going to have to brave the wrath of the IFAB and suggest rules that go beyond those allowed by fiat. And we will have to do it without changing the essence of the game; because if we change the essence of the game, then the robot-human match will no longer be a test of whether robots can play soccer.

Preserving the Essence of Soccer in a Human v Robot Match

There are three alternatives for defining the essence of soccer, each of which leads to very different rules for a match between robots and humans. The first alternative is to define soccer as essentially a game played by humans. In that case, there is no way for robots to participate.

The second alternative is to treat soccer as being defined essentially by its rules. According to this view, the current rules of soccer should be altered as little as possible to accommodate robots. If people can build robots that run twice as fast as people, that can shoot the ball into the corner of the net every time, or that can prevent any shot from scoring (a robot wall), then robots are better than people at soccer, end of story.

The third alternative, and the one we espouse, is to identify soccer as being defined essentially by the set of possible behaviors and strategies that can be used. This alternative is the trickiest to specify. This set of behaviors and strategies is already constrained by the *Laws of the Game*, but not enough for a human-robot competition. From our perspective, a game without teamwork, passing, and creative movement off the ball would no longer be soccer. If the robots can easily and reliably score from any location on the field, therefore never needing to pass or move, then even if they can win a game of soccer according to the current rules, we would not be comfortable saying that they are better at *soccer*.

In taking this perhaps controversial position, we don't seek to deny or remove the physical component of soccer. This physical component is what makes our task different from defining the rules of computer chess in which the computer and the person are constrained by the game to have identical sensing and action capabilities. They can both see the whole board and they have the same moves available to them. Thus computer chess programs are (usually) completely free to solve the problem in their own way, such as searching millions of board positions and storing large databases of positions. In the same way, it's important to us to allow robots to excel at soccer in their own way, including its physical components. They should be free to trap the ball and dribble with as much finesse as they can muster. But we are concerned that if we do not place any limitations on their speed and power, the essence of soccer will be lost.

The challenge is to give a set of rules, to add to the *Laws of the Game*, such that if they were used for a soccer game between humans and robots and the robots won, it would become clear that robots were better at soccer than people. For this to happen, the rules would have to preserve the essence of soccer and also be fair to both the people and the robots.

Rules to be considered fall roughly into four categories: Individual robots, teams of robots, coaches of robots, and humans. (Those rules we endorse are bulleted in the sections below.)

Individual Robots

We must place some restrictions on individual robots in order to prevent unfair advantages, such as being able to block the whole goal. One key limitation that we propose for the robots is that they should have roughly human form: two legs, two arms, and similar sensing and motion capabilities to humans. The robots should have arms and hands to execute throw-ins, but of course they must not touch the ball with their arms during the course of play.

This restriction on form is somewhat more subtle than it appears on the surface. For example, if a robot has two legs and two arms, but no torso (the legs go all the way to its head), is that permissible? Similarly, the exact definition of "leg" needs to be specified. On the fiip side, need we place any new restrictions on the human participants? If the robots must have two arms, can a person who has lost his arms play soccer?

Can the people have any artificial or robotic parts? Such a question came up in the 2008 summer Olympic games when Oscar Pistorius, who was was born without tibia bones in his legs, wanted to compete with the prosthetic devices, or blades that he uses to allow him to walk and run. Just as Pistorius was not allowed to compete, presumably because his blades could give him an unfair advantage, we suggest that the people must not have significant robotic parts. But this still leaves many grey areas, such as whether a person should be allowed to use a hearing aid. For now we prefer to leave the rule somewhat ambiguous, subject to interpretation based on the medical and robot technology of the day:

- **The robots must have two legs, two arms, and a head where any visual and audio sensors can be located. They should have at most two cameras for visual sensing, placed side by side such that the field of view is similar to a person's.**

- **The people must not have artificial parts that endow them with any superhuman capabilities.**

In addition to restrictions on form, the size, weight, and various capabilities of the robots must be restricted to ensure fairness. If no such limitations were in place, it would be possible to play with robots that could run twice as fast as any human, or that could shoot the ball at such a speed that no person would step in front of it.

Again, it can be tricky to figure out exactly what the restrictions should be. On the one hand, we do not want the robots to have an unfair advantage by being significantly bigger, faster, or better shooters than people. On the other hand, we do not want to limit the robots excessively so that they have no chance.

To this end, we propose limiting any *individual* robot to being no bigger or better than the *biggest* or *best* human professional soccer player. We compare against soccer players rather than against all humans for the practical reason that the robots will be playing against them rather than against Olympic sprinters or sumo wrestlers. We also believe that it would not be fair for *all* of the robots to be as fast as the fastest human player, and we'll come back to that.

It may always be a technical challenge to build a robot that can run as fast as a person. If so, this restriction will be unnecessary: the robots may always be slower than people so that the people always have an advantage in this regard. But if it turns out to be possible to build robots that can run faster than people, then we believe that they will need to be restricted in order to preserve the essence of soccer.

To this end, we propose the following rules on robot capabilities. The first is necessary; the other five are debatable.

- **No individual robot should be heavier or bigger (in any dimension) than the heaviest or biggest professional soccer player.**

- **No individual robot should be able to run faster than the fastest professional soccer player.**

- **No individual robot should be able to kick harder or more accurately than the best professional player.**

- **No robot should be able to execute a throw-in that is farther or more accurate than the best human soccer player's.**

- **The robot goalie should not be able to jump farther or higher than the best professional goalie.**

- **The robot goalie should not be able to throw or punt harder or more accurately than the best professional goalie.**

In order to enact these limitations on the robots' capabilities, there will need to be a way to measure the abilities of both humans and robots. How exactly do we measure things like kicking strength or accuracy? When measuring speed, do we measure top speed, acceleration, distance running, or some combination of all three? Do all of the human players need to be measured, or is sampling sufficient? How are the robots tested? Must there be hardware limits, or is it sufficient for the limits to be in software? We leave these details to be determined in the future.

Two other concerns related to individual robots are stamina and safety. The robots should be able to operate autonomously for a full forty-five minutes without any intervention, including battery changes or refueling (though one might argue that a battery change or refueling is akin to a human drinking water, which is permitted). On the other hand, humans get tired as the game goes on, so it is tempting to require that the robots get tired as well. However it appears to be too difficult to precisely measure "tiredness" to place a restriction on the robots in this regard. How do you model the ability to "dig down" and find the energy for one last sprint in the ninetieth minute? We therefore suggest that robot stamina should only be limited by what is possible based on battery and power management technology. It is for this reason that we suggest prohibiting battery changes except at halftime.

Similarly, we do not suggest placing limitations on the robots' abilities to plan ahead, react quickly, or "read" the opponents. In some sense, this is exactly what we aim to test: whether a team of robots that have similar physical characteristics to humans can be programmed with better ball-manipulation, passing, and decision-making skills than people.

Finally, if we really intend to stage a match with the rules we're proposing, it's essential that we consider the human players' safety. The humans will—rightly—never agree to play such a match without some assurances that the robots are not likely to injure them seriously. The robots must place human safety above all other goals, including winning the match. They may commit intentional "professional" fouls for strategic reasons, but only in a way that does not endanger any person.

Again, the method of enforcing such a restriction is not straightforward. After all, the best way for the robots to minimize the risk to humans is to stand still the entire game, which is clearly not our intention. Perhaps the robots should be required to generate a log of all their decisions so that, after the fact, it could be determined whether there was any "intent" to injure. But an unethical programmer could easily bypass such a requirement by generating false logs. In practice, we will probably need to rely on the robot developers' sense of the high cost of human injury (at least in today's climate, a single injury to a human star could spell the end of human-robot sports forever) to make sure that the robots are as careful as can be in this regard.

Based on this discussion, we thus suggest only two additional rules with regards to individual robot capabilities, the second of which is again open to interpretation and further specification:

- **The robots must be able to play completely autonomously for the entire time that they are on the field: program changes and battery changes are not allowed.**

- **The robots must not plan to commit any dangerous fouls and must make every reasonable effort to avoid injury to the humans.**

The basic principle behind these rules is that soccer is essentially a game played by players with *limited* capabilities. An essential quality of the game is figuring out how a *team* of players can compensate for the limits within the team and exploit the opponent team's limitations.

Robot Teams

A team is defined not just by the capabilities and limitations of its individual players, but also by how the capabilities of the *different* team members interact. In principle, the robot team could be built with identical characteristics in each of its players: once we've discovered how to make one robot run as fast as the fastest professional soccer player, we could easily build all robots to run at the same speed. However, we feel that a team of identical players violates an essential component of the game. Rather, we suggest stipulating that no two robots on the team can be identical in their combination of speed, size, weight, kick strength, and kick accuracy. Just like in human soccer, different robots will be best suited to play different roles on the team based on their particular skills.

One way to implement this requirement that the robots not be identical is to have a total "budget" for each skill to be distributed among the team. Just as we suggested limiting individual robots' characteristics based on the characteristics of the best individual human players, we also suggest limiting the team based on the collective characteristics of the best professional soccer teams. Suppose that a team's speed is defined to be the speed with which the team could run a relay race in which each team member ran 400 meters.

We propose that the robot team be limited to run the same relay no faster than the humans (when each robot is running as fast as it can). Similarly, there should be team budgets for all the other important player characteristics, such as total height or weight of the set of robots. The robots could be designed so that one player is a superstar, able to run and kick as well as the best human player. But then the rest of the robots would need to be limited significantly. On the other hand, the robots could have skills that are more evenly distributed among the team, subject to the limitation that no pair be identical. Just as human coaches need to select carefully a mix of players for their team, the robot designers will need to trade off between the various robot capabilities.

- **The total budget of speed, size, weight, kick strength, and kick accuracy must be distributed across the robot team so that the total team capacity in each dimension is no better than that of the fastest, biggest, heaviest, and best-kicking human professional teams.**

- **No two robots can have an identical (or close to identical) set of these characteristics.**

- **The robot team should be allowed the same number of substitutions as the human team. Robot malfunctions should be treated in the same way as human injuries with regards to whether they need to be removed from the field, when they can re-enter the field, and how much injury time should be added.**

In addition to a soccer team consisting of players with differing capabilities, a second essential team-related property of soccer is that the players can communicate with one another. In human soccer, the players may communicate in any language and by any means, including gestures and body language. Typical things that are communicated are marking assignments, directions regarding where to move, forewarnings of future actions ("I'm going to pass to you"), or multi-player play calls ("give and go"). However robots could potentially also be equipped with wireless communication that would allow communication of much more detailed information, such as the precise location of the ball, and a player's full conception of where all the other players are on the field. Such wireless communication would be imperceptible to the human players, thus not revealing anything about the speaker's location, as happens when a person speaks.

Just as is the case for running speed and kick power, our intention is to prevent capabilities that would enable unsoccer-like strategies. It is tempting to suggest a limitation either on what is communicated or on the communication "bandwidth" (rate) so that the robots may not communicate more information than humans can. However, like stamina, the bandwidth of human communication is difficult to define, especially when things like tone of voice are taken into account. Thus, we suggest for now that robot communication should only be limited to be in the same medium as that of humans, and that body language of any form be allowed:

- **The robots may not emit any signals for the purpose of communication other than sounds of limited volume that are perceptible to the human ear.**

If it turns out that the robots are able to communicate much more information than humans in this way, then it may eventually be necessary to find a way to limit communication rate or content.

Coaching

A team of robot soccer players may have two types of coaches. There will certainly be human coaches, including the engineers and programmers, that prepare them for the match ahead of time. There may also be a "robot" or software coach who observes the game and imparts strategic information to the robot players during the game.

Devising strategies suited to a particular opponent is an important part of the game, sometimes consuming the attention of many people for countless hours prior to an important match. There will be no bound on the amount of coaching the human players get prior to their match against the robots, and similarly, we do not suggest any limitations on the human coaches of the robots.

However once the game has started, it is an essential quality of the game that the players must decide for themselves what to do. A robot (or software) coach may yell information from the sidelines. But it may not take advantage of its global view of the field to "micromanage" the players, telling them where to pass or where to move at every instant. Thus the robot coach should only be able to communicate in the same way as the players: orally and with limited volume.

Even this restriction may not be enough to prevent the coach from micromanaging. It may be possible to devise a language that the robots can speak and understand quickly enough for the coach to call out every pass decision to its players. For this reason, we also suggest borrowing a technique from the RoboCup simulation league and requiring that coach messages be delayed by five to ten seconds. The coach will submit what it wants to say to a separate computer program that will then emit the sound after the delay. So the coach will only be able to communicate strategic information that is relevant over long periods of time, not instantaneous action decisions that should always be the responsibility of the individual players.

- **The robot team is allowed a software coach who may have an overhead view of the field, but who can communicate with its team only orally with limited volume and with a five to ten second delay.**

As with the players themselves, we do not recommend placing any computational restrictions or bounds on the "intelligence" of the coach.

Human Players

So far the only restriction that we have placed on the human players is that they should not have artificial parts that give them superhuman capabilities. The only other restriction that we envision needing to place on the human players is that they not intentionally engage in any activity that disrupts the robots' communication or other normal mode of operation through any form of deception or trickery. They should play soccer as they do when playing against other humans.

This restriction probably does not actually need a special rule as it can fall under the current law of the game that "unsporting behavior" is a cautionable offense.

Will It Work?

The rules given above have been designed with an eye both towards fairness and towards faithfulness to the essence of soccer, so that the team that wins a match played under these rules can credibly be seen as being better at *soccer*. In designing the rules, the essential elements of soccer that we have preserved are the following:

- **Soccer is a game played between teams of players with *incomplete sensing* and with *different capabilities* and *limitations*.**

- **The players move and kick at *roughly* the same speeds, thus requiring passing and *movement* off the ball for effective play.**

- **The players can *communicate*, but with limited bandwidth.**

- **The individuals are completely *autonomous* while on the field.**

- **The coach can provide only *strategic advice* during the game.**

The rules should be taken as a starting point to be modified based on the technological state of the day. Though a lot of our focus has been on limiting the robots to be no better in any dimension than the humans, it is quite possible that such a perspective is overly optimistic with regards to robot technology. Robots may never be able to run as fast as people, or kick as hard and as accurately as people. In that case, many of the rules we proposed will be irrelevant. However if we had to bet, we would say that eventually, robots will indeed be able to run faster and kick better than people.

While the rules have been designed with an eye towards the theoretical goals of fairness and essence preservation, we also want the game played under these rules to determine whether robots can *play* soccer. Towards that end, there are some pragmatic questions concerning these rules worth considering:

Aren't these rules 'stacked' against the robots?

Some readers of this chapter will conclude that the rules are rigged so that the humans will always win. There are more limitations on robots than on humans, making the robots more 'human' and less 'robotic'— they take away any inherent advantages the robots may have. On the contrary, we propose these rules precisely so as to give the robots a chance of decisively demonstrating that they are better than humans at soccer. If there comes a time when a team of robots defeats a team of humans under these rules, then no spectator will be able to cry "foul!" The robots will not have won because they were all faster than the humans, nor because they used wireless communication. They will have defeated the humans because they had better finesse with the ball, they worked better as a team including managing the players' strengths and weaknesses, had better vision with regards to passing, and had better movement off the ball. In other words, they were better at the essential components of soccer. Only then will we be able to say with confidence that the robots can *play* soccer.

Will human players agree to play?

People are only likely to be willing to play against robots if they are confident that they are no more likely to sustain an injury than were they playing against other people (or at least they will require much higher payment for playing if injuries are likely). Even once the robots have a credible chance to beat a human club, it will probably be a long and involved process to convince the team to actually risk their players in such a game.

One possible way to ease the transition would be to first allow the human players to play in friendly matches on mixed human-robot teams, where the robots act as teammates to the humans. In fact, within the RoboCup initiative there has already been a brief experiment with such mixed teams in which Segway-based robots teamed up with humans riding Segways. The rules were carefully designed to prohibit any direct contact between the humans and the robots: any player with the ball was given a one-meter buffer zone, but was not allowed to dribble (similar to the rules of ultimate frisbee). It is possible that if players initially gain experience playing *with* the robots in such a setting, they may become more confident that it is safe to play *against* them in a regulation match.

Will fans be interested?

Soccer is enjoyed by both fans and players worldwide, and their enjoyment is one of soccer's most important qualities. When the first robots versus humans soccer matches are played, the level of enjoyment and acceptance by fans may reveal a lot about what is essential to soccer.

If fans are not interested in watching robot soccer, it may tell us that the players being human is important to soccer's essence. Without human players, including their limitations, motivations, and emotions, soccer may not be the same game. Then again, it may turn out that fans flock to the games because the robots play better, more precisely, and even more creatively than humans, implying that the skills and the game are more important to soccer than who or what is playing.

A side-effect of trying to preserve the essence of soccer in our proposed rules is that we believe that the resulting matches will indeed be entertaining and compelling to watch, especially when the robots and humans are relatively evenly matched and the games are close.

But an FC Bot-celona?

Let's assume that all agree that our proposed rules preserve fairness and the essence of soccer, and that the pragmatic questions can all be resolved. Will the robots win? Even if the robots lose, will the match be enjoyable and identifiable as soccer? Will we be able to conclude at the end of the match that robots can *play* soccer?

We don't know. There is no way to know until the match takes place. In that way, it's a lot like the human matches we all love: it will have to be decided on the pitch. Though today it may seem like a long time before a humans versus robots sporting event could be held, the incredible progress of roboticists around the world, including our many RoboCup colleagues, is making the prospect ever more realistic. We hope that we can be in the audience for the first World Cup match between robots and people![1]

―――――――
[1] Thanks to David Levy for helpful discussions related to the rules of the first human-computer chess matches, Manuela Veloso for helpful discussions related to RoboCup, Jeff Andrews for comments regarding the nature of the human game, Ted Richards for his graceful edits, as well as many of our colleagues from the RoboCup initiative for their ongoing inspiring efforts towards the point where this chapter could be put to practical use.

7

The Hand of God, and Other Soccer . . . Miracles?

KIRK McDERMID

June 1986: It's early in the second half of a scoreless World Cup quarterfinal at the Estadio Azteca. Argentina's Diego Maradona slips the ball to Jorge Valdano, who tries to play it back, but is closed down by England's Steve Hodge. The ball deflects high off Hodge's shin, into the path of Maradona and the advancing English goalkeeper Peter Shilton. They both jump—and Diego tips the ball into the net, over Shilton's outstretched fist.

What?!? Maradona out-jumps Shilton? Incredible! Unbelievable! Miraculous . . . ? At the time, even the BBC's commentator didn't notice the how the goal was scored—and Tunisian referee Ali Bin Nasser surely didn't, either. But replays and photographic evidence soon revealed the truth: Maradona had used his hand to tip the ball over the onrushing Shilton.

Maradona celebrated the goal as if nothing special (well, over and above an opening goal in a World Cup quarterfinal!) had happened, cheekily remarking in post-match interviews that God had a hand in the goal: it was scored *"un poco con la cabeza de Maradona y otro poco con la mano de Dios* [a little with the head of Maradona and a little with the hand of God]." This quote delighted the Argentinians, and gave the English fits. In the larger context—a history of imperial colonialism, previous football grievances, and most significantly the recent Falklands Islands conflict—this appeal to providence struck many Argentinians as a perfect response. They took the outrageous goal and Maradona's glib account of it as poetic justice delivered by a nation victimized by the English, as confirmation that they were and would in the end be favoured by God. The English, of course, heard Maradona's description as a continuation of a despicable act; a bald-faced, villainous lie perpetrated on

89

the pitch now extending beyond the Azteca. Only nineteen years later did Maradona publicly acknowledge the way he had scored that opening goal.

In the game, Maradona added to his legend just minutes later with an individual effort that left more than half the pitch and five English defenders (plus Shilton, again) in his wake to score FIFA's "Goal of the Century". Gary Lineker's late goal brought the English back into contention, but too late: the Argentines won this quarterfinal 2–1 on the way to their second world title, avenging their controversial loss to England in the 1966 World Cup.

Okay, So It Wasn't Really a Miracle . . . Was It?

Few took Diego's claim of divine assistance literally . . . but what if we do? What would it mean, if that goal was scored "a little with the hand of God"? How could this be a miracle, given that we know the cause of the goal was a mere mortal hand—captured in video and still photos, no less! No divine intervention seems required, here: Diego was responsible for that goal, legitimate or not. Even if it was God using Diego as His bodily instrument, how could we ever really know that was the case? (Could even Maradona himself know that God had performed a miracle through him?)

The fact is, that goal didn't look particularly miraculous—especially if you were English. But the second, scored just a few minutes later? We might be able to make a better case for that goal's status as a miracle. Maradona deftly dribbled and carved through half the English team, contending with a less-than-pristine pitch in the process, to slide the ball past Shilton again. Jimmy McGee, calling the game for Irish television, commented that Maradona had delivered "a goal for the gods." Given the quality of that play we could fairly ask whether McGee got it backwards, that Maradona received rather than delivered. Even Sir Bobby Robson, the England manager, described it as "a miracle, a fantastic goal." It was eventually voted as FIFA's "Goal of the Century." Though I'll only be discussing this game, I'm sure that any soccer fan can recall equally amazing moments of the greatest significance for their team, which we might wonder about: were they just the product of human toil and skill, or was there a little bit of divine aid playing a role as well?

What Are Miracles, Anyway?

One of the problems with discussing miracles, for philosophers, is that this is one of those words that is just a little too familiar to the everyday speaker—it seems to have a perfectly understandable meaning, even to those without any particular religious background, until we realize exactly how flexibly the word is used. Sometimes, it seems almost secular, meaning something close to "improbable." (Most sports fans are familiar with this sort of usage.) But then it doesn't seem to have to have that meaning at all in other contexts: take for example 'the miracle of birth', which happens thousands of times a day, all around the world.

So what does "'miracle'" really mean, then? The Italian theologian and philosopher, St. Thomas Aquinas, identifies two crucial elements that make an event truly miraculous: "those things are properly called miracles which are done by divine agency beyond the order commonly observed in nature." (*Summa Contra Gentiles*, III). To count as a miracle under Aquinas's definition, the event in question first needs to be an *intentional supernatural action*. That means it can't be accidental, or a by-product of some other thing God did intend to accomplish. (So, the rippling of the net as the ball nestled in the back of Shilton's goal is not, by itself, miraculous.) The event also has to be legitimately divinely caused, not just inspired by God. Secondly, the alleged miracle needs to be "beyond the order commonly observed in nature." There seems to be roughly two ways to read this: either it just means the event is improbable or unexpected, if we stress the 'commonly observed' part of the phrase, or it means that it could not possibly have occurred naturally, if we stress the 'beyond natural order' part.

Does this help us figure out whether either of Diego's goals were miracles? It's just a start: we have to dig deeper into these components of miraculous action, to see how they might work in these two cases. We'll have to see what philosophers and scientists understand the 'natural order' to be, and what it might mean to go beyond it—that's the philosophical study of reality, or *metaphysics*—and we'll also have to explore what it means to be able to identify a miracle, or be justified in believing that one did occur. That involves the philosophical study of knowledge, or *epistemology*.

Identifying a Miracle

I'm going to start by granting that there aren't very many people who would say the "Hand of God" goal was a miracle: Maradona's statement in the press conference was just the off-the-field portion of his guile and personality. Especially with the multiple camera angles and still photos, this looks like a simple case of handball. But, this raises the question: what do 'real' miracles look like, then, if they don't look like this?

This question is one of knowledge and evidence: what signifies a miracle? Is there a tell-tale sign, like stud marks or a ripped jersey that reliably indicate a foul? It's not as if there's a neon sign over every miracle, attributing it to God. One of the oldest traditions in philosophy is *scepticism*, the idea that we don't or can't know some of the things we think we know. A popular argument for scepticism has to do with accessibility: often, we don't have direct access to the object of our knowledge. What we have direct access to, perhaps, is only our perception of an object, not the object itself. This is a subtle but very important distinction for epistemologists! (We know our perception isn't always direct, because we sometimes perceive nonexistent things—we hallucinate.) This presents a problem, because if all we have are indirect methods (like our senses) for getting at the truth, then we can't ever be sure that we've really reached the truth. Some might claim they have direct intuition or revelation of God's work, but one problem with that sort of knowledge—if we admit it *is* knowledge—is that it's not inter-subjectively verifiable. We can't share it with others, so it's much less robust, in terms of surviving criticism or testing, than publicly shared evidence. If we limit ourselves to the sorts of things that are publicly experienceable, like visually verifiable facts about the actions of a player on the pitch, can we say anything about what might count as evidence for a miracle?

Well, we might start our search by looking at the event itself: is there any *intrinsic* (internal and essential) feature of an event that 'labels' it as a miracle, some sort of metaphorical "I did it" sign that God can hang on his handiwork? After all, some historical accounts of miracles seem to have such features—a visually remarkable or even magical nature that believers and non-believers alike realized was an indicator of divine activity. Sometimes, the sign was simply the massively improbable, unusual, or impossible nature of the event. (Think of Moses and the parting of the Red Sea, especially as envisioned by De Mille!) There are a couple of competing arguments for and against miracles being obvious, ostentatious displays of God's power like this. In favour of "flashy" miracles is the idea that miracles are at least partially intended as signs for the faithful and unfaithful alike, undeniable evidence of God's providence over the natural world. Subtle miracles might be overlooked! But there are reasons to think that our popular ideas about the flashiness of miracles might be wrong, or at least not required.

First, we have to appreciate that the observer of an event is, to some degree, in charge of how they perceive that event. Neither of Diego's goals was "just" a goal. Their significance was in part due to the larger context of the rivalry between the nations both on and off the field. A Ghanaian or American, or even an Argentinian or Englishman ignorant of recent history, would have 'seen' these goals much differently. Think of showing a soccer fan just a highlight of Maradona's Hand of God goal, without providing context. Would they just shrug? Probably. Considered on its own, there doesn't seem to be any intrinsic features of the goal that even hints at its miraculous nature. Given Diego's character and drive, you could make the case that this goal was really pretty unsurprising. We might have expected, before the match, that Diego would score, and that the goals could contain some element of controversy— that's just Maradona, after all.

There may be other ways for God to convey the message that He has performed a miracle—in particular, by the timing and larger effect of the intervention, rather than by the actual details of the event. Perhaps miracles can be identified as miracles not because of some intrinsic feature of the event considered by itself, but only by considering the event in the context in which it occurs—the *extrinsic* features of the event. In this case, the fact that the goal was the opening goal in a very important game would be a start in identifying this as a miraculous occurrence. Add in the footballing rivalry from 1966's quarterfinals, when these teams were involved in a highly charged match where the Argentines—and others—thought they had received the short end of the stick in terms of refereeing decisions. (That match was filled with fouls, bookings, and plenty of ill will. Among the incidents: Argentine captain Antonio Rattin was sent off controversially in the thirty-fifth minute, for dissent, and England manager Sir Alf Ramsay forbade his players to swap shirts at the end of the game, calling the Argentines "animals" for their behaviour.)

But of arguably more importance would be the political context surrounding the match. This 1986 meeting was the first between the two soccer powers after the 1982 Falklands/Malvinas Islands conflict, in which Argentina failed to reclaim a small group of islands off their coast from the British. In particular, the illegal manner in which the goal was scored could be highlighted as significant, as it mirrors what Argentines perceive as the lawless actions of the English in the history of their occupation of the islands. Altogether, the underlying sense of injustice that Argentines felt before the game and the retribution that this victory represented could be seen as contextual signs of divine influence. Yes, outrageous infractions of the rules do happen without the referee seeing them—but to happen there, in *that* game, between *these* two nations, and involving *the* brightest star of Argentinian soccer (who also happens to be almost a foot shorter than the English keeper) . . . the significant coincidences abound! It is this larger context, and not the play on the field, that does most of the work in providing suggestive evidence for this goal's miraculous nature.

But this raises an important issue: given those extrinsic identifiers, is it *just* this goal that is "the miracle"? Imagine that the game had proceeded as it did, except that in addition to his first goal, Lineker somehow found a way to get his head on Barnes's cross in the final minutes of the game, sending it to extra time—and the English (for the sake of this argument) go on to win in extra time, or on penalties. (I know, just bear with me.)

If that's how the game had played out, would the Hand of God be anything more than pub quiz trivia? The important thing, arguably, was that the Argentines won that game, avenging the loss in 1966 and their perceived political mistreatment. So the 'real' miracle was winning the game, of which the Hand of God goal was only a part. A crucial part, perhaps, but just a part. This goes to show that even if we can agree that something miraculous has occurred, it might be really difficult to figure out what precisely it was that occurred miraculously. Was it Maradona's handball? Hodge's clearance? Bin Nasser's blown call? Or was it the much-earlier selection of a Tunisian referee instead of an official from a more recognized soccer federation, more familiar with the rivalry and Diego's character?

Part of the difficulty, beyond trying to pin down what identifies a miracle, is determining what those identifiers might say about the *scope* of the miracle. If we focused on the footballing context—just the rivalry arising from the way the 1966 match had been officiated—then perhaps the goal in itself could be the miracle. But the Hand of God by itself seems insufficient response by God, if he was intending to redress the injustice of the political situation. In that case, the goal would only be a part of a larger miracle, and may not have been a part of the game that God intervened in to bring about an Argentinian victory at all.

On the other hand (sorry), Maradona's second goal seems to have more intrinsically miraculous attributes. Yes, it was important in the larger context that this goal was scored—it was the winning goal after all—but the intrinsic features are much more prominent. We can make a better case here that this goal was miraculous regardless of the final result. The touches of Maradona in that surge forward (with Jimmy McGee of Irish television fairly shouting all the way through, "a different class! A different class!"), the almost inexplicable melting away of the English defence, the last-second touch to send the ball past Shilton before finally getting tackled, all combine to form a very extraordinary package of skill when considered all on its own. Showing a fan a highlight of "the Goal of the Century" surely wouldn't elicit a shrug!

So, the occurrence of these goals does provide us with some reasons to think they might be miraculous. But we need to ask: are these 'signs' sufficient? Calling any event a miracle is an extraordinary claim. Is there ever a case where we can collect enough evidence to justify it? We'll get to this question later, but before we do we ought to switch tactics and shift our attention to the other half of Aquinas's definition, and explore the mechanics of miracles. How does God actually bring them about, in a usually orderly and natural world?

Natural v Supernatural: Can God Score at Will?

Aquinas's definition of miracles as 'beyond the natural order' seems to many to imply that miracles violate natural laws, break causal chains of events and disrupt the lawful regularities that order natural occurrences. Characterizing miracles as just unusual or improbable events seems inaccurate, as we typically think an essential part of an intervention is that it alters what would have happened, had God not stepped in. Though this antagonistic idea of the relationship between miracles and natural law seems compelling at first glance, most modern theologians and philosophers think that miracles don't break laws at all.

This doesn't seem to make much sense, though: if God is doing something that natural laws forbid, then of course he's breaking those laws—right? Not quite. We can explain this idea by analogizing with the laws of soccer: players who handle the ball are violating one of the laws of the game—Law 12 (*Laws of the Game*, International Football Association Board)—but not the keeper within the penalty area. The keeper in the area is *exempt* from that rule, and can freely handle the ball. It's not that he's breaking the law at all: that law just doesn't apply to keepers. We can say the same thing about God and natural laws: like the keeper's very restricted special status that allows him to handle the ball, since God isn't natural, he is not bound by natural law. An even better analogy might be spectators: they aren't constrained by the laws of the game that the players have to live by, in any respect. Spectators can't be offside, be guilty of handling the ball, or of simulation, or violate any other regulation of the game because they aren't '*in*' the game. This is how we can think of God as interfering, without breaking laws: He can do whatever He wants, because, if He does it, it's not against the rules.

But this way of thinking about God's actions in the world is unsatisfying. Though it seems indisputable that a supernatural being just isn't constrained by merely natural laws, there still seems to be something wrong with the picture that God can, on a whim, divert the natural course of events in any way he sees fit. This kind of limitless capability is certainly possible, but it just doesn't seem *fair*.

There's a good reason why spectators aren't allowed on the pitch. Imagine we let a few fans loose on the field during a game. Now, strictly speaking, their actions—whatever they may be, but you can probably guess—aren't going to be illegal according to the Laws of the Game. The Laws state that the referee's role is in part to ensure, "that no unauthorized persons enter the field of play," but practically, this authority is limited at best. The referee won't be able to discipline fans, and he can try to compensate for the rogue fans' activities, but likely that effort will be fruitless. That's why, though the referee can't directly control "outside agents"—what the laws of the game call fans and their pitch invasions—he does have the authority to suspend the match until they stop. If there was a significant pitch invasion, it would be wildly surprising if anything resembling a soccer match appeared. Only self-restraint by the spectators, or some other imposed 'meta-rules' (rules imposed by a higher order of law) governing spectators' actions would keep the game from becoming not a game at all.

So while God, the original "outside agent", may be capable of a 'pitch invasion', there seem to be awfully good reasons to restrain Himself from doing so—especially since he's the one who set up our game to be played under these rules in the first place! Still, one might wonder if there are 'gentlemanly' ways to influence the proceedings, without directly interrupting the players or trumping the rules of the game. This would be the equivalent of crowd chants, or coaches shouting tactical instructions (though possibly more effective and efficient than these mortal examples!). In other words: are there ways for God to intervene that don't override the laws of nature, but instead work in a supplementary fashion, in areas where the laws don't proscribe what's permitted and what isn't?

There is such a way. The idea is to exploit 'silent' parts of natural law to perform miracles, without doing things that are contrary to nature. By 'silent', I mean aspects of the natural world that the laws don't speak to at all—elements of the natural world that aren't lawfully governed. In soccer, there are rules that constrain the action, but there are very many things that players and managers can do that aren't in any way dictated by the rules. For example, though the laws constrain the number of players fielded (ten plus one goaltender) and the allowable number of substitutes, they don't say anything about formations or tactics. A team can line up with eight strikers, or three left midfielders. Players have an almost limitless number of possibilities to pass, dribble, and shoot. The laws of the game are "silent" on these issues, as long as the things the laws do speak about are respected. So, the possibility is there that the same sort of thing could be done with miracles and natural laws. Are there areas where the laws are silent, so that God can intervene without running contrary to them?

Performing this kind of miracle would have other advantages over the earlier-discussed 'exemption' type of miracle, besides avoiding the 'pitch invasion' problem. In particular, this kind of miracle has the virtue of making sense of "Hand of God"-type miracles, where nothing 'unnatural' apparently happened. It's compatible with photo and video evidence of normal natural behaviour, unlike the 'exemption' miracle, which seems to require at least some (detectable?) overriding of natural behaviour.

The Mechanics of Miracles

What sort of space might natural law give to God, to display His skill? It depends on what the fundamental natural laws are, of course! Without getting too much into modern physics (this is a philosophy book, after all), there seem to be two ways the world could be: either all natural events happen the way they do because they were caused that way by other natural events, or there are some events that happen for no good natural reason. The first kind of world is called *deterministic*, because the way things are at one time uniquely determines how they will be at any later time. *Indeterministic* worlds don't have that sort of predictability about them, because some of the things that happen aren't determined by anything—they happen randomly or arbitrarily. (It could be that the randomness is rare, and most events are predictable, with only a very infrequent occurrence of random events. Indeterminism comes in many different degrees.) So how would God manage to perform miracles that don't override natural laws, in these sorts of worlds?

If a deterministic picture is right, then the entire world including soccer matches is like a great big Rube Goldberg device: a whole bunch of interconnected parts being influenced by and influencing other parts in specific, fixed ways. Once things are set in motion, there is only one outcome possible—no randomness, no open alternatives. This doesn't sound much like soccer—players have many options open to them at every moment, and rarely is a result truly a foregone conclusion. (As many colour commentators put it, "this is why we don't play the game on paper, but on the pitch.") Natural laws, in this sort of world, connect the past, present, and future arrangements of things very rigidly: given that the past is the way it was, there is only one way for the present to be, and only one possible future too. For a world to be deterministic like this, there cannot be *any* events that natural laws remain silent about; the way that every event occurs depends on the way that past events occurred, exactly.

Soccer's rules are not even close to being deterministic: they do constrain some events, but they aren't nearly so comprehensive as to dictate exactly how a game will be played down to the smallest detail! In a soccer game, there is plenty of room for a player to improvise. But, if the natural world is deterministic, that is an illusion: the choices that appear to us to be free and unconstrained (by the laws of soccer, or anything else) are in fact not choices at all, but strict reactions to previous events. In other words, a deterministic world only appears spontaneous and creative: Maradona's mazy run for his second goal was determined, every footstep dictated, by the positions of the other players, his balance, the position and speed of the ball, and his brain's reactions to all of those things. Given the circumstances, Diego could not have done anything but score the goal, exactly the way he did. In such a world, God could not intervene as He might like, for to do so would require overriding the course of nature in a way that was contrary to natural law. If we're okay with God exempting Himself from natural law, then fine—but here, we're trying to find out if there is a way to perform miracles that doesn't require acts contrary to nature.

If God wants to influence the way things play out in a deterministic world, without interfering with natural laws, then He will have to find another way. It turns out that there is one. Though natural laws strictly dictate every detail once the game is underway, they don't say anything about the initial setup. Natural laws typically only apply to the evolution through time of a system; they don't specify what state the system would start out in. (This 'split' is technically known as the difference between *dynamics* and *initial conditions.*)

In a deterministic soccer match, there would be rules that strictly governed every player's actions on the pitch—the dynamics of soccer—but there wouldn't be any that applied to who was selected for the team, or how they lined up—the initial conditions. And, as we all know, team selection and formation can have a great effect on games! To use this method of miraculous intervention, God would have had to intervene in the set up of the Argentina-England match in such a way that

Maradona's goal (or whatever was intended as the miracle) would happen, given the strict deterministic unfolding of the match. It's analogous to a person setting up a complex chain of dominoes: they have to set them all up in the exact right positions, so that when the first domino is tipped and the law of gravity takes over, they can be confident that the last domino will fall.

It seems very difficult to see how that could be managed for a soccer game—it's not quite as simple as a set of dominoes! Bringing about a specific series of events (like those required for either of Maradona's goals) would plausibly require precisely setting up a whole host of initial conditions very carefully. God would have to use every bit of his omniscience to know how to arrange both teams, the pitch, the ref, and every other influence on the game, to achieve the end He desired. And, it's actually worse than that, because if the world as a whole is deterministic, then God can't just muck around at the start of the match, because how the match started was itself determined by earlier events, and on and on to the beginning of the universe. So, to accomplish the "Hand of God" goal—or any other miracle in this fashion—God would have to set it up at the moment of the Big Bang itself. Now *that's* vision!

What if the world isn't so strictly governed? What if natural laws don't fix every last little detail in such a way that the present is determined, uniquely, by the past? ? In this sort of world, some events happen the way they do for no reason at all as far as the laws of nature are concerned. One of science's most successful theories, quantum physics, describes a world like this. In quantum physics, some events are as random as we'd like to think the pre-match coin toss is—there are clearly describable alternatives, but no fact of the matter about which one will be realized. (It's important to be clear here: it's not that we don't or can't know the outcome of this kind of event ahead of time. It's that there's *no* knowing, because there's no fact about the outcome to be known—until it happens.) Instead of certainties, we have only probabilities.

Could God take advantage of these unregulated events, and "load the dice" to make sure that things go the way He wants them to? In a quantum world, most events have some indeterminacy in them—popularisers of quantum physics will talk about objects being "smeared out,", and not having fixed positions until they are observed in one spot and not another. This uncertainty, however, is only supposed to exist at the microscopic level. Once we scale up to human-sized objects and events, this uncertainty is supposed to 'wash out'. Think of microscopic uncertainty and macroscopic predictability like form and class: both are important to a team or player's performance, but over the long term, variations in form even out, and class is what determines success. But what about very sensitive large-scale events that might have turned out differently if one small thing had been different?

Let's take Maradona's second goal, the "Goal of the Century", as an example. Part of what made this goal amazing was the ball control Maradona maintained throughout the play, on a less-than-perfect pitch while under great pressure. Each touch seemed perfectly weighted, each step tuned to take the ball away from tackles and towards open space. But the result of each touch, arguably, depended fairly sensitively on a myriad of factors. If those factors had been different, even slightly, then perhaps a move would have failed to beat a defender cleanly, and the play would have been snuffed out early and unremarkably. If part of what went into each touch turning out the way it did was an element of chance, then in this sort of world God might be free to guide the result by ensuring that those random factors turned out "just so."

This sort of meddling would only work out, of course, if there were such chancy events available for God to interfere with. That would depend on the details of the situation, and what sorts of things in that world were undetermined. Quantum physics describes a world where everything has a non-zero chance of being found somewhere else (of instantaneously 'teleporting', in effect), but the odds of that occurring with anything not microscopic in size are ridiculously miniscule. Even the small chance that natural law allows means that it's not illegal, so God could make the physically improbable happen, without overruling natural law at all.

There is one caveat: though indeterministic natural laws like the ones in quantum physics might not fix exactly what happens, they do fix exactly the *odds* of something happening. Depending on different technical views of probability, it might be against natural law for God to meddle with those naturally-fixed odds, even if the specific event itself is undetermined by natural law. Think of it this way: strictly speaking, a game where someone has been bribed to play poorly is still a game where anything can happen. But, because the chances of the bribed player's team winning have been affected, we would protest the result as not being a fair game. Likewise, even though natural laws may be silent about which way a random pre-match coin toss goes, we may insist that one thing they aren't silent about is that it should be fifty–fifty odds—and God stepping in to ensure that it lands "heads" is overruling natural law in that respect.

But Can We See Any of These Miracles?

There seem to be some ways that God might have managed to inter-vene, to 'help' Diego score his first (or second) goal. Even if we require divine interventions to respect natural laws, there still might be room to perform miracles. What we mere footballing mortals might want to know is: can we know that the miraculous account is *correct*? In partic-ular, perhaps you have a very dim view of Maradona's post-match claim about his first goal . . . but is there *any* case where we could be justified in believing a miracle has occurred?

One of the things that makes Maradona's post-match claims about the goal simply outrageous is that at the time, there seemed to be only a very few people who didn't know it was a mundane, non-miraculous hand-ball. The English players immediately protested, holding up their arms; Diego said much later, "I was waiting for my team-mates to embrace me and no one came. I told them 'Come hug me or the referee isn't going to allow it'." Just moments later, the broadcaster had multiple angles replayed showing fairly conclusive if blurry evidence of the handball, and shortly after the match, very clear and damning photos were pub-lished. Attributing his goal to divine intervention was the height of cheek, since Maradona had to know that this kind of evidence was out there. It seems to be an event particularly ill-suited for the label of 'miracle', given the evidence we have about exactly how the goal was scored, and very plausible natural explanations for each event in the sequence occurring as it did.

In contrast, we might have a harder time defending the idea that his second goal was entirely naturally caused: the specific moments of skilful ball control on that mazy run downfield, the sometimes perplexing deci-sions of the defenders to give him the space they did, and engage in the tackles they apparently half-heartedly committed to, seem to give some room for the possibility that there could have been more subtle, more eas-ily-missed moments of divine input in that play. A difference between the goals is the longer chain of events that the "goal of the century" was made of, with many of them very sensitively determining the overall outcome. The greatness of that goal, from a technical standpoint, was the *sustained* quality of the dribbling and ball control. A patch of sod upturned, a mus-cle twitch astray, an eye blink at the wrong time, and Maradona might have mishandled the ball enough to allow a defender time to steal it. The sensitivity of each touch, and the closeness of failure to success (in terms of a touch that kept the ball where Diego could advance with it and score) makes it harder to establish conclusively that no unnatural causes were at work there, because though the difference between a supernaturally-aided run and a natural one might be great, no particular event in the sequence need differ by more than a fractional amount, not capturable on film.

But would it be defensible to believe that the "Goal of the Century" was miraculous? One eighteenth-century Scotsman would likely disagree. (Yes, a Scotsman defending the English!) David Hume was an *empiricist*—someone who thought that all knowledge ultimately came from our senses only—who concluded on that basis that we could never be justified in believing in miracles. (No matter how ostentatious or visually remarkable they were.)

Why is that? Well, he thought that our knowledge of the way that nature worked—including our knowledge of the order in it—came from generalizations formed from our experience. The laws that scientists have established as regulating the world come entirely from their empirical investigations, from the collected experience we have of the world. To call any event a miracle, for Hume, was to say that your evidence that this event didn't follow the normal course of nature was weightier than all the evidence you had that nature did have regularities. For Hume, no matter how ostentatious the miracle was, there was always some alternative law-abiding explanation which has all the evidence of your past experience going for it. It was always more reasonable in his estimation to believe that an event was unusual but natural, rather than miraculous. Even if it actually was a miracle, says Hume, you shouldn't believe it was one. As an analogy, think about a referee deciding whether to award a penalty or book an attacker for simulation after a challenge in the box. Without the benefit of slow-motion replays, the evidence a referee has can often be very ambiguous—but if the past experience of the referee is that the attacker is a notorious diver then we know who's going in the book, don't we? In such cases, it might be hard to criticize the referee even if the replays later show a clear foul.

The decision, for Hume, is between two ways to account for an experience that *seems* contrary to nature. First, it could be a real miracle that is contrary to nature, and we accurately perceived it as such. Or, it could be that we misperceived a natural occurrence for some reason, and nothing contrary to nature actually happened. That is, we hallucinated, or were deceived, or had some other shortcoming as an observer exploited—which is occasionally expected in nature. (We have abundant evidence that, at least periodically, we can be and are mistaken about what happened. Just ask any player called for a foul: really, they got the ball, ref.)

Hume says that we have only the experience of the event itself to support the miracle interpretation, but that we have all our past experiences supporting the hallucination/mistake interpretation, because those same past experiences are what we have used to define 'the normal course of nature'. So, if your senses are what you rely on to gain knowledge, you will *never* have enough experiential evidence of a miracle to outweigh your past experience. It will always be most sensible to think that a remarkable, unusual but natural event occurred, or that you just went crazy for a bit.

Maradona's Hand of God goal is a perfect example of this: it seems really bizarre to think of it as a real miracle, when it's just so patently obvious that there is a much more plausible, mundane explanation for this unusual occurrence. Sure, it's *possible* that God was involved here, but in this case we don't have anything that's even remotely mysterious or difficult for nature to account for. Whatever evidence you may marshal for a miraculous interpretation, Hume says you're up against the combined weight of all your past non-miraculous experience, which supports an interpretation that's in character with that experience. In this case, that footballers at the highest level are insanely competitive, a little mischievous, and willing to bend or break rules to find an advantage. And, that referees occasionally miss even obvious calls.

But even where we might have had the soccer equivalent of seas parting (as the English defence appears to emulate in the Goal of the Century,) Hume would argue that we still cannot reasonably believe a miracle has happened. (You can almost hear him scoff, "The presumption! To believe a miracle is required to get the better of an Englishman!") There are just too many other potential explanations that have the virtue of conforming to our past experiences: lapses of concentration or poor communication among defenders, Maradona just having the lion's share of luck, along with his skill, seeing his touches executed so perfectly. Any of these natural explanations is superior, simply because they are natural: "unlikely" beats "wholly beyond experience" every time. For Hume, there is simply no justification to do more than marvel at the unexpectedness of this wholly natural event; to think that it's the result of some supernatural activity is to go well beyond the evidence at hand.

Added Time

So, as is fairly typical in philosophical discussion, we haven't really come to many concrete conclusions. It is logically possible that both goals (or neither) were miracles. Each goal on its own might have been a miracle, or just small parts of a larger miracle. God could have brought them about in several ways—by ignoring this or that natural law (as arguably is his prerogative), or by only intervening in things not determined by natural laws (like initial conditions, or the outcomes of random processes.) Trying to pin down some defining characteristics of the miraculous is difficult, too. There seem to be a cluster of suggestive properties—improbability, unusual skill or ability, political or religious (or sporting!) significance—that aren't sufficient or necessary to qualify something as a miracle.

But, as is also true of philosophy done right, there are some things we can say with relative confidence. If we confine ourselves to empirical, publicly sharable, observation-based evidence, it seems that we cannot ever conclude miracles occurred. Only an interpretation of observational evidence that brings in other sources of knowledge could possibly justify a belief in miracles. On the other hand, we can't ever know empirically or scientifically that miracles *don't* occur. Strict empiricists—those who rely only on past observations, and not on intuition or other ways of knowing—can't make any definitive pronouncements about the existence of miracles, one way or the other. The metaphysical issue of miracles is just beyond where mere experience can reach.

Does that mean that miracles are just a matter of interpretation and opinion? Not *just* . . . There are standards ("ground rules," if you will) that we've found to constrain our arguments about the miraculous. And at least in that respect, this discussion seems very much like almost any other soccer-related discussion: supporters of any view can make a fairly compelling case for their side that a non-partisan fan would have to take seriously.

The Unwritten Rules

8

What's Luck Got to Do with It?

YUVAL EYLON and AMIR HOROWITZ

The missing of chances is one of the mysteries of life.

—SIR ALF RAMSEY, Player and Manager, England National Team

Love of football is almost universal. To many, love of football and love of sports are synonymous. Yet there are some sports fans who actually don't enjoy football. The existence of such people has long puzzled students of the human psyche. Many explanations of this phenomenon have been suggested, including football's low scoring rate, too few commercial breaks, too much violence, too little violence, and so on.

What is it that some fans find so exciting and profound while others are blind to or annoyed by? One answer concerns the significant and mysterious role that luck plays in football. For some people, the element of luck adds to football's allure and excitement; for others, it is frustrating and even disturbing.

"We Were Unlucky"

Football is considered a sport, not a game of chance. As a sport, it's supposed to reward talent, ability, hard work, determination, and performance. But compare the following utterances. First, imagine a track and field coach who explains the defeat of one of her sprinters at the postrace press conference: "She ran magnificently, and completely outran her opponents. She was really unlucky to finish fourth." Clearly, this will not do: if the athlete actually did outrun her opponents, how come she finished fourth? Our imaginary coach is making a very bad excuse; perhaps even an incoherent one.

The analogous case in football is not so odd. Any football fan over the age of three has heard a manager explaining a draw or a loss by saying, "We completely outplayed our opponents. We were plain unlucky." As fans, we hear this time and again, and have probably said something similar ourselves. The point is that commonplace explanations for defeat such as the one just mentioned are sometimes perfectly acceptable.

A football team can play better than its opponents, yet fail to win, or even lose. Unlike sprinting, football is susceptible to luck. It's important that the team actually plays better, and is not merely the better team on paper—the better team in terms of potential, overall ability, or achievement over time. If football is distinctive, it is not because upsets exist—that the better team on paper might lose because it had an off-day, or a weaker team can prevail because it played exceptionally well, or tried harder. Although such occurrences are common enough, they are hardly unique to football (even though they are more common in football). Additionally, such upsets need not involve luck—the favorites might lose because they performed poorly. Instead, the point we are highlighting is that the team that actually outperformed its opponent can still fail to win the very match in which it outperformed its opponent. It is as if a sprinter can actually outrun her opponent, yet fail to beat her.

Clearly, there are types of luck that plague other sports more or less than they plague football. Luck includes referee mistakes that distort the outcome of the match, freak weather conditions and other occurrences such as the landing of swallows, pitch invasions, the goal-posts collapsing, injuries, and pitch conditions. (Legend has it that Israeli free-kick expert Uri Malmilian used to aim his free kicks in his shambolic home stadium toward some holes in the grass in order to mislead the opponent's goalkeeper.) In addition, a team might benefit from the unintended consequences of actions: a player might attempt to cross the ball into the box, but accidentally misdirect her strike and score a surprising goal. Such incidents are rare, or even impossible, in some other sports (can a swimmer unintentionally swim faster?), but all in all there is nothing really unique about football in this respect. Lightning does strike, on occasion, determining the outcome of contests.

All these types of 'fluke-luck' surely plague football as well. But when we discuss the unique type of *football luck*—the type of luck our distinguished manager invoked above—we can disregard the types of luck that are shared with other sports. In all likelihood, this is not what the manager was speaking about. Instead, he was referring to that frustrating and familiar occurrence: a team outplays its opponent, dominates, creates chances, hits the woodwork half a dozen times, concedes a silly goal, and ends up losing one-nil.

This type of luck seems to typify football and afflict other sports to a much lesser extent, and it is this type of luck that gives rise to the accusation that football is a game of chance. Any game can be hit by chance, but only in football do we encounter this type of chance so often.

The point about football luck transcends style of play and does not typify attacking teams. We're referring to any team that outplays its opponent: be it attacking or defensive. A team might enjoy the majority of possession, and attack for most of the match, yet be outplayed by a defensively oriented and efficient (perhaps, Italian) opponent who prefers the odd counter-attack. Nevertheless, even the defensively oriented team can neutralize its opponent, yet end up losing just by being unlucky.

The Accusation

The existence of football luck suggests that football is not much of a sport—that in an important sense, football does not reward ability or performance. The question this raises is: How can the role of luck in football be explained and tolerated? Are football fans nothing but chanting and scarf-wearing equivalents of the people who gather round a roulette table? The suggestion that football is, to a large extent, a game of chance suggests the unthinkable: that football does not reward performance, and therefore it is not really a sport or a worthy pursuit, appearance to the contrary notwithstanding.

There seem to be two main strategies for responding to this accusation: flat-out denial of the existence of football luck, or shameless bullet-biting—embracing luck but denying that it undermines the value of football in any way.

Flat-out denial concedes that football luck *seems* to exist, but insists that it doesn't really. The idea is that if there is such a thing as footballing skill at all, then we must also insist that football luck is mere appearances: in reality the better team invariably triumphs (unless lightning strikes, or, in the more likely event, the referee has been bought). If football luck cannot exist, then the appearance that it does is simply that—a mere appearance, an illusion. In reality, what we call "football luck" is really either fluke-luck in disguise (the team failed to score because the referee through error—not malice—stopped them every time they had a chance, and disallowed a couple of perfectly legitimate goals), or else not luck at all (the team failed to score because they are exceptionally inept in front of goal, or because the referee had been bought).

The denial response rests on the claim that football luck cannot exist. Outrageous as this denial might seem, it is a link in a long line of philosophical positions that deny appearances as a consequence of some argument or line of reasoning. The most famous example is perhaps that of Zeno who denied the existence of motion almost 2,500 years ago. His argument that Achilles could never overtake a tortoise who got a head-start has enjoyed a long and prosperous career. Zeno did not try to argue that objects appear stationary. What the paradox purports to show is that despite appearances, in fact motion cannot exist and therefore does not exist. It follows that its apparent existence is precisely that, *mere* appearance: a chimera, a figment of our collective imagination.

But why would anyone in their right mind think that football luck cannot exist? The gist of the reasoning behind this move is that playing well (or better) in football simply is doing what it takes to win. There is no other available sense to "playing better." Since playing better simply is doing what leads to winning, one cannot do better and yet fail to win.

The reason for this claim is that the rules of football not only regulate the competition, they also define the ability to play football. Sporting contests in general, and football matches in particular, are designed to measure a skill (in a wide sense of "skill" that includes effort, determination, and tactical nous): who is the best swordsperson, driver, tennis-player, football team, synchronized-swimmer, overall athlete, beer-drinker, or soothsayer.

How can skill be measured? Obviously, through performance— through a controlled exercise of the ability in question. The required performance has to fit the designated skill. If we wish to find out who the quickest runner is, we must arrange a race, not a tennis match. But simply requiring an exercise of the relevant ability will not do. A well-designed competition is usually required in order to truly measure the relevant abilities. Consider swordpersonship; the best swordsperson is the one who slays all the others, in a fair and well-organized tournament. If the rules allow mediocre swordspersons to habitually vanquish better ones, the rules should be improved. Similarly, the best driver is the one who survives the longest driving in Italy or Israel and lives to tell the tale, not one who outruns her opponents in a footrace.

So a contest involves an exercise of the relevant ability. But this is not always easy to arrange, and it is possible to get it wrong. For example, the rules might fail to disallow bringing a gun to a fencing contest, or the structure of the contest might be unfair creating fatigue in some (but not all) athletes. This means that it makes sense to ask: do the rules regulating the competition successfully determine that, barring fluke-luck, the best swordsperson will prevail?

Since the ability is given independently of the rules, a competition can be better or worse at measuring it, just as two different thermometers can be better or worse at measuring temperature. In the cases of fencing or driving the competition is *designed* to decide who is better at some prior and independently defined activity, namely, fencing or driving. The rules regulate the competition by eliminating non-skill related factors that might intervene and determine the outcome of the competition, for example, by verifying that the athletes are similarly armed—for example, that no one brings a gun to a swordfight, that both are "ready," that both are in good health, that the spectators do not interfere, and so forth.

The relation between the rules of a contest and the designated ability explains why the coach who excuses her sprinter as unlucky sounds so strange. It seems that in a skill-measuring contest, one can outperform her opponent but lose only in one of two ways: the intervention of fluke-luck (lightning strikes the athlete right before the finish line), or if the contest fails to reward the designated skill.

So when fluke-luck did not intervene, the track coach who insists his losing sprinter actually out-ran her opponent can only be claiming that the rules of sprinting are at fault. But this is indeed a strange claim to make. Why? Because as a matter of fact, it's highly unlikely that a sprinting contest would fail to reward the best performance—the fastest sprinter on the day. True, it is possible, in theory, to get it wrong: to try and find the fastest sprinter by holding a marathon, a tennis-match, a beer-drinking contest, or just a badly arranged sprint. But actually, we manage to "get it right" and the rules of sprinting are faithful ones: they guarantee that the winner is indeed the fastest sprinter.

Of course, this is only roughly true: the rules do sometimes demand a somewhat modified performance. An example would be the 400 meter race that requires completing a lap and thus involves running in an arc, and not merely straight forward sprinting. (As far as we know, only Michael Johnson has been reputed to be as fast running the arc as running straight.)

Defined by the Rules?

What about football luck? We claimed that football luck differs from fluke-luck. Could football luck then be the consequence of the rules of football failing to reward playing well? In other words, could it be the case that whereas in most sports the contest "fits the bill," football matches do not ideally determine the best football-team? That unlike running faster, playing better simply does not guarantee winning?

The answer seems to be a resounding "No." In the case of sprinting the negative response was factual (the contest does reward the fastest sprinter), here it seems to be conceptual. Recall that in the case of sprinting there was at least a theoretical possibility that the rules would fail to reward the best performance. In the case of football, however, it seems that is not even a possibility. This is due to an important difference between football matches on the one hand, and competitions such as sprinting, slaying, or driving-in-Italy on the other hand.

The difference is that in football, unlike in some other sports, there is no "prior" skill, given independently of the rules. The rules not only regulate measuring the skill—they actually define it. When it comes to slaying, the rules are regulative: they are supposed to make sure the competition measures the skill we want to measure, namely the skill of using a sword to severely harm others. The skill, alas, existed independently of the development of contests: people mastered using the sword, and even used and misused their swords, regardless of the existence of contests. Similarly, people (at least on occasion) drive their cars around for noncompetitive purposes. So in the case of fencing or driving, the rules of competitions merely regulate measuring an existent skill, namely, fencing or driving.

In football the competition is not designed to measure some independent skill. Instead, the skill of a footballer is simply what it takes to win football matches, as defined by the rules of football. It's not necessary that the rules of a contest constitute a skill: it is possible to simply reward someone whenever the coin falls on "tails." But when the rules of a contest do require performances, and not mere lotteries, they define a skill. Therefore, skill in football simply is whatever contributes to winning football matches, as constituted by the rules. So a good or better football performance is a winning performance. There's just no other meaning to what a good performance, and a good footballer, is. This is the crux of the argument denying the existence of football luck.

The point can be summed up thus: in fencing the direction is from an identifiable ability, to a performance that is a fine display of that ability, to regulative rules designed to ensure that only such performances are rewarded. In contrast, in football there are rules that define which performance is rewarded. A fine performance is identical to a rewarded one, and therefore it seems impossible to perform well without winning.

But if a winning performance is identical to a good performance, then luck cannot enter the picture. There simply appears to be no room for it. Appearance to the contrary notwithstanding, even Gerd Müller could not find a crack to sneak through. Therefore, the manager is contradicting himself: if his team played better, it *follows* that they must have won. Playing better than the opposing team and losing to them is not even possible.

There's More to It than the Rules Can Say

The denial of the existence of football luck depends on the claim that a good performance is identical to a winning performance. As we saw, this means that football performances can be assessed as "good" or "better" only to the extent that they contribute to winning. There are ways other than winning, however, to evaluate performance. Although these other ways are intimately related to what it takes to win football matches, they retain a life of their own. And it is these dimensions, and the possible leeway that exists between them and winning, that pave the way for football luck.

In discussing fluke-luck, we mentioned in passing the possibility of a team enjoying the unintended consequences of some actions. For example, consider a player who tries to cross the ball, but accidentally surprises the opposing goalkeeper and scores. If *only* winning defines playing well, then all is well: the accidental cross is a winning cross, a winning cross is a fine cross, and therefore the player actually played very well. So why do we feel such unease about its being unintended? If winning—if the consequences—are all that count, then the player who failed to cross really did play well.

What the unease with the accidental goal reveals is that what we are interested in are not merely consequences. What we are interested in is performance. And performance is the *intentional* exercise of abilities. So when we look at the cross, we see that the player actually failed to display footballing ability. Therefore, he did not play well, although he did play fortunately.

This doesn't mean that winning is irrelevant to playing well. The ability to cross, or any other of the innumerable footballing skills—dribbling, passing, crossing, tackling, heading, shooting, and the like—are the abilities whose use normally contributes to winning. But these abilities have a life of their own: a performance is a good performance if it displays these abilities within the context of a match. A player might dribble well past a couple of defenders, yet fail to pass; pass well to a teammate, who then squanders the opportunity; jump exceptionally high and head the ball well, but hit the post.

So, how can a team outplay its opponent yet fail to win? How can a team perform well and exercise the relevant abilities yet fail to be rewarded? The story is common enough: a team dominates play and enjoys the majority of possession, for the most part it executes its game-plan, creates many chances, yet fails to score. Naturally, all this takes place while stopping the other team, depriving them of possession, disrupting their game-plan, and preventing them from creating any chances whatsoever. Still, the opposing team manages to utilize the only half-chance they accidentally get and score the winning, and only, goal of the match.

Why does our team fail to score? The familiar tale recounted in the paragraph above suggests several ways in which luck enters the picture.

Almosts

One possibility is that its players are utterly incompetent and useless in front of goal. But in such a case, it is not really luck. A team that habitually fails to capitalize on its chances does not lose because it is unlucky. It loses because it can't afford a decent striker or find one. This is a matter of ability—or inability.

But there's another possibility, implied by the claim that playing well is identical to displaying abilities, not identical to contributing to winning. According to this possibility, our team fails to score because it only produces many near-misses: the ball hits the woodwork many times, but that's that. The key concept that allows for the appeal to football luck is that of an "almost": the team almost scored and won, but it didn't.

What is an "almost"? An "almost" is a failure to score, but had things been *slightly* different, it would have been a success. Thus, if a player kicks the ball and misses by an inch, he "almost" scores: had things been slightly different, he would have scored.

So one response to the question "How can a team exercise the relevant abilities yet fail to win?" is that exercising the abilities can sometimes lead to an 'almost' just as it might lead to scoring goals and winning matches. A team that hits the woodwork many times displays the same ability to shoot as a team that also hits the woodwork many times, but manages to hit the inside post just once.

The idea underlying this claim is that in football the ability to shoot from a distance, for example, is such that successfully scoring by hitting the inside post rather than hitting the outside post is a matter of luck— it is not "up to the player." For comparison: it might be that no human observer can, from a great distance, tell the difference between two distinct but quite similar types of sheep. A gifted observer will be able to identify the animal as a sheep (and not a dog), but not quite identify which type of sheep, though he might guess which type and be right half the time. Similarly football players—good football players—who shoot from twenty-five meters on the run, facing a defender, can sometimes shoot the ball more or less towards the corner of the goal. But whether they hit the inside or outside of the post is *not* a matter of ability—human footballing ability is not fine enough to differentiate between hitting the post and scoring, from such a range—it is a matter of luck.

The Sum of Many Almosts

The possibility of 'almosts' shows that the argument from the constitutive nature of football to the absence of football luck falsely presupposes that ability and success can never come apart. There may be a dispute concerning the extent to which 'almosts' are prevalent and can fully account for football luck. (In fact, the two authors of this chapter disagree on just that point.) But 'almosts' of this kind are not the only way in which luck intervenes.

While almosts of this kind concern even an individual action, luck also attaches to the accumulation of actions—to series of actions. Consider the following scenario: Roritania City plays Roritania United. Each team shoots eight times. To make matters simple, suppose the shots are equally difficult as far as range and the positions of both attackers and defenders are concerned. City contrive somehow to hit the wood-work eight times. United, on the other hand, badly miss seven shots—they go all over the place—but the eighth is a goal. This solitary goal decides the outcome of the match. United win.

There is a clear sense in which City played better, and their fans are justified in feeling short-changed: hitting the wood-work is better (at least in the relevant respect) than hitting innocent bystanders in the stands or the corner-flag. Hitting the post is better—football ability-wise—than badly missing the goal altogether. Furthermore, these instances add up: the overall performance of City is better. This is because the ability that usually underlies winning is better displayed by City's performance.

We can view the situation like this: a team whose performance resembles that of City's would normally score more goals than a team that performs as United did. Why then didn't City score in that particular match, whereas United did? The explanation is "luck": although taken in isolation, none of City's misses was particularly unlucky, overall City were unlucky; and although United's goal in itself was not a particularly lucky goal, overall they were lucky to score.

Chances

Now consider another, though related, respect in which ability and success come apart in football. City heavily attacks United; its players create many chances for scoring. United, on the other hand, hardly creates an opportunity. Yet while City does not manage to capitalize on any of its many attacks and fails to score, United does score in one of its rare attacks and wins the match. Significantly, there are no 'almosts' in this scenario: City outplays United, but its misses are more pronounced than 'almosts'. In spite of losing, there seems to be a clear sense in which City played better than United, even if City's performance was not good enough.

What is the content of the idea that City played better? The obvious response is that City created more scoring chances. The idea of a 'chance', in turn, can be cashed out in terms of probabilities: creating a chance to score is bringing about a situation in which the probability of scoring is relatively high.

While this way of cashing out the notion of 'chance' is on the right track, it won't do as it stands. Strictly speaking, City did not create a higher probability of scoring than United. United did score, and thus created a situation in which the probability of scoring is 1. This probability is higher than the probability of any situation in which no goal is scored.

We can, however, amend the definition of a "chance" to better capture the idea that City outplayed United. We need to abstract away the event of scoring (the ultimate part of the *process* of scoring). The process of scoring in football is on many occasions a process made up of several distinct stages. Doing well in each requires the exercise of ability. So a team can do better than its opponent in this respect: deprive the opponent of possession, pass well, attack well (up to a point), and so forth. The successful completion of such stages (a fine tackle, a nice pass) increases the probability of scoring. Thus, City in the scenario envisaged does better than United in increasing the probability of scoring, and in this sense plays better than the United.

A few points should be noted. First, the sense in question of "play better yet lose" is deeply connected to the constitutive aim of football, since the probability that is in effect here is the probability of achieving this aim, namely the aim of scoring (or scoring more than the opponent).

Second, since more than one non-scoring stage is often involved in the process of scoring, one may wonder where we should draw the line: a successful but trivial action near one's own penalty-box may increase the probability of one's scoring. Should we then say that a team that does better than its opponent in this respects plays better? This seems absurd. We would say that a team plays better than its opponent in spite of losing only if its successful performance increases the probability of its scoring in a more significant respect (for example—and this is *only* an example— if those successful performances occur near the opponent's box).

Why in Football?

This account of playing better yet losing is available in some kinds of sports but not in others. It's available only in those sports in which such a separation between stages is possible. Consider a competition of penalty kicks. In such a competition, no separation of different stages of performance is possible, hence no sense can be given to the idea of increasing the probability of achieving the aim of the competition without in fact achieving it (perhaps bowling is a real example of such a sport).

So one feature that renders football vulnerable to this type of luck is the complexity of the actions involved. Yet this type of complexity characterizes other sports, such as basketball, that are less prone to luck. Why is this the case? One reason is that in basketball chances abound. If the match between City and United would last 900 minutes, and City would hit the woodwork eighty times, this would be similar to basketball luck. But of course the more chances in a game, the less chance of a series of misses. Put differently, in opportunity-rich games like basketball luck cancels out. In football, sometimes it does not. This difference between football and other sports also explains why upsets are more abundant in football. The prospects for an amateur team to beat a major champions league club in football are significantly higher than in most other sports.

So What?

So, the existence of football luck cannot be ignored; denial is not an option. The accusation stands: Are football fans really the colorful equivalents of roulette-fans? Well, in a sense, they surely must be. But what of it? Why is the role of luck so troubling?

The accusation that football is—to a significant extent—a game of chance goes to the heart of what sports contests are all about, and why we care about them. The point is that sports contests are supposed to reward talent, determination, skill, and hard-work. Take this away, and we are left with nothing but a bunch of people exerting themselves aimlessly in a gigantic lottery.

The existence of football luck undermines the standing of football as a sport. Stripped from the rhetorical comparison to roulette, the accusation is that susceptibility to luck rewards the undeserving. The moral relation between luck and desert is straightforward, and is summed up by what is called "the control condition": people should be rewarded or punished, blamed or praised only for what is under their control.

At first glance, the control condition seems like something no one would dispute: luck and desert are mutually exclusive. We deserve what we deserve—praise or blame, reward or penalty, winning or losing—for what we do; not for what happens to us, for what is beyond our control. The idea is simple: if you viciously foul an opponent from behind, you should be sent-off. If a totally unexpected and incredibly powerful gust of wind fortunately or unfortunately hurls you at the legs of opposing player, there's no reason to send you off. Similarly for praise: kicking the ball out of bounds in order to allow an injured player to be treated is praiseworthy. Badly mistiming a shot and hurling the ball out of bounds, thus creating a stoppage of play which allows for treatment of an injured opposing player is not similarly praiseworthy.

The same goes for winning: the team that played better deserves to win. The team that did not, does not. And if football rewards the team that played worse, then football is immoral and unfair: it rewards the undeserving. Furthermore, football is worse than roulette: whereas roulette is manifestly a game of chance, football pretends to be a sport, while in reality being—to a significant extent—a game of chance.

Luck Is Everywhere

This critique of football stems from the control condition. But if football-fans resemble roulette-groupies, then we all do! According to the control condition, no-one should be blamed or praised for things that are not under his or her control. On closer inspection, this seemingly innocuous and intuitive claim entails some unnerving consequences.

Consider two assassins on a mission to murder someone. Both fire simultaneously, from different angles. The first assassin hits the target in the heart. The bullet fired by the second, however, is intercepted just before it hits the target in the heart by a suicidal swallow. The first assassin is a murderer; the second is not. The law and conventional morality distinguish between the two. But clearly, according to the control condition, this distinction is unfounded: the intervention of the swallow was not under the control of the second assassin. The actions under the control of the two assassins were similar. The only difference in consequences stems from the interference of unexpected factors beyond their control. So morally, they are on a par.

Well, perhaps they are. Perhaps the distinction between the two assassins should be dumped. After all, the control condition is clear, and by it the lucky assassin is just as culpable as her colleague. But consider instead a tale of two referees. The first referee is bent, and regularly accepts bribes. The second has never accepted a bribe. But the only reason the second referee has not accepted a bribe is that none was ever offered. As a matter of fact, if someone would approach him, he would also gladly accept the money. True, nobody approaches him, nobody knows that he is in fact of corrupt character, nobody even suspects as much (least of all himself), but the fact remains: if someone would approach him, he would accept the bribe. Again, according to the control condition, both referees are morally on a par: the only differences between them are due to circumstances beyond their control—the offering of a bribe. Yet the law, and conventional morality, sharply distinguish between the two: you are not guilty unless you actually commit the crime.

Luck as Anathema

On the one hand we have the control condition which seems not only intuitive, but necessary for the very idea of "morality": what is left of the notion of moral desert if people are blamed or praised for what is beyond their control? Surely without the control condition, our thinking about our peers is indistinguishable from magic: someone is blamed not for what he did, but for what happened to him, what he would have done, and so on.

On the other hand, we have the idea that people should be rewarded or punished only for what they *do*, not for what they *would have done* (in various counterfactual circumstances), or what *happens* to them: a would-be murderer is not a murderer, a referee who did not accept a bribe is guilty of nothing. This idea seems to be an integral part of our moral thinking.

Our aim is not to try and resolve this conflict between the control-condition and many of our basic moral intuitions. What we wish to highlight is that the conflict is troubling: it goes to the root of our moral and political beliefs. Typically, avowed and considered modern conceptions of merit and demerit rely on the control condition.

Modern morality tends to ignore, dismiss, or downplay the challenge presented by luck. This blindness is important: much of morality, in the broad sense that also informs politics, seem to depend on it.

Consequently, the explanation for the hostility some sports fans exhibit towards football is simple: football serves as a constant reminder of the ubiquity of luck. It exhibits a sensitivity to luck—a team can out-play its opponent, yet fail to win. Clearly, fluke-luck can afflict other sports, and no one in her right mind would question or doubt the role of fluke-luck in our lives. But football is not only susceptible to luck; it manifests it. This is what the difference between the reasonable manager and the absurd athletics coach teaches us: luck and football are inherently and manifestly related. In other words, the susceptibility to luck is a part of the game. It is always there—in fans' hopes, fears, and concerns. It does not matter how well you played, or whether you are ahead or not, its always the case that luck might intervene.

Yet the vulnerability football manifests and highlights is not that of a pure-lottery, but of an activity designed to reward performance—to reward merit, and indeed it is not a game of chance: normally, the better team does win. But it does not always win. This inescapable vulnerability to luck is precisely what makes football troubling to some.

Despite the prominence of football luck, football is less susceptible to luck and rewards merit to a greater extent than "real life." Not less. In football, luck cancels out in the long run: over a whole season, or decade, the better team will probably be rewarded. In life, however, luck persists. The lives of the referee who was unlucky and was offered a bribe, of the football lover born without talent, or born to support a losing and frustrating team, of the lazy, of the ill, of the poor, of the man who almost gets the girl, of the entrepreneur who almost succeeds—all those lives are forever shaped by fortune.

There's another side to the coin. Luck adds to the excitement and profundity of football. Recall, for example, the concept of an 'almost': 'almosts' don't count, and in this respect football is an all or nothing sport. This endows football with much of its excitement (along with the frustration that often accompanies it). It is what makes scoring so important and glorious; it is responsible for the tension and curiosity that characterize watching the game.

In general, we'd rather give up the role of luck in real life, in spite of its dramatizing effect and the excitement that goes with it. We invest a great deal of effort in reducing the role of luck in our lives and nullifying its effects. In contrast, as far as football luck is concerned, luck is an essential part of the beauty of the game. And nobody who loves the game would have it any other way.[1]

---

[1] We wish to thank Alon Eran and Ted Richards for reading earlier drafts of this chapter and giving their comments and suggestions, Yonit Efron and Michal Merling for helpful discussions, and Johan Cruyff just for being.

9

What's Wrong with Negative Soccer?

STEPHEN MINISTER

> The great fallacy is that the game is first and last about winning. It is nothing of the kind. The game is about glory, it is about doing things in style and with a flourish, about going out and beating the other lot, not waiting for them to die of boredom.
>
> —DANNY BLANCHFLOWER, English soccer great

Soccer is unique among professional sports. In no other game can one team slow the game to a crawl by deciding to play only defense. While strong defense is important in baseball, basketball, and American football, playing only defense in these sports would be either impossible or disastrous. In soccer, however, if one team sits back and keeps all their players between the ball and their goal, they can create so much congestion in the final third of the pitch that their opponents will find it nearly impossible to score.

While a team won't win the game this way, they can stifle their opponents in the hopes of securing a nil–nil draw. Since a draw is better than a loss, teams that find themselves with no hope of winning have nothing to lose by adopting this tactic. This style of play, putting an extreme emphasis on defensive solidity to the near exclusion of offensive adventure, has been labeled "negative soccer." This approach has recently become common when low ranked clubs or national teams play against teams with clearly superior talent.

Because negative soccer renders a game dull, uninspiring, and not worth the cost of admission, some commentators have voiced concern that use of these tactics will decrease soccer's popularity. This is a sociological claim about how people in general would act under certain circumstances. Though that's important, as a philosopher I'm more

interested in the ethical claim that teams should not employ negative tactics because there is something wrong with them. In recent years some
form of this criticism has come from the lips of major club managers like
Sir Alex Ferguson of Manchester United and Arsène Wenger of Arsenal.
Even former Chelsea manager Jose Mourinho, who isn't exactly a disci-
ple of free-flowing soccer, once complained about Tottenham's tactics,
saying they had, "parked the team bus in front of the goal." Are such
negative tactics legitimate or is there something wrong with them?

Whenever someone criticizes something as bad or wrong, he or she
is implicitly appealing to an ethical standard that determines what is
good and what is bad. Actions are not wrong in themselves, but only by
reference to this standard. Certain actions are widely condemned since
they will be judged wrong no matter what ethical standard is used.
Whether you base your ethical judgments on the Golden Rule, respect
for the dignity of persons, sympathy toward others, or simply following
the rules, you're likely to think that it's bad to go into a full-blooded,
studs-up tackle in the hopes of seriously injuring another player. When
Zinedine Zidane head-butted Marco Materazzi in the 2006 World Cup
Final, or Eric Cantona did a flying kung-fu kick into a Crystal Palace fan
after being red carded, we all pretty much agree that they were in the
wrong and should be punished for their actions (even if we don't care
much for Materazzi or verbally abusive Crystal Palace fans).

The case of negative soccer is less straightforward. It isn't illegal
according to the laws of the game. It doesn't cause physical suffering,
nor does it disrespect others' humanity. And it's not clear how the
Golden Rule would help us here. So, are the critics of negative soccer
wrong to claim that it's bad? I don't think so, but in order to justify their
criticisms we're going to need a different ethical standard. I think the best
ethical standard philosophy has to offer for soccer comes from the much
maligned (and sometimes rightly so) German thinker Friedrich Nietzsche.

The Good, the Bad, and the Beautiful Game

Nietzsche, writing toward the end of the nineteenth-century, was concerned that modern ethics had become a matter of obeying rules that
held people back rather than helping them flourish. He thought that in
order to flourish, we need to pursue excellence by cultivating virtues like
creativity, strength, courage, freedom, and honor. But by its very nature,
obedience to rules handed down by authorities, whether it be the state,
religious authorities, or simply tradition, discourages freedom and creativity. In place of strong, courageous, and honorable character,

Nietzsche worried that modern ethics based on rule-following encouraged a petty legalism.

If modern ethics doesn't actually help people flourish, where did it come from? Nietzsche attempts to answer this question by giving a genealogy of morality, tracing the roots of modern morality to what he calls a "slave-revolt" in ethics. Nietzsche thought that an ethics that discourages flourishing wouldn't have come from those who were flourishing, but must have been motivated by resentment toward flourishing people. As such, it must have come from people who weren't flourishing—people who were weak, timid, and constrained. Nietzsche thinks it is slaves who, unable to rebel against their masters physically, would rebel against them morally by creating an ethics that rejects or constrains the power of their masters. As such, ethics becomes a matter of controlling people and keeping them in check rather than helping them to flourish.

Instead of liberating the slaves, this ethics enslaves all those who accept it. Far from spurring us on toward excellence and the cultivation of virtues, modern ethics allows us to focus on our narrow self-interest as long as we follow a few basic rules, such as not violating the rights of others. It encourages a comfort-seeking, "safety first" mentality rather than the kind of risk-taking that excellence requires. Because Nietzsche thinks we should encourage excellence, he wants us to stop thinking of ourselves as selfish creatures seeking comfortable lives who are forced to obey certain laws; instead, we should try to live lives of creativity, honor, strength, courage, and freedom.

I think Nietzsche's ethical framework is well-suited to sports since the end goal of sports isn't simple rule-following or even winning, but excellence. Sports need to have rules to define the game (scoring goals is good, no handling the ball, no late tackles), but the point of sport isn't simply following rules, but playing the game with creativity, strength, courage, and honor. Though winning is a byproduct of excellence, it's not the end goal in itself. If Manchester United wanted only to win all their games, they could easily accomplish this by withdrawing from the Premier League and joining a local pub league. Winning the Premier League is much more difficult, but precisely because of that much more meaningful since it demonstrates excellence. The goal isn't simply to whip up on easy teams or cheat your way to the top, but to achieve greatness by overcoming worthy opponents.

Though excellence is the goal of sports, this goal can be abandoned in favor of a petty legalism and the narrow self-interest of a win-at-all-costs mentality. When players act this way, they not only betray the spirit of the game, but reveal their own lack of honor and strength. Examples of this are all too common in soccer, from feigning injury in the hopes of getting an opponent carded to wasting time by kicking away the ball when one's opponents have won a foul. Even some highly-skilled players exhibit this mentality as is clear from Cristiano Ronaldo's unprovoked "superman" dive during a 2006 World Cup game against France or Didier Drogba's histrionics at the slightest contact in the box. (This is to mention nothing of Maradona's infamous "hand of God," which was not only petty, but clearly illegal.) In moments such as these, players give up on trying to overcome their opponents through their own strength, creativity, and excellence, and resort to dishonorable tactics.

Though such incidents have sadly became a part of the game, there are other moments that indicate players' capacity for honor. In injury time of a tied game in 2000, West Ham's Paolo di Canio memorably caught a crossed ball in his hands to stop play because the Everton keeper had gone down injured on the edge of the box. With the keeper away from the goal, he had an excellent chance to score the match-winner, but chose honor over self-interest. More recently and in stark contrast to the cases of diving, Arsenal's Andrei Arshavin protested against a penalty kick he was awarded in a game against Portsmouth in 2009 because he knew that the defender's tackle had been clean. Though the referee didn't change the call, Arshavin's appeal for a corner kick instead of the penalty showed his desire to win through excellence rather than injustice.

When individual players engage in dishonorable tactics, it's comical if they succeed only in making a fool of themselves, but maddening if they make a fool out of unwitting referees. Increased penalties for play-acting and time wasting, along with the widespread ridicule players receive when branded a "cheat," seem to have curbed some of this behavior. Though it won't ever be eradicated, individual behavior is not an existential threat to the game.

Negative soccer, however, is just such a threat since it represents whole teams giving up on the pursuit of excellence. Negative soccer mimics modern ethics as Nietzsche describes them quite closely. It begins when teams recognize the superior talent, creativity, and ability of their opponents and so, in slave-like resentment, redefine the end goal of the game. Excellence and flourishing are replaced by a narrowly self-interested, don't-lose-at-all-costs mentality. Negative tactics are adopted as a "safety first" approach that eschews risk-taking and seeks only to neutralize the excellence of others. In the place of creativity, courage, and strength, negative tactics amount to an admission of weakness and the reversion to a predictable, timid defensiveness. Sometimes teams will even employ time-wasting tactics from the very beginning of the game. Though legally within the laws of the game, negative tactics betray the sporting nature of soccer, turning the beautiful game into an ugly, boring standoff.

Negative soccer was on full display during the 2008–09 English Premier League (EPL) season. Though actually watching a game is necessary to determine the intentional use of these tactics, a quick review of some statistics illustrates the problem. When Sunderland visited Old Trafford to play Manchester United they had just 28% of the possession and didn't manage a single shot on goal. In their match against Arsenal at the Emirates, Bolton picked up 24% of the possession, with only two shots and not a single corner kick. In these games the tactics ultimately failed as Manchester United and Arsenal each scored goals in the final five minutes to grind out dull one-nil wins. However, Stoke City's use of these tactics on their trip to Anfield was successful as they held Liverpool to a nil-nil draw despite having only 24% of the possession and zero shots on goal. When one team is content to concede three-quarters of the possession to the other side and not make a serious effort to attack, we can be sure that they've given up on the pursuit of excellence. Because of this, we can rightly say that negative soccer is bad and should be discouraged.

Soccer-nomics

We know that the resentful tactics of negative soccer are bad for the game. But are they inevitable? Nietzsche seems to suggest that they are. According to him, some people are just naturally superior and others naturally inferior. There will always be some players who are exquisitely talented and others who get by only because of their aptitude for getting away with shirt-holding and pushing. Though this is true on the level of individual players, it doesn't seem to apply to teams. Is Manchester United naturally superior to Sunderland? Is Liverpool naturally superior to Stoke City? The rise and fall of club fortunes through the years suggest that nature isn't the answer.

Whereas Nietzsche thought the inequality between people is natural, another nineteenth-century German thinker argued that much of the inequality between people is simply the result of economic forces. This thinker is none other than the influential economist, sociologist, and philosopher Karl Marx. Though Marx is best known as the theorist of modern communism, the bulk of his work is devoted to tracing the ways in which economic forces affect people's lives. In his enthusiasm for economic explanations, Marx comes to believe that economic forces can explain every aspect of our lives, from politics to morality, family life to religion. Economics can even, Marx thinks, predict the future—beware the coming communist revolution! Though Marx gets a bit carried away with the power of economics—especially the prospect of using it to reshape human nature—he's right to be attentive to the way in which economic pressures shape our lives and decisions, for better and for worse. Can the inequality between teams and the negative tactics that arise from it be explained in terms of economic forces?

A quick look at the financial realities of the EPL returns a resounding, "Yes!" The gap between the wealthy clubs and the lesser clubs is so big that Peter Schmeichel, Gianluigi Buffon, and Oliver Kahn couldn't guard it working together. At the most basic level, smaller clubs can't compete with the gameday revenues of the larger clubs. While a club like Manchester United piles more than seventy-five thousand fans into their massive Old Trafford stadium for each game, clubs like Portsmouth and Wigan can't even muster twenty thousand in their much smaller stadiums. To make matters worse, the bigger teams tend to have more gamedays because they survive longer in tournaments like the FA and Carling Cups.

The top four teams in the EPL each year also get a chance to play in the Champions League against the best teams from all over Europe. In addition to the extra gamedays this provides, the teams receive cash bonuses simply for participating in the league, as well as additional bonus money for winning games and progressing into the later stages of the tournament. Simply making it to the knockout round of the Champions League, as the English clubs usually do, can bring clubs an extra $50 million. The rich get richer.

In addition, the global popularity of teams like Manchester United and Chelsea creates a massive market for club-related products. To put it mildly, Bolton and Sunderland shirts don't exactly fly off the racks in Hong Kong, Tokyo, and New York the way that Ronaldo, Lampard, and Torres jerseys do. This popularity also makes possible lucrative sponsorship deals. Manchester United's sponsorship deal with AIG (yes, that AIG) was the most valuable of its kind in English soccer, and Nike paid over half a billion dollars to become Manchester United's official uniform producer and merchandising partner.

As if these differences weren't enough explanation for the inequality between teams, by far the biggest advantage the rich clubs have over the poorer ones is their rich owners. The most notable example so far is Roman Abramovich, the Russian oil tycoon who turned cozy relationships with the Kremlin into a massive fortune when Russia was denationalizing its state industries. Abramovich used his new wealth to buy Chelsea in 2003 and has since pumped close to a billion dollars into the team. This added capital has allowed "Chelski" to pay—some say over-pay—to stock their team, including their bench, with world-class players. The inflated transfer fees and wage packages that result from this infusion of cash make it impossible for the smaller teams to attract the most talented players.

This practice is also financially unsustainable as Chelsea now finds itself saddled with massive debt, albeit mostly to its owner. Though Chelsea has been the most conspicuous example of this so far, similar situations are playing themselves out at Liverpool, Manchester United, and Manchester City, where the new Abu Dhabi-based ownership group seem intent on making Abramovich look miserly. Of course, as Newcastle demonstrated in 2009, having a rich owner isn't enough to guarantee success; you also need to spend the money wisely. In a turn of phrase that Marx would regard as telling, FIFA President Sepp Blatter has criticized the financial practices of these clubs as a "wild-west style of capitalism." The advantage of having a wealthy owner willing to pour money into player transfers and wages in addition to the massive revenue disparity leads to a very uneven playing field.

Relegation and Alienation

Financial inequality by itself might not have been enough to encourage negative soccer were it not for the very serious financial threat posed by relegation. Each season the bottom three teams in the EPL are demoted, or relegated, to a lower league, in turn allowing three teams in the lower league to be promoted to the EPL. Relegation from the EPL is disappointing for clubs and frustrating for fans. Relegated teams frequently lose their best players who seek transfers to teams still in the Premiership, thus spurring a rebuilding phase at the club. As if these difficulties weren't enough, relegation can also put clubs in serious financial straits.

Smaller clubs trying to avoid relegation frequently must acquire new high-priced players in the hopes of being competitive and in so doing become dependent on the additional revenue, especially from television rights, that they receive for being in the Premiership. If they're relegated, they lose an estimated $55 million a year in revenue, while still having to pay debts from player transfers and Premier League size wages. Though the EPL has established a "parachute payment" to help relegated clubs cope with these realities, the existence of this payment only demonstrates the severity of the financial risk of relegation. The financial pressures of soccer have put some forty English clubs into administration, including major clubs like Leeds, Southampton, and Leicester City.

The connection between relegation and negative soccer was neatly summed up in former Sunderland manager Ricky Sbragia's response to criticism of his tactics after a dull nil-nil draw with Arsenal in 2009. "It would be fantastic if everybody played fast free-flowing football, but unfortunately we are miles behind Arsenal. At present we are fighting for our lives. If one of the bigger clubs were third-bottom, would they be playing flowing football?" In the dogfight to avoid relegation every point matters; securing a draw against one of the bigger teams through the use of negative tactics can be the difference between Premier League safety and financial ruin.

However, Sbragia's comment also indicates that using negative tactics isn't Sunderland's primary desire, but simply the necessary response to their situation. This point illustrates Marx's fundamental concern with economic inequality: it limits the possibilities for the full flourishing of all persons. Marx, writing at a time when slavery was still legal in the American South and English factory workers (including children) labored for long hours in dangerous conditions, believed the economic inequality tended to lead to what he called "alienation." Rather than their work being a freely chosen expression of themselves, laborers' position on the lower end of the economic scale forced them to play roles that kept them from flourishing.

Players on teams that employ negative tactics reproduce this notion of alienation, albeit in a much less severe fashion. Though Premier League players are far from impoverished, when economic pressures force them to adopt negative tactics, they are unable to express themselves in their playing, to become the creative, courageous, and honorable players they might otherwise have been. This contrasts sharply with the top teams who explicitly talk about finding "joy" in their game, playing with their own "style," and even "expressing themselves" on the field. The players on these teams have the luxury of pursuing excellence because they need not worry about the economic pressures of relegation.

Does Life Imitate Soccer?

Like Nietzsche, Marx's goal is to encourage human flourishing, but unlike Nietzsche, Marx thinks the main obstacle isn't personal weakness or wrongheaded ethical standards, but economic disempowerment. The example of negative soccer, where financial pressures force players to give up on personal flourishing and the pursuit of excellence, lends credence to Marx's concerns. Soccer officials have floated various proposals to mitigate the financial inequality between teams (such as salary caps or luxury taxes) and it seems inevitable that leagues will eventually adopt some such regulation.

However, the philosopher in me can't help but wonder if life imitates soccer. If so, does the example of negative soccer have something to teach us about the pursuit of personal flourishing and excellence amidst the economic pressures in our own lives? For those of us who are not independently wealthy, how do our financial circumstances inhibit the creativity and freedom to express ourselves? Does our struggle to make ends meet lead us to forsake honor for pettiness and narrow self-interest in our dealings with others? Do we have the courage to work against the powers that be to make a difference in the world or do we timidly give up the hope of overcoming adversity? What would it take to make personal flourishing and the pursuit of excellence attainable by all in a world where Premier League players make $150,000 a week while almost a billion people suffer chronic malnutrition? I don't have the answer to this last question, but I've no doubt that finding that answer would require courage, strength, creativity, and honor.[1]

[1] I would like to thank my research assistant Kyle Rogers as well as Dean Carrell for comments on an earlier draft of this chapter.

10

He Had to Bring Him Down!

DAVID WALL

Defenders get a raw deal. Not for them is there the acclaim and adulation given to the forwards; they're rarely the recipients of awards for player-of-the-year, player-of-the-tournament, or top goal scorer; they miss out on the fame and lucrative sponsorship deals. If a defender tries a trick to show off the skills he spent his youth practicing he's as likely to hear a rebuke for recklessness from his manager as hear the roar of the crowd. And even if he starts his career with looks fit for a poster he'll soon lose them after sticking his head where it hurts for a few seasons.

But defenders have at least one advantage over their teammates: they're more likely to have the chance for genuine moral action on the pitch. That's because they're more likely to be in the position where they might commit a professional foul. Doing so, in very specific circumstances, can be a genuine moral action, in a way that is difficult to perform in other situations during a match.

How can it be moral to commit a professional foul? After all, doing so breaks the rules of the game. Moreover, it's contrary to the spirit of the game as it, somewhat cynically, prevents a clear goal-scoring opportunity; it is in conflict with the very aim of football. That's just the reason why the laws were changed, initially in the early 1980s and then more explicitly in 1998, so that it would be punished with a mandatory red-card. And it's true, in most cases it's a bad thing to do. Indeed, if it involves a particularly brutal tackle then it can be little more than an act of thuggery.

Of course, in purely pragmatic terms it's easy to see how a professional foul can be the right thing to do. It can be necessary to achieve the team's practical aim of stopping the opposition from scoring and helping your side win the match. And that's what the commentator means when he says the defender "*had* to bring him down." But we don't think that ethics is the same as pragmatics. If we did then we could endorse all kinds of underhanded tactics, such as rotational fouling of the opposition's star player to avoid any particular member of your team getting carded, getting the tea lady to put laxatives in the away-team's pre-match drinks, or bribing or intimidating the referee. Obviously that kind of thing isn't acceptable to anyone but the most Machiavellian of Old Ladies. So if professional fouls are normally a bad thing to do, and if defenders are typically more likely to be the one faced with committing one you'd have thought that they were less likely to be able to do something morally good, not more likely: They seem cursed with having to be the bad-guys! So how might the default wrongness of a professional foul be over-ridden so that it can be the right thing to do?

There's no 'I' in 'Team'

What makes a particular action morally right or wrong? There is a great divergence of opinion about this issue, but a number of ideas seem to persist throughout the disagreement. First there is the importance of having regard for others. For example, according to Deontological views, such as those of the eighteenth-century German philosopher Immanuel Kant, an action is right only if it is endorsed by a principle that is universally acceptable. That is, as Kant argued, for an act to be morally right it must be in accordance with a rule that every rational person would accept. Yet it's plausible that the only rules that are universally acceptable are those that are fair to everyone (otherwise the rule would not be acceptable to those who it discriminates against). A rule that said that only those teams that traditionally play in stripes can score directly from a throw-in, for instance, wouldn't be acceptable to those who play in hoops, cheques, and plain shirts. Such universalizable principles, and hence right moral actions, will therefore be respectful of others, not just the agent herself.

Similarly, according to Utilitarian views, such as those most commonly associated with the nineteenth-century philosophers Jeremy Bentham and John Stuart Mill, the right action is the one that produces the best consequences, where this is typically understood in terms of the outcome in which the well-being of the people involved is better than it would have been as a result of any of the other actions that could have been performed. The most plausible versions of Utilitarianism place equal weight on the well-being of each individual involved. That is, Utilitarians like Bentham and Mill typically claim that what is important is to maximize the average well-being of all those affected, where the well-being of the agent herself is no more important to the moral worth of the action than that of any other person. An extreme Utilitarian might then think that it was right for the referee to favour the home team as a win for them would be better for the home fans, even if he himself was in the lesser-numbered, disadvantaged away-support. Right moral actions will therefore be actions that pay regard to others and not just the agent.

The importance of regard for others is not merely a theoretical proposal but is also part of common-sense morality. We all recognize that the Good Samaritan does the right thing when he inconveniences himself to help the injured man he encounters on his journey. In contrast, we recognize that those who ignore that man in need of help for reasons of self-regard—like being in a hurry to get to their destination, or distaste about involving themselves with someone who has been involved in violence, and so on—are not acting morally.

A second common theme in thinking about morality is the importance of someone's motivation for acting in a particular way. Just as a winger loses credit for scoring from the touchline if it turns out the 'shot' was a mis-directed cross, when we're deciding whether someone acted morally it matters what they were trying to do. We think that the Good Samaritan is acting morally not merely because he helps the injured man but because he does so *out of a desire to help that man*. If we thought instead that what was really motivating the Samaritan was the thought that he might be rewarded by the man he helps, or that he might be acclaimed for his actions, or some other such self-beneficial outcome, then we would be less likely to judge him as performing a good act. Similarly, we're more likely to excuse someone from blame or condemnation for performing an action that hurts someone or has a bad outcome if we think that she was well-intentioned in acting that way. We think there is at least something good about someone who tries to be helpful even if she fails because of circumstance, or ignorance, or accident.

This is emphasised in moral theorising as well. Kant claimed that actions were only good if they were done out of "good will." He didn't merely claim that an action had to be in accordance with a universalizable principle in order to be good. The person also had to have been motivated in her action by *trying* to act in accordance with such a principle. So according to Kant, only those actions that are motivated by a regard for others are moral. Utilitarians typically place less emphasis on the agent's motivation but it is notable that as Bentham and Mill first formulated the view it was, in part, a view about how a person should be motivated. They claimed that we should be motivated by trying to bring about the best consequences when deciding how to act in particular situations.

So it's a common theme that being motivated by regard for others is necessary to make an action morally right. Or, at least, that an action is more right to the extent that it is motivated by a regard for others.[1] This would have to be qualified in certain respects. For instance, there would plausibly have to be restrictions on whose well-being was being taken into account in performing an action, as well as the particular character and outcome of the action. If a referee was motivated to fix a result by the benefit he could bring to the members of a gambling cartel, who were betting on the outcome, by doing so we would nonetheless think that his action was wrong (even if the referee received none of the winnings himself). But concerning everyday actions then, other things being equal, there is some plausibility that being motivated by a concern for others is a feature that contributes to making a particular action good.

This is the idea that an action is more moral to the extent that it is *altruistic*. (Or more precisely, an action is more moral to the extent it is *psychologically altruistic*, to distinguish this view about an action's motivation from *biological altruism*, which is a view concerned with whether or not an action is of cost or benefit to an individual's reproductive fitness, or the number of offspring it would be expected to have.) This may offer a chance for a professional foul to be the right action to perform. It might be that the morally right thing to do, on balance, is for a player to commit a professional foul if it was motivated solely by concern for others and not for himself. The goodness of the act would lie in the defender sacrificing himself for the team.

An Absence of Team Spirit?

Suppose that this is correct, and that a professional foul could be morally right if it was psychologically altruistic. We still might doubt whether there ever actually are any psychologically altruistic fouls. According to *psychological egoists*—like François de La Rouchefoucauld, Michael Slote, and (more controversially) Thomas Hobbes—all motivation is ultimately

---

[1] It would be over-demanding to insist that any self-regarded motivation for acting in a certain way would prevent one from acting morally: it doesn't seem necessary to be a saint or martyr in order to be moral. There can be situations that only concern the agent herself so that she is the only person relevant for consideration: in those situations there wouldn't be any appropriate other-regarding actions yet we don't think that any such action performed is automatically morally wrong.

self-interested. These egoists deny that there can be any psychologically altruistic actions. Even where an action appears to be motivated by concern for someone else, they claim that it is, in fact, motivated by a concern for oneself. A psychological egoist would claim that when a forward squares the ball for his teammate to finish into an open net, when he could just have easily have scored himself, it isn't because he wants his teammate to have the enjoyment of the goal, but rather because he thinks it will bring acclaim for himself as a 'team-player', or make him popular in the changing room, or some other such thing. When Paolo Di Canio caught the ball rather than putting it into an unguarded net when playing for West Ham against Everton in 2000, the psychological egoist claims that this wasn't because of a concern for Richard Wright—the Everton 'keeper who was lying injured—but rather because Di Canio wanted to be feted as a bastion of sportsmanship and to be recognized and rewarded for his fair-play.

Should we accept psychological egoism? There is some initial appeal to it as it would help explain how we can be motivated by the results of our practical deliberations. When we deliberate about what to do and decide that a particular action is the best course of action available to us we are typically motivated to act in that way. This is especially the case in moral deliberation: we tend to be motivated to do what we think is morally right and think there is something psychologically wrong with those who are not similarly motivated. This doesn't mean that we expect people always *will* do what they think is the right thing to do. Their motivation to do the right thing might be overridden by other, conflicting motivations that they have. Nonetheless, we expect them to at least have *some* motivation to do what they think is right, that would have to be overridden if they act in a different way. If all deliberation about how to act involves our desires for ourselves then this is easy to explain: someone will be motivated by an action she takes to be getting her something that she wants.

There are also good reasons, however, to reject psychological egoism. In *The Possibility of Altruism* (Princeton University Press, 1970) Thomas Nagel has famously argued that if someone was a psychological egoist then she would, in fact, be incapable of practical reasoning or deliberation. According to Nagel, practical reasoning requires someone to recognise that if a consideration in favour of her performing a particular action is a reason to perform that action then it should also be a consideration for anyone else to perform that action were they in the same situation. That is, recognising something as a reason requires recognising considerations in favour of different ways of acting from an impersonal point of view. In order to properly engage in practical reasoning we have to be able to recognise something as a reason. But it seems that a psychological egoist can't recognise considerations in such an impersonal way: she can only be motivated by considerations related to her. So a psychological egoist could not properly engage in practical reasoning. Yet, clearly we can engage in such deliberation about what to do so, Nagel concludes, we cannot be psychological egoists.

Even if we think Nagel's conclusion is too strong, there seem to be examples of actions that psychological egoism cannot account for. Think of the soldier who throws himself onto the grenade in the knowledge that he will be killed but in the hope of saving his buddies. There doesn't seem to be any interests that the soldier might plausibly have, or that he might think he has, that would be served by that sacrifice. Thus, since psychological egoism cannot explain how someone can be motivated to perform such an action, it can't be true as an explanation of all our behaviour.

Nonetheless, not all actions are as extreme and obviously self-less as the soldier's sacrifice. In most cases we can identify some interest or other that an agent might plausibly have that would be served by her action either directly or indirectly. Accordingly, most actions could plausibly be explained in terms of self-interested motivation. This is just what is claimed by a more moderate view, *predominant egoism*, as proposed by Gregory Kavka (*Hobbesian Moral and Political Theory,* Princeton University Press, 1986). Predominant egoism holds that even though psychological altruism is possible it is very rare, and most cases that appear to be altruistic are, in fact, egoistically motivated. If that's right, and if we need a professional foul to be genuinely altruistic for it to be moral then it might be that there never are any good professional fouls. Can someone commit a professional foul out of no interest to himself? Or is it true what is often said about modern players—they don't play for the team at all but are just playing for themselves?

Keeping a Moral Clean Sheet

How might a professional foul be altruistic? As we've seen it has to be motivated by the interests of others, which means that it has to be done deliberately. So we can rule out the accidental foul like the clumsy trip or the mis-timed hack. That kind of case doesn't seem to be motivated as a foul at all. We might think it is less bad in certain respects than fouls committed on purpose, being the product of incompetence and certainly not the product of malice, but it also can't have the goodness of being altruistic. This might be difficult for someone watching the game to judge: it's a notorious problem for a referee trying to decide whether to award a foul in some cases, and to decide what kind of offence it is, that often it depends on what the player was aiming to do. But at the least, there has to be some intent to commit the foul if there is a chance that it is to be an altruistic one.

It also has to be carried out in a way that does the least possible damage to its victim. There are more and less violent ways that a defender can commit a professional foul. He might bring down the forward with a wild, two-footed lunge, or a swinging elbow as he surges past. Think of West German keeper Harald 'Toni' Schumacher and his apparent attempt to decapitate Frenchman Patrick Battison in the 1982 World Cup semi-final when he was through on goal (more galling still as he managed to remain on the pitch and take part in the penalty shoot-out that West Germany won). But a defender might stop the forward's path to goal just as effectively with a subtle trip or sly bit of shirt-pulling. Given that violent methods are unnecessary, a good professional foul couldn't be one that employed them: the harm that would likely be caused to the attacker would add to the default wrongness of the foul. There would then be little chance that this would be overridden so that it was the right thing to do even if it was motivated in the right way.

Finally, it has to be done genuinely from a desire to benefit others and not oneself. The most obvious group that could benefit would be the defender's team mates, but it might also include the team's manager and fans. So it must be done in a situation where, by committing the foul, the player believes that it will make a difference that helps his team: it is a situation in which preventing the opposition from scoring will affect the result in his team's favour (at least at the point in the game when he does it). That rules out instances when the game is all but over, say when you're already on the wrong end of a hiding, or when you're a few goals ahead and there is no chance of a come-back. Even a centre-half who has headed away too many crosses is unlikely to believe that their dismissal would help the team in those cases.

Furthermore, given the doubts about the frequency of genuine altruistic actions raised by predominant egoism it has to be a situation where the defender who commits the foul cannot derive any personal benefit from his action. That seems the best way to ensure it isn't one of those actions that appears to be altruistic but is in fact motivated by self-interest. So it probably rules out fouls in run-of-the-mill league fixtures or early rounds of a cup competition where the player will benefit when he returns to a side that is three points better off or playing in a later round after his suspension for a game or two.

These are tight constraints on a morally good professional foul, that we can be sure has the altruistic motivation required to override the default wrongness of the offense. Are there any that meet them all? The last constraint in particular suggests where to look, in the semi-finals of a knock-out tournament. If you're sent-off in that game then you're sure to miss the final. So you would miss out on the chance for a winner's medal, a place in the history of your team, the excitement of the build-up, and even a cup-final suit. Moreover, you would commit the foul in the knowledge that you are likely to suffer all of that because, as we've seen, you would be doing it in the belief that your action will result in a victory for your side but will also earn you a red card. We could be confident that someone deliberately committing a professional foul in that case was altruistically motivated as there's no plausible benefit he might believe he'll get for himself.

All of this means that genuinely moral professional fouls are going to be pretty rare. The right kind of fixture only occurs a few times each season, and most of these games will never be in such a close balance that such a foul will make the difference between victory and defeat. Moreover, it will depend on being in the right part of the pitch when the need to sacrifice yourself for your team arises.

One contender is Michael Ballack's foul on Lee Chun-Soo when Germany played South Korea in the 2002 World Cup semi-final: it earned Ballack a second caution in the tournament and ruled him out of the final, a game that his goal had put Germany in line for, it probably prevented a South Korean equaliser, and was commended as a "tactical foul" by coach Rudi Voeller. But because Ballack wasn't the last man and thus knew (or at least was pretty sure) that he would stay on the pitch, we can't rule out his being motivated by what he might do in the rest of the game. So we can't rule out that his foul was self-interested.

Other potential examples similarly fail to satisfy one or other constraint. Had Schumacher been sent off for his foul on Battison, if the referee had done his job properly, then despite it being in a semi-final, and in the right situation in the game and the right area of the field, his methods would have prevented his action from being good no matter what his motivation. More recently, both Darren Fletcher of Manchester United and Eric Abidal of Barcelona were red-carded for professional fouls in the second-legs of the semi-finals of the 2009 UEFA Champions' League, so that both missed out on a place in the final.

Both dismissals were controversial but even if we agree with the decisions of the two referees neither Fletcher nor Abidal meet all of the conditions for the foul to be ethically worthy. In Fletcher's case his foul made no difference to the outcome of the tie: United were 3–0 ahead at Arsenal (and leading 4–0 on aggregate) so were already securely into the final. And by fouling in the area he conceded a penalty so failed to prevent a goal anyway. In contrast, when Abidal was sent off the tie was still in the balance; Barca were one goal down but would go through on the away-goals rule if they levelled. By preventing Nicklas Anelka from doubling Chelsea's lead it meant that Iniesta's stoppage-time equaliser was sufficient to win the tie so the foul did help get his team to the final. Nonetheless, Abidal's offense couldn't have been altruistically motivated as it wasn't motivated at all: any contact between Abidal and Anelka was accidental, a clumsy clip of the heels. Accordingly, he can't be praised for deliberately sacrificing himself for the team. So neither Ballack, Fletcher, nor Abidal have the fact that they did the morally right thing to compensate them for missing the biggest games of their careers.

Forwards Win Matches but Defences Win Trophies

We've seen that someone can be acting morally by committing a professional foul, contrary to what we might initially think. But we've also seen that only rarely will such a foul meet the tight conditions for being the right thing to do: this isn't an endorsement to go around hacking at anyone in shooting range. Still, it does suggest one way in which it pays to play in defence rather than midfield or attack. Defenders are more likely to be in a position where they might have to commit a professional foul at all, something that is normally a bad thing to do. So they're more likely to have to do something morally wrong to achieve the team's aims. But in some cases they might be in a position to commit a professional foul in a way that satisfies all of the constraints for it to be a moral action. Given that few actions that a footballer can perform on the field seem to be genuinely good then it's the defenders who are most likely to come out as the saints of the team, albeit, saints with poor disciplinary records. A reversal of their normal role as the sinners of the team. Perhaps they might then be excused some of the criticism to which modern players are frequently subject. It should be some consolation that they can be in the right when at the wrong end of the pitch.[2]

---

[2] Thanks to Daniel Friedrich, Adam Palmer, Ted Richards, Kirk Surgener, and Eric White for helpful comments on early versions of this paper.

SECOND HALF

The Beautiful Game

11

Why Playing Beautifully Is Morally Better

VÍCTOR DURÀ-VILÀ

Morality and aesthetics are not notions we immediately tend to associate with football. Some may even wonder if we should apply these concepts to football at all. Not only should we look at football from the standpoint of morality and of aesthetics, we'll see that the morality and the aesthetics of football are related. It's morally right to play beautifully.

Right and Wrong Actions on the Pitch

Let's take morality first. I'm not interested here in off-the-pitch moral behaviour connected to football: it is morally wrong (and criminally punishable) to bribe or blackmail a player or a referee. Nobody challenges this take on morality with respect to football and in this regard football is not any different from other human activities. It's wrong to bribe a referee, just as it is wrong to bribe a university professor, a policeman, a politician or a judge.

What's more interesting is morality in the game itself. In a narrow, straightforward sense of morality, it's wrong to dive to simulate a foul in an effort to draw a penalty or to pretend that your rival has hit you to get him sent off. Not everything needs to be negative, although negative examples tend to capture our attention more powerfully. It is morally positive to see examples of sportsmanship and fair play on the pitch, particularly when the match is very intense and important.

Many of the ways we respond to these moral matters in football are different from the responses generated in other human activities. People tend to accept morally wrong conduct on the pitch much more easily than they do in other walks of life. We're much more lax when judging deception in football (the proverbial dive to provoke a penalty) than in other situations (say, cheating on an exam or on our taxes). These different levels of tolerance can't be justified because of the consequences of the actions: a penalty that may allow a team to qualify for a final or avoid relegation can have an enormous economic and psychological impact on people and institutions. In some football circles, these dishonest actions may be considered acceptable, but in fact the justifications for such conduct given by some managers or players are both embarrassing and downright irresponsible. "It's okay if you can get away with it" is not acceptable in society at large and neither should it be in football.

Different people in different countries tend to have different thresholds of permissiveness. In the UK, commentators and supporters alike are much less tolerant of sneaky players than in Latin countries. As a Spaniard, I find it fascinating to listen to a British broadcast of a *La Liga* match, particularly with regard to the comments about the various tricks that players try to (shamefully!) get away with: the notion that touching a player's shoulder causes the collapse of his legs is remarked upon with a degree of exasperation unknown south of the Pyrenees. The climax of this type of criticism is achieved when a player who used to belong to the Premier League adopts the much more feeble resistance to a challenge customary with the game in Spain: "No way he would have fallen down because of that challenge when he was in the Premier."

If these types of (clearly immoral) tricks do vary from country to country, it is obvious that they don't belong to what football is. We can also presume that these attitudes have evolved over time, probably for the worse. I have it on good authority (my grandfather's) that half a century ago players were not as prone to sneakiness as they are today. Moreover, we can all think of other sports where attitudes are very different and the threshold of honourable behaviour is much higher than in football.

Positive and Negative Values

There is a broader notion of ethics, not so much in the sense of doing things rightly or wrongly, but of conducting one's life in a fulfilling way. In the narrower sense, we can say that faking a foul when there's been none is wrong: a player ought not to do such a thing. The broader sense has to do with values and ways of conducting ourselves; ways that may be uplifting and positive or, by contrast, demeaning and negative. This is ethics as a way of living one's life in a right and fulfilling manner, rather than as a theory for generating do's and don'ts or, more precisely, moral must's and musn'ts.

If we think about football, values such as creativity, the emphasis on skill over brute force, on technique over physical strength or the use of intelligence and vision instead of unthinking discipline can be taken to be good or positive in this broader sense. Moreover, these values have a clear moral aspect to them, easily accessible to everyone, the importance of which should neither be underestimated nor overlooked.

Morality Beyond the Pitch

It would be good to discuss moral matters in football (and sports in general) more than we do. And to do so with a greater degree of subtlety, going beyond the merely obvious blameful actions such as doping and bribing. This would be good, not only for the sake of the players themselves, but also because of the influence that football might have in terms of projecting moral attitudes and values off the pitch, not the least with regard to young uncritical children.

We shouldn't overestimate the power of football and naively blame it for every wrong action, either. But the risk right now lies much more in ignoring the moral influence of football rather than overemphasizing it.

The Aesthetic Aspect of Football

To note that broadcasters, sport journalists and supporters use phrases such as 'beautiful' and even 'aesthetically pleasant', 'an aesthetic triumph' or 'aesthetic values' might help my case, but can't, in itself, prove that we're justified in talking about aesthetics in football. Nobody will deny that such expressions have been used frequently to characterize the football style shown by FC Barcelona or the Spanish national team recently, but we might worry that people are misusing the words here.

Some may say that the 'aesthetics talk' that we may employ in relation to a symphony or a poem can't be appropriately used to describe the latest goal by Messi or an old gem by Maradona. However, we don't need to equate a football match or a fragment of it to a work of art (which, unless speaking figuratively, would be mistaken) to defend the idea that there is such a thing as a beautiful or ugly way of playing, or that a football play can provoke aesthetic satisfaction or dissatisfaction. This way of talking seems to come to us very naturally; for instance, people understand me perfectly when I say that, all things being equal, football aficionados prefer to watch a match involving FC Barcelona rather than other teams on the grounds of its being more aesthetically attractive.

Two Ways of Approaching Football

There is a *one-dimensional* way of understanding football: only the results matter. Success is measured along one axis only: keeping track of the score. Alternatively, there is a *two-dimensional* way of thinking about football: the score, on the one hand, and the aesthetic pleasure elicited by the way of playing, on the other. For those persuaded by the second option, going far in either of the two directions is not enough.

These different ways of approaching football explain why people who think one-dimensionally about football are so puzzled when they witness, say in the stadiums of FC Barcelona or Real Madrid, that local supporters are genuinely angry or deeply frustrated if the standard of playing is not good enough, despite the victory of their team. If one understands football two-dimensionally, the demands on your team are far more stringent than if you assume that only results matter.

The Brazilian and Dutch Schools

Historically, the kind of football that we have deemed beautiful has been associated with the so-called Brazilian and Dutch schools. This is a way of playing where attacking is the norm, where technique, skill and engagement with the ball are paramount. In other words, the polar opposite to the ultra-defensive approach associated with the Italian tradition.

Without trying to give a historically exhaustive account, many of the Brazilian national teams (alas, not some of the recent ones!) throughout the glorious football history of this nation have been thought of as paradigmatic examples of beautiful football. The same is true of the Dutch national and club teams. In the case of the Dutch, it is easy to point out one manager and one team as the most prominent example: Rinus Michels and the Ajax of the early 1970s, with Johan Cruyff in the role of the star player. The Dutch national team that got to the 1974 World Cup final, managed also by Rinus Michels, is another highlight of this tradition.

The term 'total football' is used to describe the type of football practised by Michels's teams and their followers in the Dutch tradition. While it is clearly a very good example of the beautiful football I am alluding to, it would be wrong to think that total football is the only way to play beautiful football.

FC Barcelona and the Dutch Connection

If there's one club team that has benefited from this legacy, it is without doubt the FC Barcelona of the last two decades. While it had a very impressive roster of Brazilian players that exemplified the virtues of technique and skill (Romario, Ronaldo, Rivaldo and Ronaldinho), it is the Dutch connection, personified in Johan Cruyff in his role as manager (1988–1996), that gave to the Barcelona team its character as the world's best repository of the values associated with aesthetically satisfying, beautiful football. Johan Cruyff put in practice from the bench the values that had made him a famous player.

Although Rinus Michels had been the FC Barcelona manager (1976–1978) before the arrival of Cruyff, it was not until Cruyff's long tenure as Barcelona's manager that the values of positive attacking total football became part and parcel of Barcelona's football identity as they are today.

With the ups and downs that are only natural in a football club, his legacy has been preserved and pushed forward in the best versions of the Barcelona teams managed by Frank Rikjaard and, now, Josep Guardiola; both of them were players under Cruyff's orders in Ajax and Barcelona, respectively.

Beyond Barcelona

Although I believe that, worldwide, FC Barcelona has a privileged position in advocating a two-dimensional, aesthetic way of playing, it would be wrong to single it out as the only remarkable example of this type of playing. In Spain alone in the last two decades, teams under the direction of managers such as Jorge Valdano, Manuel Pellegrini, or Víctor Fernández, to name but a few, have showcased a very attractive attacking football. However, putting FC Barcelona to one side, no other team has exemplified this style of football as well as Real Madrid. With an impressive roster of technically very gifted players and supporters who demand a high standard of football playing, Real Madrid has embraced football values that are similar to those of Barcelona. In this respect, it is rather remarkable that in the last decade or so Fabio Capello has left Real Madrid (twice!) immediately after winning the Spanish championship amidst the uneasiness, or downright exasperation, of the supporters who hated how their team was playing. These feelings were reproduced in the 2008–2009 season on account of Juan de Ramos's very result-effective but aesthetically disappointing style of football.

Outside Spain, Olympique Lyonnais and Arsène Wenger's Arsenal have, over the last few years, been good examples of a way of playing that is attractive and emphasizes skill over muscle and technique over physique.

Finally, in the national team sphere, the very obvious FC Barcelona lineage of such Spanish national team players as Xavi Hernández, Andrés Iniesta and Cesc Fàbregas has crucially contributed to the Spanish team opting for a football style which has received unanimous praise as one of the most technically gifted, pleasant-to-watch teams of the last decades.

Why More Beautiful Means Morally Better

Looking at morality in the broader sense, we can see that a philosophy of football that promotes an aesthetically satisfying way of playing will, in turn, encourage the positive values of creativity, skill, technique, vision over discipline, improvisation over dullness, and individuality over uniformity. I think that this has the effect of postulating positive and uplifting values for football; values that do not need to be confined to football, but can easily inform other aspects of our lives.

The traits just mentioned and which are associated with beautiful, eye-pleasing football are not embraced at the expense of renouncing values such as solidarity, commitment and hard work. Actually, the contrary is true: in order to sustainably play in an aesthetically satisfying way and to not disintegrate into a disjointed, horrible-to-watch group of show-offs, the values often claimed by disciplined and dull teams, along the lines of hard work, focus, concentration and commitment, are totally necessary. Over the last two decades, this point has been well exemplified by the ups and downs of teams such as FC Barcelona or Real Madrid or, more recently, by the success of the Spanish national team. The difference lies in either putting those values at the service of dullness and predictability or using them as the basis from which to launch creativity and skill. To think otherwise is a misunderstanding.

When we turn to the narrower sense of morality, the link is weaker, but I believe that I can still make a good case for it. In principle, a dull-playing team could be morally flawless in the narrow sense. They could play with ten men behind the ball, hoping to score in a one-off counterattack, just to quickly retreat in a defensive mode for the rest of the match and yet not do anything morally unpalatable, such as faking fouls, committing cynical challenges, or stalling to preserve a one-nil advantage.

The opposite could be (and indeed sometimes is) true. A team that plays beautifully can very well have cynical players who will take advantage of the moral laxness that players, managers and supporters alike show with respect to sneaky conduct in football. For instance, they may play beautifully, but if they can take advantage of a non-existent foul by way of theatrics, so be it: it's part of the game.

So while acknowledging that this is not only theoretically possible, but that it does indeed happen, I argue that unethical play not only is more easily found, but also makes more sense for teams whose philosophy is 'the result is all that matters' than for teams whose philosophy admits and encourages other values. There is a good reason for this: if winning is everything, then it will seem more palatable to try to get away with as much as you can in order to win. Conversely, an approach to football that promotes skill, technique, and aesthetic satisfaction should leave less space for those tricks that are more often needed by technically limited players and advocated, or, at the very least, condoned by, results-only-minded managers and supporters.

In this sense, players who cheat, and belong to teams that play admirably, not only do a great moral disservice but also clash aesthetically. Unfortunately it does happen and one would hope that the aesthetic drive would serve as an extra-motivation to help to eradicate this morally undesirable conduct. That's not to say that, purely on moral grounds, irrespective of football styles and philosophies, morally degrading conduct should not be avoided and denounced: it should be at all times and regardless of any other considerations.

My claim is that playing beautifully makes playing immorally, in this narrow sense, more difficult and even more perverse. As for the broader sense related to the promotion of life-enhancing, positive values (values that can be exemplified in football, but that can be extrapolated from football to other walks of life), there's no denying that, while playing beautifully promotes these values, playing in an ugly, result-minded manner tends naturally to their rejection.

Nowadays, it is not usually the case that playing football beautifully is an inherent part of a team's identity or the deeply ingrained expectations of its supporters. While supporters welcome entertaining and aesthetically satisfying football, where technique and skill give a good spectacle and add value to a match, a one-dimensional approach to football predominates.

Nobody is happy if their team loses and few will be unhappy if it wins, no matter the style or the aesthetics of the game: winning is everything. In some places, however, the style does matter. I hope that I have made a case for actively endorsing and positively promoting an aesthetically satisfying way of playing football, not only because it makes it more fun to watch, but also because it makes it a more morally uplifting, life-enhancing activity altogether.[1]

---

[1] I dedicate this chapter to Mark Textor whose devotion to Frege is exceeded only by his devotion to Werder Bremen.

12

How to Appreciate the Fingertip Save

EDWARD WINTERS

For Patrick Buckley—el Hombre de Negro[1]

Within football, players and spectators alike think of various moves, strategies and phenomena as belonging to general categories or types— through balls, long balls, dead balls, back-heels, tap-ins, bicycle kicks, spot kicks, corner kicks, diving headers, goal-line clearances, chest-traps, body-swerves, chips, drives, lobs, curlers and dippers. The ever popular goal scored from distance by a fierce shot is described in the vernacular as "giving it laces" or putting one's "foot through the ball." Midfield play-makers, when they are not putting their foot through the ball, can "put their foot on the ball"; and in this they are admired for making space and time. (There is surely philosophy in this last, since it is not clear that even The Divine Providence supposed by the theologians—existing as He does outside of space and time—could have made either.)

One maneuver guaranteed to generate a groan from the home stands, the ultimate spoiler, is the away goalkeeper's fingertip save. The supporter's muscles tighten as the keeper extends himself to his limit. The fingertip save is the utmost frustration, as it prevents the anticipated climax of the game: a spectacular goal. Still, arguably, the fingertip save makes the game more beautiful. For all the vexing disappointment it produces, it itself is a distinctively aesthetic aspect of the game.

---

[1] Patrick Buckley played goalkeeper as a schoolboy with Real Madrid. He was in competition for the first eleven goalkeeping place with another fine keeper, Julio Iglesias, who went on to become the celebrated *jongleur*. Patrick has since played for the Tufnell Park Rangers, where he was variously known as 'Pat the Cat' and 'The Man in Black' (an English translation of his Spanish soubriquet, 'el Hombre de Negro'). Asked why he had wanted to become a goalkeeper in the first place, he replied imperiously, "The uniform!"

The Goalkeeper: A Queer Position

Part of the unique beauty of the fingertip save is that it is performed by the goalkeeper. In this the goalkeeper is alone. At the very last, only he stands in protection of his vulnerable goal. The penalty shoot-out, a relatively recent contraption, serves to heighten our sense of the goalkeeper as the guardian of honor.

The goalkeeper, all things considered, is the oddest character to grace the pitch. Regarded as a lonely figure, the goalkeeper wears a different colored jersey from his team-mates; and he alone is licensed to handle the ball on behalf of his team within their defending penalty area. Goalkeepers will wait to greet each other at the end of a game, recognizing in each other the strangeness of their calling. Goalkeepers are notoriously "stark mad" or "deranged"—outsiders. They are the inverse of the footballing hero, the superstar striker. Their task is to prevent goal-scoring and hence thwart the aspirations of the marauding opposition.

It's a tradition in England for the mass ranks of loyal support to stand behind the goal into which their team will attack for the second half. During the first half the supporters are literally behind their team. Through the first half, the fans enjoy their relationship with the goalkeeper, which is unlike that enjoyed by any other position. Confined to his goal-mouth for most of the game, the keeper often enters into badinage with his home support. Thus, there grows an unequalled affection between the keeper and the fans. Something of this affection is caught in Simon Armitage's "Goalkeeper with a Cigarette," (reprinted in his, *Selected Poems*, Faber and Faber, 2001, pp. 84–85, and used here by permission):

That's him sat down, not like those other clowns,
Performing acrobatics on the bar, or press-ups
In the box, or running on the spot,
Togged out in turtleneck pyjama-suits
With hands as stunted as a bunch of thumbs,
Hands that are bandaged or swaddled with gloves,
Laughable, frying-pan, sausage-man gloves.
Not my man, though, that's not what my man does;
A man who stubs his reefers on the post
And kicks his heels in the stud-marks and butts
Lighting the next one from the last, in one breath
Making the save of the year with his legs,
Taking back a deep drag on the goal-line
In the next; on the one hand throwing out

Or snaffling the ball from a high corner,
Flicking off loose ash with the other. Or
In the freezing cold with both teams snorting
Like flogged horses, with captains and coaches
Effing and jeffing at backs and forwards,
Talking steam, screaming exhausting orders,
That's not steam coming out of my bloke, it's smoke.

The poem catches the loneliness of the keeper in his confinement, forever watching the play, consigned by his responsibilities to spend most of the game observing; removed from it until called upon as a last desperate hope of preventing a goal. The keeper's job is to frustrate. It is the most dangerous job since goalmouth incidents occasion the raw, unbridled ambition of the goal-hungry striker who slides in stretching his foot out, studs first, in his eagerness to make contact with the fifty-fifty ball.

Why, then, would anyone want to become a goalkeeper? Accordingly goalkeepers, alone amongst the other positions, have the psychologies of the outsider—that wonderful brooding character celebrated by existentialist novels. Albert Camus played goalkeeper for Algiers and is often quoted, "All that I know of morality I learnt from football." (Exceptionally, the film *Zidane* by the artist, Richard Gordon, imbues the French-Algerian midfielder with a dark and brooding character, befitting the existentialist mood of the outsider.[2])

Goalkeepers smother, parry, punch, kick, block, and catch the dangerous balls that come their way. But the fingertip save is the crucial province of the keeper at the liminal threshold between conceding and preventing a goal. Keeper and fan rejoice in the fingertip save, just as they share the deep anguish of conceding a goal from a penalty when the guardian of the posts has "guessed the right way" and "got his fingers to it." For a goalkeeper, his fingertip save is the image that recurs in his mind and sustains him during the week between games. It is a vivid mental picture that diverts him from the cold rain at the bus-stop or in the middle of the night as he tries, in vain, to sleep. Proprioceptively, he *feels* the save he made last week as he stands huddled in the cold; or sits bored in some committee meeting.

---

[2] The ninety minutes of the game between Real Madrid and Villareal at the Bernabeu on April 23rd, 2005, is filmed entirely tracking the movement of Zidane. The psychology we encounter when looking at this solitary figure in isolation from the team foreshadows his exit from the game at the 2006 World Cup Final between France and Italy. Having been sent off for ungentlemanly conduct, Zidane trudges from the pitch, despondent, head hanging, alone at the last and never to grace a football pitch again.

Proprioception: Being Able to Put Your Finger on Your Nose with Your Eyes Closed

The light dove cleaving in free flight the thin air, whose resistance it feels, might imagine that her movements would be far more free and rapid in airless space.

—IMMANUEL KANT, *Critique of Pure Reason*

There's a sort of architecture in the fingertip save. An architecture in type and style, if not detail, similar to that of skateboarding, freerunning and dancing. Propriocpetion is the key to understanding and appreciating this architecture.

Proprioception is a standard means of engaging and negotiating the world. However, in non-normal cases such as skateboarding, free-running, dancing, and keeping goal, the agent manoeuvres his body in response to an unusual constraint that is placed upon him by the activity in which he is engaged. The skateboarder learns the ways in which she can negotiate a terrain exploiting her board as she comes to terms with steps, curbs and railings—feeling in her bodily movements the limits of the environment in which she is able to extend her repertoire of timing and movement. She adjusts her negotiation of the environment in light of skills and techniques developed in her proprioceptive awareness of herself in space and time. (On the relationship between skateboarding and architecture see Iain Borden, *Skateboarding, Space, and the City: Architecture and the Body*, Berg, 2001.)

Free-runners exploit architectural features in ways unforeseen and probably unforeseeable before the practice was inaugurated. Architecture is designed to accommodate our embodied ambulatory selves. Change the nature of that self by radically altering the terms in which the environment is negotiated and you call upon change in the nature of the architecture constructed to fit our newly acquired purposes.

In this respect, skateboarding, free-running, dancing, and goalkeeping share a common ground. The articulation of the self—as it bends, twists, stretches, adapts its posture in response to the pull of gravity; and as it relates itself to an external stimulus—calls upon the skateboarder, the free runner, the dancer, and the goalkeeper to work against these constraints as he or she adapts their movement to circumstances beyond our more ordinary environmental behavior. In football the timing of the sliding tackle or of the diving header are exercises in proprioceptive knowledge. The fingertip save is a matter of timing the leap—and of twisting and stretching within that leap—so as to maximize the chance of deflecting the ball.

Unlike Kant's dove, the engaged agent articulating its body in pursuit of desired ends celebrates rather than laments the constraints of the urban environment (including the skateboard); the rhythm of music as it enters into the bodily response; the compliance of the self in response to another's bodily movement; and the contortion of the self in order to intercept and deflect the trajectory of the goal-bound ball.

Terms of Engagement

Embodiment is not only required for skateboarding, free-running, dancing and goalkeeping—clearly it is—it is also required as a component of our *understanding and enjoyment* of these modes of activity. In *The Re-Enchantment of the World* (Oxford University Press, 2007), Gordon Graham has argued for a conception of aesthetics that engages agency. Graham wants an aesthetics that *includes* life rather than forming a gulf between life and the object at which we gaze. The problems Graham sees for modernism in painting and in literature derive from the separation of art from life—a separation that did not figure when art belonged to the enchantment of life by religious belief.

Graham takes exception to Kant's view that we respond aesthetically to formal patterns in mere reflection. Graham instead favors the view of Nietzsche, who identified two views of art, ascribed to the Greek gods Apollo and Dionysus. The Apollonian conception of art involves only passive contemplation, whereas the Dionysiac requires our *participation* in the art.

Music is Dionysiac, with religious composition enmeshed in the ceremonies for which it was written. Indeed the concert hall with its Bach recital, its concert-goers sat in an audience, is a degradation of the original intention; which was for music to accompany the liturgy of the Mass—where 'accompany' is to be understood as 'integrated into' rather than as 'sitting beside'. Music, perhaps more than the other arts provides an image of what enchantment means in terms of religious feeling. It is this that is missing from the secular world and it is this that needs to be replaced by the development of an aesthetic attitude, if aesthetics is to be recruited to the task of re-enchanting the world.

We might think that watching football in a stadium or sports bar is engaged. We think our shouting matters—as if it is some sort of prayer that might miraculously get answered. But the football fan feels as if he is part of the action.

Football as Magic

Graham's conception of enchantment and magic is both interesting and illuminating, particularly in the light of the intelligibility of religion in the context of secularism. Here the notion of magic is used to fill out the idea of an emotional engagement with the world. Dionysiac magic is not the audience we give the conjurer; nor is it the belief in some causal power that cannot be explained by science. It is the emotional coloring that we are able to give to the world in virtue of some activity in which we are *engaged*.

Graham cites the war dance of the warrior about to engage in battle. The war dance is undertaken in order to summon up courage, to bind the warriors together as a fighting unit; and to identify a people against its enemy. This form of magic can be found in the singing of national anthems before international football matches, where again it is undertaken by nationals, both spectators and players, to bring into focus their unity and patriotism. The role of music in religion, then, can be seen as the magical engagement that colors the emotional response to the ceremony under way. It is to be heard as part of the activity that provides the ceremony with its celebratory force. Moreover, its contribution is integrated into the ceremony not as a mere external adjunct, but as an internally related constituent. The ceremony would not be the ceremony it is without the music.

The enjoyment we can get from attending to the performance of some activities as they are undertaken by the highest level practitioners, is similarly embodied. The feeling that we have is as of our own movement in relation to the movements of the performer. The old aunt and uncle who sit swaying in time with the music at a wedding dance look on not as spectators but as participants. In moving with the music, albeit with modest exertion, they move with the other dancers and thereby become a part of the dance they feel in their bones. We can carry over into aesthetics more generally the thought that our responses to art engage our embodiment.

Our embodiment may even get into our appreciation of painting too. As Ruby Meager once put it, first asking Wittgenstein's question, then answering it:

Wittgenstein: "When I see the picture of a galloping horse—do I merely know that this is the kind of movement meant? Is it superstition to think I see the horse galloping in the picture?—And does my visual impression gallop too?" *Answer:* "Who knows, but the gallop can certainly get into my imagination, and, whatever Wittgenstein may say, into sensations in my muscles and my joints, too. That is, if it is a really good picture of a galloping horse." (Ruby Meager, "Seeing Paintings," *Proceedings of the Aristotelian Society*, 1966, p. 66)

Ruby Meager's sense of a response to pictures being such that the gallop can "get into sensations in my muscles and my joints, too" is of a piece with her love of cricket. Meager was an Oxford Blue at cricket in the 1950s. In lectures at Birkbeck College she often referred to a particular stroke of the bat by the left-hander David Gower as an example of beauty. (It is the continuity between our attitudes toward works of art and our attitudes to the more hum-drum world of sport that exercises me in writing this essay.)

If Meager's thought on our responses to pictures has anything in it, then we can understand the participatory nature of the old aunt and uncle as they sway with the more agile dancers. And as I watch a game, can I not feel (as if from the inside) the deft turn of the forward; the anticipatory reflex of the goalkeeper as he twists in mid-air to touch the ball round the post? Hence it is common parlance to speak of managers, most of whom have played the game at a high level, that, whilst they are confined to the touchline, they "kick every ball."

It's not just the managers: the spectator also feels proprioceptively the movement of a player in the game as he imagines himself playing it. He internalizes what he sees; and so proprioceptive imagination connects the spectator to the player with whom he is able to identify.

The Shape of the Dance

No one would deny that ballet is a form of high art. And it would be churlish to recoil dismissively from the modern choreographed pieces written for film or performance in architectural spaces, such as the beautiful contemporary work of the choreographer Gaby Agis. (See Gaby Agis and Company at www.londondance.com)

Unlike skateboarding and free-running the choreographed piece is rehearsed and acted out according to a score. The dance is scripted, even if there's room for interpretation by both director and dancer. But as we step down from the heights of such delicately crafted movements in the art of dance to the floors of the municipal ballroom we find nonetheless an aesthetic practice that observes the patterns that make up a particular dance.

If we move from the high art of ballet with its practiced set pieces—the *pas de deux*, for instance—to less formal dance, where there are accepted moves but where, traditionally, the man leads the woman, we can see that types of step can be practiced if not choreographed. I am thinking here of the tango. In the Buenos Aires *milongas* there are rules to be obeyed in the choosing of a dance partner. However, after three to five dances (a *tanda*) there is a clearance of the floor (a *cortina*) so as to facilitate the changing of partners.

The improvisation of the dance, directed by the male but whose directions must be interpreted by the female, provides the space in which sexually charged emotion can be expressed. (The tango is a dance emerging from the slum streets and brothels of Buenos Aires in the late nineteenth century.) There are basic steps that each must learn before moving on to the more creative expression of the dance. And once the basic internal structure of the dance is mastered, the wonderful flourishes, which earn the great tango dancers of Buenos Aires their revered social status, can be seen as lifting the dance into the realm of the beautiful. Notwithstanding the nature of the architecture constitutive of the observed patterns which cohere as the form of the dance it is—the improvisation thus afforded is what makes the dancer's personality.[3] Put another way: the very strictest of ballroom dance forms facilitates rather than impedes the emergence of personality (and thereby expression) in the dance. (We remember Kant's point that the dove *needs* the resistance of air.)

In the very poor area of the Boca in Buenos Aires there is a similar pride rising from the street—where football is pursued with similar passion. Boca Juniors is the team of the people. Maradona is treated as a figure of adulation in Argentina—and his emergence from the slums is an important element in his popularity.

Grasping the Game

The rehearsal of moves, on the street, in the dance studio or on the training ground, gets the actor to be comfortable with a particular situation as

---

[3] Patrick Buckley, the goalkeeper to whom this chapter is dedicated, served as foreign correspondent for Reuters News Agency throughout Central and South America in the 1970s. *La cueca chilena* is a national dance of Chile involving two dancers each with a handkerchief to be waved whilst circling the partner with much stamping of feet. Buckley invented the move of leaving his kerchief on the woman's shoulder, wheeling away from her and then spinning in something of the manner of a Dervish; before returning to recover the token with his teeth. Such is the risqué interpretation of the less constrained foreign dancer. The move is admittedly Latin; but proved too European for the more modest dancers of the Bar Cinzano, Valparaiso; its decadence frowned upon by the haughtier, more conservative, *bailador*. Contrapuntally, Buckley's Latin American

it is eventually to be embedded in the full performance of the routine. In understanding the development of a whole game; and the part that an entire move—a passage in the game—'means'; we have to look for patterns of intention. It is unclear as to whether we should attribute meanings to games of football as a whole or moves within it as constituent parts of games.

We see the back-heel as wrong-footing the opposing defence and releasing the winger into a space which can be exploited in our attack, for instance. And now the particular back-heel is understood in terms of a strategic move that makes sense in the game as a construction of moves and counter-moves, the players from each team using the skills they have mastered in training to control the play in the hope of outwitting the opposition—of outplaying them.

If the moves that are rehearsed in training are to be understood as embedded in the game as particular actions, we have a way of understanding this back-heel or diving-header as a unique example of a general type. We can understand general types of action as being exemplified by particular instances—Ronaldo's swerving free-kick against Porto; Essien's volleyed goal against Barcelona; and Adebayor's chested control and then bicycle kick against Villareal (all in the 2008–09 European Champions' League). It wasn't just a swerving free kick; not just a volley; not just a bicycle kick. It was *that* free kick, *that* volley, *that* bicycle kick.

But our understanding brings the particular under the more general; and that is how we make sense of the play. Here we might think of our aesthetic responses more broadly. When we see or hear something beautiful, we do so by seeing it or hearing it under a description that makes general sense of this particular instance. And in football, just as in the arts, we might think that the place to look is in the broader context within which this token appears. It is not just that Rothko uses *these* muted colors. It is that he uses them in the context of earlier paintings of his own; and in the context of the painters of the American Sublime; and in the context of J.M.W. Turner's great seascapes. In football we recognize the ability of a player to bend a free-kick, Beckham's free-kick against Greece at Wembley in 2001—a last minute goal that meant qualification for the 2002 World cup finals—calling to mind Garrincha's swerving shots from the 1970

---

connections in London served to provide Tufnell Park Rangers with an international squad at ease with a relaxed, flamboyant, even audacious, style of football more usually found in the Americas.

World Cup, or Roberto Carlos's goal-scoring free-kick for Brazil against France in 1997.

The Loneliness of the Goalkeeper (Again)

The unique position of the goalkeeper can be brought into view by considering Peter Handke's *The Goalie's Anxiety at the Penalty Kick* (Farrar, Straus and Giroux, 1972), later made into a film by pre-Hollywood Wim Wenders as *The Goalkeeper's Fear of the Penalty*. Handke's anti-hero is a goalkeeper, Bloch, who has just strangled a girl he picked up at the cinema. Bloch, the goalkeeper and murderer is in a border town awaiting his eventual capture and punishment. He is conversing with one of the border guards concerning the nature of the guards' defence of the border against smugglers. The guard confides in him:

> And then if somebody suddenly steps in front of you, you don't even know how you should grab hold of him. You're in the wrong position from the start and when you finally get yourself right, you depend on your partner, who is standing next to you, to catch him, and all along your partner is depending on you to catch him yourself—and the guy you're after gives you the slip.

Here, the border guard sounds like any member of the back four, defending as part of a team—assisting his partner but with only collective responsibility for defence. Later, at the very end of the book, Bloch is at a football match. The referee awards a penalty. Bloch cannot bear to look. All the spectators rush behind the goal. As the area is cleared in anticipation of the kick Bloch reflects:

> "The goalkeeper is trying to figure out which corner the kicker will send the ball into," Bloch said. "If he knows the kicker, he knows which corner he usually goes for. But maybe the kicker is also counting on the goalie's figuring this out. So the goalie goes on figuring that just today the ball might go into the other corner. But what if the kicker follows the goalkeeper's thinking and plans to shoot into the usual corner after all? And so on, and so on."

The goalkeeper has no choice and little chance. He must stand quietly facing what is almost an inevitable outcome. The fans are already celebrating the award of the kick—already anticipating the goal to come. The striker volunteers to take the kick. He expects to score—anticipates the celebration of his team-mates, expects to be mobbed in his glory.

The goalkeeper looks forward to punting the ball back to the centre-circle for the game to re-start. The keeper foresees his own dejection as his opponents rejoice.

Individual moves in games are to be seen in the broader context of the game in terms of the strategies available to players whose task it is to outwit and outplay the opposition. The dancing guests at the wedding do not claim to be fine artists. Nevertheless their activity is interpretative. The man leading needs to dance in such a way that his partner can respond appropriately. In football the interpretation is both positive—in that one's team mates need to understand your intention—and negative—in that the opposing players are to be deceived by your move.

However, the wedding guests offer us some insight into the values we find in both playing and watching football. The dance is to be enjoyed proprioceptively by its performers and its spectators alike. So too is football. In seeing the complex relations of interpretation on the football pitch under such terms we can see why the appropriate response to football is aesthetic.

The goalkeeper, however, is called upon to make the save when all else fails. His efforts are 'last ditch'. His fingertip save contains desperation. And his confrontation with the penalty taker is at the limit of the attempt to foil the opposition. Only he stands between the opposition and the goal. The goalkeeper is a lonely figure; his fingertip save, when pulled off, the act of a hero.

This fingertip save is to be seen in the context of the current desperation, the conclusion of an opposition raid on our goal. The save is all the better if the opposition's move was of such a calibre that it deserved a goal—as if a goal were inevitable given the build-up play. We, the spectators, engaged as we are in the game, have already as much as conceded when the goalkeeper's heroics prevent the concession we reluctantly embraced. Gordon Banks's magnificent fingertip save at the foot of his post after a downward header from Pelé in the 1970 World Cup Finals in Mexico was no ordinary save. It was against (arguably) the best player ever to grace a pitch. It was for England against Brazil.

But the fingertip save, more than the back-heel or the diving header, puts us in touch with the goalkeeper as the outsider. Alone in his ability to handle the ball, alone for the best part of the game, alone in terms of team tactics, he is a character that gives the game a romance it would not otherwise have. The fingertip save is at the limits of what it is possible for a man to achieve in stretching himself to his proprioceptive limits.

Arguably, football is not a fully fledged art. If, however, we take seriously Graham's conception of Dionysiac aesthetic engagement, then football can certainly be located within the aesthetic realm. Football is an institution which calls upon us to invest our emotions and to identify with the players as they make use of talents we can only imagine as our own. The goalkeeper's repertoire is set apart from that of the outfield player, but in him we see the aesthetic character of the man who abides on the outside looking in. The fingertip save is a wonderful thing.[4]

---

[4] I am grateful to Derek Matravers and to the artist Marcus Rees Roberts for reading and commenting on previous drafts of this chapter. Marcus Rees Roberts played as a midfield playmaker with both The Slade All Stars and Tufnell Park Rangers. I am also grateful to David Davies for his insights into *The Goalie's Anxiety at the Penalty Kick*.

13

Is Ronaldo a Modern Picasso?

TIM ELCOMBE

On May 5th, 2004, an anonymous buyer purchased Pablo Picasso's painting *Garçon à la Pipe* at a New York auction for $104.2 million. Painted by the celebrated Spanish artist during his "Rose Period" in 1905, the price paid for the nearly hundred year old *Boy with a Pipe* made it, at the time, the most expensive painting in history. Just over five years later La Liga football club Real Madrid made similar news, paying English Premier League champion Manchester United $131 million for the rights to reigning World Player of the Year Cristiano Ronaldo. The June 11th, 2009 transfer fee paid for the Portuguese winger crushed the record set only one week earlier by the same Real Madrid club—$92 million to AC Milan for Brazilian star Kaká.

On the surface, comparing the sale of a Picasso painting with negotiations for the services of a soccer player (beyond their shared record setting transfer fees) may seem trivial. But there is much to compare. In addition to their connection with Spain (Picasso's nationality and the home of Ronaldo's new club) and ages (Picasso was twenty-four when he painted *Garçon à la Pipe*, the same age as Ronaldo at the time of his Real Madrid transfer), there is the question of their relative greatness and future legacy. Pablo Picasso clearly stands as one of the most influential artists of his time, and among the most celebrated in modern art history. Current debates about the best footballers near the end of the twenty-first century's first decade always include Cristiano Ronaldo—and some suggest his sublime talents and performance on the biggest soccer stages may eventually lead to his inclusion in the pantheon of all-time footballers.

But there is one more interesting comparison to consider: does Ronaldo occupy a similar role in culture as Picasso did during his lifetime? Put another way, can a footballer such as Ronaldo be considered an "artist" just like the great twentieth-century Spanish painter and sculptor Pablo Picasso? Is the "beautiful game" a place in which art can happen?

Soccer as the Beautiful Game

Soccer, as a relatively simple game to play and understand, holds an unparalleled reach into the hearts and minds of people around the world. A sport that requires little in terms of technical equipment to play, soccer typically stands as one of the most popular—if not *the* most popular—games in most countries and regions. On a global level, only select mega multi-sport events such as the Olympic Games approach the interest generated by elite soccer—particularly World and European Cup championships, the Champions League tournament, as well as major professional league play in Europe and Latin America.

Beyond its accessible nature and long history, interest in soccer also stems from the fact that it is the world's "beautiful game." Usually aesthetic titles or descriptions of this kind are reserved for sports that use judges to determine better from worse in terms of beautiful movements, such as gymnastics, diving, figure skating, and synchronized swimming. You probably wouldn't find fans of other popular sports referring to their games on an aesthetic level—like hockey as the "game of icy elegance" or American football as "grace on the gridiron." Yet fans and aficionados of soccer welcome this aesthetic title. As Uruguayan author Eduardo Galeano writes in *Soccer in Sun and Shadow* (Verso, 1998), "I go about the world, hand outstretched, and in the stadiums I plead: 'A pretty move, for the love of God'" (p. 1).

Occasionally "beggars" for beautiful soccer like Galeano get their wish. Those fortunate enough to watch the world's greatest soccer legends—including Pelé, Diego Maradona, Zinedine Zidane, Bobby Charlton, George Best, Franz Beckenbauer, Lev Yashin, and Johan Cruyff to name a few—witnessed their ability to display an exquisite style of play on the pitch rarely matched.

Not all modern soccer is considered "beautiful." Many analysts and fans complain about the lack of "beauty" in most action. Yet others, particularly those with the most vested in the outcome (including coaches, owners, and gamblers), will quickly trade what they see as the extravagance of aesthetic play for cold efficient results. To this, Galeano writes, "The history of soccer is a sad voyage from beauty to duty. When the sport became an industry, the beauty that blossoms from the joy of play got torn out by its very roots" (p. 2).

Still, some modern players provide moments merging usefulness with a pleasing style that helps soccer retain the title "beautiful game." From the daring relentlessness of Lionel Messi, the ball handling wizardry of Ronaldhino, the impenetrableness of Fabio Cannavaro's defense, the completeness of Steven Gerrard, the technical mastery of Kaká, and of course, the offensive brilliance of Cristiano Ronaldo, the game's beauty can be spontaneously revealed. But just because a game can have instances of the "beautiful," does that qualify it to be considered "art"?

Midfielders and Metaphysics

To really tackle this question, it's important to first consider the branch of philosophy called metaphysics initiated by Ancient Greek philosophers Plato (429–347 B.C.) and his student Aristotle (384–322 B.C.). Plato believed in a realm that existed beyond the natural world (thus "meta"-physical) in which pure "forms" existed. Plato argued that one true, unchanging perfect image of something we call a midfielder existed in this realm. To prove his point, Plato might ask us to close our eyes and imagine a midfielder. Although we might all picture a different particular midfielder (size, shape, gender, skill set, space on the pitch covered, emphasis on pushing forward or supporting the defense, primarily a scorer or a passer), we still all likely share a conception of what a Midfielder with a capital "M," or "midfielderness," is. Plato extended this use of metaphysics beyond "things" like midfielders to ideas such as goodness and beauty. In doing so, metaphysics for Plato served as the key to understanding our world and how to best live within it.

Aristotle held similar views about metaphysics as his teacher Plato. Unlike Plato's appeal to some kind of supernatural realm of perfection, however, Aristotle would use keen observations, like a referee looking for fouls, to identify the "necessary and sufficient" characteristics that determined "midfielderness." Aristotle's "inductive" method would involve studying many examples of midfielders and come up with a list of essential qualities shared by those worthy of categorization under the title of Midfielder.

Despite their different methods, Plato and Aristotle agreed on the need to come up with "universal" characteristics for virtually everything. By doing so, on some level anything could be evaluated against a perfect form to determine its status or adequacy. Midfielders in the real world come in a variety of imperfect forms, however to rightfully identify someone as a "midfielder," or to determine if something is truly "beautiful" requires meeting certain universal criteria.

The challenge for both Plato and Aristotle, and the many philosophers that apply this basic understanding of metaphysics, is to clearly identify and describe these perfect forms. We all may be able to picture a football or point to an official FIFA ball, for example, but for everyone to come to full agreement on a single definition of "footballness" (color, size, material, design) is like everyone agreeing on who is better: Ronaldo or Messi. Aristotle's method also results in problems—there are always more things people call footballs to study that might throw a wrench into the "necessary and sufficient" characteristics of "footballness." Kids in an impoverished region might use different materials to make their own, in contrast to someone given an official FIFA ball; some balls might bounce enough that it blurs the line between Football and Basketball. As a result, traditional metaphysics always end in long debates. If the lines around what counts as something, like a football, are drawn too narrowly, than many objects that people might consider a "football" will be excluded. If the lines are drawn too broadly, than almost anything can be called a "football."

Portraits of Ronaldo and Synchronized Swimming

So how does this quick sketch of Plato's and Aristotle's metaphysics apply to the question about soccer as art, and Ronaldo as an artist? The reality is that many modern conceptions of art rely upon Plato's and Aristotle's basic ideas about metaphysics. To qualify as "art" means that certain metaphysical criteria must be satisfied—criteria that usually fail to gain universal acceptance. For example, if Beethoven's music counts as art, what differentiates it from music not considered art? Is music from the Beatles art? Frank Sinatra? Enrique Iglesias? Brittany Spears?

The same questions can be asked of other art forms when determining if some products are onside while others are offside as Art. Are Picasso's paintings art in all cases? If so, is there something that separates a Picasso work from paintings such as Coolidge's *Dogs Playing Poker* collection? Can a portrait of Ronaldo painted by a new Real Madrid supporter count as art? One way traditional metaphysicians address these tough calls is to refer to all of these as art, and then find further ways to subdivide them into categories such as "fine" or "high" art versus "popular" art. An opera performance will usually be considered fine or high art; whereas a rock'n'roll concert might still qualify as art, but more likely as popular (and thus lesser) art. In the end, the key from a metaphysical perspective is that some unchanging definition of Art, and its subcategories of fine or high and popular art, exists to clearly determine what is in play, and what is in touch when it comes to Art.

Similar metaphysical arguments often occupy philosophical discussions about sport. There's a long history in sport philosophy debates over what counts as Sport, and how to go about reaching these conclusions. The two most often argued about activities are those with a heavy reliance upon technology (such as auto racing) and "judged" sports that rely upon qualitative assessments of "beauty." Sports identified earlier as "aesthetics sports"—gymnastics, figure skating, diving, synchronized swimming—although popular and included in the Olympic Games, generate debates as to whether they actually are Sports. Some argue that the determination of superiority through subjective judging rather than the completion of some clearly defined objective task (such as kicking a ball into a goal) makes aesthetic activities non-Sports. Others, like in art, avoid the Sport/non-Sport division by categorizing them into purposive sport (such as soccer, hockey, basketball) and non-purposive or aesthetic sports (gymnastics, figure skating, diving, synchronized swimming) where aesthetically pleasing movements serve as the core of the activity.

Soccer, of course, never generates debate in terms of its qualifications as a sport. But to firmly remain a Sport, from a traditional metaphysical perspective, soccer's aesthetic elements must remain a byproduct of the game. If, for example, the game added judges as assistant referees to qualitatively award bonus points for stylish play, critics would probably consider dismissing soccer's status as a real Sport. So based on this traditional metaphysical perspective soccer might have "beautiful," even "artistic" qualities, but it is not Art.

Challenging Art

What results from this traditional metaphysical approach is the conception of Art as a special, disconnected realm. Like a national team, many strive to make it as Art, but only a limited few find places on the squad. Some tangible, finished products, such as paintings, sculptures, poems, songs, and photographs earn caps on Team Art and thus are distinguishable from non-Art. Consequently, the value of art (like the value of a professional footballer) becomes quantifiable. A Picasso painting such as *Garçon à la Pipe*, despite criticisms that it is not his best work, objectively gains status as the artist's most "valuable" art product. While paintings, sculptures, poems, songs, and photographs may use soccer as its subject matter (probably as "popular art"), the

actual game cannot qualify as Art. Soccer is a Sport, something completely different from Art on a metaphysical level.

Pragmatist philosophers such as John Dewey (1859–1952) attacked
this traditional approach to metaphysics, and subsequently the modern
notion of Art. Metaphysics from a pragmatic perspective is less about
conceptualizing perfect forms to use as evaluative tools and more about
focusing on "working definitions" that can change based on our real-
world experiences. It might be important to identify the shared characteristics of "midfielders," "footballs," or "art," but only from the
perspective of functionality. Pragmatists always allow space so that our
ideas about "midfielders," "footballs," and "art" might change if it
becomes more useful to think of them differently.

A great example of this experientially-based approach to metaphysics is art. What is most important from a pragmatist perspective is
not what characteristics distinguish Art from non-Art, but how art is
experienced, how art is used, what work art does in the world. In his
1934 book *Art as Experience*, Dewey tackled analytic metaphysical
approaches and challenged us to rethink our modern conception of art,
the importance of aesthetics, and how we live more generally. Arguing
that the conception of art based on traditional metaphysical foundations limited its real world impact, Dewey instead emphasized art's
experiential and functional possibilities.

To give support to his offensive, Dewey criticized the growing adop-
tion of a "museum attitude" toward modern art. Too often, he suggested,
its place in a museum or a private collection determined the worth of art.
While a supporter of museums, Dewey felt the *emphasis* of setting aside
and protecting art in antiseptic, controlled environments separated from
everyday life limited its potential. In fact, Dewey attacked the field of
aesthetics as a whole, suggesting the emphasis on "specialness" or "dis-
connectedness" left it on the philosophical sidelines when dealing with
the "big" questions that impacted everyday lives. Traditional conceptions
about art, and aesthetics more generally, emphasized "escape." The privileged persons with access to museums and private collections left the
real world behind and entered a "special" place to stand back and view
"true art" and "real beauty."

Soccer as Art

To pragmatically rethink art is to consider what art does, rather than focus
on what art is. Dewey believed artworks stood as the consummation of
human experience. In other words, art at its best exemplified the richest

way for humans to exist. Always grounded in human transactions with the world around them, good art heightens human experience, taps into our emotional depths, and reveals the constraints and possibilities of our existence. Rather than "losing ourselves" in a different realm beyond the ordinary, artworks immerse us more fully in our world while taking us beyond the routine and mundane that often characterizes our daily life.

Historically, traditional forms of art like painting, poetry, and music succeed in performing the role of engagement and illumination. A great painting by someone like Picasso uses shapes, colors, and forms within a defined space to engage us immediately and to see the world in a different, non-mechanical manner. A poet fuses words and sentences together in novel ways to capture some part of our humanity beyond the use of simple, robotic description. We "feel" great art rather than "know" great art. It captures us, pervades our memory and reflections, generates discussion and interpretation, challenges how we look at the world. After witnessing great art, our lives and our worlds are never the same.

Whether art qualifies as "fine" art is not a question of whether the work of art is a certain type of product, its price, its popularity, where it's placed, or its pedigree. Instead, "fine" art generates a sense of meaningfulness and vibrancy, lifting us beyond the mundane to see life in new ways. "Fine" art stimulates imagination and creativity, engagement and communication between the artist, the artwork, and its witnesses. Art*works* do real work and one does not need to set out to create art in order to make art. In fact, most art from the pre-modern era was never intended to sit in a museum—these works existed for some function while simultaneously transforming their time and space. Any product or action holds the potentiality to become an artwork—sometimes slipping in and out of artwork status over time and in different contexts.

Based on this pragmatic understanding of art and aesthetics, anything can serve as a context in which art might spontaneously "happen"—including the soccer pitch. Players use "ordinary" human movements in combinations most of us can only dream of to control the ball, to move with it through bounded time and space against the resistance of defenders, to pass it with precision to a teammate, to strike it with incredible power towards a defined target and past a goalkeeper. They do so with the same forces of gravity acting upon them, the same degrees of freedom in their bodily movements, the same rules and boundaries that confine the recreational player.

Yet once in a while, a moment in life seemingly lifts out of the ordinary and reveals the "thatness" of experience—*that* meal, *that* storm, or in the case of soccer, *that* move, *that* pass, *that* ball strike, *that* goal.

Sometimes these moments are pleasurable. Other times they reveal problematic situations. In any case, we reflect upon these seemingly extraordinary experiences, discuss them, interpret them, try to repeat or avoid them, seek more or less of them. These are the moments that Dewey refers to as art.

From a pragmatic perspective, the greatest enemy of art is the mundane or the routine at one extreme, or the chaotic at the other. If nothing in our daily existence draws us to the potential "thatness" of experience, or if we live lives of disconnect and meaninglessness, we miss the potential for living artfully—we live a numb or "anesthetic" life. Soccer, however, provides us with a durable context—the lines of the pitch and the always moving clock as a frame for space and time, the history of the game as an evolving foundation, the rules of soccer to define actions. Within these parameters are the opportunities for dynamism, for creativity to push the boundaries of what humans can do within the context of a game. Rather than stand as non-Art from a traditional metaphysical perspective, soccer instead serves as an ideal locale for art to do its work. We may not immediately "know" why something happening on the pitch is meaningful and artistic, but we certainly "feel" it.

Cristiano Ronaldo as Artist

So the big question: Can we view Cristiano Ronaldo as an artist like Pablo Picasso? It is probably fairly obvious at this point that the answer from a pragmatic perspective is yes. But to arrive at this conclusion requires a reorientation away from the traditional conception of art. If this move is made, Picasso becomes an artist in the active moments in which he creates a painting or sculpture that captures our attention and transforms the way we see the world. In the same vein, Ronaldo becomes an artist on those occasions when his play engages us, leaving with a feeling that something meaningful just happened. Neither is an "artist" in a traditional metaphysical sense all the time—only when in the act of creation within the parameters of their crafts.

Ronaldo, for example, might only handle the ball forty to fifty times during a ninety-minute match, make twenty to twenty-five passes to teammates, attempt five to seven shots on goal. Most of the time he covers around ten kilometers of ground over the pitch without the ball, waiting for a moment to create something that is at once productive from an objective sense, and at the same time can collectively engage us as spectators to lift us beyond the mundane. As Galeano writes, "[The idol's] acrobatic art draws multitudes. . . . The ball laughs, radiant, in the air. He brings her down, puts her to sleep, showers her with compliments, dances with her, and seeing such things never before seen his admirers pity their unborn grandchildren who will never see them" (p. 6).

For Ronaldo to produce artworks—the kind of imaginative actions that transform the way we see the world—he must do so within the durable bounds of soccer. If, for example, Ronaldo suddenly picked the ball up with his hands, ran towards his own goal, stopped to perform some amazing juggling tricks, and then launched a powerful bicycle kick into his own goal, it would likely fail to resonate with us as artful. Certainly such a display would qualify as creative and novel, however its randomness and disregard for the objectives and boundaries of soccer would render it fairly meaningless—unless we collectively decided this was more interesting than traditional soccer.

Great artists do challenge the status quo, transforming what is considered possible; but they do so by building upon the durable qualities of their environments and their histories. Picasso's paintings came after Rembrandt's, whose works came after da Vinci's. Painters may experiment with new mediums, subject matters, dimensions, styles—but their works are not completely random. Ronaldo can push at the boundaries of what might be considered possible in the game, but his playing grows out of the always moving evolution of soccer, from its long and storied history. Ronaldo's artistry grows from Zidane, from Maradona, from Cruyff, from Pelé.

Not every painting, every meal, or every touch on the soccer pitch points to the "thatness" of experience. Often, paintings, meals, and soccer play can fail to strike us as extraordinary, fall short of immersing us more fully in the world that we live within. Instead, the mechanical demands of life can take over. Galeano criticizes soccer for too often promoting such an environment: "The technocracy of professional sport has managed to impose a soccer of lightning speed and brute strength, a soccer that negates joy, kills fantasy and outlaws daring" (p. 6). The same can be said for paintings, musical compositions, and meals trading the potential of "thatness" for efficient results.

But then, sitting in an all-seater or watching at home on television, Ronaldo strikes a free kick so startling in its power and its precision that we jump up and shout "did you see *that*!" It is at these revelatory moments, at the intersection of the possible and impossible, the durable and the dynamic, that great art happens. We as a collective are better for it after witnessing such moments. Food tastes better, bodies gain energy, conversations become more interesting—life becomes more meaningful after watching Ronaldo explore the limits of space, force, movement, speed, and touch on the soccer pitch.

Ronaldo's magical play, occurring within the bounds of soccer's rules and dimensional restrictions, perfectly embodies Dewey's active, functional notion of art. Growing out of the place in soccer history he finds himself, Ronaldo, like Picasso, pushes the bounds of what is thoroughly humanly possible. As spectators, we gain the opportunity to more fully connect to our humanity, to experience life more meaningfully, through Cristiano Ronaldo's play.

Beyond Picasso and Ronaldo: Living Artfully

Dewey spent a lot of time during his final decades of writing focusing on transforming ideas about art and aesthetics. He did so because he felt a better understanding of these concepts would help us in the search for the good life. Living artfully, Dewey argued, was the best way for humanity to exist. To live artfully means we are engaged in our world, trading the coldness of a numb, mechanical anesthetic existence for a life of depth, vividness and meaning.

The pragmatic turn here is not about making the argument that activities like soccer can be art, and players like Cristiano Ronaldo can be artists in a traditional sense. It's not about elevating the cultural status of soccer to that of "high" art. Instead, it is about completely reconsidering what art does in the world, and thus reorienting what counts as art. In doing so, art becomes less disconnected, less of a special realm inspiring only those fortunate enough and sufficiently cultured to access and appreciate art products such as paintings, sculptures, music, and poetry. The potential for artworks from a pragmatic perspective is all around us, in our daily activities, our hobbies, our games. To ignore these opportunities leaves us trapped in the mundane, the meaningless, the anesthetic.

Seeing the art in soccer, in the play of Cristiano Ronaldo is vitally important. His play stimulates our imagination to see the world anew; engages us in the here and now of our lives; gives us reason for communication. Dewey saw in art the possibilities of genuine democracy and the roots of ethics. Once we learn to appreciate these artistic moments, to seek out that which is truly valuable, we can make better moral judgments and live together more harmoniously. What better display of the potential for democracy is there than an Arsenal or Barcelona or Messi fan as a true soccer aficionado finding the beauty in the play of Ronaldo? The aesthetics of soccer, the artistry of Ronaldo and others, can create the groundwork for genuine communication, for shared values, for the fullness of possibilities.

It is not just players at the level of Cristiano Ronaldo who can live artfully through soccer. All players, of all ages, of all abilities, can find artful moments within the game (and beyond). Ronaldo's artistic advantage, like Picasso as a painter, is his expansive ability to imaginatively test, challenge, and reconfigure the game's possibilities. But the difference is in degree, not kind. The six-year-old willing to test her limits on the pitch, exploring new ways to move with the ball, to control it, to interact with it, lives artfully. She makes a turn, moves past a defender unlike any time before, and reflects upon the moment as "*that* move!" This is what Dewey encourages us all to do—find ways to live artfully.

Consequently, art and aesthetics serve a central role in the development of democracy and fulfillment of human existence. Since artworks embody experience in its richest sense, cultivates a sense of imagination within the context of the here and now, and irreducibly fosters social communication, art moves from the museum to the pitch, and aesthetics no longer stands as a special, politically insignificant branch of philosophy. Instead, art and aesthetics emerge as a centrally important aspect of our existence and for cultural development. Thus soccer (and the game's "artists" such as Ronaldo) becomes an important contributor to human existence and social flourishing, rather than a simple game featuring players merely kicking a ball around a field.

Since its purchase in 2004, few people have seen *Garçon à la Pipe*. Its owner and location remain a secret. Consequently, it does very little work in the real world. Cristiano Ronaldo, on the other hand, displays moments of artistry on the pitch regularly, and to a wide, diverse, passionate audience. This is the difference between traditional conceptions of art and a pragmatic understanding of art. Many art aficionados would certainly bristle at the claim that a footballer performs a more valuable artistic role in culture than a rare and priceless Picasso painting. But for pragmatists, the potential to realize beauty and value, and the contributions such moments make to the good life, come from the everyday, from the simple, from soccer, from a Portuguese winger.

14
Kant at the Maracanã

LUCA VARGIU

Taste is the ability to judge an object, or a way of presenting it, by means of a liking or disliking *devoid of all interest*. The object of such a liking is called *beautiful*.

—IMMANUEL KANT, *Critique of Judgment*

The chairman had one eye on what was happening on the pitch, and the other on Dosrius, who was mingling with the spectators on the terraces, a philosophical onlooker apparently unconcerned by the way the match was going.

—MANUEL VÁZQUEZ MONTALBÁN, *Offside* (2001)

Kant at the Maracanã? How come Immanuel Kant is at a soccer pitch? That same philosopher commonly described as grave, methodical, a creature of habit, married to his studies and his daily walk?

Well, why not? It's not as absurd as it sounds. After all, we've already seen him as a player at the Olympiastadion in Munich! All this happens in a Monty Python sketch presenting an improbable match between Greek and German philosophers. And, in the German national team, managed by no less than Martin Luther, Kant just had to be there, lined up, only heaven knows, as a defender with the number two. (For your information, it was Greece that won the match 1–0, thanks to a goal scored by Socrates at the eighty-ninth minute: the referee Confucius validated the goal despite complaints by German players).

If Kant has played soccer, or so it seems, I would like to imagine him as a spectator, enjoying an equally improbable match with the best stars of *futebol bailado*: Garrincha, Didi, Vavá, Pelé, Dirceu, Falcão, Zico,

Sócrates (a case of coincidence of names), Romário, Ronaldo, Rivaldo, Ronaldinho . . .

Where? As I already said, at the Maracanã, in Rio de Janeiro. Why? No need to explain, it's the stadium where Brazilian soccer belongs. Where is he? In the grandstand. How come? Is there a particular reason? Well, yes. It's okay to allow our imagination free rein, but it's just too much to swallow to picture him on the lower tier with the *torcida*, cheering and jeering, among choruses, flags, banners, roars and smoke bombs with a painted face! Much better to imagine a quiet eighteenth-century Prussian gentleman sitting in the grandstand. It's more likely and more suitable for his personality.

What's more, the grandstand corresponds better to his philosophy, in surely one of the best known and seminal aspects of his thought: *aesthetic disinterest*. What is aesthetic disinterest? Good question. In the *Critique of Judgment*, published in 1790, Kant wonders if, and how, we may conceive of an aesthetic judgment like when we say "*x* is beautiful (or not)." To this question he answers that if an aesthetic judgment is possible, first of all we have to see if we can imagine a kind of pleasure or pain not connected to interest in the object of our judgment's existence. That is, interest related to what we can know about that object, or to its use for instrumental or moral purposes, physiological or psychological needs. If such a pleasure or pain were thinkable, this would be a necessary feature of aesthetic enjoyment as seen in its purity. Or as Kant puts it: "Interest is what we call the liking we connect with the presentation of an object's existence" (*Critique of Judgment*, §2). It's always part and parcel of desiring, whether it regards the senses, or its use for a purpose, or its moral goodness. Instead, simple aesthetic judgment is independent of the existence of the object and, therefore, disinterested.

Kant, who was very aware of everything that went on in the world, gives us various examples. A negative one is that of "that Iroquois *sachem* who said that he liked nothing better in Paris than the eating-houses" (*Critique of Judgment*, §2). Who knows, perhaps it was not only the Native American chief, torn away from his land and accompanied to one of the biggest European metropolises, who thought so. But, in Kant's example, it's a fact that those who like the eating-houses are interested in their existence!

Let's give another example. If I like a boy or a girl, am I interested in their existence, or not? Do my female students who like, say, Kaká, Cristiano Ronaldo or Cannavaro (as they are handsome, that is), forget about Kaká's, Cristiano Ronaldo's or Cannavaro's existence? They may forget they are soccer players, but that they aren't interested in the existence of those guys seems unlikely to me. Well, the discussion is neither easy nor short. However, I find it meaningful that in Italy you can often hear, or read on the stadium bleachers, "Thanks for *existing*!" (*Grazie di esistere!*). (I don't know whether this saying is related to Eros Ramazzotti's song with the same title, or not. Has Ramazzotti read Kant?)

On the contrary, says Kant, the judgment of taste is "merely contemplative," that is, it's "indifferent to the existence of the object" and "considers the character of the object only by holding it up to our feeling of pleasure and displeasure" (*Critique of Judgment*, §5). One of the philosophers who had studied Kant's aesthetics a great deal, Hans-Georg Gadamer (1900–2002), observed that there are two aspects at stake here, a negative and a positive one. Defining the aesthetic pleasure as disinterested has the negative sense of ruling out that the object of one's judgment could be employed as useful or desired as good. But it also means, positively speaking, that the existence of the object neither adds nor takes away anything from my pleasure's content. (*Truth and Method*, Continuum, 2005, p. 482). The existence of a work of art I'm contemplating doesn't add anything to the fact that I like it, or don't like it.

Some soccer stadiums are noteworthy works of architecture. There is the Maracanã itself, planned by a team of Brazilian architects, or the already mentioned Munich Olympiastadion, by Behnisch and Partner, with particular canopies by Frei Otto, or, in Munich still, the Allianz Arena designed by Herzog and De Meuron, the same architects who built the Beijing Olympic Stadium. One day those stadiums might no longer be there because their respective administrations may decide to tear them down. Well, I might get upset that these stadiums no longer exist, and I might also get upset because they were beautiful works of architecture. However, they were beautiful before, and they'd be beautiful now as well. Their existence allows us to admire them, but it doesn't increase their beauty. On the contrary, if I admire the stadium but, at the same time, I think that I can take away a piece so as to bring it home as a souvenir, or to sell it on eBay, or I wonder what its economic value is and how different my life would be if I were the owner—well, in all those cases I'm polluting the aesthetic judgment with an interest (besides being a vandal).

In the Bleachers

Let's put ourselves in the shoes of a sporting event spectator. We do it along with another distinguished scholar, the philosopher and art historian Erwin Panofsky (1892–1968). In line with Kant's thought, in a 1940 essay Panofsky writes that every object, "natural or man-made," can be experienced aesthetically. We do this, he adds, when we look, or listen to it, "without relating it, intellectually or emotionally, to anything outside of itself." Some examples make his thought clear. A carpenter looks at a tree associating it with the various uses of the wood, while an ornithologist associates it with the bird that might nest in it; someone betting on horses associates the race with the desire that the horse on which he has put his money will win. All of these people are relating the object under consideration to an interest: the carpenter is interested in the instrumental purposes of the wood, the ornithologist wants to know something more about the birds, and the gambler is interested in the chances of his horse winning. Panofsky concludes: "Only he who simply and wholly abandons himself to the object of his perception will experience it aesthetically" (*Meaning in the Visual Arts. Papers in and on Art History,* Doubleday, 1955, p. 11).

From a racetrack to a stadium, from horse racings to soccer matches, the gap is narrow. How can we make the most of Panofsky's insight? By saying that just those people who go to the stadium for the simple delight of enjoying the match adopt a disinterested and contemplative attitude. It's Kant who talks about contemplation with regards to the aesthetic judgment. So we can already guess why someone with a contemplative attitude (Kant himself) stays in the grandstand and not with the supporters, singing, dancing, and fooling around. What's more, some observations on language: "to contemplate" comes from "*templum*", a Latin word meaning "temple." Haven't people compared the great stadiums with temples more than once? Isn't the Maracanã known as the "temple of world soccer" (*templo do futebol mondial*)? May we not say the same for Wembley, Azteca, San Siro, Santiago Bernabeu . . .?

Very good, we seem ready for the kick-off. Kant is contemplating in the grandstand, the players are lined up, the *torcida* is hot. . . . But let's wait for a while. Let's reflect a little bit more and wonder if Kant is alone or not, with his disinterested attitude, among the spectators (it's not fair if you answer that he's with Panofsky, though it's implied).

Panofsky talks about the gambler and tells us that this spectator is interested, and how. Thus we observe he doesn't share his attitude with Kant. Yes, we may think that he knows how to isolate himself and enjoy the match just for the pleasure of the match. Of course he'll be able to appreciate a beautiful goal aesthetically, regardless of who has scored. However, the hope that the team will win is always bound to come out.

Among the spectators we can find, first of all, the supporters and the *torcida*, with their choruses, banners, cheering, and choreographies. What about them? What do they have to do with disinterest? Let's start with the language. While "supporter" is more or less a neutral word, "*torcida*" is surely more emphatic. Its etymology refers to the Portuguese verb "*torcer*", which means "to root for," but also "to wring" and "to turn," as if to emphasize the inextricable tie with a team. The English term "fan" has lost its power, or so it seems nowadays, but let's not forget that its root is "fanatic." It should imply some form of fanaticism toward their favorite team, not unlike religious fanaticism ("fan" comes from the Latin word "*fanum*", from which the poetic English "fane": a synonym for "temple" again). "You shall have no other teams before me"? We run the risk of being blasphemous and politically incorrect. Then, one remembers the small altarpieces dedicated to their favorite champions, like those built in Naples when Maradona used to play there, between kitsch and degeneration of traditional popular culture.

The Italian terms "*tifo*" and "*tifoso*" are at least more secular. They come from the Latin "*typhus*," meaning "typhus" (what a surprise), "fever," and indicate, therefore, such a strong engagement that soccer becomes more than a passion: it becomes a disease. It is the soccer disease described by novelist Nick Hornby in *Fever Pitch* (Riverhead, 1998), contracted "suddenly, inexplicably, uncritically" (p. 15). The pre-match rituals (here again, something related to religion), the feeling of a nervous stomach churning before the match, the tyranny of supporting, with its overarching influence over weekends, holidays and all commitments, the search for an identity, or the awareness of being incapable of relating to the other people if not through soccer. We can read all this in *Fever Pitch*, a sort of supporter's "sentimental education," with their enthusiasm and their depression, dreams, obsession, priceless emotions and bitter disappointments. It's a state of elation that, as we all know, can even cause heart attacks or degenerate into violence, as the "hooligan phenomenon" unfortunately shows.

Like "fan", the word "*tifo*" has become weaker along the way. It's hardly surprising that we've coined new words to denote the wildest supporting groups: beside the *torcida*, there are the *ultras*, but these *ultras* are of course *ultrafanatic* and *ultratifosi*. Supporting represents a very strong element of identification. Being a fan, a *tifoso*, a *torcedor*, means not simply taking part, but engaging with the event, with the other fans, feeling and sharing the emotion of a lot of people and of the whole supporting group. It means expressing ourselves by saying "we," not "the team", nor even "my team". "We won 3–1!" "We tied." "We lost the match, but the referee didn't give us the penalty." Using "we" means that I too am member of the team. As Hornby writes, "I *was* Arsenal," "It was *us*, and I was a part of us."

Fever, typhus, passion, disease. How do you associate all this with disinterest and contemplation? It doesn't match, evidently. Like the gambler, the supporters don't seem to share their attitude with Kant. However, unless they've been blinded by passion, they can't avoid recognizing if the opposing players have played well, and praising the beauty of a goal or of a action, from whatever team they come from. This means that, for the fan as well as for the gambler, a disinterested attitude is possible, although it isn't the most frequent or usual.

In the Middle of the Pitch

While we're reflecting on the spectators, the referee has already blown the starting whistle and the match has begun. We make the most of it in order to get close to the pitch. We neither want to plan an invasion at the end of the match with the fans, nor do we want to burst into the middle of the pitch during the match—as certain crazy people do—in a strange costume or totally naked. Instead, we want to observe the match, saying hello to Kant and Panofsky in the grandstand, and relate the question of disinterest to the people who are either on the pitch or sitting in the bench.

Might the players, the referee and his linesmen, the coach and the whole staff adopt a disinterested attitude while the match is on? Let's focus on the players. Needless to say, they must watch out for the development of the match, the movements of the opponents, the coach's indications. At no moment can they distract their attention.

Who of you knows the manga and anime *Captain Tsubasa (Flash Kicker)*? In the cartoon, in order to emphasize the narration and make it more epic, there is a certain use of slow-motion that may be excessive. The pitches look kilometers long (you can perceive even the curve of the Earth's surface) and the matches last twenty episodes. When I was young, my friends and I always wondered—and I am still wondering— how long the pitches in *Flash Kicker* are. This time and space expansion should allow us, as spectators, to share the involvement of the players during the match, their concentration and effort, as if we were playing that match. So, never mind if we perceive the curve of the Earth: suspending the normal conditions of experience can help us become aware of how much of a struggle a goal or a save can be.

In this context "involvement" is another word for "interest." For the spectators this means engaging with the event. And for the players? For them this means that a disinterested attitude seems impossible during the match. Attention, concentration, and struggle are all enemies of contemplation and disinterest. In this light, the players have a lot to share with the fans, coach, mates, opponents, but nothing to share with Kant. Nevertheless, we can hypothesize that, in certain moments, they're able to isolate themselves from the match, so as not to distract themselves (never ever!), but to admire a save, a goal, a dribble, a free kick, regardless of who has carried them out, a team mate or an opponent. Once again, contemplation is possible, but not usual.

In fact, in the event of a favorable or unfavorable moment, the players don't limit themselves to contemplation, but share their joy or sadness with the whole team, the staff and the fans.

> In the far goalmouth, unbeaten,
> the other keeper stays put. But
> his soul refuses to be left alone.
> In rapture, his arms are thrown
> up to blow kisses across the field.
> This party—he says—is my party too.

So sings the Italian poet Umberto Saba (1883–1957) in his poem "Goal."[1]

Post-Match Commentaries

Final whistle: it's already time to take stock. In their more usual and more frequent attitude, the fans are not disinterested, the players mustn't be that way, and the observations we've made about the players are the same for the referee, the linesmen, the coach and all the staff. There is no doubt that it's a possible attitude, but it isn't a usual one. Are there people who go to the stadium and "simply and wholly" abandon themselves to the object of their perception, as Panofsky says? Surely not many.

Nevertheless, from Kant's point of view, what matters is that disinterest is possible. Kant is anxious to investigate the conditions of the possibility of the judgment of taste, before he considers if it's real. He wants to see if and how an aesthetic judgment is possible. This implies that, for Kant, such a judgment is "a methodological abstraction," as Gadamer says (p. 39). Maybe merely disinterested aesthetic judgments will never

---

[1] The translation is by Tim Parks <www.abc.net.au/rn/bookshow/stories/2007/1954136.htm> and is used with his permission.

exist, but what is important is that we may conceive of them, as a matter of principle. So, what's the meaning of the aesthetic judgment? Why does Kant need to reflect on something that perhaps will never exist?

Kant's *Critique of Judgment* is a milestone in modern aesthetics, and modern aesthetics arises, firstly, to face a series of problems intimately related to the philosophical thought. Its constitution in an autonomous field of studies is connected with the attempt to find a form of regulation in those spheres of human experience in which every effort to formulate rules and criteria fails: for instance, the spheres of politics and of social and communicative action. To give an example, taken from economics: Are there strong reasons why the chairman of a soccer club would prefer a cautious policy in order to keep the team finances in the black, or it is better to have unscrupulous behavior so as to grab the best players? When I say "strong reasons," I mean as strong as the laws of physics. Are there such reasons? No. But then, the curious philosopher asks, how do chairmen make such economic judgments?

The aesthetic judgment shows this, meaningfully. In its sphere, there aren't universal rules, as in the case of scientific judgments, but not for this reason does it remain a field free from judgments. You can apply it to the discussions where one ought to break away both from the absence of rules (according to the proverb "there's no accounting for taste"), and from rules valid in every time and place (which would reverse the proverb: "there's accounting for taste"). This is the space of communicative action. It's the space of dialogue, of argument, of agreement and disagreement; it's the space of social and political debate, which opens with the rise of public opinion. It's not an accident that Kant, in his political writings, stands up for freedom of thought and of the press (as he does in *What Is Enlightenment?*). Hence, the two traditional branches of philosophy, theoretical philosophy (as for the conditions of the possibility of the judgment) and practical philosophy (for social and political action), find their common ground precisely in the *Critique of Judgment*, and in the exemplary significance of aesthetic judgment.

Kant investigates such a judgment by considering it as if it were in a lab, keeping it away from every possible disturbing element and trying to imagine it in its purity. Here he pinpoints some essential features, among which is disinterest. Do disinterested judgments exist? Who knows, but what matters is, above all, that it's possible to think so.

Actually, disinterest isn't the only feature of such a judgment. Another one, no less important, is the ability to share it. If the space of aesthetic judgment is the space of dialogue and agreement, when we say that a certain thing is beautiful, we indirectly mean that everybody can agree.

Otherwise we wouldn't have said "*x* is beautiful," but "I like *x*." However, we already know that in aesthetic judgments there aren't strong reasons and universal rules, as in scientific judgments. When we say "*x* is beautiful," this judgment doesn't have the same validity and the same strength as judgments like "the ball is round" and "the pitch is rectangular." That Cristiano Ronaldo is handsome may be discussed, we may agree or disagree. That the ball is round is undoubted. So, we have to do with a strange judgment, which can't depend on objective and universal rules, but nevertheless asserts the (potential) agreement of everybody. Kant calls this feature of the aesthetic judgment "general validity."

This is the problem that emerges when we want to vote for the greatest goal in the history of soccer. What's the most beautiful goal ever? A lot of polls put Maradona's second one during the 1986 Mexican World Cup quarter-final at the top. It was when the Argentine ace left half the English team behind. This way (maybe), he was able to be forgiven for the first goal, scored with his hand (the "hand of God"). That goal, for example, has been voted "Goal of the Century" in a FIFA poll, followed by Michael Owen's goal during England v Argentina, 1998 World Cup, and by Pelé's one during Brazil v Sweden, 1958 World Cup. However, is this poll based on something objective? No, in fact we can carry out other polls and another goal would come top of the league. However, the result of that, or any other poll, aims to be shared by everyone and to reach an agreement, even if not on objective ground. Actually, if I say: "Maradona's second goal during Argentina v England is the most beautiful ever," I say that because I expect my judgment to be shared. Otherwise I wouldn't have said: "That goal is beautiful, or better still, the best", but I'd confine myself to saying: "I like that," perhaps adding: "What do you think?"

General validity and disinterest are closely related. If we want to share our judgment, our judgment must necessarily be disinterested, because every interest can't but be personal. If it's Maradona's agent speaking about Maradona's goal, we may even suspect that his judgment is biased. If it's a fan speaking (Maradona's, not the agent's!), somebody who even has an altarpiece at home, here again we may have our suspicions that such a person can't be disinterested.

TV Appointments

And now, let's ask Kant to leave the Maracanã's grandstand, and come home with us, to watch the match again on TV. Can we find the disinterested attitude while watching the match, or the programs on soccer, in the comfort of our living room?

What happens to us as TV spectators? Enjoying a match at the stadium is different from enjoying it on TV. The environment is different, the atmosphere is different, the medium is different, and hence the point of view is different, thanks to all the possibilities offered by technology (replay, slow-motion, super-imposure, multiple views, commercial breaks—ouch). In 1978, the year of the Argentinean World Cup—won by the host—Serge Daney in the famous French review "*Cahiers du Cinéma*" proposed a three part typology of the TV audience:

1. **the "pure ones," those who love sports;**

2. **the "telephiles", those who are addicted to the imaginary on TV;**

3. **the "metalinguists," those who in every moment, even in the most intense ones, prefer to analyze how communication works.**

Can any of these TV viewers attain a disinterested attitude?

The pure viewers, despite the differences, have the same attitudes as the stadium spectators. Among them, we can especially meet fans, *ultras*, *torcedores*, and *tifosi*. Sometimes, when they're in group, even with choreographies and painted faces. Hence, not much contemplation. The telephiles are too TV-addicted to be able to adopt a contemplative attitude as well. The metalinguists no doubt feel pleasure in analyzing the mechanics of communication. However, it's about an intellectual pleasure, which comes from knowledge and learning, and which is related not directly to the program's content (the match, the interview, the talk show), but to the way the content is presented on TV.

Knowledge and Pleasure

Here arises a problem that has interested students of aesthetics for ages. Does knowledge add pleasure, or not? Put another way, do those who lack knowledge feel less pleasure, more pleasure, or enjoy in a different way? It's not only the metalinguists, interested in the "how" and communication, who feel an intellectual pleasure. Every soccer lover can feel such a pleasure, and if we focus on the game, we'll be able to see it. We can ask the question this way: How shall we consider the pleasure of a spectator who doesn't know the soccer rules in comparison with someone who knows them inside out, and is able to recognize an offside, a penalty foul, a throw-in, and so on?

Kant, who is now comfortably seated on the sofa, reminds us of his distinction between *free beauty* and *accessory beauty*. Accessory beauty is "attributed to objects that fall under the concept of a particular purpose," where free beauty, "does not presuppose a concept of what the object is meant to be" (*Critique of Judgment*, §16). Knowing what an object is for, how it works and what its destination is, implies that we enjoy that object not only with the senses, but with reason as well. We join the "aesthetic liking" to the "intellectual liking." According to Kant, there is a gain, but such a gain drives us beyond mere aesthetic judgment, as it concerns not the rules of taste, but rather the "rules for uniting taste with reason." This doesn't mean that Kant prefers free beauty (of an ornament or a flower, for example). It means that the aesthetic liking as such has nothing to do with the knowledge of the rules of the purpose of our object of pleasure.

Let's take the action of a forward who scores by breaking the defenders' offside trap. We can enjoy it because we know the offside rules. So, what's the difference between us and those spectators who enjoy the same action without knowing the rules? This is what Kant is talking about. No doubt those who know the rules really enjoy the action, and it's a bit difficult to understand the pleasure felt by those who don't know anything about soccer, when they watch twenty-two people in short trousers chasing a ball. This confirms that the pure aesthetic judgment is just "a methodological abstraction" and that, in everyday life, it's easier to find a mixed pleasure, both aesthetic and intellectual (the same at the stadium as in front of the TV).

All those who know the rules, first of all know the aim and the purpose of the game. What's more, they know the aim and the purpose of every action. Hence, an interesting question. Let's imagine a spectacular play: does it create more pleasure when it ends with a goal, that is, when it fulfills its purpose? Or is the pleasure independent of the way the action ends? Here it seems tough to find the answer. There's always a union of aesthetic liking with intellectual liking, but in the first case the action succeeds, and in the second case it doesn't (we might even judge the action to be merely fruitless and ineffective).

A player of undoubted class like Denilson, master of dribbling, has often been reproached for not being so effective, especially in front of the goal, and for dilly-dallying with superfluous preciosity, useless to the team. His "samba-dribblings," as the press has called them, a lot of times have been as amusing as they are inconclusive (who of you remembers Brazil v Netherlands in the 1998 World Cup semi-final?). That's why his career hasn't been as rewarding as everybody expected. Other wingers have been more effective. If we make the comparison with Garrincha, then, there's no contest. He was not only a skillful illusionist, able to hide the ball from the opponents, not only the greatest dribbler ever, not only an "angel with bent legs" (*anjo das pernas tortas*), as a beautiful poem by Vinicius de Moraes (1913–1980) sings, but also a formidable scorer (283 goals in 714 matches).

VHS, DVD, YouTube

Let's sit in front of the TV again. It doesn't seem that we'll find disinterest here. Yet there is the possibility here of a regular and consistent contemplative attitude. Everybody knows that the video-recording of an event for TV (a sports match, a concert, or a theater play) make it possible to watch the event again, and again, and again—a potentially infinite number of times. A match, or a single play, can be unique and unrepeatable—and a pity for those who miss it—but it can be re-broadcast, or I can watch it again, as many times as I want. It's no longer the event that is unique, but rather its live broadcast. This is well known by those fans who, if they can't watch the match, record it so as to enjoy it later. Meanwhile they warn everybody—relatives, friends, neighbors and acquaintances—not to tell them the result nor the way the match develops, so that, when they watch it, it will be as if they participated in the event, as if it were played in that very moment in front of their eyes.

But what sense does it make to watch an old match, or a video showing us the feats of the great one-time champions? Let's see. It may be out of a scientific interest, similar to that a sociologist or an anthropologist may have if they go to the stadium. Here the historian joins the sociologist and the anthropologist (not necessarily a soccer historian). If it's fans watching old videos of their team or favorites, maybe a nostalgic attitude will prevail. In this case, however, they are more disinterested as well. They already know the result and, perhaps, they also know the actions in detail, of who has scored or saved, the yellow cards, in short, the whole development of the match. What's more, nobody puts their money on it, because there can't be bets on the past.

All this leads the fan to a more contemplative attitude, in which the aesthetic point of view plays a more important role. If a fan prefers to watch a certain match again, and not another one, it's also because that match is more beautiful and more exciting. In that match his or her team has played well and there have been beautiful actions. We're getting closer to disinterest. The spectators of an old match can't have the same interest in the existence of their object of pleasure as they have when the object is (in the) present. Desiring that a past match exists doesn't make sense! At most, I may be happy that the match has been recorded and that I can watch it, and watch it again. But in such a case the interest moves from the match to its recording.

The Internet (for example YouTube) offers lots of possibilities. In its huge image archive, you can even find videos dating back to the first World Cup, that of 1930 in Uruguay. Leaving aside the scholar and the nostalgic fan once again, the Internet allows us, more than elsewhere, to activate a contemplative and disinterested attitude. It's true that the fact of singling out the match's highlights, or of making a compilation of actions—goals, dribbles, tackles, and saves—may have celebratory intent and may be a dedication from some fans to their team or their champions. However, that video can be watched by everybody, by people who aren't fans of that team or that champion. This suppresses its emotional power and, somehow, neutralizes it.

For Kant, after all, being indifferent as regards the existence of the object of my judgment of taste, means that I consider that object as if there were just the image of it. If in the disinterested pleasure the real existence of the object is indifferent, then that pleasure isn't related to the object, but to the object's image. Thus, maybe just on the Internet, one of the symbols of our civilization of images, we may abandon ourselves to the disinterested contemplation, more than elsewhere. From the Maracanã grandstand to the sofa in the living room, now Kant sits in front of a computer screen. Who knows, perhaps he's watching the Monty Python sketch and disinterestedly enjoying the vision of himself playing soccer![2]

---

[2] I would like to thank all the friends and colleagues who have helped me and without whom this chapter wouldn't exist: Ted Richards (coach), Tina Onnis (referee), Rossella Aramu, Maria Luisa Dessì (assistant referees), Paolo Piu (fourth official), Pilar Garcia Perez (goalkeeper), Ignazina Buzzo, Sabrina Figus, Bettina Ruggeri (defenders), Pierpaolo Dore (libero), Mauro Murgia, Federica Pau, Simona Pau (midfielders), Emanuele Melis, Piergiovanni Morittu (wingers), Paolo Meloni (center forward), Nicoletta Atzori, Francesca Garau (ball girls).

15

Embellishing the Ugly Side of the Beautiful Game

JESÚS M. ILUNDÁIN-AGURRUZA
and CESAR R. TORRES

*With three English players nipping at his heels, Maradona takes posses-
sion of the ball on the Argentine side. "El Pelusa" rushes forward, feints
right, dodges another defender to the left, goes between two more players,
dribbles past another one, and bypassing the rushing goalie, as the last
defender slides to tackle him, he kicks the ball into the net! A most beautiful goal.*

"The beautiful game." English speakers the world over know this refers to
football, if their smarts and sports savvy are a notch above those of a
guppy (some would call it "soccer," but they know better). In the
Portuguese and Spanish speaking worlds *jogo bonito,* or *juego bonito,* refer
not to the game of football itself, but to a way of playing that's nothing
short of sporting wizardry—just swap the wand for an official FIFA ball.

In this chapter, we play both senses back to back. Indeed, football is
the kind of game that can knock your socks off, literally and figuratively.
But we have a confession to make: this isn't just about the good-looking
side of things: it's more about the "bad-looking" one. We organize this
philosophical foray into football in an aggressive, maybe insane, 4–2–4 formation to run the ball, er, arguments direct and fast along the touchlines.

To begin, a *Blitzkrieg* move: for Albert Camus, who knew his football, "crushing truths perish from being acknowledged" (*The Myth of
Sisyphus,* Vintage, 1955, p. 90). For us, this means that to fully appreciate football, we have to dance with the ugly one. The goal we'd like to
score entails a revaluation of contemporary manifestations of the sport
by *facing the uglier side* to bring about a more robust expression of the
game. Put another way, for football to flourish and merit being called *the*
beautiful game, we must confront the unsightly.

What we have in mind here are *displays* of football that are either cosmetically embellished with cheap make-up tricks that lack the craft to color ill-intentioned fouls, or worse a warts-and-all shameless hubris that twists and breaks rules at will for the sake of goals and results. Unless we face these head on, things will deteriorate even further. The greatest game in the world deserves no less, we have little to lose and a lot to gain (unless we wish to keep dancing with the ugly one).

With a Striking Game

Before a big game, a good training regime is always advisable—who wants to pull a muscle after managing to get past the last defender, or (worse still, if that's possible) strain a neuron thinking too hard? Let's begin ours with a set of basic concepts applicable to football—and thus by extension the world of sport generally. Over time, humans, thanks to those restless ones, have created incredibly numerous, complex cultural phenomena. Philosopher Alasdair MacIntyre calls them social practices. These practices cover any endeavor that falls under the rubric of art, science, humanities, crafts, sports—you name it. Keeping the ball close to our interests, there are many sports involving spherical objects, of which football is one. (We realize it's not *just* one among many, but for now let's keep that to ourselves, shall we?) To cut the play short, practices are complex forms of cooperative social activity characterized by the internal goods and standards of excellence they realize.

Football involves certain actions and outcomes that are proper and unique to, and considered good for, the sport precisely because of the type of game it is, of how it is played. To skillfully maneuver the ball with feet rather than hands, to dribble, feint, and lob just so, to create spaces or develop a "silky touch," are all skills characteristic of football valued and valuable within the framework of the game. Off the pitch, say on your job as a plumber or accountant, the skill to pass a lobbed ball or control it with a chest trap isn't worth a used subway ticket, really. These skills are called the internal goods of the game among those in the know. These internal goods are non-instrumental because they are pursued for themselves: they're not means to something else, but simply part and parcel of the process of playing football. They have intrinsic value only for those of us who love football. (As for those who don't swoon over it, try pity before scorn.) What's more, the process trumps the end result, that is, the emphasis is on how the game is played not the outcome. We say *emphasis*, it doesn't mean results are not important.

If your cousin plays striker *just* to get more dates because of the cool factor, his or her interest is extrinsic: the game is an instrument, a means to get some action—the wrong kind when we're concerned with football. On the other foot, if you play goalie because the very idea of defending the posts, catching the ball, and outsmarting forwards despite the risks of being kicked, hit full-force by the ball, or pummeled by sliding attackers (are goalies closet masochists? Just wondering), then you have an intrinsic interest in the game. You could be Sisyphus pushing the rock; so long as you had an intrinsic interest in doing so, the gods be damned, it'd be fun and worth it! That's the beauty of *primarily* being intrinsically interested in activities (or people) in non-instrumental ways, without turning them into mere means: you always "win." Even if you lose the game in terms of scoring, so long as you enjoyed it, you've already won—in a deeper sense. If you actually score more goals, well, then you get to gloat!

To turn the intensity up a notch, let's dribble in the technical concept of constitutive rules. These rules give the game its internal logic or structure. They give football its personality and set it apart from other sports: it's not American football or, lord forbid, curling. These rules define and limit permissible ways to achieve the aim of the game, and prescribe less efficient means to accomplish them: they create artificial obstacles. In football the goal is to score a goal (how fitting!) by putting the ball past the line under the opponent's goalposts. Among other things, the rules limit the spatial boundaries within which play must take place, and exclude the use of hands to contact the ball (excepting goalkeepers, we *know*). More efficient ways to make the ball cross that accursed line could resort to the use of all extremities, or better yet a cannon.

For the kick off, let's engage the standards of excellence. How we satisfy the internal goods is assessed by criteria that specify what counts as excellent. In football, there are better or worse ways of achieving the aim of the game. Getting past an opponent by dribbling and using one's ability to control the speed and direction of the ball within the rules cultivates this excellence, whereas overcoming an opponent by poking his eye as you willfully kick his shin undercuts it. Excellence depends on minding the rules: exemplary and skillful plays by them result in brilliance and quality. Cheating, bending rules, and forsaking the internal goods make the game all the poorer. In the Turkish League, the match between Galatasaray and Fenerbahçe on April 12th, 2009, went from boring to bad to disgusting as it degenerated into a fight of very confusing boundaries that just went on, and on, and on, in the best Energizer Bunny fashion.

Crucially for us, there's another angle to this that bridges sporting values and skills to ethics, namely sportsmanship and fair play. These bind players to honor the rules of the game in a noble way (explained later). Playing the beautiful game beautifully partakes of this overarching excellence. Practices flourish when this excellence is cultivated—or else they wilt. When teams don't try their best and play below their abilities because they have nothing riding on it, and say, the other team is at risk of going to a lower division, this falls short of these standards. But not all involved in the game follow such standards. Carlos Bilardo, who coached Argentina to victory in the 1986 World Cup, was fond of bending and breaking rules. As Eduardo Galeano tells: as "a player he'd prick his opponents with a pin and look innocent" (*Football in Sun and Shadow*, Verso, p. 174). As coach, should the other team be particularly skillful, he would flood parts of the pitch with water. Neither of these shows one iota of concern for excellence in the game.

To cast this all into a seamless, speedy play: football players willingly abide by the rules of the game because they have an intrinsic interest in it—they love it—as they seek to cultivate the type of excellence proper of football. Two reasons for this technical training are that it shows the inner workings that make football special, and it equips us to work with the dark side of football.

Where the Beastly Play

The counterpoint to the opening vignette recounting Maradona's goal comes handed (!) down by him as well via the infamous "hand of God goal"—which the Ultimate Referee Himself would be loath to call. That goal, result of an (un)timely arm-directed ball that contributed to victory in a decisive match, regardless of whether it's condoned or not, remains clouded in controversy. (No need for dirt here, this is no paparazzi-fed tabloid sort of book . . . actually, we get to this in a moment.) The problem lies in the very controversy. Great plays like the opening salvo by "el Pelusa" are not contested but celebrated. The divine or devilish hand, ultimately and sadly, doesn't add but depreciates the internal values of football worth embracing. There's many a blemish—each deserving a colored card or a pertinent punishment and condemnation—that detract from the good looks of the game.

We enter now the ugly side of football with a critical line up of the six most notorious culprits. Before passing the ball to you, we want to stress that this unattractive side isn't merely aesthetic, as in a match with poor play and skill, but more significantly it is ethical, in the sense that these are ignoble or dishonorable. Unless we look at these we act like the proverbial ostrich, hiding our head in the sand to wish it away. With this strategy, things stay bad before they get worse. To create a better, handsomer football we must fully own up to the nasty side. (Advisory: what follows isn't pretty. Parental Guidance is fully recommended. Some readers may find it prudent to close one eye).

First, the players. They are the stars of football. But all too often, they forget their gravitational pull. To be sure, football is very physical. Thrown into the fray and fighting for a ball, it is understandable that one may kick too high or too hard. That's the reason for referees and codified do's and don'ts. Players, however, often willingly rely on dubious tactics to influence outcomes that no self-respecting player or follower should condone. Perhaps the most common way for players to vilify the game is faking a foul; either by miming contact when there isn't or by embellishing contact by pretending to be in excruciating pain. They have always been part of the sport. They are "tradition." Tradition, however, isn't a reason that justifies itself: there are awful traditions we're better off without, like human sacrifices to appease volcanoes. For many this passes as player's savvy. Until this works against them, then they are the first to complain. Besides, not only does this make players look like wimps—compare them to Tour de France cyclists who finish 130-mile mountainous stages with broken bones—but worse, it sports the same flaw as the next risqué example, which spices things up.

On November 16th, 2008, Catania played Torino in the Italian *Serie A*. With a free kick against Torino a few minutes before half time, three Catania players drop their shorts and moon the goalie to block his view. The ruse worked. Catania scored to put the game 2–1 and end up winning 3–2. This is certainly not sexy football, mostly notably for goalie Matteo Sereni who had a first row seat to the show and is probably being treated for posttraumatic stress disorder syndrome. Since there was no provision against this in the rulebook, it was allowed. This wasn't against the explicit rules, but is a clear example of an action that is unsportsmanlike, seeks an unfair advantage, and goes against the internal goods and the pursuit of excellence. In short, dropping your shorts is never justifiable in principle if we play by the "spirit" of the rules.

Can it get uglier yet? You bet. Let's not pander to our lower instincts and focus on the hard tackles, of which there are horrific stories. Well, maybe we should, but only for the sake of academic thoroughness: Real Madrid defender Pepe, during a match against Getafe on April 21st, 2009, takes Javier Casquero down hard in the penalty area. Not happy with this, he kicks Casquero, still on the ground, twice more. Pepe gets a red card. Now really unhappy, he loses control and tries to punch Juan Albin. Some behaviors incompatible with sportsmanship fit quite well in drunken sailor brawls, but are clearly out of place on the playing field.

And let's not forget the physical and verbal baiting meant to make opponents lose their cool. The father of one of the authors played professionally in Spain in the 1960s (we're going to the game's dark ages here!). Murcia was playing Osasuna. Ilundáin senior had played for Osasuna, his hometown team, but now was a center forward for Murcia. This didn't sit too well with an Osasuna defender (name withheld by the old man because the chap's still around) who was pestering him with an impious litany of kicks, jabs, and shoves. Ilundáin senior thwarted the defender and turned his methods around by egging him with a rhyming couplet: "Sure, kick me instead of the ball, 'cause you aren't going to get it at all." As the defender lost *his* cool, he scored. On the verbal side, today's footballer bards are quite "creative" with their insults, which question the legitimacy of matrilineal genealogy or discuss espousal comings and goings in ways that would make the coarsest truckers blush. (Note: our illustrations were censured after readers reported dyspepsia and acute discomfort.) Just as unbecoming are the resulting actions should the epithets succeed. Think of Zinedine Zidane: a most wondrous player who created spaces where there were none. We bet we know what you're thinking: the head butt incident! Sadly, his reputation will forever be tainted by that moment of ugly football. Instead of legacy we have ignominy. Not good. Not pretty.

The referees come second. Who among us hasn't been on the brink of a myocardial infarction or an embolism because of a referee's horrible, terrible, dreadful, atrocious, very bad call? To which we have to add the guilt for musing about how to skin, chop and boil him. Yet, referees are human—well, most of them anyway—and they can make mistakes. But at times they abuse their power in ways that determine the end result. And this crosses the line. When journalists write about the referee and not the match, the referee should be placed under a Witness Protection Program—mostly to get him out of the game. In the 2008–09 season the Spanish *Liga* reaped a good crop of unwise referees. The Award for Most Outrageous Referee goes to Alfonso Pérez Burrull. The game, on January 19th, 2009, was between Osasuna and Real Madrid. Juanfran, a *rojillo* Osasuna player, was the victim of two penalties a blind man could have seen in a cave. But not only were these not called, he was actually given two yellow cards that kicked him out of the game as the referee admonished him to learn how to fake falling down. The national media, which don't agree even on the current day of the week, unanimously called this as a case of thievery and plunder.

Third, the fans: in particular, hooligans and ignorant aficionados (some manage to be both). Hooligans bring gratuitous violence to the game, often harming others. Think of the nasty 2006 Basel Hooligan Incident, or even worse the gruesome 1986 Heisel Stadium Disaster. With Liverpool and Juventus playing, what should have been a day of glorious football turned into a calamity where thirty-nine people died because of these self-righteous bastards. Ignorant followers profess to love the game, but really don't know a lick about it. How does one recognize them? Their team *never* does anything wrong, it's *always* the opposing team that's at fault, and referees *invariably* have it in for their guys. These misguided "enthusiasts" disrespect the internal goods and misuse the game as a means to deal with whatever dysfunctional issues they have. In their case we should speak of moral and aesthetic subtractions from—rather than contributions to—football. They form a very select club: the United Cretins F.C..

FIFA is next. Despite its Armani clad lawyers and honorable lineage, it isn't off the hook either—there's plenty of blame to go around here. More than actively causing the unattractiveness we have alluded to, they have dropped anchor in a comfortable past and refuse to move. Where should they go? How about forward? Instead of resisting the use of technology, such as instant replays or the RFID (radio frequency identification) chips against "ghost goals", they could embrace it. Too techno-geeky? Maybe they could budge regarding their reluctance to modify rules. Consider the controversy over football matches at high altitudes, where certain countries, Bolivia, Colombia, or Ecuador are embattled with FIFA and flatland world powerhouses such as Argentina and Brazil. With a fine chip shot, not a cheap one, let's lob the argument past FIFA's Procrustean goalkeepers: a great match is an articulate, artful dialogue voiced with the legs and lungs of the players as they punctuate their plays with the ball. Were FIFA to engage these issues with transparent, open dialogue rather than by means of "executive orders" from backroom dealings, we'd get a game with a heart of gold that keeps on giving.

Our fifth candidate: the "political protagonists." Here we include presidents and other high-ranking elements of clubs, legendary managers, prominent ex-players, and politicians who butt their way in. Whenever the ball passes from the field to the presidential box, or other platform outside the sidelines, there's an ugly issue lurking behind. Real Madrid's Ramón Calderón's distasteful shenanigans before bowing out as president in January of 2009, the smaller of which was rigging a trustees' vote by planting friends and family members, were a beautiful example of this. With regard to a well-known coach, you're already familiar with Bilardo. As Galeano recounts it seems that he once put a sleeping-aid substance in the drink of Brazilian Branco, who was giving his team plenty of trouble—lest Bilardo loose sleep over a loss (*Football in Sun and Shadow*, p. 174). Or, to bring a currently "popular" politician into the fray, Iranian President Mahmoud Ahmadinejad, amid the controversy of his re-election in 2009, responded to the popular unrest by comparing it to the aftermath of a football match where there is a confrontation with the police, implying that the disturbances are not a problem. These responses not only belittle the reaction of a large part of the Iranian citizenry, but more relevantly for our purposes, also show a deep misconception of what passes for normal in football. The fact that violence and football can be so readily associated and used to diffuse or make light of other types of serious confrontations is troublesome. Talk about giving football a bad rep.

And sixth, the mass media. At their best they are Platos speaking the truth about the Byzantine world of football, Homers singing the feats of the players, Shakespeares voicing our very passion for the game. Okay, we're overdoing it a bit. But they do write tremendously influential narratives that guide the minds and hearts of fans. This influence can bounce like a capricious ball, deflecting in unintended directions, or it can be manipulated (or pedipulated?) so that at their worst they become confabulators that abet many of the flaws we've mentioned in order to have all the news that's fit to print or fabricate, twisting things so that artificial controversies arise. Then there's the allure of gossip and triviality dressed as breaking news. How many articles about the Beckhams are written in football magazines that have nothing to do with the David's game?

Scandalous! Isn't it? True football lovers should scream for reform. All of these *directly* affect what happens on the green pitch. The result is that we get football where the ball is flat. The game becomes unsporting, unethical, and all the "uglier" ultimately. It may be age-induced nostalgia on the authors' part, or perhaps today's "instamatic-all-you-can-consume" access to information makes it appear so, but the affronts seem to be on the rise. No matter, these unattractive facets won't go away by themselves. They're like athletic tape on a hairy leg: very, very sticky and painful to deal with. The solution is not to kick the ball out of bounds to buy time either. The tape will still be there when the whistle blows to resume play.

So we've danced with the ugly and played with the beasts, but why are such monstrosities still part of the modern game? Why haven't they been run off long ago, instead of breeding like bunnies on the loose at *La Bombonera*, Boca Juniors' stadium in Buenos Aires? It doesn't take fine legwork to cover the requisite ground and realize that extrinsic motives are the usual suspects, such as making it to the next round no matter the cost (ends justify means), or the indirect but very tangible goods likely to come if one scores or blocks the goal: improved reputation that leads to higher salary, endorsements, and the like. This sets up—like a ball delivered on the bounce for a half-volley—the philosophical tension between, on the one boot, the requirement to mind the rules of the game (remember, they actually make the game possible) and its internal goods, and, on the other boot, bending or breaking the rules and forsaking the internal goods for extrinsic motives.

Mind you, it is not that everything extrinsic is evil. These "fringe benefits" have their right place on and off the field. Things become unattractive from a moral, aesthetic, and sporting sense when the game becomes a mere means, an instrument to the latter. In the best cases, they're compatible, but it's the love of the game and the pursuit of excellence within the rules that (should) bring the rewards. We're fallible, and the temptation to act in ugly ways is human, all too human. However, understanding why and how this works, if anything, takes away the excuse. It also opens the way to a much better game.

Contenders for the Beautiful

The match is gaining in intensity in the last minutes; we up the tempo, dynamism, and density of the plays. These lace suggestions to redress the above with a defense for the beautiful *sides* of the game. Three aspects constitute football: technical or kinesthetic (ably embodied movement), aesthetic, and moral. In practice these are interwoven and happen simultaneously as embodied actions on the grass, or the enveloping combination of actions, perceptions, and utterances of the world of football made up of players, fans, officials and all the rest. But, this doesn't mean they can't be conceptually distinguished. The same action, a glorious assist from Andrés Iniesta to Samuel Eto'o, unfolds as a blend of refined skills to feint and lob the ball, which are imbued with the aesthetic qualities of finesse and accuracy, and a willingness to play by the rules, honoring fair play and sportsmanship.

This analysis gives us a deeper understanding of and appreciation for good, beautiful football. In turn, it helps us revalue and enjoy football more deeply and meaningfully, adapting our moves to the harsh plays of the ugly team without cowering or pretending they're not there. Rather, its skillful plays look all the more beautiful as they accommodate the ugly plays within their own graceful moves. We focus on the ethical facet—the technical and aesthetic ones have been richly explored by others—chiefly because it adds a subtler but more fundamental reason as to what makes football beautiful (or ugly in its absence).

To bring the ethical side in a fashion that isn't preachy and moralistic, let's line up two prestigious Greek players, Plato and Aristotle. In Brazil, Pelé's *chilenas* or bicycle kicks and Sócrates's heel kicks—he played in the national team in the 1980s, and given the company he seemed fitting—drove crowds mad with excitement. For their part, the pair of Greeks brings to the pitch a move called *Kalon* that is no less thrilling. In ancient Greek thought *Kalon* is a concept that concerns well-being and the good life, and translates roughly and poorly into "noble," "fine," or "beautiful." It does double-duty, playing both for a club and the national team: an action, idea, or person displays *Kalon* when they are aesthetically beautiful *and* morally commendable. To refine this, *Kalon* is about nobility, which connects naturally with the concepts of fair play and sportsmanship.

When an action in life or on the pitch exhibits nobility, it is imbued with this deep sense of honorable beauty. Some football plays exemplify this. For instance, *Kalon* is exemplified when a player kicks the football out of bounds upon realizing that an opponent appears injured. By the same token, it's realized when the football is returned to the team that kicked it out of bounds once play is resumed. Early in 2006, Italian midfielder Daniele De Rossi demonstrated *Kalon* in a match between Roma and Messina. De Rossi diverted a cross with his hand into the net to put Roma up 2–0. Although the goal was originally awarded, De Rossi told the referee that he had handed the ball to score and the goal was immediately disallowed. *Kalon* is the *beau geste*—the beautiful gesture. At its best, football is *Kalon*. To boot, it aligns perfectly with the non-instrumental conception of games and sports embraced here, for it requires players to play by the rules *even* when it costs them. We propose to adjectivize the use of *Kalon* very much like *kosher* is used in the US to express something as fine or genuine. Thus, of a play or game that exemplified this high aesthetic and moral quality we could say, "Hey, that header assist from Amauri to Alessandro Del Piero was *Kalon*, very *Kalon!*"

And here comes an unexpected and very exciting twist to the game. Surprising fans and opponents alike, we force a play that actually has the beasties playing "for us" in spite of themselves. Because they roughen up their game, and not just push but tear the envelope, actually enhances the good, beautiful football of our game. This really burns them. Their lack of technical or kinesthetic, aesthetic, and moral resources are all the more obvious when contrasted with the creativity and finesse of our team. To continue Iniesta's play with Eto'o. Paul Scholes comes at him with a sliding tackle that could send the African back home without going to the airport first. Scholes's tackle highlights Eto'o's filigree and artistry as he envelops the ball in a half twist and seems to float above Scholes. To add mirth for us and rub salt in the wounds of those who would inflict them on our team, Eto'o then bounces the ball off Nemanja Vidic, who intended to take his knees out, on his way to assist Lionel Messi, who scores a classy goal. This doesn't mean we cannot have exciting *Kalon* actions that shine on their own, as when two teams play to their best honoring each other and the rules (something we'll see in a moment). Only that the nasties actually make us look even better. Being realists, we know the "dark side" has a good number of dedicated players, who will probably continue to bring dirt to the turf. However, when the talent and luck are on the side of the nice guys, it is poetic justice indeed.

To celebrate and enjoy beautiful football like great art or excellent wine, we need a prolific imagination and a discerning palate. Knowing what poor art, cheap wine, and ugly, ignoble football are all about is helpful. After having tackled the ugly side of football, we can now truly appreciate, celebrate, and play the beautiful game so much more richly. We admire a verily difficult feint and half-turn pass to avoid a charging defender for the right reasons: not just because of the technical skill (it'd be easier to handle with a dirty play), but because this silky move has been developed and implemented precisely to handle a difficult situation while minding the rules. It is a beautiful move kinesthetically, esthetically, and ethically. Nothing's lacking!

This all may seem Quixotic, but stay with the ball a bit longer. Consider what has moved football forward, what makes people dream, and what constitutes its greatness. You'll find that these issue from how innovators play, daring to explore the technical and artistic limits of the sport, risking and having the guts to dream, doing it for the love of the game, and a yearning to win *Kalon*, nobly and beautifully, according to the standards of football. Had this not been so, we would still be making simple direct passes and there would be no chip, bicycle, banana, lace, or tunnel kicks or even mere juggling, not to say *jogo bonito*. And that's not fun. If not in this ideal, where are we to find the passion and the soul of the game? In statistics and numbers? In ugly wins? In uninspired newspaper match reports? No need to answer, they are rhetorical questions.

It'd be illuminating, or at least amusing, to compare beautiful and ugly football side by side. How about Barcelona and Real Madrid during the first half of the 2008–09 *Liga*? Journalist Jesús Alcaide writes: "To compare the football of the 'azulgrana' with that of the 'blancos' is almost as sacrilegious as officiating as priest at the Vatican and demanding that one begin to teach Secular Education in all seminaries. Barcelona sweeps to victory and conquests, the Madrid cheats and barely manages to survive with a despicable game" (*El Mundo*, January 19th, 2009). Do you prefer to play and win with Barcelona's *jogo bonito*, a model of the beautiful game, or play as Madrid, epitome of the sooty, tricky, and base? Who says nice guys finish last? These aren't rhetorical questions, by the way.

Goals for All Ages and All Occasions

Football is at its best when players, fans, referees, officials, all who line up for a game, enjoy themselves because of the quality of what happens on the grass regardless of the outcome. When it can be stated "This was a great game" for and by *everyone,* celebrating the event even with the disappointment of a loss, recognizing the opponent's worth even with the exultation of the win, then this is indeed *the* beautiful game. And this comes from a popular and populist "game" that purportedly began some- where in medieval England with the severed head of an opposing army's leader being kicked around . . . Not too shabby!

What sorts of games exemplify this kind of football we celebrate? A great, recent match is the Arsenal v Liverpool encounter that took place on April 21st, 2009. It had it all. The result was a 4–4 draw that saw Liverpool's Fernando Torres (no connection to the current author) and Yossi Benayoun score two a piece, and Arsenal's Andrei Arshavin get an "arsesome" four. The following highlights from a review by Arsenal's own Chris Harris give a taste: the encounter was "pulsating" and "incred- ible;" "the pitch was perfect and pristine for a game of passing football" and "that's exactly what we got;" "the pace was relentless;" and our favorite comment: "Frankly, neither side deserved to lose" <http://www.arsenal .com/match-menu/3121545/first-team/liverpool-v- arsenal?tab= report>. All was very *Kalon* indeed! Arsenal had a lot riding on this match, but still celebrated great football first and foremost.

A swift play scores our goal, which has amounted to *embellishing the ugly side of football with a striking game where the beastly play, con- tenders to the beautiful goals for all ages and occasions.* Indeed, the kinds of goals, footballing or intellectual, we have put into our opponent's net are those that can be celebrated by all—fans, players, referees, officials, the whole lot—no matter when and where. After confronting those who play ugly across the field and beyond, and feint, dribble and outrun them, the resulting, resounding "goal!" should make football as deeply beautiful as a game can be: truly sublime and fun. More importantly it should leave no doubt as to which is *the* beautiful game on earth and, let's be modest, the solar system, and the universe.[1]

---

[1] The authors wish to thank Halit "Cem" Kuleli, philosophy student and true football fan, for all the great examples and discussions.

FIRST EXTRA-TIME

Fandom

16

Is It Rational to Support Aston Villa?

DAVID EDWARD ROSE

It is some time ago now since I perceived that, from my earliest years, I have supported without question Aston Villa above all other football teams and followed their fortunes with an avid partial interest, but I also perceived such support was based on insecure origins, so I resolved to undertake seriously once in my life to begin afresh from the foundations, if I wished to justify something firm and constant in my life that constitutes such a central part of my identity.

—after *Meditations on First Philosophy* by René Descartes

There are a few, but very real, oddities about my support of Aston Villa. If you asked me why I'm a Villan, I would be at an initial loss to respond: I am too distant to attend home games and rarely travel to Villa Park; I do not now nor have I ever lived in Birmingham or even in the West Midlands; nor were any members of my family or my friends ever Villa supporters; and the support in question began at a very, very early age. The denouement of this chapter may well reveal an error made on my part in my infancy concerning a 1978 Panini sticker book (those wonderful books which were never filled with the players' stickers no matter how many ten-pence packets—with free bubblegum!—were bought from the local newsagent).

What, you might well be wondering, do such personal ruminations have to do with philosophy? You may not care why David Rose supports Aston Villa and have no interest in finding out why he does. Surely he should be musing in a more appropriate context: in the pub amongst friends or on the psychiatrist's couch (since it seems so very important to him!). However, if you're reading this book, you probably support a football team. And your support for that team makes you act in certain ways:

you cheer when that team scores and groan when that team concedes. Your reaction to other teams scoring also relates to the support of your team: whether you move up or down the league table or whether they are your team's bitterest rivals, for example. Your support of that team dictates certain behavioural patterns. If you support Aston Villa, you ought to—all things being equal—rejoice when they score. The support of that team constitutes a part of your identity and determines both how you *do* and how you *should* behave.

A bit like ethics.

What is right or wrong is for the most part due to a tradition and a culture. You have found yourself inheriting a particular set of values that you share with your fellow 'supporters' and these values dictate how and when you show approval or disapproval. For example, we collectively boo when the opportunities of a minority are curtailed just because they happen to be a minority and we collectively cheer when the government is judged offside as it tries to store information about the genetic material of innocent people. We do this because these judgements stand in a rational relationship to the claims that liberty and equality are values worth maintaining and promoting. We support the whole Western team of liberty, equality and so on. We also disapprove of different values held by other supporters; we see those values as making no sense and their actions as wrong. So, for example, individuals from another society may well withhold the right to vote from women because they reject the belief that men and women are equal and instead hold that men know what is best for their female relatives. But the only difference seems to be that they were raised in a specific culture and we were raised in another.

They support one team and we support another.

Hold on a minute, though. Someone, perhaps you, might want to argue that morality and supporting a football team are just different kinds of things. We tend to think that the values which constitute our moral identities as something more than a gift of a tradition or a contingency of our births. I may well be an atheist because I am born into a secular, post-industrial culture, but no matter where I was born or how I was educated, I would surely think that liberty matters or that hurting others without any good reason is just wrong. I would think so even if I were born into a pre-industrial, theocratic culture.

We would like to believe that the values we hold—liberty, equality, compassion, welfare—are somehow rational and not mere historical accidents, passed down to us because we live in the area, or because my dad believes them, or because I happen to abide by them every match day. We tend to think that they are true and that they can be justified to all rational agents; that if someone refuses to acknowledge them, then we can just stop talking to him because he has denied our values at the cost of his own rationality. You might want to hold that we are a human being in spite of all the cultural and social pressures which batter against us and our very humanity commits us to certain patterns of behaviour that all human beings, if they were rational and moral, would endorse.

Well, at least this is the normal way we think about things. On the one hand, morality is like supporting a football team because we just happen to adopt certain patterns of behaviour due to historical and geographical luck; but, on the other hand, morality is unlike supporting a football team because we can justify our commitments since they are rational and not just accidental. So, we ordinarily think of ethical positions as rational and football support as non-rational (that is, neither rational nor irrational, just a brute contingent fact).

But is it as simple as all that? Morality is perhaps more akin to supporting a football team than we philosophers are inclined to admit and, what is perhaps most interesting, is that ethics is all the better for such a kinship.

What You Ought to Do

Let's at least try to be rational about this. For the most part the team one supports is a hereditary or geographical 'gift' from your tradition. You just happen to support them and have never felt the need to justify that support. I ought to cheer when Aston Villa score *if I happen to be an Aston Villa fan*. And *I just happen to be* an Aston Villa fan. There is no compelling rational reason to be an Aston Villa fan (or even a football fan, for that matter). Let us pretend that this is different in kind from the system of ethical values we endorse. It is not the case I ought to deplore discrimination against women *if I happen to be a member of, say, the secular English liberal tradition*. It is rather that I ought to deplore discrimination against women because it is immoral and, being a human being, I am (not happen to be, just am!) a moral agent.

It's possible that the difference between being an Aston Villa supporter and being a moral agent is the difference between two different senses of the word 'ought' and this is the origin of our confusion. When we say, "an Aston Villa fan ought to cheer a goal," we mean, "for Aston Villa supporters the most probable or normal course of action on their scoring a goal is to cheer." If a supporter doesn't cheer, then his deviation from the norm is explained by an appeal to other factors: he's on anti-depressants, his dog died that morning, and so on. However, when we say, "You ought to help the man in distress," we mean that, "It is right or good that you help the man in distress." When passersby see a person needing help on the street, they will in all probability pass them by, but that doesn't make it the right thing to do! They *ought to* help even if, in all probability, they won't.

Then again, if the agent doesn't help, there may be good reasons why not. If asked, he may reply, "I'm rushing to fetch my friend the MD," or, "He isn't that badly hurt and I am carrying blood to the hospital for a small, dying child." It seems that, although the value of compassion ought to be accepted by all moral agents, the actual behaviour of the moral agent is also a probable event. So, there is no real difference in the use of ought at this level of explanation of behaviour. Whereas "You ought to help" (and its equivalent, "You ought to support Aston Villa") refers to one use of the word "ought," both "You ought treat his wounds" (and its equivalent, "You ought to cheer when Villa score") refers to another use, that is probable behaviour given certain conditions.

For all that, something doesn't seem quite right. It is possible for someone to say (and say rationally), "I didn't cheer because I don't support Villa." But the statement, "You ought to help," is different because we cannot truly say (and remain rational), "I didn't help him because I'm not a moral agent." The deviations from the norm were explained in terms consistent with moral action: the best course of action, if we want to improve the man's welfare, is to fetch my doctor friend rather than help him myself. If you support Aston Villa, you ought to conform to certain expectations of behaviour. If you're moral, you ought to conform to certain expectations of behaviour. But, where we can say, "You ought to be moral," meaningfully in rational argument, we cannot do so with the statement, "You ought to support Aston Villa."

Or, can we?

Scoring a Goal Is Good

Both being a moral agent and being an Aston Villa supporter commit us to certain expected behaviour. However, we think that we *all* ought to be moral agents. Could there be any real sense to the phrase, "You ought to be an Aston Villa supporter"? If I am a supporter of Aston Villa, I must be committed to watching them on TV in preference to other sides, going to the stadium given half a chance and willing them to win. It would not be unintelligible to make such prescriptions. I must also be committed to statements such as "Aston Villa scoring a goal is good."

Let me list the main reasons I have for supporting Aston Villa which would stand in some sort of rational relationship to the statement, "Aston Villa scoring a goal is good':

1. **They were my local team;**

2. **They won the European Cup in 1982;**

3. **I liked the colour of the strip;**

4. **They are the best team full stop (or period for the US audience);**

5. **They are the best team where 'best' is evidenced by their success (number of championships, FA cups and European cups);**

6. **They are the best team where 'best' is evidenced by their glorious history and tradition;**

7. **They are the best team where 'best' is evidenced by their identification with legendary players (Eusebio, Maradona, Zidane . . .);**

8. **They are the best team where 'best' is evidenced by their playing the best football.**

Let's look at each of these in turn. 1 is empirically false (in my case). Psychologically, 2 may well have had an impact on me in my infancy (I would have been nine years old) since events in our childhood do determine later commitments and beliefs. However, I distinctly remember that the day after the final a 'friend' of mine spitefully declaring that Villa didn't deserve to win and that Munich were robbed (on watching the game recently, he certainly had a case), so I was already a supporter prior to the game. Then there's 3, which I'll come back to (but please don't hastily scoff until you get the full story!). It is obvious, though, that 3 could be a reason for me but not for you (and definitely not for my Italian wife who *knows a priori* that the colours of claret and blue clash). But none of these reasons *justify* supporting Aston Villa—that is, give a reason to do so, if you do not—only perhaps *explain* why I (David Rose) support Villa. They are all reasons *for me* to support Aston Villa but not for anyone else.

4 is probably false or at best controversial, although the use of the word 'best' is one we ought to think about as reasons 5 through 8 seek to do. If I say that the steak is the tastiest dish on the menu, or that it is 'better' to buy a house with a garden than without, then I am offering reasons to do certain actions rather than others; reasons for both myself and other people. And with football teams, it could be possible to say that Aston Villa is the best team where 'best' is given some sort of quantifiable definition.

Unfortunately, none of these are applicable to Villa. Success has been sparse except for the European cup in 1982, so 5 is false. History and tradition are probably just a vaguer version of measurable success since those teams with the most glorious histories (Real Madrid, Inter Milan, Liverpool, and so on) are generally those with the most competition wins. To cite legendary players, as in 7, also offers no reason to support Villa: the players who I can personally cite from my thirty-six years' experience are Peter Withe, Gary Shaw, Nigel Spink, Gordon Cowans, Paul McGrarth, and David Platt. None of these fits the epithet 'legendary'. The first three were also immortalized by the victory in the European Cup and most legendary players belong to winning sides (as the perceived difference between Zidane and Cantona attests), so competition wins again remains the best quantifiable way to select the 'best' team.

Finally, number 8 is definitely false in Villa's case and, in addition, is problematic in two ways. We would find it hard to all agree on what the 'best' type of football was: total football, catenaccio, long ball, wingless wonders, and so on. One way to resolve the contested nature of playing the best football is to say the team that plays the best football is the most successful one and so we return to number of competition wins. There is, however, a further problem: even if we could agree on a criterion for the best football and it were true that Aston Villa played the best football, then perhaps they played the best football this season but won't the next and if this were the reason, then I would yo-yo between teams. I would be a Villa supporter one moment, an Arsenal supporter the next, then my head would be tilted by Ajax and finally seduced by Barça. No such yo-yo could ever be considered as the behaviour of a true supporter.

So, is it possible to stand back and apply the one rational or 'transcendental' (that is, not due to our social circumstances or cultural upbringing) reason to choose the team who 'score' the most points in terms of success measured by competition wins (that is number 5)? Could I conceivably use my reason to override my allegiance and ask other supporters to do likewise? Such a reasoner would not be a real supporter, not in the sense in which we use the word (or, at best, they would be a Man United fan). Try walking into your local club or pub and stating openly: "Look, I once supported Aston Villa, but they scored only three points on the Rose-*calcio* scale and Real Madrid scored a whopping 546. I am now a Madrid supporter and, if you were rational, you would be too." To change allegiances according to reason is to contradict something integral to what it means to be a football supporter at all.

Torturing Children Is Bad

Comparing the statement, "Aston Villa scoring a goal is good," with the moral statement, "The torture of children is bad," seemingly reveals the difference between being a supporter and being an ethical agent. What could be the logical foundations of such a moral belief? Here's a list:

A. My friends, family and culture agree that torturing children is wrong;

B. In 1953, a child torture ring was exposed and it was horrifying for society at large;

C. A society that condemns and prohibits the torture of children is more stable than one that does not and a stable society is something we want;

D. I don't like the torturing of children, it is unpleasant;

E. It is just wrong to torture children, full stop;

F. The torture of children is harmful to their welfare;

G. If asked, the children would express the wish not to be tortured, so they would not consent to the practice and if you do then torture them, you are infringing their liberty to decide what to do.

Now A isn't a good reason. What if my friends and family believed otherwise? Would the torture then not be bad? B makes the wrongness of the action contingent on an historical event and if it hadn't happened (or hadn't been exposed), then torturing children would be fine. And beneath A and B, we see an old logical fallacy—the genetic fallacy: explaining how a belief came about is not the same as justifying a belief. If you just happen to think that torturing children is wrong because your culture thinks it is wrong, that does not justify your belief (that is, demonstrate why it's true), it only explains why you believe something to be true. C also poses a problem. Imagine that society could be made stable by the wholesale and gratuitous torture of children. Would you happily pick up the pliers? D is unpalatable: the torturer could conceivably find it pleasant. So a reason for you is no reason for him to stop and surely you want to make the statement, "You (and me) ought not to torture children." Imagine the nonsensical rant: "You say 'I like cheese,' but you can't like cheese, you ought not to like cheese, because it is horrible. . . ."

Herein apparently lies the difference between supporting and being ethical. On the one hand, there can be reasons for me to support a football team—reasons that explain the historical or personal circumstances of supporting Aston Villa—but no reasons why anyone *ought* to support them. These 'reasons' are explanations and not justifications. You support a team and that is just a contingent historical fact—it is trivial—even if it can be explained. On the other hand, there are reasons for *all of us* to support the values of liberty, equality, and welfare and to let them determine our behaviour whether this be because liberty is a good, or welfare is a good, or human beings are autonomous, and so on and so forth.

And morality is different because it can offer reasons for all of us to behave in a certain way. But what are these reasons? E is incomplete because saying something is wrong 'full stop' is a bit like saying a team is the best 'full stop' without saying what 'best' or 'wrong' actually means. Both F and G aspire to put some meat on the bones of what 'wrong' may actually mean. F may strike some of you as a good reason: pain is obviously bad and so torture is bad since it causes pain. But what about a surgical operation which causes pain? Ah, you say, but short-term pain can be traded off against long term benefits, in terms of welfare. Welfare not pain is what we are actually interested in. Whose welfare matters? Everyone's, you say, otherwise I wouldn't care about children being tortured unless they were my own or I had to watch. So, I ask, is the torture of the terrorist's child justified if it will reveal where he has planted the bomb that will kill thousands unless it is found? We still need a way to decide what to do even if we agree welfare matters.

G is sort of Kantian, but we force children to take their medicine, to eat their greens, and we don't let them watch *Ben 10*, with little or no consideration of their wishes. We could say that it is what they *really* wanted, even if they were unaware of it ("I know the medicine tastes horrible, but it will make you better, so you *do want* to take it!"), but that means there is a 'true' self with preferences, wishes, projects and reasons that they (and we!) may not be aware of and others may know better than themselves (or even ourselves).

Seemingly there are good reasons not to torture children, reasons that all rational agents agree to. These good reasons are determined by asking not what 'me' as a particular agent would want, but what a rational agent would want. There are special procedures for doing this: the impartial spectator of utilitarians or the original position of latter day Kantians, for example. These are the procedures for finding out what we (and others) *really* want and not what we just *happen* to want.

The benevolent spectator holds that we ought to put aside our particular preferences and our own commitments and projects and ask ourselves, if I were a benevolent spectator who was not directly involved in the outcome of the course of action, what prescription would result in the best outcome for the most number of agents. If you ask why I should do this, you are just not capable of moral agency. The original position holds that, if I were behind a veil of ignorance and unaware of my biological sex, gender, class, level of education, sexuality, and other circumstances that could compromise my impartiality, then I could propose values or motivations which all rational agents, if they are not being partial, would agree to. Again, asking why I should do this, excludes you from the rational and moral domain. Moral values that determine our behaviour, on both these views, can be judged rational or not from a privileged methodological position (and not just historically explained).

Both modern positions in ethics rest on the ideal of impartiality and it is obvious that a football fan should not be impartial; impartiality is anathema to being a real or proper supporter of a team. Occupying the original position or being a benevolent spectator as a model of choosing which team to support commits us to an absurd description of the supporter akin to the Rose-*calcio* scale described above. So, maybe, supporting a football team and being an ethical agent are just different in kind. Ethical dictates will be: impartial, universal (that is every rational agent ought to act on them and not some select group, such as Aston Villa supporters) and rational (that is, logically related to the first-principles). These first-principles (act so as to maximize welfare; never coerce or exploit other free beings) are independent of particular and social commitments on the agents' part and are arrived at by asking ourselves what all human beings would endorse if they were rational (as determined by being a benevolent spectator or occupying the original position).

But, of course, the claim that supporting a football team is not rational is hardly Earth-shattering. Well, it isn't if rationality is defined as coherence with standards of right. The odd thing is that if ethics thinks of rationality in this way, then it is peculiarly 'irrational'. It is like having a Rose-*etica* scale which distorts our actual moral experience and makes us into agents as 'irrational' as the supporter who follows my Rose-*calcio* scaling procedure.

The Rational Irrationality of Ethics

If I agree that everyone's welfare matters and I can either spend my well-earned thirty pounds on a ticket to see Villa play Newcastle or I can donate it to charity, according to the benevolent spectator, it ain't going to be me benefitting and getting the pleasure from going to the match. Should I spend my time writing this chapter or helping other people? The latter would be the course of action suggested by a benevolent spectator. And the upshot is that rational ethical action is so demanding that it frustrates my own projects and plans and damages the integrity of my identity: I must commit myself so much to the welfare of others that my cares, aspirations and ambitions are sacrificed. We need to be a little egoistic or partial to members of our family and our friends over strangers even if it can't be 'rationally' justified. Otherwise we wouldn't be 'rational' as we would intuitively understand it!

Consider the manager of a Premiership club who needs a new striker and his son is just out of the team's youth academy. The coach knows how difficult it is to get ahead in football even if you have the talent (which his boy undoubtedly has). He stands back into the original position and applies himself to reasoning impartially and with respect for all individuals and their rights. Should he show impartiality and get his Board and the team's scouts out on the road to fill the hole in his team or should he be partial towards his son? Being a moral agent seems to commit him to doing the 'right' thing at the cost of his own family obligations. The idea of an impartial ethical agent is incoherent with a normal understanding of agency. One cannot act in a moral way unless one knows the relevance of moral distance between oneself and others, between strangers and family members, or one knows how to resolve seemingly contradictory duties in a rational way.

Finally, the rational first-principles of ethics that we can, in virtue of being a human being, all agree on from the standpoint of a rational procedure will include prescriptions such as, "treat others with respect." Yet, that in itself does not tell us how to behave—that is, how to actually respect others and the micro obligations such a macro prescription involves. Do we look them in the eyes or avert our eyes? Do we shake their hands or bow our heads? Do we allow them to wear their burkha or demand they cast it aside for their own liberty? The rational ethical principles that all humans, in all times and all places are supposed to agree on (that is, are universal) are so abstract that they cannot determine actual behaviour in the real world. That is left to the particularities and commitments of our social selves. Those social selves we just happen to be because of historical rather than rational reasons.

I can walk into the pub and proclaim, "Look, I once endorsed the values of order and security, but they only scored three points on the Rose-*etica* scale and liberty, equality and welfare combined scored a whopping 546. So, I am now going to give all my money and time to others at the cost of my own future aspirations, never favour my family or friends over strangers and live only by abstract prescriptions untainted by social commitments. I expect you all to do the same because you are all rational." Being rational in this sense seems to come at the cost of our own rationality.

So what if ethics were more like supporting a football team after all, would it be so irrational?

Supporting a System of Ethical Values

Ethical principles are in no way separate from a framework of social goods and meanings that make them intelligible. A moral agent knows how to act because he is thrown into a social tradition with all of its mores, expectations, oddities and etiquette. To bracket off the social elements of agency from the moral sphere is not only disingenuous, it also distorts how we actually reason and how we determine our behaviour in moral ways. The moral sphere cannot be isolated from the social sphere as the 'rational' models of ethics would have it without it becoming too demanding, susceptible to conflicts of duties or simply too abstract to actually determine an agent's behaviour. We are thrown into a community with its values, meanings and reasons produced from a long tradition and history. And thank goodness for that, otherwise we would never know how and when to apply the expectations and nuances (such as, at times, putting ourselves before others) that truly determine our behaviour.

So, what if ethics were more like supporting a football team? What difference would it make? It would be a matter of thinking what values matter and how to apply them in a way that your peers in your society would see as 'rational' (like behaving in ways that identify me as an Aston Villa supporter to others). We don't need to consult some true self separate from society, but rather a collection of others who—like ourselves—are already submerged in society. The advantages are obvious. One, it wouldn't be too demanding: you ought to give to charity but not to such an extent that you frustrate your own personal cultivation. Two, all our duties could be prioritized, and partiality towards friends and family justified (if the moral costs are negligible). And three, prescriptions will not be too abstract because they will be interpreted through a social system of meanings that determines our action effectively.

If a moral agent is more like a football fan, then he can perform his duties immediately because they constitute his identity. I care because I am the father, I generate wealth because I am a unit of the market, I cheer the goal because I am an Aston Villa fan and I act morally because I am a member of the liberal, English tradition that understands the macro value of liberty, equality and welfare as well as all the micro determinations of action that these entail.

The idea of rationality to which ethics has always aspired is akin to being a football fan in the abstract. Prescriptions would involve impersonal commitments such as: one ought to cheer when a goal is scored, one ought to attend the home games of the team one supports, and so on. But, without that little engagement on the part of the agent that states *which* team he supports, then these prescriptions cannot determine behaviour. Being an abstract football fan does not determine my behaviour one way or another.

Where's the Rationality in All That?

There is, though, a problem. In ethics, we suppose that standing back from our immediate, contingent commitments is possible and rational, and we do so because it is possible that the historical values and duties of my culture are abhorrent. We assume that even if I were born in a culture that routinely discriminates against women or tortures children, we would be able to reject such actions as wrong. Even if such actions could be justified by a system of beliefs (such as what matters is not individual welfare or liberty but social order, harmony and might), we would still deny them. By using the procedures of the original position or the benevolent spectator, we could reveal that the values are false and endorse the goods of equality, liberty and individual welfare.

What if, God forbid, I were a supporter of Millwall? Are we free to support who we wish or free to change our allegiance? Am I able to—in a midlife crisis that has seen one too many defeats—give up and adopt a new, more successful team than Villa? By assuming that ethics is more akin to supporting a team than is commonly thought, then we are faced with this problem of allegiance to a tradition (or team). Just as we cannot reject Milwall (even if we should), we are also unable to reject easily the values of our culture, even if we perceive them to be unjust, wrong or unpalatable. And that is surely wrong.

The social ethics presented here contains the spectre of relativism and the challenge that one becomes a 'real' supporter at the cost of free choice. In ethical terms, the motivations of one's culture are immediately binding just because one happens to belong to that culture and not for any normative worth at all. There must, though, be an exit strategy for any supporter, otherwise unethical prescriptions and injustice would be unassailable. We need to show again in what way the statement, "You ought to support Aston Villa," and, "You ought to endorse the axiomatic values of liberty, equality and respect," are rational. Remember that the latter can no longer be justified by an appeal to a special reasoning procedure because that makes the moral agent incoherent with actual moral action.

So, what is the alternative?

A Different Kind of Rationality

When I asked whether it could be rational to support Aston Villa—that is why I (or someone else) *ought* to support Aston Villa—I concentrated on a rationality of standards, of finding the way to objectively understand the meaning of 'best' when applied to the concept 'team'. This was absurd. There's a different way to understand rationality. If I didn't support Aston Villa, or I didn't support any team at all, I think it would be impossible to understand and participate in watching the sport. It is a truism that one cannot be neutral whilst watching football and enjoy it: the natural experience is, very early on in a match, to 'take sides'. This is rational because otherwise those forms of behaviour associated with being a football fan would not be possible. Supporting a team is rational because it allows the agent to watch the game. Supporting one particular team means I can choose which game to watch on TV, when to sacrifice watching a game to take my kids down the park (only if Aston Villa aren't playing!) and decide who I would most enjoy talking to in the pub. Social commitment of this sort makes rational action possible since without this prerequisite of choosing a team I would be unable to act in so many ways.

This sort of rationality can be carried over to ethics. The social commitment to traditional values (liberty, equality, welfare) and all the micro obligations and values these entail (specific ethico-social commitments) enable the agent to be moral. Social and cultural involvements allow me to order and prioritize my desires: I learn when to respect others and what is most important to me and others. I learn when I shouldn't do what I most want to do or, at least, I learn when to put it on hold for another day. Through society, I learn when to put others before myself and when not to. I learn when to do things for others and how to gain their trust, and also earn and repay their trust in me. Through a moral culture, I know immediately what is right and good without having to stand back and reason, which would make my actions in the world slow and ponderous. I just keep my promises, and hold doors open for others, without having to decide whether this is good or right at each moment of the day. If I wasn't a member of a moral culture, if I didn't just support some values, then I just couldn't be moral at all. And that is surely a measure of its rationality.

A Rugby Supporter Watching Football?

But surely, just as supporting any team, enables you to understand football, so endorsing any values whatsoever will make you moral. Even if I endorse the values of order, harmony and might, then I am rational. This seems to suggest there can be no rational preference for one society over another as there can be no rational preference for one team over another.

There is no rational preference for one team over another, however, because supporting any team will allow you to make the sort of rational choices a football supporter ought to make. But supporting a rugby team or a cricket team will distort your experience and engagement with the game of football (without, it should be noted, making it impossible to participate but only in some rather confused, erroneous way). Correspondingly, not all societies and systems of values will allow you to make the sorts of rational choices a moral agent ought to make. Why not?

Think once more of the example of the society that discriminates against women because they don't know what is best for them or because social order is more important than individual liberty and equality. Participation in such a society allows agents to be moral and so it seems to be rational. However, these agents may well be only *partially* moral. It is akin to supporting rugby (or NFL) and watching football. It will allow action that simulates aspects of moral action, but is at base a distortion of what moral experience should be because it does not allow all individuals of that society to learn the prerequisites of morality as called for by a moral culture. A bit like cheering when a goal is scored because it is like a try (or touchdown) being scored. The learned behaviour from corrupted relationships generated by this model will generate historical conflicts that will demand resolution: one can easily imagine that a society that puts the state's order before individual needs will face demands from those individuals when it expects their allegiance, or a society that discriminates against women may well generate conflicts for enlightened husbands who wish to put their wife's needs before those of their male colleagues. Again, 'like' not seeing anything wrong in a full-blown shoulder charge on the football pitch because it wouldn't be condemned on the rugby (or NFL) pitch. Such societies won't be fully rational because moral agency won't be truly possible: the agent will not know how to act in certain situations and will, at times, find the prescriptions of that society either nonsensical or contradictory.

So Why Do I Support Aston Villa?

Is it rational to be an Aston Villa supporter? If you mean, "Does it meet some standard of objective rightness or truth?" then the answer is no. But, if you mean, "Does it make sense and is it a worthwhile pursuit to support Aston Villa?" then yes.

And there are two levels to ethical questions. "Is it wrong to torture children?" The answer is yes according to standards of rightness central to society. "Is it rational to endorse these social values?" Well, if you mean, "Do they meet some further standard of objective rightness or truth?" then the answer is no. But, if you mean, "Do these values lead to the possibility of moral agency and moral action?" then the answer is yes. We sometimes mix these two levels of rationality up.

Let us return to a more pressing issue. Why do I support Aston Villa? I have said there is no rational preference for one team over another; it is just rational to support a team at all. And that's true even if it is based on an error. I think that my support grew from seeing a sticker of a West Ham player in my brother's 1978 Panini sticker book and (not being able to read) telling my Dad I supported the team in those colours (claret and blue). He wrongly thought I meant Aston Villa. And so I am an Aston Villa supporter.

And even that is rational in a certain sense.

17

The Evolution of the Football Fan and the Way of Virtue

ANDREW LAMBERT

As a child growing up in the English city of Liverpool two things dominated my life: football and the Catholic Church.

At church on Sunday with my mother, I always knew what I would pray for. During the few moments of silent reflection that followed Holy Communion I would petition God to permit my beloved football team, Everton, to win their next game. And if I'd been particularly well behaved during the previous week, I might inquire whether Everton could finish the season as champions. However, as I grew older I became more aware; perhaps other boys in churches around the city were also petitioning God for victory, and some of them would be fans of our fierce rivals, Liverpool FC.

I became unsure about what to pray to God for, mindful of the bind facing him when Everton played Liverpool in the local derby game. The children of Liverpool would ask him to do two things simultaneously that he could not possibly do: grant victory to both teams. Perhaps because of this worry about the limits to God's power, as time passed and my reflective tendencies grew, his interventions faded from the scene. My philosophical doubt turned to the other passion that had structured my formative years: football.

The early 1990s brought the founding of the English Premier League and huge investment in the game. Interest in football surged, as did players' wages and the proportion of the team who were not born locally, or even in the British Isles.

As I aged and ticket prices rose, I came to wonder, of my longstanding commitment to football, with its practical and psychological costs, is it worth it? Is it *rational?*

Perhaps, the global rise of football is merely good marketing and the skillful development of a form of mass consumption. Or, beyond the commercialism, are the institution of football and the life of the football fan ways to live well in the modern world?

What the Critics Say

Our contemporary liberal sensibilities offer a quick reply to this problem. As long as no one is harmed, individuals should be left to pursue their own interests. We all need pleasures, and football is just one of innumerable stress-relieving hobbies and activities that can be incorporated (or not) into a life, fitted in around the more serious business of employment, family and the law.

But this response isn't quite enough. I don't want to understand a love of football by focusing on what it does not do (harm others); I want to know whether it's *worth* it, whether it has *value*. If it's not worth it, then the commitment of time, passion and other resources to football should be pruned. Then it truly would be like a hobby, never a cause of harm to others because it mattered so little to oneself; one would not risk conflict or make sacrifices to pursue it. We can get some idea of the worth of the football fan's life by asking: what benefits does being a fan bring to the fan?

Popular opinion can be quite critical here. Some think the football fan is merely a consumer, focused on the passive enjoyment of a pleasure of questionable worth. A football match is a mildly confusing event, akin to watching a flock of hungry birds fight for a rotund piece of bread, but also stimulating for those with simple needs. When not watching the match, this fan is restlessly longing for the next one, or participating in a meandering and futile thread of gossip concerning player injuries and transfers. Football is thus a trivial pleasure, like a narcotic. Further, it is argued, the football fan becomes active only to emphasize tribal differences and even to engage in violence, partly through misplaced loyalty, partly through misplaced delight in physical confrontation and danger.

Some alternative appraisals of the fan do acknowledge something of value. Playing and watching the game and engaging with other fans and non-fans in a variety of social contexts is something more than passive stimulation. Thoughtful activity is involved. However, its critics say, football squanders valuable energies on a lifestyle with limited prospects for growth and enlightenment. Despite well-meaning intentions, this is a lifestyle of escapism and bad faith, a lack of courage to face more demanding but more rewarding challenges in the arenas of community, economy, politics, and on the global stage.

So, does an interest in football and a life shaped by it lie outside the higher realms of human experience and excellence?

No, it doesn't. Such reductive judgments of football's value reflect a limited understanding of it. Rebutting such judgments requires looking in more detail at both football and modern life.

Supporting the Football Fan

The following is a fan's view of the worth of football. But there is a twist. T he wisdom of being a fan can be shown by first occupying the ground usually claimed by social commentators and norm setters, and providing an analysis of modern social life. This will make clearer football's virtues. The key idea of this approach can be summarized thus:

> *Football is a way to get the skills and character that are needed to do well in modern life.*

This approach draws on the thinking of the ancient Greek philosopher, Aristotle. Some readers will know him from his role as sweeper for the Greek team in Monty Python's famous "International Philosophy" sketch. Aristotle was interested in what it took for an individual to live well. For Aristotle, in order to live well an individual had to be able to act well within his or her social world. Aristotle identified a variety of virtues or excellent qualities that, when cultivated, secured such good living. These included things like courage, practical wisdom, temperance, and the right attitude to honor.

Aristotle's claim that to live well an individual must be able to respond well to his or her circumstances seems plausible. The capacities to judge fairly and manage our time and practical goals are important. But his account met with objections. Critics claimed that his list of virtues presupposed a generic and universal human nature—a way that, ideally, all humans are—but that actual humans just aren't like this. Rather, they are shaped by their social world, and different societies and different times have called for different values and virtues. The Athens of Aristotle's time faced ongoing war and so, unsurprisingly, prized courage. But Athens was also a class-based society that accepted slavery and denied women a place in public life. From a contemporary perspective, such values are alien and objectionable. While some values might be enduring, we have also come to embrace values not recognized in earlier eras, such as kindness and respect.

We should retain Aristotle's basic idea that living well consists in responding to the society we live in, which means developing the appropriate sensibilities and abilities. However, rather than look to ancient Greece for values or an account of human nature, we should focus on the features of contemporary society—let's call it Western liberal consumer democracy—and the particular qualities relevant to living well here and now. And football, understood as all activities and institutions that a football fan engages with and as an ideal standard of play, is one way to acquire the relevant 'modern' personal qualities.

Football is not the only means to acquire such capacities; but it is a reasonable, accessible, and popular way. Contrary to its critics, football fans are neither consumers nor escapists but rational souls.

Claiming that football has value because of its contribution to well-being leads to two issues: what are the important features of modern life—what demands and pressures does it put on the individual—and in what ways does football create a person who is able to meet these challenges?

Making Space for Football

To answer the first of those two questions, let's look at five important aspects of social harmony and individual well-being. Each implies a corresponding virtue or sensibility that enables its possessor to live well.

1. The Possibility of Finding Comfort in Beauty

Life in a competitive market-orientated world awash with demands for greater efficiency can be tough. You snooze, you lose. Employment brings with it the unspoken threat of replacement or the non-renewal of a contract; financial worries are ubiquitous. In addition, media broadcasts create an ever-greater sensitivity to interpersonal comparisons by constantly reminding us what to look like and how to live.

As a result an individual can feel forced to develop a strong sense of self-interest, and a heightened concern with securing those interests. People find themselves taking a critical and calculating approach in areas of life where they instinctively feel it is inappropriate. We want to save the environment, but the family is just so damn safe inside an SUV, protected from all the other SUVs on the road. Making one's way via a clear sense of self-interest seems *de rigueur,* since everyone's doing it. But it can come to feel a little excessive, as if some kind of meaning has been lost.

Faced with such pressures, people need a forgiving refuge. They might find it in pleasure, or in opportunities to observe and appreciate something beautiful. The experience of beauty is a release, since it's insulated from endless comparison and expedient reasoning. At the same time, however, beauty can only have its effect if it is available; access cannot be too restricted, conditional on things such as access to the bank account of a superstar professional footballer.

2. The Need for Catharsis

Catharsis (the original Greek word meant 'purge' or 'purify') is the idea that people need opportunities to regulate potentially harmful emotions. This can mean identifying with something bigger than our own lives, like a great charitable cause, or witnessing some climatic event that puts our own life into perspective, or finding the opportunity to freely express our emotions—to 'vent'. Catharsis is a way to keep ourselves mentally healthy.

Modern social structures, however, limit when and where this process can arise. Partly for laudable reasons of fairness and partly as the result of increased impersonal bureaucracy, emotions must usually be censored so as to be inoffensive to those who share the same social space. Going berserk in the desolate mountains might pass unnoticed, but screaming and raving and just letting it all hang out in the city is likely to bring the police around. The challenge of modern living is to find a forum in which one's emotions find relatively free expression and yet cause minimal offence.

3. The Desirability of Maintaining a Sense of Belonging

Modernity has challenged traditional values and social structures. Individuals are no longer determined by roles defined by their community but can choose their own identities and lifestyles. Generally, this has been welcomed. Racial segregation has gone and equal rights for women have come. But this sweeping liberation also has costs. We must find meaning in a less familiar and more impersonal and secular world. To orientate ourselves in such an environment we look for identities and perspectives that seem deeper and which offer ways of relating to the world more substantial than the consumer's choice. Some people join religious groups, others make a commitment to the environment. Some don't do anything but still sense they should "give something back" to someone or something.

At the same time there are limits on the kinds of attachments and commitments that are accepted or tolerated. What are required are identities that both integrate an individual to a larger network of meaning but are also compatible with accepted values like respect and tolerance.

4. The Ability and Willingness to Take Part in Public Discourse

The people are not deprived of a voice in liberal consumer democracies, but awareness of the importance of public discourse and encouragement to participate in it are limited. Low voter participation in key elections concerns some social commentators, as does the shaping of public policies by secretive or unelected committees and lobbyists. It seems like a good idea that taxpayers have a say in how taxes are used. What is needed is an incentive to take on the role of citizen or stakeholder.

While getting involved in the largest communities is important, participation in formal political processes can start from a focus on something more local and personal. Small-scale events can inspire a sense of concern, a willingness to participate and a grasp of the basic rules of discourse; these are part of the identity of the modern citizen and important political skills.

5. A Need to Generate Altruistic Concern and to Maintain an Appropriate Regard for Others

Modern social arrangements complicate our attitudes towards other people. In times of less social mobility and diversity, an individual's relationships with others in their community were defined by familiarity, habit and clear expectation. But as discernible class divisions and social distinctions have blurred and personal aspirations and mobility risen, so interpersonal relationships and attitudes have become more nuanced. In addition to family and friends, we have to deal with people in various contexts and communities: bus driver, celebrity, Facebook friend, work colleague and so on. Then there's a growing global awareness of the interests of people we have never met but stand in some relation to: in some cases, we buy the products of their labour; in others, a sense of fairness, righteous anger or pity move us to respond to their interests.

Individual mobility and autonomy has been largely welcomed, but they raise difficult questions: in what relationship do we stand to these people? What do we owe to them? How strong is the spark of altruism within the individual when it is not fanned by forces of custom and social expectation? One powerful response has been to seek commonality between people or even common features of humanity, with the hope of creating goodwill. And if a feeling of goodwill is too much to ask, we need at least to find ways to cultivate self-restraint when dealings with others who seem different from ourselves.

Living Well in the Modern World

These five features of modern life constitute a significant challenge to the ideal of living well. Fortunately, there are ways we can meet this challenge, and football is at the heart of one possible response. It provides opportunities and reason to develop attitudes and abilities relevant to each area.

1. The Game and Its Beauty

Pelé subtitled his autobiography "My Life and the Beautiful Game". In doing so, he captured an important truth: football is a source of refined and comforting beauty. But what makes football a beautiful and affecting spectacle?

One explanation is the range of bodily expression found in the sport. Unlike many sports, football uses minimal equipment, freeing the body to move in ways not conditioned by the repetitious use of some stick or racket. The game involves one inflated sphere, moved within a wide-open space, with few restrictions on bodily movement. Olympian strength, speed, bodily control, balance, coordination and spatial awareness all have their place on the field of play.

The interface of body and ball is also a site of skill and grace. One of the game's artistic offshoots, freestyle football, testifies to this. You're probably familiar with its creative, dance-like performances. In all forms of the game, physical prowess must be orientated towards the ball, and it is the ball that moulds awesome physical strength into an art form by introducing sensitivity, awareness, imagination and ball control. In the free play between body, mind and ball, the only means of control excluded is the most common and thoughtless human means of interacting with the world—the hands and arms.

Beauty is also expressed through distinct forms and techniques, such as shooting, trapping, dribbling, tackling and passing. Consider volleying and trapping the ball. The perfect volley is violent, explosive, and exhilarating; yet such force must be regulated by excellent timing and precise skill, otherwise the final product is comical. When the greatest players bring a high, swirling sixty-yard punt to a dead stop on the grass at their feet, the watcher is thrilled by the feeling that something unnatural has occurred; the gaze keeps on moving, past the player, trying in vain to locate the moving ball, incredulous that such momentum could be nullified.

Football's claims to beauty are thus varied. Observers not only delight in the athleticism, balletic grace, creative vision, use of the ball and the perfect execution of recognizable forms, they also respond to the endlessly novel and flowing events that combine all of these.

Such aesthetics are, however, just a part of explaining the affecting spectacle that is football. The beauty of the game has another source: its simplicity and the emotional depth this generates. Football is moving because it is easy to be moved by it: the techniques and forms are difficult to master, but easy to appreciate. The rules are also generally simple, apart from offside, featuring only one type of scoring. And the spectacle is not complicated by argument, allusions, or social commentary.

This is not to say that anyone, simply by watching a game for a few minutes, will understand and be gripped by it. As with any activity, some learning and habituation is needed. The excitement and enjoyment of football does require putting the scene into context. Knowing that one's team is only 1–0 down, that five minutes remain and that a goal takes only a second to score combine to generate a hopeful feeling. Similarly, awareness of the rules for scoring creates excitement as the ball enters the penalty area. But such background knowledge remains unobtrusive; the 'story' of a football match is always present before the observer and this allows the game to achieve a balance between the visual and the cerebral.

This achievement should not be understated. A visual spectacle can be exhilarating briefly, but easily descend into a confusing mix of sight and sound. The motion-filled scenes of Hollywood's commercial action movies become unwatchable because they are senseless; they lack structure. On the other hand, the affective qualities of a ponderous live performance can be lost when the observer must sink into thought to figure out what is going on. Some kind of balance is needed between the visual and the mental in order to arrive at something scintillating, and football has this balance. There is sufficient framework to guide and incite the emotions but not so much that the experience becomes largely cerebral and reflective.

Football's simple and affecting beauty is different, but not inferior, to artistic forms that rely on a more complex narrative or a plot to achieve their full effect. But football also has narrative, social commentary, and allusion. They are written separately from the spectacle—before and after the game in the sports pages of national dailies, in official and unofficial histories and by fans.

With just a little observation and learning—of vocabulary, history and motifs—football proves to be a source of beauty and a refuge from a tough world.

2. The Distinctive Emotional Experience of Football

The beauty and simplicity of football also contribute to the second requirement of modern life, catharsis, by providing relief from and so perspective on other, more demanding aspects of life. In addition to the physical grace and the beautiful forms, the game evokes and structures emotions in another way. Good football is a game of sustained anticipation punctured by climatic moments.

Football has its obvious and attractive features; but football can also surprise. Part of its appeal comes from what we can't quite grasp or didn't foresee. With the finest, fastest free-flowing football, the viewer's comprehension of events is challenged; the continuous and rapid flow of both ball and players around the pitch moves ahead of the observer's predictive powers. We just can't quite see what's about to happen. Like a huge sea monster emerging from the depths of the ocean, the waters foam and churn and a dark shape appears under the surface, but no concept forms in the mind.

The concrete expressions of this are seated fans involuntarily standing up as one. This inchoate sense of something being about to happen creates a sustained state of expectation and arousal. The effect isn't present for the entire match, but it's palpable when good teams create forward movement. Hope rises as the ball approaches the opposition's penalty box, quickly giving way to fear and dread as play switches and the bad guys close in.

The rules of the game heighten this sense of anticipation by giving us a climactic moment: the scoring of a goal. To understand this, consider the experience of watching high-scoring sports. Individual scores bring pleasure but multiple scoring dilutes their impact, dispersing it throughout the duration of the game. In football, goals mark a great rupture: a single event, a single goal, can be the difference between the immortality of winning the World Cup and becoming forgotten losers. It is the difference between zero and one. The dividing line is clear and the experience of crossing it correspondingly more affecting. The infrequent and abrupt arrival of a goal produces a more dramatic and satisfying emotional discharge. Mayhem, in fact.

Football also provides a space for the expression of these intense emotions, particularly those that could not be expressed in other social contexts without a degree of embarrassment or offence.

Numerous social roles and norms of conduct constrain civilized living. Many of these propagate shared emotional experiences that, in remaining within certain limits, minimize conflict. But such constraints are not the full story of how to treat our emotional side. Alternative or intense emotional experiences can be educational. They deepen understanding of our own conduct and habits; through them we leave behind the familiar roadmap of social interaction and risk a few risqué interactions. Football helps here by granting certain temporary freedoms—to feel and express in ways that transcend everyday responsibilities. Football creates an arena for us, a site to express raw and powerful emotions, whether it is a stadium, a private living room or a bar showing live matches. Others can be forewarned of the football match, so that behaviour that might appear eccentric or 'out of character' in other contexts is given an interpretative framework. For onlookers, the frenzy is no longer so alien and threatening since it has a clear cause and a scheduled ending (although if extra time is played the return of normality, like the news, might be delayed).

This is not to deny that truly objectionable behavior can still happen, and it should not be excused. But the social utility of allowing people to indulge in some temporary mild rule breaking and role forgetting is what matters. And not only are goals celebrated with Dionysian frenzy: players, well-compensated for their troubles, are fervently abused for their mistakes or for just belonging to the wrong team; fans sing songs badly that question players hairstyles, social habits or sexuality; and fans bait opposition fans. The final result is that the fan leaves the football arena having thoroughly exercised his or her emotions and released pent up frustrations, able to return, refreshed, to normal duties.

3. Football Facilitates the Development of a Personal Narrative

Football fans can tell themselves a wondrous story. They locate themselves on a footballing timeline that stretches back before they were born and will continue after their exit from the scene. Their world is a busy one, crowded with faces, events and places, and there they find an identity that is personally reassuring. Independently of the ups and downs of life there will always be football. But it is not a simple safety blanket. Individuals can use football to tell many different stories about themselves, about who they are, and these stories provide guidance when faced with practical dilemmas and uncertainty about how to act. These action-guiding stories derive from three sources: football-*qua*-sport, the family, and clubs.

Football is an organized, global sport with a long history, and its key moments have been televised (sometimes) and documented often, creating a common memory for many people. Some remember where they were at the time of President Kennedy's assassination or Princess Diana's death. Football fans remember themselves through World Cup wins, manager's sackings and relegation.

In the family, fans are often raised among generations of supporters, with football a conventional and difficult-to-question commitment received from parents and elders. The game reaches across generational gaps to create shared passion between fathers and sons, juniors and seniors, prompting dialogue and keeping alienation at bay.

And as a fan of a particular club, one shares with many others in its history: the revered figures, its role models, and its experiences of triumph and tragedy. People are married at grounds and their ashes are scattered there; they collect the relics of the club and create social safety nets for former heroes. In short, clubs become part of the fabric of the communities in which they are embedded. For example, an Everton fan, David France, recently sold to the club his private memorabilia collection, described by a famous auction house as the largest collection of memorabilia relating to a single club in the world. It is being held in public trust by the city of Liverpool's records office and the collection has recently been digitized and made available online, in addition to being exhibited in local public museums: <www.evertoncollection .org.uk>. Aside from recording the events of a football club, the collection is a social history, documenting the region over the past 125 years.

Another charitable venture, the Everton Former Players Foundation, raises funds and cares for ex-players facing financial difficulty who served the club when wages were modest. The foundation provides hospice care and medical services, maintaining a sense of continuity between past and present, and the link between players, club and fans. In its most comprehensive forms, football is more than either a sport of a business; it is a way of life.

Football is not the only source of a good story. Other sports are potentially similar in having a global reach, a history, and consecutive generations of fans; and some decisions in life must be made by putting football into perspective. But as a matter of contingent historical fact, football is the sport with the most varied and coherent story, one with innumerable practical implications.

4. Football as an Invitation to Rational and Public Discussion

Caring about the game of football naturally leads to an interest in talking about it, and this leads to the skills and motivation to engage in extended social discourse.

Inspired by love of a team or the game in general, constructing one's own viewpoint, and persuading others of how reasonable it is, suddenly matters. This obliges one to learn the rules of public discourse: justifying one's claims, turn taking in dialogue and understanding the interlocutor's viewpoint. In public debate, people who mindlessly insist on a claim, or are dismissive of another's ideas, are quickly excluded.

Supporters also realize through such engagement that romantic and wondrous claims are often ill-supported by reality, and what felt so certain should be understood as merely personal feeling. Football is thus an education in truth-seeking debates. The fan believes in the truth and seeks to articulate it, but all such claims are contested. In this way, the game inspires intricate arguments and refutations about matters such as tactics, the greatest ever player or team, the laws of the game or the rights of football fans.

Further, social and technological change have strengthened the motivation to engage others and granted a wider range of voices access to the public domain. Homes and pubs were once the place for football talk, with friends making up the audience. But new channels of communication such as websites, blogs, and fanzines have enabled fans to create a culture of debate and hone their public persona. The chance for unconditional and frank exchange leads fans to embrace another important political virtue: dissent. Many fans find the information and encouragement to challenge official voices, so-called experts and watery TV punditry; disagreement with the guardians of the game leads to supporter-led campaigns (for new amenities at grounds and against moving to a new stadium) and a vocal presence at Annual General Meetings.

Finally, the fullest engagement with the public realm and the ultimate political act of the fan is ownership: effective control of his or her football club. According to the UK organization Supporters Direct <www.supporters-direct.org>, which advises fans on club takeovers, sixteen clubs in England are now under the control of supporters' trusts, including the Football League sides Exeter City and Brentford FC. In U.S. Major League Soccer, the Seattle Sounders democratic system of decision making allows fans input into team tactics, the matchday experience and even provides for a vote of confidence on the general manager.

Being a football fan still involves the anonymous participation in wordless cathartic rituals, but a sense of self-determination is also emerging. Public engagement and the awareness of collective interest marks the final stage of evolution of the football fan: from the caged-in working class spectator found on crowded terraces a few decades ago to enfranchised property owner, a common motif of contemporary life.

5. The Genius of Football in Generating Mutual Affection and Respect

Football influences people's treatment of each other beyond the conventions of public debate. It has the power to generate and propagate altruistic feelings that defy cultural and social divisions: it reminds us how the discovery of common passions creates mutual goodwill and expands social cooperation. But football also teaches how to get along with others in the absence of such feelings, how to marry passionate personal commitments with a reflective and reasonable treatment of those with different interests. It's an education in respect.

Football is often called a global language. The simplicity outlined above means that, globally, people can easily identify with it. A ball and a space to play, a few gestures or simply the names of a few players are sufficient to start a conversation in a foreign land. The language is primitive but the emotional and practical implications are great. Recognising a passion for football in a stranger often initiates a different view of that person. They are transformed from a mere generic other, to whom we owe minimal duties of respect or non-interference, into a particular person. This gestalt switch, this waking up to another, can initiate chains of altruism-tinged action. The fan feels goodwill towards another fan's friends because they are *his* friends. Even if other circumstances and other personal differences cool the initial warmth, at least the opportunity for bridge building was created.

One memorable occasion when football was a conduit for goodwill was the 'Christmas Truce' of 1914 during the First World War. British and German troops temporarily ended hostilities on and around Christmas day and gathered to play football. The game gave expression to forgotten feelings of altruism and mutual regard at a time of hostility.

Football is also a useful way of channeling existing altruism. Few material costs mean the game is open to all social and economic classes; and large-scale altruistic and charitable projects inspired by football can be organized with relatively limited resources and produce substantial intangible benefits. Witness, for example, the work of the UK's *Guardian* newspaper in Northern Uganda, where football has been used to sow the seeds of unity in a conflict-affected region <www.guardian.co.uk/katine/football>. Football appears to generate mutual affection far out of proportion to the value of a mere game or hobby.

The powerful effects of recognizing commonality and unity are not confined to football. The feminist movement offers a similar story of solidarity achieved through simple commonality. Still, the 'rationality' of the football fan, as someone moved to create social cohesion in the face of difference, is clear. And though the fan's disposition to feel altruism is selective and imperfect, it stands in contrast to lifestyles that obsess over personal goals or with projects that interest only an immediate circle of acquaintances.

In addition to altruism, football is involved in cultivating another stance towards others: an attitude of respect and tolerance. Football generates such respect by contributing to greater self-understanding. It enables individuals to gain critical distance from their experiences of passion and strong attachments, and so limit their influence on behaviour and reduce interpersonal conflict.

In football, the key to this education lies in a mature approach to the dual and potentially conflicting identities of a football fan: those of 'loyal football fan' and 'fan of football'.

The loyal fan occupies a world colored by intense passions, directed towards his team. The world and his attitude to others is defined in terms of the particular, an awareness of group attachment and outsiders, and a sensitivity to comparisons. This leads the loyal fan to relate to others in a mildly antagonistic fashion and to engage in playful derision and romantic claims of superiority and inferior. And this has its advantages. After all, some relationships—including friendships and romance and those in the workplace—can benefit from a sense of challenge and a degree of tension. The loyal fan's psychological profile is also useful in a competitive market-orientated world. There might be merit in challenging the orthodoxy that affirming others and eliding personal difference is the best approach to interpersonal interaction.

However, loyalty can mutate into a fascination with exclusion and difference and it is clear that the partiality and tribalism of football breed discrimination, favoritism and aggression—values which are at odds with social ideals like respect and tolerance. There is much evidence that football engenders conflict and violence; perhaps the most famous case being the 'Football War' that broke out between Honduras and El Salvador, following the two countries meetings in qualifying matches for the 1970 FIFA World Cup. Numerous other acts of hooliganism also come to mind.

Perhaps the way to limit the dark side of the loyal fan is to develop the outlook of the 'fan of football'. This fan delights in the game itself and finds a rationale for limiting the excesses of the loyal-but-selective fan. She realises that behind an identity founded on partiality is a deeper commitment, a passion for football as a game and as an institution. She comes to realize that the people with whom her team loyalties conflict share a common cause. As a result she gains perspective on her sense of loyalty, its passions, and her habitual division of the surrounding social world into 'us' and 'them'. She still enjoys the experiences of the loyal fan—the depth of feeling that accompanies the ups and downs of her team and its community. But now she can also see its limits. She knows when it can be fully enjoyed and when other values are more appropriate to the situation.

Passionate-but-reflective fans of football thus learn to take an 'ironic view' of their more intense passions; they allow them space for expression and enjoyment but are also aware of their contingent and subjective nature. Consequently, they come to have more regard for others as generic football fans, those with different loyalties and aroused by different particulars.

Such an advance in self-understanding has an important parallel in the wider social world, where the same insight, moving from the particular to the general, is instrumental in creating civil society and resolving personal antagonisms, especially when caused by mere differences in personality or personal preference.

This sketch of the football fan's inner life also helps us understand the venerated ideal of 'respect'. This is sometimes portrayed as a simple, single attitude that ought to define the relation of the modern self to others. But as the above suggests, perhaps no such purity is possible. Ambivalence and antagonism might be an ineluctable part of living with difference. But while implying the elusiveness of one wholesome ideal, football also reassures—reminding us that what really matters for social unity is sufficient ironic detachment from our passionate commitments. We can live with conflicted feelings and a fractured self, as long as another view of ourselves can take over to ensure social harmony.

A Final Doubt about the Football Fan's Life

We can now see why a life structured by an interest in football is a fulfilling one. But one important doubt is worth reprising: the worry that the fan's energies are somehow naively misdirected. Despite the valuable features of the football fan's lifestyle, it might be a failure to participate fully in social and political life. This includes democratic participation as a citizen, as well as identifying and acting for collective interests that arise through employment, basic human needs such as health, and global issues. Arguably, a fully developed and virtuous life goes beyond what football can offer. How should the football fan respond to this?

My aim here has been to establish that the identity of football fan is a rich source of value, well suited to modern living, rather than claiming that it is somehow the best kind of lifestyle. The practices of football are not in obvious conflict with more politically-minded activities. Football fandom cultivates sensibilities and skills that can then be used in these other areas. In a balanced life, an interest in football co-exists alongside other roles and commitments, some of which will be of a more political nature. Whether or not football, to some inordinate degree, diverts a person's energy away from other urgent social issues can only be answered on an individual basis; it is not something internal to football.

But even if football was, in some sense, a diversion perhaps it is a reasonable one. The modern political arena is a specialized one, populated by professional politicians and technocrats. Under this division of labour, the citizen's role is to understand various issues in outline and vote for representatives accordingly, not to directly participate in the making of policy. In so far as one accepts and has faith in this system, the football fan can also satisfy his political obligations. Whether or not the system is sound is a question for the reader's own judgment.

Further, the equating of a valuable life with active political participation begs questions about the relative merits of two different lifestyles: one centered on political activity and one on aesthetic and artistic delight. Is it wrong to enjoy looking at something beautiful more than it is be involved in political bargaining? What the football fan loses in being naïve about the political and social world, he might gain back through a focus on what is beautiful and absorbing.

The Final Whistle

When football is examined within the framework of the pressures and demands of modern social life, its worth emerges and an answer to its critics is found. Football fans can be assured in their sense of vocation.

Let me finish our discussion with a demonstration of the 'respect' that football can initiate. As an Everton fan, the greatest leader of our greatest rivals, Liverpool FC, might be our greatest foe. But legendary Liverpool manager Bill Shankly recognized football as something beautiful, as a source of community and as an exception to prejudice and sectarian divisions that sustained identities in a 1960s industrial city. He saw that the usual animosities did not arise in football, and that the game could redirect peoples' lives to produce concord and solidarity in the face of hardship. So while the loyal fan begrudges the final word going to another tribe, the fan of football admires his insightful observations. Commenting on the mix of antagonism and camaraderie between fans in the city, Shankly said:

> You get families in Liverpool in which half support Liverpool and the other half Everton. They support rival teams but they have the same temperament and they know each other. They are unique in the sense that their rivalry is so great but there is no real aggro between them. This is quite amazing. I am not saying they love each other. Oh, no. Football is not a matter of life and death—it's much more important than that.

18

Playing the Derby

KRISTOF K.P. VANHOUTTE

> This city has two great teams—Liverpool and Liverpool reserves.
>
> —BILL SHANKLY

When I moved from my home and country to the house where I live now with my wife, there was only one thing that I could not bring with me. It's nothing special really. In fact, it's a simple piece of clothing, a shirt. I think it is still locked up somewhere in my closet in my parents' house. The reason I couldn't bring it was not because my wife thought it was ugly. It wasn't even because it didn't fit anymore. The reason why I couldn't bring it was simply because it was considered pure evil. No such thing was ever going to be present in *our* house. It was her or the shirt, and so I had to agree. It's my poor old Lazio Roma shirt which I bought years ago. Bringing this into a family of AS Roma fans would have meant, if not a serious declaration of war, at least a very bad start for me.

When two teams meet to play a game of soccer, both teams want to win. Professional sports brings the obligations of winning for colleagues and for the fans. Fans from each side will probably not like each other during the game, but when the final whistle sounds all will go home and be happy or sad—according to the result.

But when two teams of the same city meet, the story changes completely. The derby is not just a game that has to be won. Make no mistake, derbies have to be won, but there is much more at stake than just the league points. Derbies are about honor, about cultural confrontation, about *territory*. They are about the right to brag. They are about the fear of humiliation. They can easily be qualified as the definitive moments in the season for the fans.

Often these rivalries have been caused by differences in social or cultural backgrounds. When we look at the history of some of the most famous derby-clubs in the world we can see that most of the typical social and cultural oppositions can be found in these soccer clashes: rich versus poor, city-folk against peasants, industrials contra the working class, even political (right-winged against left-winged) or religious (Catholics versus Protestants) differences enter with the players during the derbies.

Most of these ancient oppositions have now faded but they remain firmly present in the historical and cultural baggage of the clubs. When these teams meet, at least twice a year, all of this is remembered and thus plays a fundamental role. It is easy to imagine how these matches are not merely temporary demonstrations of one's superiority. They are still about honor and about social or religious belonging. As such these rivalries—and this is contrary to most of the other games of the season—do not finish with the final whistle of the referee. The rivalry lasts the whole season and is combined with a profound and lasting inner feeling of aversion for the other team.

The Origins of the Derby

There exists no absolute certainty on the origins of the concept of a derby. While most of the time a derby is a game between two teams from the same city (*intra*-city derbies), sometimes games between two different cities are classified as derbies (*inter*-city derbies), as are some of the most famous games between different national teams. The most famous of the inter-city derbies are the games between Real Madrid and Barcelona in Spain, Manchester United against Liverpool in England and Juventus from Turin and Inter(nazionale) from Milan in Italy. Some of the more emotionally loaded international derbies are the games between Brazil and Argentina, England against Argentina, Italy versus Spain, and The Netherlands against Belgium.[1]

Some say that the term 'derby' originates from the first match between Liverpool and Everton (both clubs are in fact from the city of Liverpool). The story goes that their "territories" was divided by some property of the Earl of Derby. This, however, seems a bit poor as proof for the origins of the derby. A more plausible explanation for the derby could be found in the matches played between Derby County and Derby Junction at the end

---

[1] This chapter will focus mainly on the 'intra-city' derbies because most aspects of the intra-city derbies are also valid for the inter-city and national derbies.

of the nineteenth century (both teams are, as can be easily deduced, from the English city of Derby). It could be that people started naming these games simply the derby, but there is no proof of any of this and Derby Junction did not exist as a club for that long a time. Derby Junction, in fact, stopped existing around 1895, when it merged with Derby County.

Another possible and much more interesting option for the origin of the derby can be found in the centuries old *Royal Shrovetide Football match*. This strange game seems to have been played since the twelfth century and could explain a lot about the peculiar nature of most derbies. The game is still annually played over two days (Mardi Gras and Ash Wednesday) in the town of Ashbourne (*Derby*shire, England). Except for the monuments and cemeteries, the whole town is the playing field. The two teams that play are made up of hundreds of people. The point of the game is to hit one of the two ancient mill stones, depending on which team you are, three times with the ball—a sphere somewhat larger than a normal football that has been decorated by the local craftsmen for the occasion. Popular tradition holds that the ball used to be the head of an executed criminal and even though this particular aspect of the game has changed over time the original rules are still the ones used: no hiding of the ball, the game finishes exactly at 10:00 P.M. and murder is prohibited (general violence is however tolerated). Or, as described by a local in a small documentary on YouTube,

> A person coming into town in a car would think, "What is going on here, all these people, congregating?", and then, all the sudden you'd see a great rush, of people, and, surrounded by a lot more people. And they would think, "I can't make this out." And then they see them pushed up against a wall, and they think, "What is going on here?" And they wouldn't have a clue what it was all about. But when you have been brought up around here, you know exactly what it is. There is a saying that there are no rules. In fact the only rule that I know of is bang the ball three times against the 'pling', you know, the goal. That is all they can do. So no other rules.

Even though the written transcription is comical, the spoken version of this mostly incomprehensible rambling is worth the viewing!

Forming the Fan-Community: 'We' Won

Although there is no certainty on the historical exactness of any of the origin stories, the *Royal Shrovetide Football match* is by far the most intriguing. Not only is it the oldest tradition, it shares some of the more characteristic aspects of the current derbies. First, with the exception of the cities where there are more than two teams, the contemporary derbies involve the whole city and divide the citizenry into two distinct groups. And, unfortunately, violence is often present before, during, and after the modern derby games even though, and this contrary to the Shrovetide, it is not condoned.

In fact, there seem to be two fundamental aspects that characterize every derby-city and its fans. The division of the city into two clearly distinct groups brings an enormous sense of *belonging* that is very strongly felt by the fans of the competing teams. The second characteristic, which differentiates the modern derbies from the Shrovetide, is the continuous hatred that exist between the teams and its fans. Let us, however, start by taking a closer look at the sense of belonging.

The derby is won or lost, first of all by the team, and, secondly, by the whole community of fans. Winning the derby, or the championship as a team that belongs to a derby-rivalry, is something that is done as a group. Characteristic for this is the fact that the pronoun 'I' is very rarely used. As the famous quotation goes: "There is no 'I' in team," and one could add that there is no 'I' in fan either. It is not without meaning that Liverpool fans start every match of their club by singing their club song "You'll Never Walk Alone." The language used in team sports and by the fans is a language that has been restricted to the plural. Nothing is done alone.

When taken literally however, this 'we won', as pronounced by fans could seem to be rather meaningless. Only the players on the field, and maybe even the coach, win the game. But people do not question this sentence because they are aware of the meaning of this "we won." Every soccer fan understands this sentence perfectly and would not question it. (I actually hope nobody ever tries to convince a fan that *he* did not win anything, this could end up rather badly.)

In fact, in soccer there even exists an expression that describes precisely this sense of belonging of the fan-community. One could even think that the expression 'the twelfth player' was invented especially to create this sense of belonging and participation in soccer. This twelfth player is essential in soccer, especially during derby games, and the fans want to be considered as essential. They have all become that twelfth player. They have all individually become one, a collective. The game is also played when there are no fans, but, as everybody has probably experienced when watching a game of soccer behind 'closed doors', the game is not so real and definitely no fun at all to watch on TV.

That the twelfth player is essential should not surprise. In fact, it is a fundamental part in the construction of the fan-community. As such, this can be considered from the point of view of the formation of collective identities. The formation of collective identities consists primarily of the production of boundaries, boundaries that separate the 'them' from the 'us'. It consists of a dynamic duality that, in order to be able to produce some effect, has to be structured in a stable enough way for it to have some meaning and to be recognizable and understandable for its members, that is, for the members of that group. So on the one hand there will be the boundaries of that what makes the us 'us' and, on the other, there will be certain identifiable boundaries that will enable us to separate 'us' from 'them'.

An excellent example of this strong, one might even say extreme, form of belonging can be found in the Istanbul derby between Fenerbahçe and Galatasaray.

The Clash of Two Continents

The stakes in the Istanbul derby between Fenerbahçe and Galatasaray are just a bit higher than those of your regular, run of the mill derby. This is because the Istanbul derby is a derby between two continents. While in the same city, Fenerbahçe is Asian and Galatasaray European, with the Bosporus Strait separating them. In the hall of fame of most spectacular, most tense and most explosive derbies, this game is number one. (No need to take my word for it, the Fenerbahçe-Galatasaray derby is ranked #1 at www.footballderbies.com.) There is also another soccer team in Istanbul, Besiktas, and although the matches between Besiktas and the Big Two are also derbies, the fact that Fenerbahçe and Galatasaray have both won more championships and are so different in background makes those derby matches much more tense than the ones with Besiktas.

The high ranking of this game in the derby classification is, however, not caused by the fantastic games that one can see on the field during derby days. If that were the case, the Bosporus derby would probably not even get one star. But one generally does not participate in this derby for the soccer but for the incredible atmosphere on the stands. The most extravagant things have been said on this game and probably most of them are also true. "It may not have been hell, but a Stygian gloom drifted over the Bosporus" is how *Times* correspondent Rick Broadbent described the atmosphere during this derby. Remembering that the mythological river Styx separated the world of the living from the world of the dead makes everything perfectly clear.

This unique derby is felt so strongly by the fans because of the different social backgrounds of the teams and because it is a cultural clash of two continents, which gives it an extra allure. Not only is Fenerbahçe the Asian team, it is now a very wealthy club owned by one of the richest business people in Turkey. Originally, however, it was founded as a team of and for the working class. So the feeling of "having it made" is always present in this team and by its fans. But with the feeling of having made it comes the attitude of always having to prove oneself. This attitude has enabled Fenerbahçe to become the most successful derby team of Istanbul. Galatasaray, on the other hand, is European and was founded at the beginning of the twentieth century by students of an elite school. The mythical story of the foundation of Galatasaray states that the school was founded as a gift from a fifteenth-century Sultan. But as the founding myth continues, the school was so poor that the shirt colors (yellow and red) were chosen because of the lack of other fabric colors. So a European-oriented egalitarian feeling combined with the desire to belong, and all this in spite of economical difficulties, is what strongly characterizes this club's fans.

It's better not to tell your life-insurance agent that you are traveling to Istanbul to participate in this clash of the continents. If you go, however, you should always remember that the stakes are so high, that on most occasions the two teams don't even play decent soccer. To borrow a line from Rodney Dangerfield: if you're lucky, a soccer game might break out at the fight. This does not mean that the show on the stands is any less extreme. Flares and banners, songs and cheers that could match Cirque du Soleil are always present. In case things turn really ugly, just make sure that the shortest way back to the hotel or to your house is the one you are actually taking.

The Holy Goalie

The sense of belonging is an essential part of being a soccer fan, and that sense is felt especially strongly in derby cities. The strong sense of belonging brings with it, in a natural and almost unconscious way, the feeling that in order to *truly* belong one is expected to do certain things or to behave in certain ways. In fact, belonging to a group almost naturally imposes that certain forms of behavior will be expected. This facilitates the recognition of other members of the same group without the need to express this literally.

Some behavioral traits will be seen as normal to the members of the group; while the 'others', those who do not belong to that group, will not always be that ready to accept them. But that is exactly what allows us to feel as being a part of a particular group and not another. For those who *belong* the rules are clear.

Most of us generally don't go hugging the first perfect stranger who happens to stand next to us when something good happens. But when we are in the stands and surrounded by other fellow fans we start shouting and hugging everybody because "our" team scored. This is normal and natural and nobody thinks anything of it. For the same reason, we sing songs containing certain words which wouldn't make it into our vocabulary even if we were in a state of complete madness. I won't even talk about certain insults the referees have to hear when he whistles against one of "our" players.

Not always, however, are all the fans aware of these same rules. All heck breaks loose when players aren't aware of some of these unwritten rules. Sometimes they've only recently joined the team and still have to adapt to part of the city's behavior. When this isn't done in a speedy way, it can lead to embarrassing situations.

Celtic goalkeeper Artur Boruc was one of those who did not know the rules, or maybe he simply refused to obey them. But poor Boruc couldn't have chosen a worse derby to learn a valuable lesson.

The derby between the two Scottish teams from Glasgow, Celtic FC and Glasgow Rangers, is not just a simple derby. It is a very good example of a derby where the ancient religious and political oppositions still rule the game. The Rangers fans, in fact, can by and large be classified as Protestants who are loyal to the UK; Celtic fans are generally Catholics and Republicans. For historical reasons the Celtic fans are also closer to the Irish cause than the Scottish one. Celtic FC was in fact founded by a monk, who had emigrated from Ireland, to raise money for his charity. When these Old Firm teams meet one is thus guaranteed to witness a unique and spectacular event and thanks to Artur Boruc things got even more spectacular.

Being a decent goalkeeper and a native of Catholic Poland, Boruc had the good fortune of being bought by Celtic. (There used to be an unwritten rule for both clubs to buy only players who belonged to their own faith. When Boruc was bought this, however, wasn't really the case anymore.) Artur, however, had a particular habit. Probably nobody would consider this habit a dangerous one, but during the derby of the 25th of August in 2006 this habit (almost) cost him dearly. Maybe Boruc did it on purpose, who knows, but the fact remains that once he made the sign of the cross the Rangers fans went completely mad. The act of crossing oneself is generally rejected by Protestantism and is considered a typical Catholic superstition. In this sense one can understand the disarray created by Boruc. Luckily nobody got hurt that day and in the end the threat of legal action against this "holy goalie" was dropped. Ever since, however, no player has been spotted crossing himself during this good old Scottish derby.

The Eternal City's Derby

Soccer fans aren't only expected to do certain things but they are also expected to feel certain things if they are to retain their membership in the group.

"I hate them, and I do not use the word 'hate' lightly. I wish them ill and I want them to be humiliated in every game." This is probably the closest one could get to a general phrase usable by a fan of either of the two derby-teams. One just has to change the meaning of 'them' and the same sentence will be heard all over the city. And, in all honesty, this simple form of hatred is something that characterizes even the nicest and well-educated of fans. Simply: a *true* fan of one of the opposing teams has to dislike, or, to use stronger language, has to *hate* the other team and its supporters. The fan has to dislike the other team, and this holds especially for derby cities, because one never wins or loses alone, let alone the derby.

The derby rivalry does not exist only in the week or days that precede and follow the two derby matches. These two games are the highlights of the season (when won that is), but the derby-feelings don't end there. In fact, the derby-feeling lasts the whole year and is only dormant during transfer period. But don't be fooled! The mere rumor of a possible transfer of a player to the rival team during the summer recession will rapidly awaken this volcano from its sleep. In fact, only rarely are players welcome from the opposing team and if that would occur the player can rest assured that he will be even more hated by his former fans than the other players from his new team. This will be explicitly demonstrated at the first derby that will be played during the next season. Recently, the Argentinian international Carlos Tevez left Manchester United for their city rival Manchester City, but he was smart enough to blame United's manager. Things went different with the Portuguese player Luis Figo. He had to witness how even images of himself were burnt by Barcelona fans. This wouldn't have happened however were it not that Figo had moved from Barça to Real Madrid, the club most hated by the Catalan fans.

Confirmation of the fact that the derby hate-feeling is continuous can be found in the celebrations of the championship at the end of the season if the title is won by one of the derby-teams. A good example of this is the celebration of the Italian title won by AS Roma on the 17th of June, 2001. The streets of the centre of Rome were full and, maybe typical for the Italian sense of exaggeration, a coffin was being carried through them. This wasn't a true funeral, however. No specific person had died that day, but half of the city was mourning. The streets were colored yellow and red because AS Roma had won the championship; the coffin was white and light blue like the colors of the other team of the city: Lazio.

Following the true spirit of the derby rivalry the most important message that day was the one to the other team of the city. AS Roma did not just win the championship, no! Roma had won *and* Lazio had lost. That the other teams, especially the stuck-up and arrogant northern big teams, did not win the championship was only normal. In fact, on this particularly joyous day for the Roma fans they weren't even considered. What couldn't be forgotten, however, was the fundamental and important message to Lazio. And in case the fake casket wasn't enough to deliver the message, songs were sung for Paolo Negro, the Lazio back that scored an own goal and the only goal in the first derby of the year. The second derby ended as a draw (2–2), so Negro was the one who, ironically, had actually made the difference.

The importance of reveling in your derby rival's losses has made fake funeral ceremonies commonplace in Italian soccer. When, for example, the three remaining Italian teams in the Champions League 2009 (AS Roma, Juventus and Inter Milan) were kicked out of the competition, fan clubs from all three derby rival teams (Lazio, Torino, and AC Milan) showed funeral banners during the next Sunday game. There was no derby game that Sunday, but the fans found it important enough to bring these banners to their game and let their message be sent through the TV.

Don't Worry, We'll Be Back Next Season

However, not all derbies end with phony processions and not all championships won by one of the rival teams end with fake funeral parties. In 2009, Rangers won the Scottish championship after three years of Celtic hegemony.[2] The championship celebrations were, however, seriously damaged by the murder of a Catholic man in Ireland by raging Irish Ranger fans. Being kicked several times by this Protestant mob, Mr. McDaid died in the hospital of his injuries, leaving a Protestant wife with four children wondering about the why of this pointless and idiotic violence.

---

[2] I confront this particular incident simply because it happened so recently, not out of any desire to make the Scottish derby seem more violent than any other.

But concluding with such a negative note feels almost like losing the derby, and nobody wants to lose that game. As I have shown, the derby is a game like no other. The derbies are the best and most wonderful games of the season. The banners and songs are never as colorful as during derbies and in the moments before both teams enter the field one can almost feel the butterflies in one's stomach. Tension is high as never before and when you're a fan, it feels like heaven when you win and like hell when your team loses the derby. Even the most timid people will start hugging the first stranger they see who just happens to be "one of us".

If the game is lost, encountering your family or friends that happen to cheer for the other team will be as harsh for you as will be the press for the players. When the derby is won, making fun of them will give you a feeling you will rarely have felt. It's all part of a derby and underlines nothing but its beauty. There is however one thing that should remain clear. As David Berreby wrote in *Us and Them: The Science of Identity* (University of Chicago Press, 2008, p. xii): "the problem is not that religion, or nation, or ethnic feeling always leads to violence. It is that these divisions *sometimes* do." Clan or fan rivalries, religious and social tension have never hurt anybody, it is only when people start exaggerating these differences that people can get hurt.

It should be our task as fans to make sure that at least when soccer is involved these divisions don't result in violence. The feeling is too good when you can make fun of your friends or even laugh with a perfect stranger if they happen to cheer for the opposing team. However it's such a turnoff when things degenerate in violence for something that, in the end, is and remains *just a game.*

But, oh, what a game!

19

Villa till I Die!

ANNE C. OSBORNE
and DANIELLE SARVER COOMBS

> Loyalty to any one sports team is pretty hard to justify because the players
> are always changing. . . . You're actually rooting for the clothes, when you
> get right down to it. You're standing and cheering and yelling for your
> clothes to beat the clothes from another city. Fans will be so in love with a
> player but if he goes to another team they boo him. This is the same human
> being in a different shirt. They hate him now. Boooooo. Different shirt,
> boooo.
>
> —JERRY SEINFELD, *The Label Maker*

Seinfeld's speech is sure to generate laughs from any sports fan who has
enjoyed (or, equally often, suffered through) a long-term commitment to
a particular club. We've all been in this situation: a player who seems
central to our team's success, whose name we've emblazoned on the
back of our replica shirts and whose nickname we've screamed until
we're hoarse, abandons the good guys in a move to the Dark Side. Once
the move is completed, his reception at the old homestead is optimisti-
cally defined as, well, chilly. What does this mean? Do fans really cheer
for nothing more than a shirt?

We have to wonder because, you see, we're Aston Villa fans, and in
the past five years just about every aspect of the Aston Villa Football
Club—including the shirts—has changed. So when we stand in the Holte
End of the Villa Park singing, "John Carew, Carew. He's bigger than me
and you. He's gonna score one or two. John Carew, Carew . . ." what
exactly *is* it that we're singing for? Okay, obviously it's the Norwegian
international and Villa striker John Carew, but it's more than that. We're
also supporting the team, the institution, right? And if John Carew left us
would we turn on him? When news broke that team captain Gareth Barry

was negotiating with Manchester City after years of loyal service to the claret and blue of Aston Villa, some fans certainly weren't pleased. One message board posting bluntly affirmed Seinfeld's contention; "I will boo the @#$% out of him if he goes there!!!" Barry wound up accepting their offer, and this decision eliminated over a decade of good will accrued among the Villa faithful.

My Father's Club: Not My Father's Club

Change is something we fans have come to expect but that doesn't mean it isn't painful. Haven't we all seen a favorite player leave our beloved club in a way that felt like a lover's betrayal? Or maybe your club renovated its stadium and your seat, the one you've had for generations—where your grandfather first introduced you to the sport and you planned to someday bring your grandchildren to continue the tradition—was replaced with a swank skybox that's now completely out of your price range. In Barclays Premier League, there have been a lot of changes to raise fans' ire. Club football, or soccer as it is better known in other parts of the world, grew out of a tradition of local residents banding together to compete against others in neighboring towns or villages. It intrinsically was rooted to place. Today football has a very different look and feel. Barclays Premier League is big business, and clubs look more like international corporations than local sides.

Despite the differences between football of yesteryear and today, fans turn to the sport and their side to feel more connected with the past and their community, to resist change. Fans commonly say, "I love the Villa because it's the same club my dad and his dad before him supported." Nonetheless, change surrounds them. And some football fans feel alienated as a result of the globalization and corporatization of the game. These fans might grieve for a nostalgic ideal of Aston Villa they feel died long ago. Maybe you're one of those fans, or probably at least know one, who says, "I miss the old club. That's when football was good, real. I still support the Villa but it's just not the same."

Gabby Is Gabby

You can imagine the conversation between these two fans, supporters of the same team: one loves his club because it has remained the same, and one misses his club because it has not. It's an interesting question about the nature of identity. In everyday conversation, we tend to use the concept of identity fairly loosely, and often descriptively. We think of people as being lots of things at a time. Villa's rising star Gabriel "Gabby" Agbonlahor is a striker, English, more specifically Brummie, and fast. But this is not what philosophers mean by identity. When talking about the material world, philosophers give identity a more fixed meaning. Identity is the relationship between a thing and itself; it is the same as itself and separate from other things. Simply put, $x = x$. Gabby = Gabby.

A seemingly simple concept, identity, can be surprisingly hard to nail down. Take the tale of the Ship of Theseus. Theseus, son of Athenian King Aegeus, sailed to Crete to battle and ultimately defeat the Minotaur, a half-human, half-bull that had for years preyed on Athenian youth. The legend says that for centuries after Theseus's return, the people of Athens maintained his ship as a symbol of his heroism. Over time, as the wooden ship rotted, shipbuilders replaced every plank with an identical piece of wood. Philosophers have asked if the ship that returned from Crete was the same ship that, centuries later, Athenians sailed as a memorial to their hero. If you answer no, then at what point did it stop being Theseus's ship? Was it at plank two or plank 202? Later Thomas Hobbes proposed an extension to this paradox. Imagine, he suggested, that a second ship were constructed using all of the discarded planks from the original. Which of these compilations of wooden planks could best be identified as the Ship of Theseus?

Proud History, Bright Future

This is the same question we ask of Aston Villa Football Club. Few clubs have won more titles. Even fewer have as long a tradition. Of the twenty teams to play in the 2009–10 Barclays Premier League, none is older than Aston Villa. Sure, Bolton Wanderers can claim to have been around since 1874, but the team was formed under the name Christ Church FC and didn't become the Wanderers until 1877. Aston Villa, on the other hand, has been Aston Villa since its inception in 1874. It was a founding member of the Football League, formed in 1888. It is one of only seven of the founding Premier League clubs to have remained in the Premiership since its formation in 1992.

The Villa isn't just one of the oldest clubs; it has been one of the most successful. Villa has won the First Division Championship seven times, the FA Cup seven times, and the European Cup and UEFA Champions League. Only the current "Big Four" of Arsenal, Chelsea, Liverpool, and Manchester United have more top division titles than Villa. Only Everton has spent more seasons playing in the top division. More recently, Villa has threatened to break into the seemingly impenetrable aforementioned top four of the Premiership, finally finishing the 2008–09 season in sixth place.

It's no surprise then that the club has a deep and loyal fan base. When you're a sports fan, the only thing better than your team winning is the feeling that it has been winning longer than you've been alive and will continue to do so long after you're gone. We're fairly new Villa fans, but friends who have supported Villa for decades love the club because, they say, it's the very same club their grandfather loved and supported. Yet like the Ship of Theseus, Aston Villa's every plank has been replaced. In just the past five years it has undergone enormous changes. Longtime owner Doug Ellis sold the club to American Randy Lerner in 2006. Around the same time, Martin O'Neill replaced manager David O'Leary. The team, named for the Aston neighborhood in Birmingham where it was formed, now fields an ever-changing roster of players that include men from Togo, Bulgaria, the Netherlands, Norway, and the U.S. The crest—the very symbol of Aston Villa—has been redesigned, including a shift to using "AVFC" in lieu of Aston Villa. Even the claret and blue of today's Aston Villa are not the same shades they were just five years ago.

Aston Villa Is Aston Villa . . . Or Is It?

So here's the problem simply stated: how can an object comprising numerous parts—a football club comprising player, managers, staff, and so on—remain the same object while its parts change over time? How can AVFC in 1874 and AVFC in 2009, comprised of completely different components and existing over two hundred years apart, be the same, be identical? This is the Aston Villa Paradox.

In May 2006, when Randy Lerner invited the 1982 European Cup winning team back to Villa Park, we saw a clear example of this modern Ship of Theseus. Because the Cup was won during a short break in Ellis's ownership, he was perceived to have treated it as if it never happened. He never invited the team back, and the players were not lauded as would be expected. Lerner, however, recognized that fans craved an opportunity to show appreciation to their heroes, and marked the twenty-fifth anniversary of the victory by bringing the entire team back to Villa Park for an appearance on the pitch. The fans stood and held high scarves proclaiming "Proud History, Bright Future" on one side and "Aston Villa Football Club" on the other. They cheered for the men who won the title in 1982 with the same vigor that they cheered the men who defeated Sheffield United that day.

Imagine on that day that all members of the 1982 organization had been present, the players, the owner Doug Ellis and the manager who led the team to glory, Tony Barton. On that day in May 2006 we had two sets of people, each of which were AVFC at different points in time (AVFC82 and AVFC06). So which was the real AVFC?

Aston Villa Across the Fourth Dimension

One deceptively simple answer is that both were AVFC, at different points in time. Philosophers have offered numerous explanations of the metaphysics of how objects persist through time. While interesting, these theories of objects through time unfortunately miss the issue of identity, leaving us with an apparently arbitrary choice between two objects claiming to be the same thing.

Presentists, for example, believe only in the present. Past and future are simply human constructs. They only exist in our minds. The world and all its objects thus exist in the present moment. There is no need to account for change because each moment stands alone, distinct. We may have clear memories of watching Aston Villa trounce archrivals Birmingham City 5–1 in the 2008 "Second City Derby." We can describe the chill in the air and the energy of the crowd. But that exists at this moment only as a memory. That Aston Villa Football Club does not. Similarly, we can envision a future AVFC that will again win the FA Cup. But that reality, that football club, does not exist now. Presentism doesn't allow for any meaningful way to talk about the past or compare it to the present. This theory tells us that both teams standing on the pitch in May 2006 existed at that moment but tells us nothing about which is best called AVFC.

Eternalists, on the other hand, believe that past and future are just as real as the present and that all of these realities exist simultaneously. Four-dimensionalism, grounded in eternalism, at first glance appears to offer the greatest possibility for addressing our question. Four-dimensionalists believe objects extend across time in the same way they extend across space. Each object is a "spacetime worm." The book you are holding extends across space and has different spatial parts: the left page and the right page. According to four-dimensionalism, it also extends across time and has different temporal parts, like segments of a worm. Just like spatial parts may be different—left page v right page—the temporal parts may be different and so an object may be different today than it will be tomorrow. What we see as AVFC now is simply a part of a larger whole stretching from the past and continuing into the future, segment by segment by segment.

Four-dimensionalism may account for an object changing through time—its temporal parts are different but it is all part of a larger whole. But does it tell us which ship is the Ship of Theseus or which team is AVFC? No.

In his book titled *Four-Dimensionalism*, Theodore Sider explains that the problem arises because the spacetime worms of two distinct objects are each co-located with what we would call the Ship of Theseus at different points in time. He calls the ship maintained over time "Replacement," while the one reconstructed with original wood is "Planks." With regard to which can properly claim the title of the "real" Ship of Theseus, Sider concludes:

> The answer depends on our concept of a ship. Perhaps our concept of ship does not emphasize sameness of planks, and applies to spacetime worms that continue in ship form even if they exchange planks. The replacement worm rather than the original planks worm would then count as a ship, and the correct answer to the question would be Replacement. . . . On the other hand, perhaps it is a feature of our concept of ship that ships must retain the same planks. The original planks worm, rather than the replacement worm, might then count as a ship. (Oxford University Press, 2001, pp. 8–9)

Sider points out that four-dimensionalism (and the same can be said of presentism) can't tell us why a particular arrangement of wooden planks can be known as the Ship of Theseus while another identical ship is a mere replica. Or similarly what makes one group of players Aston Villa at one time and not at another? The theories of persistence in time allow us to consider whether the boat termed the Ship of Theseus still exists today or only existed in the past. To answer the conceptual question of which ship is that of Theseus, we must turn to a different philosophical approach: material composition.

United We Stand

Lynne Rudder Baker's "Unity Without Identity" (Midwest Studies in Philosophy XXIII, 1999, pp. 144–165) offers, we believe, the best solution to our question: How does Aston Villa persist despite changes in players, managers, and owners? And her theory also tells us something interesting about football fandom.

Baker offers *constitution* as a middle ground between identity and separateness. To understand her approach, we must define a few central ideas. First, each object is fundamentally a member of only one kind—ship, plank of wood, team—called a "primary kind." To identify an object's primary kind, we ask, "What most fundamentally is it?" Put another way, if an object stops having the properties of its primary kind, it no longer exists. While you may consider yourself a football fan, this is not a primary kind. You can stop being a fan but you won't stop being—the number of objects in the world won't change. If you stop being human, on the other hand, the number of objects will decrease by one.

Constitution explains how two primary kinds can share the same space and time. Planks of wood constitute a ship and people constitute a football club. The constituted object—ship/team—remains independent of the identity of its parts. The planks and the ship have essentially different properties, referred to as kind-properties. Because they remain independent with different kind-properties, one can cease to exist while the other remains. Imagine that owner Malcolm Glazer decided to disband Manchester United by selling off all the players and turning over the stadium and training grounds to inter-city Premier League competitors Manchester City. While all the component parts would remain and still function as they had before, the club Manchester United would not. In the same way, one could dismantle a ship but the planks of wood would retain their primary-kind identity.

A group of players may constitute a team, but that doesn't mean any time you get together eleven guys you have a football club. Imagine, for example, members of several Premier League clubs coming together for an awards ceremony. Simply because they stand together on the pitch does not mean that they are a team. They may even kick a few goals for the amusement of the crowd and still they're not a team. They need favorable circumstances. Baker explains, "where F [group of players] and G [team] are distinct primary-kind properties, it is possible that an F exists without there being any spatially coincident G. However, if an F is in G-favorable circumstances, there is a new entity, a G, that is spatially coincident with the F but not identical to it" (p. 149). A piece of paper, for example, only constitutes a dollar bill in a world that places exchange-value in currency. A hunk of marble only constitutes a statue if there is an art world. These relational properties—the exchange-value of currency—are essential properties of the constituted object. An essential property of any statue is an art world.

The Fans Keep It Real

We contend that an essential property of any football club is its fans. When the crowd at Villa Park stands with arms raised in a Villa "V," singing, "Villa, Villa, Villa," they create the football-favorable circumstances that make Aston Villa Aston Villa. This is not to say that fans are the only relational property. The Premier League structure and organization, for example, also contributes to the football-favorable circumstances. Still, fans are essential. One can imagine a group of players playing football without fans, but few would consider a group of friends playing an ad hoc weekend pick-up match to be a club. In other words, the identity of Aston Villa is dependent on the meaning the fans confer to the club as it is at any particular moment. Without these fans, the club is reduced to its constitutional parts: players as planks, uniforms as sails, and managers as giant wooden steering wheels. Only through the relationship with fans can the club become a meaningful object.

Remember that the original Ship of Theseus was so named in honor of its original primary occupant: Theseus. When this ship was first constituted, its makeup likely differed little from other similar ships of the time. It persisted through time as the Ship of Theseus, despite numerous changes to its parts, because of the emotional connection of the community who maintained it for centuries in honor of their hero, Theseus. The ship—regardless of its particular constitutive elements at any particular time—remained the object of its "fans'" affections. Likewise, Aston Villa draws its identity from how fans perceive the club. Its constitutive parts constantly change and evolve, and the modern AVFC would be almost unrecognizable to fans from 1874 (or even 1950). The club survives, however, because the appeal for fans is rooted in their relationship to the "ship," rather than its constitutive elements.

Fans are important in another way. In addition to creating the circumstances that allow the whole to exist, the fans also confer value to its parts. Baker explains that an object and its parts can borrow properties. For example, the weight of a ship is the weight of its component parts. But borrowing can also work in the other direction. The parts can borrow from the whole. Let's say, for example, that you have a pile of wooden planks, nails, and other materials, the value of which totals $5,000. Now imagine that you arrange the materials into a ship that is worth $10,000. The same materials double in value because they borrow value from the ship.

We see in the case of football that the component parts often borrow from the whole. Individual parts of a club—players, shirts, stadium—share the value fans attribute to the whole. While a replica shirt may cost $80, fans are often willing to pay significantly more for a shirt worn by their favorite player in a high stakes Cup match. The shirt borrows its value from being a part of the football club. This also explains why we boo players who leave our team. Gareth Barry's value to Aston Villa fans comes from the fact that he is part of the Aston Villa club, not from his innate ability. Once he was no longer a Villan, his value decreased.

The Limits of Change

The difficulty with the Ship of Theseus and likewise the AVFC Paradox is that we often try to offer metaphysical solutions to conceptual problems. Constitution allows us the best possibility of determining which group of men, on that day in May 2006, was Aston Villa because it brings circumstances into the question. Constitution can be fluid. Parts may constitute an object at one time and not at another and when the relational properties change, the identity of the object will change. A canvas covered in nothing but black paint is considered a painting today, but likely would not have been centuries ago. The relational property of the art world to painting has changed. So the answer depends, as Sider suggested, on what the fans conceive to be their club. Likely the relationship between the fans and the people who constituted the organization in 1982 has changed. AVFC82 may no longer be AVFC but it may now be "heroes." The same parts now constitute a different whole.

Constitution and the idea of primary kind properties also give us a way to think about why some changes work and some do not. Imagine that rather than replacing the ship's wooden planks with identical planks, the Athenians replaced each with a metal plank. The first several of these metal planks might make no significant difference in the overall identity of the vessel as a ship. But over time the object would become too heavy and would sink. It's hard for the object to still be a ship if it cannot float. If over time the oars were replaced with wings, the bow recast with a propeller, and the rudder replaced with a tail, the ship would no longer be a ship but would become a plane. The first changes might go unnoticed but over time the vessel becomes something different.

When American Malcolm Glazer purchased Manchester United, fans were furious. Believing that this particular man would be an inferior owner, fans feared that he would fundamentally change their club. Enraged fans went so far as to establish a new football side: FC United. A principle news hook in press coverage documenting the outrage of long-time Manchester United fans often focused on the fact that Glazer is American. So it was somewhat surprising when American Randy Lerner purchased Aston Villa and fans welcomed him. Both new owners were American, and much of the criticism of recent changes throughout the Premier League has focused on foreign owners invading British territory. So why the different receptions?

Primary-kind properties of each may account for the difference in how fans received Lerner and Glazer. Lerner was seen as a football enthusiast, a custodian of his team, whereas Glazer was seen as a businessman, an investor in a profit-generator. Both may own clubs but "owner" was not their primary kind, rather steward and investor were the primary kinds seen by fans. Just as the art world defines the parameters of what is and is not a statue or painting, these fans set the parameters of acceptable ownership and what they demanded was a commitment to the club not to profits. Many Manchester United fans feel their club stopped existing when Glazer took over. It was not his nationality that was problematic but his attitude toward the club.

Baker's theory of constitution offers a useful way to think about the changes facing Barclays Premier League clubs. Particularly, it gives meaning to the indispensible role fans play. Fundamentally, the Athenians wanted the ship to remain Theseus's ship, and fans want their club to remain their club. Individual players, owners, and managers may change, just as planks in a ship may be replaced. Seinfeld's joking claim that we are cheering for the shirt speaks to this dynamic: as fans, we recognize that the constituent parts can (and will) change—sometimes with alarming frequency. Each part must have a commitment to the club. When that commitment falters, the relational property between the club and its fans can change to the point that the club loses its identity. But as long as the fans are cheering the club will remain.

It's literally the fans who keep Aston Villa Football Club alive, singing:

Villa till I die.
I'm Villa till I die.
I know I am.
I'm sure I am.
I'm Villa till I die!

SECOND EXTRA-TIME

Soccer and Society

20

Tell Me How You Play and I'll Tell You Who You Are

JOHN FOSTER

A team is above all an idea.

—César Luis Menotti

Football is a simple game of twenty-two men chasing a ball for ninety minutes. In the same way, a murder trial is basically some people in wigs having an argument, and a map is just a colourful assemblage of squiggles and dots.

All true, but hardly the whole story. We might look, for example, at a match played in Kiev in 1942 between eleven Ukrainians and eleven Germans, and conclude it was simply a case of twenty-two men chasing a ball for ninety minutes. Twenty-two men, half of them English, half Hungarians, chased a ball for ninety minutes at Wembley Stadium in 1953. But these games were significant for far longer than ninety minutes, and to many more than twenty-two people. Just as a map is more than a piece of abstract art that resists attempts to fold it, and a murder trial is more than ritualized dressing up and hammer-banging, football is more than just football: its meaning extends far beyond its empirical, describable facts.

A country's most popular sport becomes disproportionately important compared to other sports. If you are Turkish or Brazilian or Italian or Nigerian, the primary pastime of your nation is football even if you personally resent the game. It takes up space in your newspapers, on your television screens, in your conversations with strangers. Victory for the national team is a cue for the whole country to jump into the nearest fountain, defeat provokes widespread despair. Politicians will make statements about great or terrible results, about an unjust red card or a penalty manqué. And not for any sport. No sky was ever filled with the exultant sound of car horns or a hail of celebratory bullets because someone somewhere won a game of rounders, because rounders is the national sport of nowhere. Football, more than any other sport, assumes this special status as the national game. And since it's the national game it's a matter of national identity.

Questions of identity are frequently mythic and sport in general is inescapably mythic. Like any constructed, 'social', reality, they are based on a set of common conceptions and ideals, sometimes with a basis in empirical fact, sometimes not (though mythic does not automatically mean false). Myths are simply a way for people to make sense of things: they are a symbolic tool for understanding the past and a guide to action in the present. Sharing in these myths gives you membership in a community. Rationality, even truth, doesn't really come into it. *"Credo quia absurdum* [I believe because it is absurd] may even become a criterion for group membership, requiring initiates to surrender their critical faculties as a sign of full commitment to the common cause. Many sects have prospered on this principle and have served their members well for many generations while doing so" (William H. McNeill, *Mythistory and Other Essays*, University of Chicago Press, 1986, pp. 19–20). McNeill wasn't talking about football, but he may as well have been.

Myths are prevalent in every aspect of the game, from players' pre-match rituals (putting my left sock on first is bad luck) to pundits' insistence on a familiar narrative (will the forward rejected as a youngster score against the club who snubbed him?). Fans mythologize teams and players relentlessly. Eduardo Galeano, unofficial poet laureate of the game, is fantastically guilty of this. His writing about football is breathlessly romanticized, but then he writes as a fan (his phrase is "a beggar for good football"), and as such he paints his tributes, homages and denunciations in suitably mythic strokes (*Football in Sun and Shadow*, Fourth Estate, 2003, p. 1).

More complex is the relationship between football and issues of identity and community, and how this relation is mediated by myth. When society and football are so closely intertwined, myths about one can have a profound influence on the other. Sometimes the myth will emerge from a society and set the pattern for the way football is played there. Sometimes football is so influential the myths flow the other way; something that begins in the stadium has repercussions in hearts and minds far beyond the touchline.

Of course, we should never lose sight of the fact that it remains "a simple game of twenty-two men chasing a ball for ninety minutes". The phrase is Gary Lineker's. "And then the Germans win," Lineker added. The phrase sums up the mix of resentment, antipathy and resignation the

English feel about the Germans when football is involved (or, if you prefer, how the English feel about football when the Germans are involved). Football is always more than just football.

Sages and Poets and Lovers and Priests v England

The first football myths predate the game itself. Football as we know it took shape in Victorian England, and consequently the Victorians' ideas about what football should be like have a lot in common with their ideas about what society should be like: manly, upstanding, and hysterically moralist.

David Winner, in his excellent book *Those Feet*, describes the beliefs and values that educators tried to instill in the youth of Victorian England, particularly that stratum that was expected to rule the world when it grew up. He explains why English football was born valuing hard work above skill, demonstrating how the whole of society made a fetish of toil and mistrusted artistry and reflection, which was unbefitting and effeminate, or worse, foreign. "The best kind of Englishmen were strong, decent and patriotic, brave and capable, men of action rather than words; honourable and chivalrous rather than cunning; daring fighters rather than sages, poets, lovers or priests" (Winner, *Those Feet: a Sensuous History of English Football*, Bloomsbury, 2006, p. 47). This, then, was the myth that accompanied the English game overseas, a way of thinking and playing that can be summed up as 'better a broken leg than an exposed one'.

Initially the game abroad was played by English expats, or by locals who played the English way. But there was a problem in transposing a style of football that was rooted in a particular myth to a society where that myth did not apply. As Jonathan Wilson puts it, "Argentinians and Uruguayans, uninfected by British ideals of muscular Christianity, had no similar sense of physicality as a virtue in its own right, no similar distrust of cunning" (Wilson, *Inverting the Pyramid: The History of Football Tactics*, Orion, 2009, p. 34). Latin Americans, especially working-class ones who didn't share the bourgeoisie's consuming deference to all things Anglo, quickly came to consider blood-and-thunder football to be particularly English, therefore foreign, therefore undesirable. But it was the formula they discarded, not the blackboard. They invented, in the words of Galeano, "a home-grown way of playing football, like the home-grown way of dancing that developed in the *milonga* clubs . . . On the feet of the first Creole virtuosos *el toque*, the touch, was born: the ball was strummed as if it were a guitar, a source of music" (quoted in

Wilson, *Inverting*, p. 34). Almost from its conception, football was different in the New World.

Accordingly, different myths emerged. Uruguayans called their tenacious and aggressive way of playing after the indigenous Charrùa Indians, despite the lack of Charrùa footballers. The name bestowed an explicitly local identity on the style that emerged east of the River Plate, and in doing so recast this foreign game in a Uruguayan mould. Similarly, in Argentina in 1931, a newspaper reported how home-grown football was "different from the British in that it is less monochrome, less disciplined and methodical, because it does not sacrifice individualism for the honour of collective values." Flair was admired above all else. A story about a player erasing his footsteps in the dust after scoring a virtuoso goal, so that his feat could not be copied, is "mythic, evidently, but indicative of the prevailing system of values" (Wilson, *Inverting*, pp. 38–40; for the story, see Galeano, *Sun and Shadow*, p. 74). This expressive style, named *criolla viveza* ('native cunning'), was formalised into a system known as *la nuestra* ('ours'). The terminology doesn't exactly demand deep analysis. Football had gone native. It had become fútbol.

But this was not simply a way of cocking a snook at the English. Just as the characteristics associated with English football were visible in the wider English cultural landscape, the Charrùa style and *criolla viveza* did not emerge without a context. A footballer who plays with *criolla viveza*—and its flip side, the passionate fury called *bronca*—embodies characteristics of that Argentinian archetype, the *compadrito*. This figure "can dance the tango as a master and play the guitar. He is an elegant seducer whom no woman is able to resist; he has been in prison and is admired because of his courage, physical strength, and capacity to cheat where necessary" (Eduardo P. Archetti, *Masculinities: Football, Polo, and the Tango in Argentina*, Berg, Chapter 5). 'Argentinian-ness' is expressed no less authentically by the knife-fighters and tango masters of folklore than by a piece of virtuoso brilliance from Maradona or Kempes, an intelligent foul by Rattín or Simeone, or by the red mist descending on Ortega or Mascherano. National team boss Daniel Passarella once called his centre-back Roberto Ayala "the best dirty little player in the world." It was meant and understood as a sincere compliment.

Pressure Down the Left

"There is a right-wing football and a left-wing football," said one of Passarella's predecessors, César Luis Menotti, who coached Argentina to victory in the World Cup in 1978. "Right-wing football wants to suggest that life is struggle. It demands sacrifices. We have to become of steel and win by any method . . . obey and function, that's what those with power want from the players. That's how they create retards, useful idiots that go with the system." (Quoted in Wilson, *Inverting*, p. 324). Menotti was not the first to project a political slant onto tactics. Many years earlier, Gusztav Sebes had said something similar. It was Wembley Stadium, 1953, and his side had just inflicted England's heaviest ever home defeat, a 6–3 rogering that flattered the hosts. The winners were Hungary, already known as the Aranycsapat (the 'Golden Team'). Sebes, a former union organiser and committed leftist, declared his side had won thanks to their "socialist" way of playing football. Well-organised, positionally fluid and tactically advanced, for Sebes they were an expression of the prime socialist myth: that socialism, the most scientific and rational system of government ever devised, would lead inevitably to a materially superior and more harmonious society (Wilson, *Behind the Curtain: Travels in Eastern European Football*, Orion, 2006, p. 78). (Robert Imre discusses the Aranycsapat, and the team's inpact on Hungary, more extensively in Chapter 23.)

In a sense the success of the Aranycsapat was down to the socialist system. Hungary's government, realizing the propaganda value of their football team, had nationalised the country's clubs and reallocated the players to benefit the national side. Most of the best ones were sent to Honvéd, nominally the army team, leading to a raft of players being 'conscripted' and given ranks and uniforms before being deployed on a militarily crucial training pitch (Wilson, *Curtain*, p. 73). Together for the whole season, the Hungarian internationals could develop a far greater understanding than was typical for national teams, and Hungary duly pulled the English apart with their movement and teamwork and tactical superiority—socialism in action, against and far above the torpid individualism of England.

But despite the efforts of Sebes and his government, the Hungarian socialist myth needed more to sustain it than a famous victory over England (or indeed, two famous victories—in the return match six months later in Hungary, England were beaten 7–1). Perhaps it even had the opposite effect. "In those days of dictatorship, it was football that united people in Hungary with the five million Hungarians living outside the borders," said Gyula Grocsis, Aranycsapat goalie and a staunch anti-communist. "There was a feeling of togetherness in the Hungarian nation, something to grab hold of and tie ourselves to" (*Curtain*, p. 79). Two years later Hungary revolted against communist rule. Soviet tanks rolled into Budapest, and most of the Aranycsapat fled into exile.

After Wembley but before the Uprising, the Golden Team were to be central actors in another timeless myth. The 1954 World Cup final, which was supposed to be the Golden Team's coronation, instead saw them lose 3–2 to West Germany in one of the biggest final upsets of all time. This match became one of the great mythic contests, not for any blow it dealt to the myth of 'socialist' football but for the shot in the arm it gave to the West German nation, which had been shorn of its national-mythic supports by the war and its devastating end. Patriotism, which had been taboo in any form for nine years, restarted in Berne in 1954. Galeano again: "It was the first World Cup that Germany had been allowed to play in since the war and Germans felt they had won the right to exist again. [The commentator] Zimmerman's cry became a symbol of national resurrection. Years later, that historic goal could be heard on the soundtrack of Fassbinder's film, *The Marriage of Maria Braun*, which recounts the misadventures of a woman who can't find her way out of the ruins" (*Sun and Shadow*, p. 94). Football, in the form of the 'Miracle of Berne', provided West Germans with the symbolic means to escape from their shattered past.

(Though Menotti and Sebes espoused very different styles of play, there is not necessarily a contradiction between Menotti calling meticulously systematised football right-wing, and Sebes calling the same thing left-wing, if we think of it not as a conflict between Left and Right but between authoritarianism and liberalism. Though economic leftists both, Sebes falls into the former camp, Menotti the latter. Here, then, we have political ideology based on footballing ideology based on political ideology: myth constructed on myth constructed on myth.)

Trouble at the Quarry

A one-club city is different, like an only child. Its obsessions seem somehow disproportionate even to other football fans. Compare Glasgow, Milan, and Madrid with Newcastle, Naples, and Bilbao. In the former, you can sense the presence of football on every corner, but there are two presences—the blue and the green, the white and the red, the red and the blue—rather than one, making the space somehow more comprehensible. You, a stranger in Milan, might not be an Inter fan, but it's okay, nor are half the people around you in the piazza. In the one-club cities, you're entirely an outsider. The one club pervades everything, and hangs heavy over every public space. There is only the black-and-white of Newcastle, the *azzurro* of Napoli, the *rojoblanco* of Athletic. The last one is an especially singular case.

Sometimes the marriage between sport and politics is explicit, a result of shared ideology rather than shared circumstance. Basque politicians and Athletic Bilbao do not just step out together in public for the sake of the cameras, they finish each other's sentences, open each other's letters and wear each other's clothes. On the club's centenary in 1994 Athletic's president, like every one of his predecessors a member of the separatist PNV, wrote: "Athletic Bilbao is more than a football club, it is a feeling—and as such its ways of operating escape rational analysis. We only wish for the sons of our soil to represent our club, and in so wishing we stand out as a sporting entity, not a business concept. We wish to mould our players into men, not just footballers, and each time a player from the *cantera* makes his debut we feel we have realised an objective which is in harmony with the ideologies of our founders and forefathers" (quoted in Phil Ball, *Morbo: The Story of Spanish Football*, WSC, p. 61). As mission statements go, this certainly knocks 'we will action new blue-sky initiatives to effectuate broader brand awareness in the East Asian meta-market' into a cocked hat.

Athletic Bilbao might not be a business concept, but they aren't just a sporting entity either. Athletic are a central part of the Basque nationalist myth, to the extent that it's hard to see where one ends and the other begins. It was ever thus. "The coincidence between the emergence of Athletic and the growing influence of the PNV in the early years of the twentieth century cannot be overestimated. Athletic Bilbao's prominence in the twenty-eight years up to the formation of a professional national league ensured that the political momentum of conservative Basque nationalism could prosper off the back of the sporting prowess of its representatives"—an example of a football club helping to prop up a political myth (Ball, *Morbo*, pp. 64–65). The interests of the PNV and Athletic's members dovetailed neatly: both groups wanted a successful Athletic and a sovereign Euskadi; many of them were in fact the same people. In a perfect demonstration of the closeness between Athletic and the PNV, the first legitimate Basque president, José Antonio Aguirre, was a former Athletic player.

The *cantera* ('quarry') policy to which Athletic's president referred, the principle of selecting only Basques, is a central pillar of the marriage of nationalism and sport, reaffirming the sense that this club is special. After all, who else but national teams make birthplace a consideration in eligibility for the shirt? As long as the Basques do not have an independent nation, with a FIFA-recognised team that can line up against (a

Basqueless) Spain as equals, Athletic is a national team by proxy, on-field ambassadors for Basque statehood.

This has posed off-field problems. Athletic have perhaps been guilty of adhering to the letter and not the spirit of the *cantera* 'law' by poaching promising youngsters from other Basque clubs, by having a rather generous definition of Basqueness, and by occasionally erasing non-Basques from the club's history. But the stakes are high. To suddenly look beyond the *cantera* would be taken as a betrayal of the club's history and identity, and therefore of the myth which the *cantera* represents. Questions might be asked about the condition of Basque nationalism if its most famous symbol (we'll glide diplomatically over ETA) started flinging open hatches battened down for generations. The myth is too important to be let go now, and given the long and ongoing struggle to preserve the Basque identity—of which Athletic is just a small part—you can understand why. The myth is ultimately even more important than the club.

The Fragrant Privies of Barcelona

In his superb *Morbo*, Phil Ball also considers the FC Barcelona myth, beginning with their famous slogan "*més que un club* [more than a club]," noting that Barça once ran an art competition so prestigious Dalí submitted an entry, that Pope John Paul II was a paid-up member, and that the club museum gets more annual visitors than the one dedicated to Picasso. "Most football supporters from Sidcup to Sydney now know these facts and could also tell you that Barça is the 'flagship' for Catalan nationalism. They might even add that the Dream Team that won the European Cup in 1992 was much dreamier than any other team in the history of the game and that even the toilets in the Camp Nou smell of roses" (Ball, *Morbo*, p. 81).

He exaggerates, but not by much. Barcelona is indeed taken to be a symbol of football the way it should be, both on and off the pitch. Johan Cruyff's 1992 European Cup-winning side featuring Guardiola, Stoichkov, and Romário remains to many the standard by which all other teams must be judged. (It may be that another Barcelona team, the 2009 *Tricampeones*—Xavi, Iniesta, Messi and company—now take up that mantle. This goes for club teams; in the international arena the unimpeachable paragon of footballing virtue is the Brazil of 1970.) Managers, Helenio Herrera and Louis Van Gaal among them, have been dismissed despite their success because they didn't win with sufficient panache. Fans of most clubs will tolerate any amount of dross as long as the team is winning, but not this one. Bobby Robson won the Cup Winners' Cup and the Copa del Rey and came a close second to a categorically superior Real Madrid in the league, all in his first season in charge. It was also his last season in charge. (It would be remiss not to point out that this attitude is hardly unique to Barcelona, but it is nevertheless more important to Barcelona's mythos than it is to any other team, Real Madrid included.)

Barcelona appeal to another sort of purist too. The team is owned by its members, rather than a faceless conglomerate or a dictatorial oligarch. No sponsor ever tarnished the *blaugrana* shirt until 2006, and even then the chosen logo was impeccably non-commercial: few observers could take the view that having 'UNICEF' emblazoned on the players' torsos meant Barça were selling out to the man. We can call the image of Barcelona as a football club in its most perfect form the myth of the fragrant privy.

The 'flagship-of-Catalan-nationalism, yah-boo-to-nasty-Madrid' stuff is certainly part of the myth too. Jimmy Burns, in his highly partial account of Barcelona's history (*Barça: A People's Passion*, Bloomsbury, 2000) describes the situation in suitably emotive language: "Much of Catalonia's history is a story of humiliation and frustration, its aspirations as a regional power curbed and stamped upon by the centralising tendencies of Madrid . . . Only at the beginning of the twentieth century did the formation of FC Barcelona by a group of enterprising Swiss and Englishmen bring into being the perfect vehicle for galvanising local pride." Then he really hits his mythopoeic stride. "Whenever Madrid tried to impose itself, Barça drew its people deep into its bosom, offering protection like a medieval castle whose surrounding village is threatened by siege. Barça's . . . is a history reinvented again and again to the level of mythology, demigods fuelled by exaggeration and by propaganda, played out by symbols, heroes and villains, demigods and devils . . . While Real Madrid became, in Catalan eyes, a symbol of dictatorship and the enforced unity of Spain, Barça was transformed into more than a club, a world in which people discovered a crude sense of what it is to feel Catalan, with loyalty and emotion" (pp. 9–10). In this passage, like the book generally, there is little mention of pro-unity Catalans, or anti-Barça Catalans (or of their football team, RCD Espanyol). Barça players, the myth trumpets, are ambassadors for their homeland. There is no room in the myth of '*mès que un club*' that FC Barcelona might not represent all Catalonia, or might in fact, at least to some, be no more than a club.

The reason this myth, a national myth for Catalonia, is important today has more to do with football than with nationalism. Catalonia

versus Castille is a crucial element of the Barça-Real rivalry, which is ran-
corous and often ugly, as you would expect from Spain's two most historically successful teams. But the nationhood question for the Catalans
today is not nearly so vexed as for the Basques. Many Barcelona players
are products of the youth team, but this reflects more on the club's footballing philosophy than any latent Catalanism. Many of Barcelona's
greatest players—Cruyff, Kubala, Rivaldo—have been foreigners, welcomed unstintingly by the club. Either Catalan nationalism is peculiarly
inclusive, or it is constructed less on territorial or ethnic grounds than on
cultural ones (in which case the very term 'nationalism' might be unsuit-
able). Or, as Phil Ball suggests, "Catalan nationalism is more about holding Madrid to as much ransom as possible . . . Calls for independence
are not canny enough for the people of this region. They have plenty of
autonomy, thank you, and know better than the Basques how to exploit
it" (Ball, *Morbo*, p. 82). Either way, the football myth has a political element, not the other way round.

When Pepe Samitier died in 1972, fans offered him the sort of tributes
normally reserved for flower-of-youth royalty. The fact that Samitier was
openly pro-Franco was overlooked: he was also very loyal to Barcelona,
and the success he represented as a Barça player was more important
than a detail like his political opinions. Samitier was Barça, and Barça is
more important than politics. Athletic is not. Hard as it is to imagine a
Francoist Athletic player, it is harder still to imagine one who the supporters would venerate like Barça venerated 'El Sami'. Unlike in Bilbao,
in Barcelona the myth of the club (the '*més que un club*,' the 'fragrant
privy') comes first and the myth of a Catalan nation a distant second.

Escapism and Victory

Our final example, alluded to in the first paragraph, is the 'Death Match'
between FC Start and a *Luftwaffe* team that took place in Ukraine in
1942. "No game," Jonathan Wilson declares, and he would know, "has
ever been so submerged in myth and counter-myth" (*Curtain*, p. 11). FC
Start was a scratch team put together by several Dynamo Kyiv players
who after the outbreak of war had found themselves working in a bak-
ery. They beat all opponents, often handsomely, and as word spread
their feats became symbolically important to a population suffering Nazi
occupation.

After Start had established their reputation, a team called Flakelf representing the *Luftwaffe* challenged them to a game (why Flakelf thought
they might win against a team filled with professionals is unclear; maybe

the potential repercussions of defeat didn't occur to anyone and they just fancied playing a top side). Start won 5–0. A rematch was arranged, which Start won 5–3 despite blatant violence from the German airmen, overlooked by the SS referee. Soon after the game, the Ukrainian players were interrogated, tortured and sent to the Syrets prison camp, where many of them died. The symbolism, which would have been enormous anyway ('the German military is beatable'), took on mythic proportions with the players' martyrdoms.

After the war this became 'official' Soviet myth, with mythic embellishments. Galeano, as so often, can be relied upon to give both the most mythical and also the best-written of all versions: "In the end they could not resist the temptation of dignity. When the game was over all eleven were shot with their shirts on at the edge of a cliff" (*Sun and Shadow*, p. 32). Wilson, equally typically, offers the best analysis: "The myth may have been better known than the truth, but the effect was the same: Dynamo became a rallying point in the darkest days of occupation, and, at least until fragmentation, retained a patriotic value as the team of all Ukraine" (*Curtain*, p. 12).

I Play Therefore I Am

Myths are contagious and adaptable. They flow from society to football and back again, whether they have emerged unbidden from the streets or been concocted in a smoke-filled room, whether they begin in a historical memory or in a famous kick. Puskas's against England in 1953, Werner Liebrich's against Puskas's ankle in 1954, Zvonimir Boban's against a policeman in 1990. This was at Dinamo Zagreb v Red Star Belgrade at the Maksimir; riots began inside the stadium, then outside, and within months Yugoslavia was ripping itself apart. Wars of independence, the most violent expressions of national identity, must by their nature have mythic beginnings. Outside the Maksimir today there is a statue and a plaque that reads "To the fans of this club, who started the war with Serbia at this ground on 13th May 1990." Other examples are legion.

This is the nature of human society, and also of football. Myth, what people believe, is more important to a constructed social reality than what is actually true. While no one can understand football from myths alone—the clash of contradictions would leave you as stranded as helplessly as a fullback caught eighty yards out of position with his shorts down—no-one can understand it armed simply with a record of the facts either. The Aranycsapat won nothing, an Olympics aside, so in a factual sense they are no more important than any other defeated World Cup finalists, Czechoslovakia in 1962 for instance. And who remembers them? Athletic Bilbao limiting their pool of players to their back yard alone? Madness. Start v Flakelf? It was only a friendly, what's all the fuss about?

The same is true of history. The taking of the Bastille was militarily insignificant for the French Revolution, but to ignore it for this reason (as some historians have) is inadmissible given its mythic, ogreish importance to the Parisians of 1789. Anyone wishing to make sense of the French Revolution has to make sense of the myth of the Bastille, while being aware of the empirical record of events. And anyone wishing to make sense of this sport has to understand this relationship between truth and myth, between the facts and figures in Rothmans Football Yearbook on one hand and the legends that emerge from behind them on the other, and our inescapable need, as human beings, as football fans, for both.

I'll leave the final word to Eduardo Galeano (*Sun and Shadow*, pp. 204–05):

An astonishing void: official history ignores football. Contemporary history texts fail to mention it, even in passing, in countries where it has been and continues to be a primordial symbol of collective identity. I play therefore I am: a style of play is a way of being that reveals the unique profile of each community and affirms its right to be different. Tell me how you play and I'll tell you who you are.

21

Barça's Treble or: How I Learned to Stop Worrying and Love the Heat

A. MINH NGUYEN

What makes a team great? An obvious answer is winning lots of trophies. But why do some teams win trophies while others do not?

Luck? But it's hard to be consistently lucky if the team lacks talent. Talent? Many teams have talent, but not all of them win because they lack discipline. Discipline? Many teams have discipline, but not all of them win because they lack experience. Experience? Many teams have experience, but not all of them win because they lack chemistry. Chemistry? Many teams have chemistry, but not all of them win because they lack a good game plan. A good game plan? Many teams have a good game plan, but not all of them win because, though well-coached, the players are not talented, disciplined, experienced, or compatible enough to execute the plan. A great team requires a critical cluster of all these things. Without such a cluster, it's unlikely to be successful, let alone great. To this list, I'd like to add passion, that special power of the heart that enables us to stand the heat and show our true worth. In many cases, what really separates the great from the good is passion.

Take, for instance, FC Barcelona's 2008–09 season. At the end of the campaign, they became *tricampeones*. The first club in Spain to win La Liga, the Copa del Rey, and the UEFA Champions League in the same season. In the annals of European club soccer, only four other teams had accomplished this treble-winning feat: Glasgow Celtic (1967), Ajax Amsterdam (1972), PSV Eindhoven (1988), and Manchester United (1999). Barcelona's *gran triplete* would not have come to be except that passion had revitalized a talented but underachieving squad and empowered them to reach the pinnacle of the game.

Logic of the Heart

A strong feeling. A powerful emotion. An object of such feeling. An outburst of such emotion. All these are passions. Passion is primarily the condition of feeling so intensely about some entity that it is poised to influence our mind and behaviour. The feeling is so intense that the motivational matrix which animates it dominates one's will and makes the will suffer and submit.

Passion is an inclination to respond to certain stimuli in certain ways. Neither the stimuli nor the responses have to be external or physical. Either can be internal and mental. Hristo Stoichkov has a passion for the game. This player-turned-coach from the Balkans would feel and act in certain ways in certain situations. A goal by Bulgaria or Barcelona would elicit cheers from him while the recall of a penalty miss would cause him anguish.

Passion is a dispositional rather than an occurrent mental state. What is the difference between mental dispositions and mental occurrences? Consider the sentence "Stoichkov has a passion for soccer." This ascription of a mental disposition can be true even if, at the time it is uttered, he is deeply asleep, hypnotized, anaesthetized, fainting, or comatose. The ascription can be true even if, at the time it is uttered, he is not feeling, sensing, thinking, saying, or doing a thing about soccer. This is the kind of case where the passion is there but not all there. The passion is present but doesn't work its magic in consciousness or manifest its power in behaviour, because the person involved is preoccupied, nonwakeful, or unconscious. When we ascribe a mental disposition such as hope or fear to a subject, or a physical disposition such as fragility or solubility to an object, our dispositional ascription is not a claim about anything that is happening at the time, but rather a claim about what would happen if certain conditions were met. Like other mental dispositions such as belief and desire, passion is capable of manifesting itself in many ways and over a span of time. Typically, beliefs and desires don't just come and go. They stick around, evincing themselves in our thoughts and actions. We don't lose beliefs or desires in our sleep and regain the very same ones while eating breakfast. The same is true of passion.

In contrast with mental dispositions, mental occurrences are transient events. Mental occurrences are so called because they occur at some particular moment in a person's mental life. Suppose you watch the televised final of the 2006 FIFA World Cup on that hot July day. You are thirsty. You reach for your chilled bottle of Heineken. You enjoy its smooth and easy flavor. You smell French fries and pizza and ask for some. You hear the fans cheering and chanting and you get into the act yourself. You see Zinedine Zidane head-butting Marco Materazzi. You can hardly believe it. You play that image in your mind. You feel confused and dejected. You remember Zidane stomping on a player in a 1998 World Cup match. You recall his brace of headers against Brazil in that World Cup final. You think the head-butt is a disgrace. All these are mental occurrences: the sensations, perceptions, recollections, mental images, felt emotions, and conscious thoughts. They can be successive, overlapping, or simultaneous.

While mental occurrences differ from mental dispositions, they interact with each other in a number of ways. Here are two of them. First, a mental occurrence can play a role in the formation of a mental disposition. My perception of Zidane's head-butt led to my belief about it. A mental occurrence, my perception, serviced the construction of a mental disposition, my belief. Second, a mental disposition can manifest itself not only in a piece of behaviour but also in a mental occurrence. There are occasions in which Stoichkov possesses a passion for soccer not just dispositionally but occurrently too. When he goes onto the pitch hungry for an early goal or runs back and forth shouting orders to his troops, feelings and thoughts about soccer are present to his consciousness. They come to the forefront of his mind. Compared with the mental disposition which they manifest, these mental occurrences are short-lived. They pass away not long after the match or the training session when Stoichkov turns his mind to something else. His passion for the game persists, which is not to suggest that it lasts forever or remains unchanged. People fall in and out of love all the time. Even when love endures, it may be more or less intense.

Intensity characterizes passion. A passion lacking intensity is an impossibility, just as a hardworking slouch is an impossibility. The intensity of feeling and emotion seldom, if ever, admits of mathematically precise determination. It isn't the sort of thing whose instances can be numerically measured, especially on a uniform scale. What number do you put on Paolo Maldini's commitment to AC Milan? What quantity do you assign to Raúl González's love for Real Madrid? We can't quantify such things. In spite of this, and in spite of the fact that there are different types of intensity just as there are different types of passion (sensual, intellectual, moral, political, spiritual, aesthetic, work-related, play-related), we often make qualitative judgments, including qualitative comparative judgments, about passions. The statement that Stoichkov's passion for soccer is more intense than his passion for mahjong is truth-assessable; one can assess whether it is true or false. The lack of precision and certainty with regard to the intensity of feeling and emotion is therefore not much of a hindrance to our understanding of ourselves or of others.

Due to its intensity, passion not only affects our decisions but also drives our lives. All passions are powerful feelings that are poised to move a person to action, including mental action. If I have a passion for soccer, then some of my thoughts and actions are directed at soccer. I think about it, read about it, talk about it, watch a program about it, write an article about it, etc. One would be hard-pressed to find a person passionate about soccer yet disinclined to think or do anything soccer-related even when she has the time and resources to do so and possesses no overriding desires.

We are often advised not to underestimate the power of passion. As Goethe put it, "passions are vices or virtues to their highest powers." What are the positive aspects of the power of passion? Some claim that passion is necessary for success or, what is more elusive, greatness. Others claim that it is sufficient. Still others claim that it is both. Does success require passion? Does passion ensure success? It is possible to succeed without really trying; people who are lucky or unethical may rise to the top without being passionate. Conversely, even the most passionate effort may not secure success. At least this is true of sporting success from a silverware point of view. Suppose every player on your team is passionate about a certain cup. Throughout the season everyone has shown commitment to achieving this goal. Does that mean that you and your teammates will lift the trophy? Not necessarily. What if the other teams are just too good? What if your team lacks good fortune, talent, discipline, experience, chemistry, leadership, followership, etc? Like passion, none of these last items is necessary for success. If a team lacks a critical cluster of them, however, it's unlikely to succeed.

Although passion is neither necessary nor sufficient for success, the positive aspects of passion enhance the chance of success. Passion enables us to engage the world with determination and purpose, and to do our best to give a good account of ourselves. This is just a special case of the widely endorsed thesis of the causal efficacy of the mental: something going on in your mind can cause you to behave in a certain way. Belief and desire, hate and love, by influencing people's actions, can have effects in the physical world. The potency of passion thus consists in its causal efficacy or its capacity to generate an effect.

When we claim that passion enhances the chance of success, we attribute to passion a causal power—the power to bring about success. According to the probabilistic theory of causation, event C caused event

E just in case the occurrence of *C* raised the probability of the occurrence of *E*. Causes raise the probabilities of their effects. Zidane's head-butt caused his ejection from the final because the former raised the probability of the latter.

Barcelona's treble demonstrates that passion reinvigorated a gifted but underachieving squad and transformed them into one of the greatest teams in the history of the game. The build-up to the second *clásico* of the 2008–09 season and its aftermath is a case in point.

Barça'ing up the Wrong Tree

On May 2nd, 2009, Estadio Santiago Bernabéu witnessed the greatest *clásico* ever. Virtually everyone had considered Real Madrid the favorites. They would play at home. They would have fresher legs thanks to a whirlwind of kicks and tackles which Chelsea had unleashed midweek against Barcelona in a Champions League semi-final encounter that Chelsea manager Guus Hiddink had glorified as "a man's match." They were all fired up. Since the corresponding fixture nineteen games ago, they had won all their matches in La Liga except the 1–1 draw against Atlético Madrid. A defeat would mean a season without silverware. A victory would cut the gap between them and the league leaders Barcelona to a single point and the momentum would propel them to another come-from-behind league title.

Meanwhile, the meltdown continued at Camp Nou. *El cagómetro*, which measured the amount of crap that Barcelona released out of fear, skyrocketed. Many attributed this to madriditis. An epidemic among *culés*, madriditis is the acute onset of paranoia in otherwise normal soccer fans in reaction to anything Real Madrid. Having played the most spectacular brand of soccer in Europe in the first nine months of the season, the *Blaugrana* had suddenly been dishing out one pedestrian display after another at the end of April. A draw against Valencia on April 25th, coupled with Real Madrid's win over Sevilla on April 26th, slashed Barcelona's once-unassailable twelve-point lead atop the league table to just four points. Three days later, a scoreless draw against Chelsea at Camp Nou in the first leg of the Champions League semi-final pushed Barcelona to the brink of elimination from Europe's premier club soccer competition.

El clásico couldn't have come at a worse time for Barcelona. The exuberance of fantasy soccer championed by the club had evaporated. Vroom and boom had surrendered to gloom and doom. Blame it on the Blues. On April 28th, Chelsea took the team bus to Camp Nou and parked it right in front of their goal. The scheme prevented Barcelona from scoring at home for the first time this season. English commentators went wild. Some hailed Chelsea's defensive masterstroke. Others celebrated their masculine virtues. Most salivated at the prospect of the second consecutive all-English Champions League final, perhaps a repeat of last year's final between Manchester United and Chelsea. The whole affair scandalized Barcelona. Immediately after the final whistle, Barcelona players and coaches rushed to the microphones to slam Hiddink's badass approach and the referee's wussy performance.

Barcelona's post-match reaction was pitiful. It took only one draw for them to panic. In his maiden season at the helm, Guardiola tried to steel his sublimely talented players with a team ethic that had been lacking in the twilight years of the Rijkaard-Ronaldinho era—an ethic based on unity, commitment, humility, and hard work. The post-match reaction cast doubt on whether Guardiola had succeeded. A sign of entitlement mentality, Barcelona's constant rant about officiating and "anti-football" grated on many fans and pundits, who wanted to think of their heroes as gutsy and hardy. Not in their wildest imagination could they conceive that the Pride of Catalonia comprised such prima donnas and drama queens more interested in "exchanging pretty pitter-pat passes" than fighting it out against "the nasty men from Chelsea," to quote Des Kelly of *The Daily Mail*. For all the valentines that they had received for their balletic performances, Pep Guardiola's team had not won anything yet. They were not in the same league as Frank Rijkaard's team of 2006, let alone Johan Cruyff's Dream Team of the early 1990s. In light of their friability, an apter object of comparison was the Bayer Leverkusen team of 2002, who not only blew the chance to win a treble but also managed to finish the season trophyless. During a fortnight, Michael Ballack and company completed a hat-trick of collapses and earned the nickname of "Neverkusen." They lost 2–1 to Real Madrid in the Champions League final, lost 4–2 to Schalke 04 in the German Cup final, and lost their five-point lead atop the league table with three games to go to allow Borussia Dortmund to pip them to the Bundesliga title.

Barcelona's breakneck schedule, together with injury and fatigue, constituted yet another reason why the odds were stacked in favor of their domestic rivals, who enjoyed the luxury of not having to worry about the Champions League or the Copa del Rey. Barcelona had been scheduled to play four games against top-notch opponents over a span of eleven days, whereas only two had been lined up for Real Madrid over the same period. To make matters worse, the scheduling gods had sandwiched *el clásico* between the two legs of the Champions League semi-final. Consequently, the goalless draw at Camp Nou in the first leg conspired with the imminent visits to Santiago Bernabéu and Stamford Bridge to increase the pressure on Barcelona. The *Blaugrana* had to decide whether to focus on the Whites or the Blues. They had to choose between the Spanish League and the Champions League. Failure to do so would set off a double disaster—nay—a treble tragedy *à la* Neverkusen (Barcelona had already clinched their place in the King's Cup final on March 4th).

Barcelona's disunited front did not inspire confidence. Lionel Messi preferred beating Chelsea over Real Madrid. Barcelona would still be the league leaders regardless of what happened at Santiago Bernabéu, whereas a victory for the hosts at Stamford Bridge would signal the end of their European campaign. An argument of impeccable logic indeed! Except that a loss to Real Madrid would shake Barcelona to their foundations. It would seal their fate not only in La Liga but also in the Champions League and the Copa del Rey. Contrary to Messi's stance, Barcelona captain Carles Puyol and his deputy Xavi Hernández rated Real Madrid as enemies number one. For true-blue Catalans like them, *el clásico* is more than a soccer match. Barcelona symbolize everything Catalan, from history and language to culture and traditions. Barcelona embody the spirit of Catalan autonomy and the resistance to Castilian hegemony. A win for Barça is a win for Catalunya. What a vein of noble sentiment! Except that their multidirectional campaign would end up in tears if Barcelona went all-in and lost. Faced with opposites, the players needed guidance. None was forthcoming because Guardiola was busy playing Hamlet. The day before the big day, this former law student and self-styled pessimist revealed that he was still debating whether to rotate his players for *el clásico* with a view to the second leg of the Champions League semi-final.

What's Love Got to Do with It?

There was much to say in favor of the above analysis. But its proponents overlooked an important point. Passion is not enough to guarantee success. True, but passion increases the likelihood of success. Passion helps us focus on the importance of what we care about, gives us the energy to act with resolve, and impels us to find ways to achieve all that we can achieve. While Real Madrid were the in-form side in the *Primera División* at the moment, form alone was not a reliable indicator of victory in *el clásico*. Passion played a key role too. The linguo-cultural and socio-political elements underlining this fixture always aroused passion. Despite recent setbacks, neither Guardiola nor his players could justly be accused of lacking passion. Indeed, this Catalan-born Catalan-bred Catalan-trained Catalan-proud ballboy-turned-waterboy-turned-player-turned-captain-turned-coach was passion incarnate. Here is Jimmy Burns's portrait of the coach as a young man in *Barça: A People's Passion* (Bloomsbury, 2000):

> The earliest and clearest image a lot of *culés* have of Guardiola is of a skinny, unshaven waterboy running out from the touch-line and embracing Pichi Alonso the night Venables's team qualified for the European Cup final. Guardiola had broken the rules but claimed afterwards that he had acted just like any fan who happens to be there at a sublime moment of victory.

The year was 1986 and Guardiola was fifteen. Here is Burns's description of the coach the day after the Dream Team had won the European Cup:

> Later, the team took their latest trophy to the Plaça Sant Jaume, showing it separately from the balconies of both the Generalitat and the City Hall. It was left to Guardiola, however, to touch the real emotional nerve of the gathering. He paraphrased the historic words of the Catalan President Josep Tarradellas on his return from exile after Franco's death—"Citizens of Catalonia, I am here!"—declaring, "*Ciutadans de Catalunya, ja la tenim aquí*! [Citizens of Catalonia, you have it here!]"

The year was 1992 and Guardiola was twenty-one.

What about now? Consider the following testimony given by Xavi in an interview with the news agency EFE:

> Guardiola transmits his passion and is so enthusiastic. If he believes something is white and you think it is black, you will end up believing that it is white. He is a very intelligent person and I think that is his secret. It is how he convinces and motivates you and treats the best players in the team. He always says that if you think about the club first then you will not make any mistakes. He is very meticulous, a perfectionist and he sees the game like nobody else. He can tell you two things, a couple of details and he need not say anything more all week. We have all felt part of things since preseason. We now battle back in games. Now the team has great professionalism and commitment. Things are better than ever.

Guardiola's passion and enthusiasm were infectious just as his conviction and dedication were profound. The Catalan-rooted coach reminded Xavi and his teammates of what it meant to play for Barça, an institution whose motto was "more than a club" and whose anthem celebrated unity in diversity. Through him, they renewed their commitment to Barça. Guardiola's passionate temperament and keen intellect, together with his Barça-first ethos and charismatic civility, helped explain several facts: why he had been commissioned to replace Rijkaard even though he had had no first-team coaching experience; why having learned soccer at the feet of Cruyff, he had been leading with an acute awareness of and respect for the club culture; and why Barça had been enjoying a superb campaign after having gone sapless, mirthless, gutless, feckless, rudderless, and trophyless for the last two seasons.

At the beginning of his tenure, Guardiola drew up a team strategy and a code of conduct. All members of the squad were required to adhere to them. The code of conduct had been implemented to ensure that all players behaved even when they were off the pitch. No more star treatment. No more slap on the wrist. The team strategy consists of two elements: possession and pressure. A possession game requires the team to win, maintain, and recover possession. A pressure game requires the team to play high, suffocate the opposition, and offer them no way out. Typically realized in an ultra-offensive 4–3–3 formation, both elements of Barcelona's game require collective effort and sacrifice. When pressuring the opposition, the players push forward *en masse*. When losing possession, the players hunt the ball *en masse*. The pressure and defense begin with the forwards. When done right, this Cruyffian strategy is highly effective. You can't score unless you have the ball. Your opponents can't score when you have the ball. By squeezing your opponents, you conserve energy. It is easier to score when you win the ball because it is closer to the opposition's goal. Barcelona players felt happy, and not just because they had been racking up points. "There is order and discipline now," said Xavi, "It's all for one; there is solidarity again."

The newly rediscovered unity and passion had produced striking results. On January 17th, 2009, the Catalan giants had notched up a record for garnering the highest total of points for the first half of a season in the *Primera División*, tallying 50 points out of a possible 57. Guardiola's side, as Sid Lowe of the *Guardian* put it, had "scored the most goals and conceded the fewest, had the most shots and allowed the fewest, suffered the most fouls and committed the fewest, enjoyed more possession, completed more passes and spent more time in the opposition penalty area than anyone else." In addition to their exploits in La Liga, they had reached the final of the Copa del Rey and were only one scoring draw away from advancing to the final of the Champions League.

Barcelona had many reasons to look forward to *el derbi español*. It was time to decide the title race. A win would practically ensure them a

La Liga crown. Buoyed by their triumph, they would edge out the home team in London for a spot in the Champions League final.

It was time to exorcise the demons of yesteryear. On June 17th, 2007, Barcelona's quest for a third consecutive league title ended. The championship was decided on the closing day of the season. Barcelona had the same point tally as Real Madrid and a superior goal difference. That proved worthless because of their inferior head-to-head record against their fierce challengers. On May 7th, 2008, Rijkaard's men had to form a *pasillo* or guard of honor to welcome their nemeses onto the pitch. Ashen-faced and visibly shaken, they stood and applauded the newly crowned league champions while the Bernabéu faithful chanted, "*Barça, cabrón! Saluda al campeón!* [Barça, you bastards! Salute the champions!]"

A title-clinching victory would put these demons to rest. Indeed, it was time to put everything else to rest: all the schadenfreude-laden and machismo-spiked yackety-yak about favorites, goalfest, madriditis, *cagómetro*, prima donnas, drama queens, pretty passes, balletic performances, breakneck schedule, relentless prep, injury, fatigue, frustration, distraction, disunity, friability, meltdown, panic, Neverkusen. After two seasons without silverware and a barrage of trash talk, Barcelona's hunger ticked like a time bomb.

The Moment of Truth

Guardiola rested no one for the biggest game of the season. The best available line-up would start. Despite falling behind as early as the thirteenth minute, Guardiola's side responded with the best performance Barcelona had ever produced. They humiliated Real Madrid with a 6–2 demolition job, with two goals each from Henry and Messi as well as one goal apiece from Puyol and Piqué. With this win, they set their own record for the most goals ever scored in a *clásico*, and achieved the largest margin of victory in an away *clásico* since 1974, when Cruyff and company had hammered the hosts 5–0. Guardiola had made a tactical change to his forward line. Instead of playing out on the right wing with license to roam infield as usual, Messi roamed freely up front with license to drift into midfield. The *Merengues*' failure to anticipate this allowed Messi to play plenty of one-twos with Xavi and Iniesta, serving up a cornucopia of scoring chances for the *Blaugrana*. "Xavi, Iniesta, and Messi can all do things with the ball and you are incapable of stopping them," Zidane declared in an interview with Canal Plus. "Even on PlayStation!" he insisted. *Diario AS* said amen. "Only in paradise can you see soccer like this," its editorial concluded.

The victory over their archrivals had given Barcelona a boost. On May 6th, 2009, Barcelona played Chelsea without three of their first-choice players: Carles Puyol, Rafael Márquez, and Thierry Henry. Chelsea drew first blood as Michael Essien smashed a left-footed volley into the top corner from twenty-five yards out just nine minutes into the game. Things went from bad to worse for Barcelona when Éric Abidal was sent off in the 66th minute. With the English hosts impenetrable, all seemed lost for the Spanish visitors as the game headed to stoppage time. It was left to Andrés Iniesta, the *anti-galáctico* from Fuentealbilla with a population of 1,846, to crack the London club's tightly packed defense. Iniesta picked up a desperate pass from Messi just outside the penalty area and fired a right-footed curling shot into the top corner to equalize the game, sending Barcelona through to the Champions League final on the away goals rule. "I can't even dream of a goal like that. I struck it with all my soul and it went in perfectly," Iniesta told Canal Plus.

On May 13th, 2009, the two most successful clubs in the Copa del Rey history faced off at Estadio de Mestalla to determine who would become the kings of the competition. Like the matches against Real Madrid and Chelsea, Barcelona conceded a goal early, thanks to a set-piece by Athletic Bilbao in the ninth minute. But it was all Barcelona from then on as they turned on the style and the goals to beat Athletic Bilbao 4–1 to win the Copa del Rey for a record twenty-fifth time. When Real Madrid lost 3–2 at Villarreal on May 16th, 2009, Barcelona's status as La Liga champions and domestic double winners was confirmed.

On May 27th, 2009, the moment had arrived for Barcelona to claim a treble. To attain that, they had to defeat a side managed by Sir Alex Ferguson. "This is the best squad I've ever had," the Scot confided to MUTV. Manchester United featured a number of the game's finest players, including Rio Ferdinand, Nemanja Vidiç, Wayne Rooney, and Cristiano Ronaldo, the last of whom had won both the European Footballer of the Year Award and the FIFA World Player of the Year Award in 2008. The English club had just won their third consecutive Premier League title. The defending champions in Europe's most prestigious club soccer tournament, they had been gunning for a double-double. The capture of both the European title and the domestic title for two consecutive seasons would ratify their claim to greatness. Ferguson had tasted greatness. In the 1998–99 campaign, he had guided Roy Keane and teammates to a treble, winning the Premier League, FA Cup, and UEFA Champions League in the same season.

Barcelona were the underdogs. Their defense was depleted. Three of their first-choice defenders would miss the Champions League final:

Rafael Márquez, Daniel Alves, and Éric Abidal. They would have to rely on the Manchester United reject Gerard Piqué and the thirty-five-year-old barely-used substitute Sylvinho playing his last game for Barcelona. To compound the problem, neither Henry nor Iniesta was fully fit. The Champions League final is a time for celebration, however. It's not a time to wallow in self-pity. According to *El Pais*, Guardiola ended the pre-match warm-up session early to show the players a seven-minute film that featured the best action from *Gladiator* and the best moves by each of the players during the season. The film concluded with a message on the screen: "We are the center of the field, we have accuracy, we have effort, we are attackers who are defending, we are defenders who are attacking, we have speed, we have the respect of our adversaries, we are each goal that we score, we are the ones who are always looking for the opponent's goal. WE ARE ONE." Guardiola then let the players enter the Stadio Olimpico in Rome without saying another word.

Barcelona withstood pressure in the first nine minutes. They went on to play assured, attacking, attractive soccer to beat Manchester United 2–0 to earn their third Champions League title and their first treble. Scoring in the tenth minute after Iniesta had played him through, Eto'o became the second player to have scored in two separate Champions League finals, the first one being Raúl. "Leaping like a salmon after peeling away from a swaying tree of a center back to head across goal and into the net in the 70th minute," as Goal.com described the action of the shortest man on the field, Messi validated his reputation as the best player in the world. In a triumphant display of the *cantera* system, seven graduates of the youth academy at Barcelona had appeared in their starting line-up, including the creator of the first goal Iniesta, the creator of the second goal and the official man of the match Xavi, plus the scorer of the second goal and the player of the tournament Messi.

The final score belied the fact that this was the most lopsided Champions League final since Fabio Capello's AC Milan had thrashed Johan Cruyff's Barcelona 4–0 at the Olympic Stadium in Athens in 1994. Anchoring the midfield for the Dream Team in that match had been the twenty-three-year-old Pep Guardiola. The emphatic victory over the mighty defending champions prompted a number of soccer luminaries to judge the current Barcelona team superior to the Dream Team. "We are not the best team in history but we have played the best season in history," said the youngest treble-winning coach and the youngest coach ever to guide a team to Champions League glory.

Barcelona's 2008–09 campaign demonstrates the potency of passion. Here was a talented but underachieving squad under the guidance of an inexperienced but dedicated coach. By virtue of his tireless industry and wise management, the coach succeeded in heating up the team. The players trained with conviction and played with resolve. Forging partnerships grounded in the club-first ethos, they pushed themselves to the limit and achieved all that they could achieve in a season—a treble. Passion empowered a side otherwise destined for failure to become one of the greatest teams in the history of the game.[1]

---

[1] Before this book went to press, Barcelona had already become the first team ever to accomplish the sextuple in a single calendar year, having won after the treble the 2009 Supercopa de España against Athletic Bilbao (5–1 on aggregate), the 2009 UEFA Super Cup against FC Shakhtar Donetsk (1–0), and the 2009 FIFA Club World Cup against Estudiantes (2–1 after extra time).

I would like to acknowledge the generous assistance of Michelle Benningfield, Todd Gooch, Kara Lairson, Tyler Nighswander, Steve Parchment, Rob Sica, and Abraham Velez during the preparation of this chapter. Special thanks to Nhi Huynh and Ted Richards for their understanding and support.

22

A 'Messi' Way of Life

CAMILO OLAYA, NELSON LAMMOGLIA,
and ROBERTO ZARAMA

> Football is a whole skill to itself. A whole world. A whole universe to itself.
> Me love it because you have to be skillful to play it! Freedom! Football is
> freedom.
>
> —BOB MARLEY (*Bob Marley Magazine*, 1979)

We all remember June 22nd, 1986. Estadio Azteca in Mexico City. Argentina v England. Diego Armando Maradona scored two of the most legendary goals in football history. The infamous "Hand of God" goal and, three minutes later, the goal that was voted as the Goal of the Century in 2002. (Kirk McDermid compares these two goals in depth in Chapter 7.) These goals triggered discussions about tactics, rules, referees, ethics, and instant replays. But we also enjoyed the game. It was a celebration of emotions. This game and those goals present an opportunity to reflect on why we love football and life.

Football Philosophies

That historic match reflects the striking difference between two styles of playing football, which was summarized in the FIFA Official Report:

> A contrast in styles provided a fascinating contest: England, playing with a classic 4–4–2, tried to launch their two forwards Lineker and Beardsley in most cases with long passes. As both strikers were marked closely by Ruggeri and Cuciuffo, they could hardly ever be brought into play. By way of contrast, Argentina played a system that was much more variable: In front of the English goal, Valdano, Burruchaga, and Maradona, being freed from a special role, constantly changed their positions. (FIFA World Cup, *Mexico 1986 Official Report*, p. 53)

In these different styles of play, we recognize two broad football traditions. We can label these styles "philosophies" of football. The first school would be the "European philosophy". We all know its characteristics: discipline, highly organized, fast pace, swift attacks based on few touches of the ball, efficiency, long and effective passes, little improvisation by players, preservation of schemas and shapes, collective tactics prevailing over individual play. Essentially, the departure points of this school are teamwork and cooperation. Of course, there is also space for individual talent; but in this philosophy, society is more than the individual. Since a match is a contest between societies, a football game resembles a chess match in which tactics, strategies, collective moves, flanks, and so on, drive understanding. Plans are required to achieve success. The prominence of the coach is a natural feature. This is the terrain of theories, schemas, anti-schemas, instructions, roles, and blackboards. It is the preferred topic for football experts—including TV commentators, the great specialists of "knowledge" of the game. This philosophy, then, favors order, planning, authority, the rule of the coach, the superiority of the team, and the power of collective action.

The "South-American philosophy" is almost the complete opposite. It is immediately recognized because of its short passes, spontaneity, possession-oriented play, slow-pace, free-style moves, dribbling, emphasis on individuality, and flexible positions. This philosophy rewards talent and creativity and points to the prominent role of the individual in breaking collective schemas—even that of his very own team! The individual seems to have some liberty to think and act independently about his own team plans, organization, or tactics. The individual player sometimes makes what he thinks is the best choice, regardless of what the coach says. Now and then, as a solitary warrior, he forgets what was agreed upon in training and faces the adversary, the defensive block or even the entire opposing team, by himself. Meanwhile, the coach suffers and screams. We usually watch these heroic tales on the highlights of sport shows. It is the triumph of the individual over the collective. It is the prominence of individual innovation. Of course, there are game plans, but often these are not the first plan. This philosophy favors liberty—liberty of the player from the coach's plans, liberty of thought, liberty of ideas, liberty of tastes and pursuits.

The Player versus the Team

A big question, as we football fans know, then arises. Which philosophy is better? Consider the statement of a very disappointed Cristiano

Ronaldo after losing 0–2 against Barcelona FC in the 2009 Champions League Final: "This is the biggest disappointment of my career . . . I'm always confident in my own ability and confident that we can win whenever we play, which makes it even more disappointing. . . . We didn't do well, the tactics were not good and everything went wrong" (*Daily Mirror Online*, May 28th, 2009). Ronaldo blamed the gameplan. He blamed Sir Alex Ferguson's choice of players and formation. Is Ronaldo right? Was the problem that tactics overrode the power of individuality? Should individual talent be first? Or must the team come first? Or can both philosophies be applied by a single squad?

Although there are no "pure" teams (there is no hundred percent European -tyle team; there is no hundred percent South American style team), and although it is evident that we are aggregating in two broad schemas a diversity of styles, football squads can be located in particular points across the continuum between these two "schools," with tendencies to one of the two extremes. In some teams, the power of the individual prevails. In other teams, it is the very team that prevails; the team is composed of eleven unknown warriors. If we could choose between these two schools, what would be our first choice? Should individuality come first? Or should the team? This tension exemplifies an age-old problem addressed in philosophy: the struggle between Liberty and Authority.

Two Types of Rules

The British philosopher John Stuart Mill is notorious for having addressed this struggle, specifically in a famous essay entitled *On Liberty*. He explored "the nature and limits of the power which can be legitimately exercised by society over the individual" (*On Liberty*, University of Adelaide Library, eBooks@Adelaide). This statement highlights everyday questions from the perspective of the individual. What are the limits of my actions? What if I disagree with prevalent customs? What about rules of conduct, traditions, ideologies, or religion? What if I disagree with almost everybody else on a particular issue; and vice versa? What should be the scope of interference of society into my own affairs? It is not hard to imagine that some rules are necessary. We human beings are not saints. Some rules of conduct are imposed by necessity. Mill recognizes two types of rules: by law, and by opinion on many things that do not depend on the operation of law.

In football, this distinction between *rules of law* and *rules of opinion* is easy to see. In any game we can recognize similar types of rules that a player faces. On the one hand, there are the rules according to FIFA:

"The Laws of the Game." Let's call this "the rules of law." For example, a player cannot touch the ball with his hand unless he is the goalie. On the other hand, we have the rules of our own team, the rules of the coach. If I am a striker and there is a corner, I know exactly in which part of the field I should be and what I should do, at least according to the opinion of the coach. Let's call these rules "rules of opinion."

Football is a game where players can break both types of rules.

Freedom from the Rules of Opinion

Mill examined the control that society should exert over the individual. His position is summarized in what has been called the *harm principle,* which states that the only valid reason to exercise power over any individual is to prevent harm to others. Mill rejected other restrictions of liberty. He rejected, for instance, the notion that an individual should be obligated to act based on morality or based on the opinions of others just because to do so is believed to be wise, or even right. He also rejected restrictions based on paternalistic reasons because others believe it will make him happier. Mill believed that we are entitled to liberty:

> Liberty of thought and feeling; absolute freedom of opinion and sentiment on all subjects, practical or speculative, scientific, moral, or theological. . . . Liberty of expressing and publishing opinions. . . . Liberty of tastes and pursuits; of framing the plan of our life to suit our own character; of doing as we like, subject to such consequences as may follow. . . . No society in which these liberties are not, on the whole, respected, is free. (*On Liberty*, Chapter 1)

Mill especially rejected the imposition of prevailing opinion and the tendency of society to impose its own ideas and practices as rules of conduct on those who dissent from them. He called this propensity *the tyranny of the majority.* For Mill, as long as the individual does not harm anybody else then he is free to act upon his own opinions.

Breaking the Rules of Opinion:
A Football Dilemma

What about football? The coach designs the gameplan; that's what training sessions are for. There are several issues to define. For instance, what's the best formation for the next game? Should we switch from our secure 4–2–2–2 to 4–2–3–1? How should we defend, man-to-man or zone defense? The coach usually makes these decisions. If he follows the European philosophy of football, then the team comes first. Always "pass and move" is a likely dogma in his trainings. Imagine now a game in which one of his players receives the ball in the midfield. According to the coach, he should always "pass and move." But what if the player has a different idea? What if he thinks that he can dribble past his next opponent? Should he go against the coach's orders? Should he go against the team's plan and take a risk? Should he follow—instead—what he feels is right? Is he free to follow his own instincts? The European philosophy would advise: "Do as the team expects you to do; follow the plan. Make the easiest play." The South-American philosophy would advise: "Follow your instincts. Play your own way."

The dilemma between these philosophies is not easy to resolve. If we examine football history there are close ties between the two approaches. We could compare results generated by both schools of thought. European teams and South American teams have each won nine World Cups. If we count the old Intercontinental Cup and the current FIFA Club World Cup, South America has taken slightly more titles: twenty-five to Europe's twenty-three. The history of football is full of moments that favor either one school or the other.

An example of the power of societies is the "Miracle of Bern" in the 1954 World Cup final when eleven amateur Germans defeated the "Mighty Magyars" led by individual legends like Puskas and Kocsis. But the German coach, Sepp Herberger, became a legend. FIFA labels him as,

> the football strategist par excellence. . . . His teams were superbly prepared, bristling with stamina, strength, discipline and fighting spirit. . . . Of all these attributes, interpersonal restraint was the most important, as he believed a side must be primarily functional as a group of people. He lived by his motto, *'You have to be 11 friends.'* (FIFA, *Sepp Herberger Biography*, Classic Football FIFA Website <www.fifa.com/ classicfootball/coaches/coach= 61547/bio.html>)

Similar stories exist. These are the cases where the "European philosophy" scores.

But there are also other myths that award the triumph of the player over the team. Perhaps the best example is the 1986 World Cup, which is seen by many people as the triumph of one man: Maradona. His second goal in the quarterfinals against England, the "Goal of the Century," celebrates the power of the individual over the opponent and over his own team plans. He took the ball inside his own half, and made a sixty-meter, ten-second run, during which he passed five English players and dribbled around the goalie to score; bringing the tally to 2–0 for Argentina. It was a goal that every football player dreams of. It was a football tribute to human genius.

Which path should be preferred, if any at all? The "Miracle of Bern" or Maradona? The coach or the player? Are there any reasons to justify the breaking of the rules of opinion by any individual?

Choice and the Triumph of the Human Character

Mill recognizes that liberty brings the possibility of brilliance. For him, genius can only grow in an atmosphere of freedom. Here Mill seems to refer to football, but that is not the case. He is referring to human life: genius is *originality* in thought and action. Similar to the way in which a player decides to create new things based on his own thoughts and through his own actions, we, as human beings, can bring creativity, innovation, and surprise to our daily lives by ignoring opinions, by ignoring traditions, by ignoring "conventional wisdom." We can, and perhaps should, challenge customs. Why? The creation of new paths relies on the power of *choice*. Mill emphasized that human faculties such as perception, judgment, discriminative feeling, mental activity, and even moral preference, are exercised only in making choices. To do something just because it is the custom is to make no choice.

Mill questioned the deficiency of personal impulses and preferences with the expression *collective mediocrity*, which is what we get when public opinion rules. For him, in such a situation it is even more imperative that exceptional individuals should be encouraged to act differently from the mass. Furthermore, Mill defended the intrinsic value of individuality, which he considered equivalent to *development* and one of the essentials of well-being. Ultimately, Mill suggests that individuality leads to happiness. Human character is developed through choice.

If we agree with Mill, then liberty promotes better human beings. This liberty allows us to enjoy the second goal of Maradona, the Goal of the Century, a monument to instinct. It is the rise of creativity, the victory of human character, the celebration of the act of choosing. Coming back to the dilemma between the European and the South American philosophies, the latter one now seems preferable: the supremacy of liberty and freedom of action. It applies not only for football but also for living a happy life. This seems an easy first-choice. But, is it really so?

Fair Play?

A possible problem with Mill's position is that absolute freedom, with no direct harm to others, might nonetheless be offensive. Mill implicitly suggests a type of *offense principle*. This is an additional restriction on liberty: individual liberty can be reasonably limited to prevent offensive behavior. Although by breaking the rules of the coach, the rules of opinion, Maradona allowed us to enjoy the Goal of the Century, it is also true that this was possible because the other players obeyed the rules of law. If an English player had fouled Maradona, then the story would have been different. But it was this respect for the rules of law that opened the space for the wonderful play. But what if the rules of law are also broken?

Let's consider now the other goal of Maradona, the infamous "Hand of God" goal, which seems to challenge our preference for liberty. Such a goal seems to represent a violation of the "offense principle." This goal not only broke rules of opinion, it also broke a rule of the game, a rule of law. Argentina won that game, and later on the World Cup, because of *both* goals. Can we accept this result? And is this outcome related to football at all?

Football Is Primarily Watched and Played by Human Beings

The "Hand of God" goal represents everything that football is. It encapsulates the human nature of football and how it is rooted in our lives, in our human experience. It reminds us that the game of football is loaded with the entire spectrum of human emotions; not only the nice ones, but also the darkest ones. Life is not only comedy. It is also drama, and in a few cases it comes with shame and resignation.

For football fans, our first lessons about emotions probably come from the game. Football teaches us what our parents sometimes fail to address. Football teaches us to love. It also teaches us the thin line between ends and the means that we use to achieve them. We become linked to football from a very early age. We grow up listening to our parents talking about that single and majestic chance that they had when they went to the stadium and watched Pelé and Brazil's national football team. It was the time when they were able to see yellow butterflies flying in the sky around the stars. For us, for the fans, football and life become the very same thing. We are born in a football field carrying a ball.

Just as no one chooses to be born in a particular country or chooses her name, no one chooses his beloved football team. It seems that we become fans of our teams on the very same days we are baptized. Life and football develop side by side. And life comes with emotions. Since the beginning, football fans learn that a single whistle may be, at the same time, one of the most joyful experiences for some and one of the saddest experiences for others. Through football, we learn how short and how long a minute can be. We learn to suffer. We learn to rejoice. All of this happens because football is an emotional compromise.

Every single person who has been to a stadium knows that football is, above all, an emotional experience. And not just that, but it is an *unrestricted* emotional experience. We have no certain idea about how many emotions we can feel. We experience happiness, sadness, anger, love, hate, fear, surprise, and pride, just to name a few. We can feel all of these emotions when playing or watching football. Emotions are the oxygen of our soul. We feel these emotions throughout our lives because football doesn't let us to forget about them. And we know that we are alive when we experience them. Football is about feeling alive. It is about feeling that you belong to something greater. Above all, it is an aesthetic human need.

The Art of Football

The arts probably have a useful function. Jorge Wagensberg is a physicist and the director of a science museum in Barcelona. He established a relationship between science and arts (in his book, *Ideas sobre la complejidad del mundo*, Tusquets, 2003). According to Wagensberg, both science and the arts are able to recreate something, to reproduce an experience, to let us experience knowledge as well as emotions. We could say that through science, we experience the emotion of certainty, or uncertainty in some cases, while arts have a broader set of options. Through the arts we can experience those emotions artists want to express. In this sense, arts have the aesthetic function of making us feel. Just consider literature or films; many of them are named by the emotions that they produce: drama, comedy, horror, romance.

Let's consider music as a form of art. There is a relationship between music and football, as the Uruguayan journalist and football fan Eduardo Galeano argues in *El fútbol a sol y a sombra* (S.XIX, 1995). This relationship becomes clearer in South America. In Spanish, the verb *tocar* ("to touch" in English) is used for meaning both "playing music" and "passing the ball." When somebody plays a musical instrument, Spanish speakers say that she *toca* (touches) the instrument. In the same way, when a football player passes the ball we say that he *toca el balón* (touches the ball). Football players *tocan el balón* (pass the ball) like an orchestra "plays" a symphony. In this way, South American philosophy is characterized by the *toque de balón* (ball passing). Johann Sebastian Bach's *Toccata and Fugue in D minor* is a representation of what we are trying to say about South American football style. It is an aesthetic experience that makes us feel emotions.

The Beauty of the Game

However, even aesthetic experiences need some sort of order. Let's consider music again. Playing the piano has certain restrictions, such as the number of keys. If there were only one key it wouldn't be so interesting to listen to the piano. It wouldn't make us feel many emotions. It would be no more than a boring experience. In contrast, an unskilled monkey playing the piano is not something that we would really like to experience. So, we enjoy music neither if it is absolutely restricted nor if it is totally free. What we call music is something between these two extremes. We admire Chopin because he is able to make us feel emotions. He was able to overcome the obstacles and restrictions of playing the piano to produce music.

In the same way, we admire Maradona, Pelé, Messi, and many others because they are able to overcome the obstacles and restrictions of playing football to *produce* football. If there were no restrictions at all we simply wouldn't—and couldn't—admire them. Playing football is not just about eleven men running behind a ball to kick it. Kicking the ball is an art. Just think about the aesthetic difference between a penalty kick and a free kick. Nobody would really enjoy watching a player scoring from the penalty mark, unless, of course, the goalie plays for the opposing team; only in this case the kick becomes an emotional experience. However, it would be pretty strange if a penalty kick was selected for the goal of the week. In contrast, a save made by a goalkeeper can be the play of the week or even the play of the year; for the goalie the challenge is far bigger. More restrictions increase the chances to enjoy a beautiful goal. Free kicks are more often selected as the most beautiful goals because to achieve them players have to overcome harder tests. On the other hand, if the restrictions are so high that the quest becomes unlikely to accomplish then the aesthetic effect disappears, for instance when the free kick is too far away from the goal. Similarly, we admire players dribbling the ball in their opponents' area, it doesn't produce any emotion when they do this in their own area.

Our heroes don't just kick balls; they play with them as Chopin played piano. Our idols overcome restrictions. This is why they are idols.

Freedom from the Rules of Law?

Apart from the "rules of the coach," restrictions in football are derived from the rules of law, or the Laws of the Game. In the book *Speech Acts* (Cambridge University Press, 1969), the American philosopher John Searle distinguishes two kinds of these rules: constitutive rules and regulative rules. Constitutive rules deal with agreements. Regulative rules guarantee that agreements are fulfilled. Just because an agreement has been reached does not guarantee that it is going to be honored. There are many agreements in football that have been agreed and are fulfilled. It would be extremely unusual to see an official football field without goal posts, players, demarcation lines or the ball. However, rules such as offside or grabbing the adversary's shirt are often broken by most players and the referee seems unable to guarantee them. Anyone who had watched a *calcio* football game knows about it.

However, there is a set of rules that needs to be guaranteed, which presents another dilemma. The guarantee of such rules has a cost, and we have to decide how much we are willing to pay for this. We have to decide how much liberty we can sacrifice to exercise power. Field players are not supposed to touch the ball with their hands. The only player who can play the ball with his hands is the goalie. Once in a while, however, a player scores a goal with his hands. It occurs in friendly matches, in the neighborhood among friends, but also in World Cup competitions. It happened on June 22nd, 1986. Maradona chased a high ball. Shilton was the favorite to reach the ball. But Maradona reached it first, much to everyone's amazement since he was by far the shortest player. How did Maradona overcome this restriction? He elected to punch the ball with his left hand. And it was a goal. The English players surrounded the referee, complaining for several minutes. But the referee wrote down "goal" in his notebook.

According to FIFA (*Laws of the game*, Zurich, 2008), "A goal is scored when the whole of the ball passes over the goal line, between the goalposts and under the crossbar, provided that no infringement of the Laws of the Game has been committed previously by the team scoring the goal." Obviously this is not completely true. The one who decides whether or not a goal is scored is the referee. A goal is scored when the referee says that a goal was scored. Argentina didn't win the quarterfinal game against England because Maradona scored a goal with his hand. They won because the referee said that it was a goal. Maradona just played by the rules. And football rules include the decisions that the referees make and implicitly establish that the referees may make mistakes and the players can cheat.

When Maradona scored this goal, he cheated the referees. At this time, many Argentineans probably felt happy, while others may have felt ashamed, and most English fans felt sad, angry, disappointed, and impotent. This is what football is all about. Football is about emotions. Football reminds us that we are humans. We make mistakes and we break agreements. It happens all the time in our daily lives.

Ethics

Those cases in which rules are agreed upon but not guaranteed become a matter of ethics. FIFA tries to guarantee that agreements, the Laws of the Game, are fulfilled. But football is a sport where the regulatory capacity of the referee is far less than the capacity required to guarantee that rules are always obeyed. We don't know if what Maradona did was right or wrong. We are not the ones to make this judgment. But perhaps because of this situation, we follow football and football players. We recognize human decisions in every game. There have been 2063 goals from 1930 to 2006 in the FIFA World Cup final phases (*FIFA World Cup Record Organization*). But, we only remember one scored with a hand, a single goal. Football's regulative rules just provide no guarantee that players don't score goals with their hands.

Football is beautiful not because it is well regulated. It is beautiful because it can be one of the most poorly-regulated sports. Beauty emerges from liberty. In the case of football, this liberty is provided by its loose regulation. Football reminds us that we don't need cameras and instant replays to do what we should. FIFA is not responsible for protecting agreements between football players or football teams. Football players are responsible for their actions. The concept of fair play is a notion that players and fans bring with them to the football field. This space between what is agreed upon and what is done is filled by ethics. As Ludwig Wittgenstein wrote in the *Tractatus Logico-Philosophicus*, "ethics and aesthetics are one and the same" (p. 183). Three minutes later, Maradona scored the "Goal of the Century" and even today Maradona thanks the English players for letting him score this goal and not fouling him in order to avoid the most beautiful goal ever scored in the World Cup finals. That's what makes us proud of being human. We are above our rational thoughts and our natural instincts. We have free will to choose what is right.

A Little bit of Messi for our Life

On April 18th, 2007, Lionel Messi, playing for Barcelona, duplicated Maradona's "goal of the century" in a *Copa del Rey* semifinal against Getafe. Messi started in almost the same position, ran about the same distance, beat the same number of players, dribbled the goalkeeper with the same move and scored from the same position Maradona had twenty-one years before. Perhaps it was not just a coincidence. Amazingly enough, Messi starred in another *déjà vu*. In the very same season, a few months later, Messi also made a perfect replica of the "hand-of-God" goal in the *Catalan Derby* Barcelona-Espanyol. With Barcelona down 0–1, Messi launched himself at a high cross and punched (left hand again!) the ball past Espanyol goalie Carlos Kameni. It was a goal. Espanyol players surrounded the referee and complained for several minutes, just as the English players did twenty-one years before. But the referee marked the play as a "goal" in his notebook. The match was now 1–1. We could explain this by saying that Messi is an imitator or Maradona's heir. But these accounts seem too simple. Perhaps a better explanation is that now and then individuality overcomes order. Now and then, humanity prevails.

We break rules from time to time, rules of opinions and rules of law. Like any other player in the field of life, sometimes we want to ignore our team, we want to ignore what the coach (society) orders, and instead we want to put our own strategy into action. Sometimes, we just want to do what *feels* right. We have a need to express ourselves as *emotional individuals*. Other times, we dive in the penalty area to fool the referee and gain a penalty-kick. We, as players, should respond to this. But small rebellions from imposed orders, now and then, might be good for us. A bit of *mess*, a bit of free thinking and free action, a bit of art, a bit of emotions, might lead to a joyful life.

Freedom from traditions and freedom from rules bring out our very essence and highlights the primacy of the human being—as unique, as creative, as different from others, as free, as ethical, as beautiful. Yes, perhaps we should break rules more often.

23

Hungary's Revolutionary Golden Team

ROBERT IMRE

6–3. In itself, not a very remarkable score.

The 6–3 defeat of England by Hungary on November 25th, 1953 at Wembley Stadium, however, was a very remarkable match.

It wasn't remarkable just because the English side lost. Sure, England at the time was seen as the dominant power in international soccer. They had not been beaten by any side from outside of the British Isles since the turn of the century. But soccer teams can win or lose on any given day.

What was remarkable was the way that they lost and the sea change in the game that the Hungarian team presaged. The *Aranycsapat* (Golden Team) was at the cutting edge of innovation with their passing attacks, their pioneering 4–2–4 formation countering the English 'W–M', and the odd v-neck lightweight shirts and boots without ankles made them a strange sight for the English fans and players alike. Indeed, the running style of the Hungarian squad was such that in the 4–2–4 it was mostly the people without the ball who did all of the running! This was the first view of what would become the modern game. The tactics produced results. England managed a total of five shots on goal; Hungary countered with thirty-five. Ferenc Puskás later remarked that if the English keeper hadn't been so good, Hungary would have had twelve goals. And not just results: the Hungarians played with such style and flair that everyone revelled in the beauty they produced. At the end of the match, the stunned English fans applauded and cheered the Hungarian *Aranycsapat* off the pitch.

Even more remarkable was that this wasn't a one-off match. In May of the following year in Budapest, the *Aranycsapat* was in the middle of its nearly four-year winning streak and the English national side still had not adapted. Subsequently England lost by a margin of 7–1, their greatest international defeat, ever. The game was so lopsided and the English so out-classed that Sidney Owen, England's cetntre-half, said: "It was like playing people from Outer Space."

While the winning run of the Magnificent Magyars sent shockwaves through international football, their impact inside of Hungary was even more profound. The rise and fall of the team mirrored, and was mirrored by, the tumultuous social and political events of post-World War II Hungary. Mirrored them so closely, in fact, that many Hungarians hoped that the success of the *Aranycsapat* would pull Hungary with it, in a triumph over history.

Revolution

There was a particular problem with Hungarian civil society in the Cold War period; there was a profound disjuncture between political representatives and the people they were meant to serve. There had long been a tradition of liberalism, as well as socialism, neither of which were Stalinist and totalitarian. Having been firmly entrenched in the Soviet camp during the post World War Two re-alignments of Europe, Hungarians revolted against the Soviet Union, or 'the Russians' as they saw it, and in 1956, managed to recapture the capital, Budapest, as well as ensure the loyalty of the countryside. Finding themselves on the world stage, Hungarians fought one last time for an identity that had liberty at its foundation. Emulating other great revolutions before them, the Hungarian spontaneous uprising was driven by a philosophy of solidarity, a newly found unity against their common Soviet enemies. In the midst of all of this, Hungarians had managed to gain some significant freedoms through civil society organizations, and even by using various arms of the state to foster independence from the state itself. To a great extent the soccer teams were a manifestation of this and the Golden Team (*Aranycsapat*) transformed from a symbol of state power, to an emblem of freedom, and then to a metaphor of freedom smashed.

Civil society is a problematic idea. Not clear, and certainly not unanimously agreed upon, it is one of those 'contested concepts' that we have a good idea about some of its characteristics, but will dispute a number of others. Nations and nation-states will often be held together, or driven apart, or secede from, rebel and revolt from, other parts of their governing bodies, at least partially based on competing understandings of what 'civil society' might constitute. Some philosophers claim that civil society must be a reasoned and rational set of voluntary organizations. This is typically seen as the result of the rejection of religion when the freedom to choose is finally delivered to a populace. The toleration of a variety of religions would eventually result in the historical formation of a people who, through reasoned discourse, will reject all forms of faith, as they realise that one form of faith is the same as another.

But can revolution deliver civil society? What is the historical process that we call revolution, and how does it come about? Would a revolution in the style of soccer aid in this transformative capacity? Is it possible to have a spontaneous uprising, and transform the political organization of a nation by sheer will? Hungary's Golden Team of the 1950s embodied these philosophical problems. In the struggle to modernise football by using the creative capacities of all of the individual members, while at the same time setting up that truly modern idea of the ideal 'system', Hungary revolutionised the game and changed the direction of soccer in the post–World War II era, forever.

4–2–4, Socialist Football, Civil Society

Coaches will often have similar impacts on soccer teams as political leaders might on national polities and civil societies. Coaches set agendas, create responses to problems during play as well as outside of the game, and any number of things. If a coach reflects political change, and delivers on the philosophical approach of the team, then s/he has done their job and fulfilled the expectations of a leader. As agents of change, coaches must also have the cooperation of their players, just as political leaders cannot act alone and must have the consent of civil society within their respective polities. Many of the teams in the early days of modern soccer were part of other organizations that reflected some kind of civil society in its broadest sense of the concept.

From the 1930s until the 1960s, many club and national teams operated as part of the national armed forces, part of the secret police, or other aspects of the society in which they lived. In the organizations of the Latin American teams from the 1930s, soccer teams reflected the way in which civil society itself was organised. The political organization of a nation, not its ideology, was often reflected in the way in which soccer was organised.

For Hungary, the soccer teams coming out of the Second World War were meant to demonstrate something about civil society. The national team was meant to be situated in opposition to 'untrue socialism' as a kind of 'real socialist' voluntarism. Gusztáv Sebes, the national coach, was a person who believed in the socialist ideal of co-operative work. This cooperative work was to be determined by the talents of each individual. These talents were to be structured in the play and flow of the game so that everyone would attack, and everyone would defend. The major innovation in the game was the advent of the 4–2–4 system which changed the idea that there were some who stood 'behind the ball' and some who stood 'in front of the ball'; some who sacrificed and defended, and some who moved forward and took the glory. For Sebes, there was a clear equality in the productive capacity for socialist football, and soccer was the vehicle to prove that human nature acting within the boundaries of civil society could achieve great things.

Sebes had been a labour union organiser in France in the 1930s and was famous for delivering left-wing political speeches in order to rally his troops. Of course, it was with a wink and a nod that his players listened. Both Ferenc Puskás and Nándor Hidegküti claimed later that they would often listen to the message, and then filter the explicit tactics out of the socialist rhetoric. These tactics were the passing attacks exposing the weaknesses of defensive formations, the newly made 'short boots' cut below the ankle, and the abilities of the whole team to stand behind the ball and flow forward and backward as the game changed throughout the ninety minutes of play. One of the most baffling of tactics for the opposition sides to grapple with was the way in which the members of the *Aranycsapat* would constantly switch positions, a tactic not seen before in the game and later emulated by the great Dutch and Brazilian sides. Inside attackers would switch sides regularly as they pressed forward, and midfielders could appear anywhere on the field—not needing direction and form from an external authority—self-organising in response to needs on the field. This capacity endeared the team to their opponents as well, since it was such a stylish system of play. Again, like the Brazilians who came later, the sheer joy of creativity, the construction of absolute beauty in the play, made everyone admire the Hungarian squad.

In this way, the victories associated with the Hungarian national team were not merely interpreted as some form of national propaganda, but quite the opposite. The overwhelming talent, creativity, and novel methods of play meant that the structural politics of the state faded into the background. The idea of socialist football was to demonstrate that *despite* the persistence of the Stalinist government of Mátyás Rákosi, Hungarians could still be clever enough to get around the authorities—or perhaps the authorities could let them get away with more since the *Aranycsapat* could deliver on an ideal of socialism. The capacity for a kind of civil society in which people could participate in various things not directly related to the Socialist Workers Party, and not directly decided upon by the Central Committee, was thus in existence. Both the *Aranycsapat*, as well as the eventual 1956 Revolution, presented a historical anti-thesis to the prevailing Stalinist reality and the abandonment of Hungary by the West. Justice was close at hand. . . .

The *Aranycsapat* played the kind of fluid and disciplined football of the later Dutch teams of the 1970s. The 'total football' of the Dutch and the legendary Brazilian sides could look to the *Aranycsapat* as a precursor to the daring and courageous way they themselves would eventually play the game. It was Coach Sebes's assistant, Béla Guttman, who took the 4–2–4 system to Brazil after the 1956 Revolution had scattered the team members.

The loss to West Germany in the World Cup of 1954 was a positive turning point for Germany in terms of its post-WWII national mythology, while for Hungary it marked the 'beginning of the end' as the solidification of the Cold War and the 'sphere of influence' of the Soviets placed Hungary in the Socialist Camp. This event entrenched a kind of Hungarian fatalism, sometimes politically quite dangerous, that no matter how hard the 'nation' tried—after all they defeated the Soviet Red Army in the Battle for Budapest in the October Revolution of 1956—they would eventually lose to the exigencies of history, as the following December of the same year proved. Talent alone would not win the day, especially if 'history' was against you. And since the overwhelming philosophy of history was that of an organic development, the loss was not viewed as the proper course of justice, but it had to be accepted since it was the 'will of history': the final synthesis

In political philosophy terms, this fatalism led to a deep-seated mistrust of civil society at all levels. In her book *On Revolution,* Hannah Arendt refers to the Hungarian Revolution as a kind of 'true' revolution:

> nothing indeed contradicts more sharply the old adage of the anarchistic and lawless "natural" inclinations of a people left without the constraint of its government than the emergence of the councils that, wherever they appeared, and most pronouncedly during the Hungarian Revolution, were concerned with the reorganization of the political and economic life of the country and the establishment of a new order. (p. 275)

But this approach was smashed when the Soviet tanks moved into Budapest in December of 1956 and installed the puppet government of János Kádár. The final act of survival was to try to make compromises with the existing government and the occupation of Hungary. The compromise with the Kádár government—Kádár himself had compromised with the Soviets—killed both existing socialism as well as possible democratic formations. This meant that in post-1956 Revolution Hungary, the only way out of the dilemma of occupation by the Soviets was to completely disengage from politics. The voluntary organizations that are prevalent in civil society, and indeed the 1956 Revolution appeared to be a civil uprising, became fragmented and compromised. There was a single set of representatives, with very narrowly defined political goals, led by Kádár as the Party Secretary, and that would close off politics in the late 1950s. The only way out of this political trap was internal disengagement or emigration.

The eventual disappearance of the main members of the *Aranycsapat* in post-1956 Hungary made the case for emigration, and also enshrined the notion of anti-politics as a way in which to prosper and further one's individual interests. Ferenc Puskás himself showed a kind of ironic retribution: he was jeered when he returned to Budapest after the World Cup defeat in 1954, banned from playing by FIFA for eighteen months immediately after the 1956 Revolution—since the Hungarian FA had banned him for refusing to return to Soviet occupied Hungary—and he re-started a soccer career in Spain in La Liga for Real Madrid where he went on to become a legend of the game.

In many ways, this destruction of the idea of the polity, the polis, or the anti-'civic republicanism' that developed in Hungary in the 1960s and 1970s, paralleled the movements in Margaret Thatcher's UK and Ronald Reagan's US a decade later. The advent of neo-liberalism was presaged by disengagement from the polis in the former 'eastern bloc' in that citizens in Czechoslovakia, Hungary, and Poland in particular, came to see themselves as capitalists trapped in a socialist body politic.

Nations and Nationalism

There is still a fundamental problem for us when we think about the political philosophy of soccer. When Hungary was playing for the World Cup in 1954, and the years leading up to this event that saw the success of the *Aranycsapat*, who were they playing *for*? The glory of 'International Socialism' as opposed to 'Stalinism'? The many hundreds of thousands of Hungarians left outside their borders as a result of the treaty of Trianon? The nearly half a million Hungarian Jews deported a decade previously to the death camps? The World War II refugees who had left East-Central Europe and went to the UK, US, Canada, and Australia, and many other places around the world?

Given these difficulties, what might we mean by the term 'national character'? Self-perceived or otherwise, a 'nation' is not a taken-for-granted entity, and those of the same 'blood and soil' seem to have a capacity for claiming they are not of the same nation. For the émigrés, the opposite was quite often true; they found it quite easy to claim they were part of the same nation, with people who were not of the same 'blood' and came from a 'different soil'. Hungarians migrating to the United States, Canada, and Australia in the twentieth Century had no trouble establishing themselves as loyal citizens of these nations along with immigrants from all over the world.

If we take the idea beyond a discussion about borders and who might inhabit them, many philosophers have also tried to discuss what nationalism itself might mean. What constitutes a nation: shared suffering, cultural mission, shared language, geographic proximity (in the same space) and/or shared geography (in the same *kind* of space), shared ethnicity, common enemies, or any other combination of things. So for us in the modern period, what does it mean? Ernest Gellner, in *Nations and Nationalism* (2006), claimed that nationalism itself is a comparatively weak force. The Industrial Revolution and the great change made in people's lives in the transition from one way of life to another is the main shift. Nationalism is simply a way to remain organised and to try to deal with the exigencies of modern industrial life. Hannah Arendt's discussions about modernity in *The Human Condition* (1958) echo parts of this in that she saw modernity as having done some significant damage to the 'human condition'. Modern nations were subject to a kind of loss of the public sphere that was a key for the realisation of cooperative civil society.

And this is where soccer, especially in the 1950s, in Hungary and other parts of the world, meant more than just a simple third-rate nationalism. It was indeed the expression of a creative human force, the capacity to voluntarily create beauty, the truest form of civil society. After all, the English squads and their fans always cheered their losses to the *Aranycsapat*, and the English players expressed nothing but admiration for their opponents.

Re-interpreting the philosophical meaning, rather than the historical meaning, of the *Aranycsapat*, as well as the 1956 Revolution, shows us how resistance and revolution as the anti-thesis to an unsatisfactory political life, can deliver the conditions of freedom. Creativity and striving for this beauty, the combined failures, or untimely ends of both of these socio-political phenomenon, shows us how the dismantling of civil society entrenched a kind of anti-politics in Hungary.

It is fascinating to think philosophically about this: what would have happened if Hungary had won the 1954 World Cup? Would this have done the same thing to Hungarian civil society as it perhaps did to

German civil society? In West Germany, the World Cup triumph meant that the world would accept a Germany that had extraordinary success in any number of fields of endeavour, a Germany that need not feel isolated, incapable of demonstrating remorse, and a Germany engaging in the world at large. Essentially, a Germany participating in some version of global civil society rather than the pre-Nazi era Germany, the inter-war Germany of the early 1930s: paranoid, delusional, seeking revenge. This changed dramatically in the 1950s as a self-perception, a civil society idea changed.

The *Aranycsapat* and destruction of the 1956 Revolution represented the end of a philosophical idea and not the beginning. The success and eventual failure of the team and its disbanding represented the end of a particular kind of civil society and the end of a particular kind of European nation. The bourgeois dream that was killed in the Second World War, that dream of triumphing over adversity through hard work and luck, was ultimately killed in the gas chambers of Europe. Hungarians sought to revive this in the *Aranycsapat*, could not accept their defeat, and fought a revolution, which they won, and then lost, only to participate in the same destruction of the Prague Spring in 1968 with the multinational forces that destroyed yet another uprising against the Soviets.

Perhaps this places too great a weight on a few games of soccer. But in a Europe deeply divided, nation-states who had felt humiliated, had the capacity to set some things right by demonstrating that they had the capacity for good in a true and beautiful approach to human contest. Soccer became this kind of contest. The *Aranycsapat* was not about smashing opponents, but rather a demonstration of skill as a symphonic human endeavour. Closing the door on this meant that frustrated nationalism remained, not as a result of the Cold War as many had thought, but rather as a result of the inability of civil society to philosophise, or think through these problems. The capacity to reconcile with past evils is just as important as some form of empirically demonstrable success.

Finally, the nation in the Cold War period became defined in strictly modern terms. This means that the borders of contemporary Hungary, with co-ethnics on the other side, were seen to define the national community. Hungarians outside of the current version of the nation-state could not be viewed as a people who were part of the same project. If Hungarians within Hungary had a difficult time co-operating in the post-*Aranycsapat* world, how could co-ethnics even begin to think that by virtue of being Hungarian, there must necessarily be a civil society link?

Extra-Time or Penalties?

Justice does not always prevail. On any given day any given team can win. History can be instrumental as well as 'true', and soccer can be a powerful nation-forming factor in the modern era. More importantly, we have learned (rather than proven), that talent and beauty can be quashed by the contingency of historical events. Truth of the talent, and the beauty of its manifestation was part of the legacy of the Hungarian squads throughout the 1950s. At the end of the day, the formation of the Hungarian nation-state was as truncated as the legacy of the Treaty of Trianon, leaving Hungary and the Hungarian nation with some unfinished business that remains to this day.

We will never know if a World Cup victory would have changed that and drawn Hungarians together and established a different set of parameters for the nation, created a different idea of what might constitute a political community. There's no answer to this, just as there is no answer to what might be more just, extra-time or penalties. One thing is certain, that the West German victory in 1954 was a catalyst for West German cooperation, and a move towards reconciliation with Jewish communities, and a positive step for the West German polis towards a more free society in the wake of the tragedies of World War II. Maybe Puskás's disallowed goal could have allowed a tie, then both nations could have claimed a victory and we need not answer that most difficult of questions: extra-time or penalties? We might have been happy with the peace.

The historical circumstances of the *Aranycsapat* in post–World War II Hungary had deep significance in terms of Hungarian national consciousness during the decades that followed. The *Aranycsapat* solidified the fatalism of the Cold War. The failure of the team to win the 1954 World Cup, and the subsequent emigration of its key players, was a potent force in the destruction of Hungarian civil society and helped in the eventual fragmentation of Hungarian groups, especially the large minorities in Slovakia, Romania, and Yugoslavia. The World Cup loss of 1954 delivered cause for a profound sense of self-doubt, fully realised in Cold War compromises, and as a result the idea of the polis became a watered-down version of a modern social(ist)-democracy. Decades later, Hungarians, whether they were soccer fans or not, still politicised this loss and claimed that Hungary was sacrificed for another, more politically and economically powerful, European country. The end of the *Aranycsapat*, was seen as the soccer equivalent of the Yalta agreements dividing Europe between super-powers, entrenching the Cold War and signalled the end of the idea of democracy in Hungary.

History and Philosophy

There are times in a nation's historical consciousness when its citizens can claim great victories. There are also those instances in which the polity can look backwards to the great failures and use them for any number of things, both positive and negative. Coupled with this, the instrumentality of history is inescapable in that people will attempt to use agreed upon facts relating to historical events for particular purposes. There are also some more ambiguous and complicated events that can be seen as harbingers of doom, then reinterpreted as something more positive, and then once again as an universal category of deeply held failure.

Sport, and soccer in particular, can play a crucial role in all of this. Local interpretations of the Canada-Russia ice hockey series of the 1970s, the North Korean soccer team in the 1962 World Cup in England, the South Korean team in the 2002 World Cup, Mexican soccer in the 1986 World Cup, recent stagings of Olympic games in both Sydney and China, and many more examples, demonstrate the hegemonic interpretation of history as both non-contingent (possessing an inner logic of progress), and instrumental. This means that political leaders seem to be able to convince people that history has a pattern that can be understood and predicted, and as such employed for some very particular purposes. These purposes might be good, bad, completely evil, totally practical, and any number of things by themselves or combined. The important point here is that the examples mentioned above are all interpreted as successes regardless of whether the sports team won particular matches or tournaments. In the Hungarian case, it is a deep national injustice to have lost the final match in the 1954 World Cup, and one that was caused by forward progress explained by the grand narrative of 'history'.

It is assumed that this pattern is also organic: it is a naturally occurring manifestation of the character of a 'people'. National characters, then, are grown from the soil, manifest in the blood of its people, like giant fleshy vegetables wandering the earth, but always deemed to be revealed by their actions in particular situations. Instead of challenging these intertwined ideas, I suggest that we take seriously, however problematic, this philosophy of history.

For contemporary Hungarians of every ilk, the *Aranycsapat* of the late 1940s and early 1950s is a special historical event, or series of events. The victories that they accumulated coming out of World War II were indeed astounding and the place of Hungarian soccer on the world stage was daunting in every way. This was meant to demonstrate the resilience of a people who had a self-perception of creativity, pouncing on opportunity, incorporating all variety of talents on the field of play, and the belief that through great achievements, justice would prevail. This would be the defeat of the Yalta, and perhaps even the Trianon, treaties.

The *Aranycsapat* went thirty-one matches without a defeat and lost their thirty-second in the World Cup final of 1954. This loss was intimately linked to the 1956 Revolution in that the Revolution was seen by many as a completely spontaneous uprising, that had been building for years, in which socialists as well as liberal reformers sought to rid themselves of the Soviet occupiers first, then argue politics later. The *Aranycsapat* could have shown the capacity for Hungarians to fully realise their destiny, not necessarily in a World Cup victory, but at least in a successful outcome of the 1956 Revolution.

This view can also be seen as a façade as well. Not the victories of the *Aranycsapat*, for that is an established fact as is the innovations they brought to soccer. But rather, it is problematic in that this helps to develop an idea of the world working against an embattled nation, a nation that was an innocent victim of greater machinations of larger empires. This cannot be the case, since civil society in Hungary consisted of people acting, making decisions, participating in political life. The last days of World War II saw the quickest expulsion by any Nazi German ally of a citizenry who were marked as being of Jewish origin. This expulsion occurred in the waning days of the war and in 1944, from May through July, over 400,000 Jewish people were sent to their deaths in the concentration camps.

These deportations solidified the end of liberal pluralism, which was strengthening in the lead up to the first World War, was placed in great danger in the inter-war years, and then ended in 1938 with the pro-fascist group holding power in Hungary. Soccer mirrored this. The idea of liberal pluralism, the capacity to accept the 'other' and make political, legal, and social space for all kinds of people in a modern Hungary, was killed along with the nearly half million Jewish Hungarian citizens deported to their deaths.

So where does this leave us in terms of the notion of a modern Hungary? With liberal pluralism dead, and the revival made temporarily possible in a two-pronged attack of 'socialist football' developed by coach Gusztáv Sebes on the one hand, and a full-blown spontaneous 'people's revolution' on the other, Hungary in the mid-1950s was set for a kind of cultural renaissance, indeed! History, the organic process, would finally allow that most Hungarian of terms, *igazság*—meaning both truth, as well as justice—to manifest in the people. The only problem was, neither the revolution nor the football team succeeded. If only one had triumphed. But *igazság* could not be in Hungary. Soccer could not overcome history.

24

When a Soccer Club Becomes a Mirror

ANDREA BORGHINI and ANDREA BALDINI

> Soccer is a metaphor of life: from Milan's success people realized that mine is a winning philosophy.
>
> —SILVIO BERLUSCONI (1994)

This quote from Silvio Berlusconi is part of the speech he gave on April 18th 1994, during the celebrations for AC Milan's third consecutive *scudetto* under his management. Suppose we take this claim seriously: what is the logic at play when soccer is linked to other spheres of life? In what ways is a team a metaphor for its patrons?

Warming Up

Metaphors stand to language as pitons, karabiners, and ropes stand to a rock-climber: they nail down and guide most of our exchange of information. They come in handy when we talk about things such as love, power, and food; yet we have come to identify them where you would not expect that much rhetoric. Most (if not all) scientific models rely on metaphors, such as those representing chemical compounds, gases and light.[1]

---

[1] If you want to know more about metaphors in science, we recommend *Models and Metaphors: Studies in Language and Philosophy* by Max Black (Cornell University Press, 1962), *Models and Analogies in Science* by Mary Hesse (Notre Dame University Press, 1966, and Part IV of *Metaphor and Thought* edited by Andrew Ortony (Cambridge University Press, 1993). For more on the theories of metaphor in general try *Metaphors We Live By* by George Lakoff and Mark Johnson (University of Chicago Press, 1980); and *The New Rhetoric: A Treatise on Argumentation* by Chaïm Perelman and Lucie Olbrechts-Tyteca (Notre Dame University Press, 1969).

Soccer can be thought of as a metaphor too. Indeed, its use as a metaphor for life is so widespread that it has come to be accepted and not analyzed. Soccer metaphors typically rely on particular features of the game that in some way resemble aspects of *normal life*. These features include items such as a player's sacrifice of personal gain in favor of the interests of the team; the due respect for a coach's deliberations; an individual player's creativity; the importance of virtuous conduct, and so on.

There are three aspects of soccer which make it highly adaptable as a metaphor for life in general:

1. **Soccer is unpredictable.**

2. **Soccer means winning or losing.**

3. **Soccer gives the ref undisputed authority.**

1. Soccer Is Unpredictable

This unpredictability can be seen at three different levels.

a. *Game unpredictability.* The peculiar rule that forbids touching the ball with hands and arms—for everyone but the goalkeeper—shapes the interaction between the player and the ball, so that the movements of the former have to be constantly responsive to the position and movement of the latter. For this reason, while scoring a point is a prosaic occurrence in most sports, in soccer it becomes a magic moment.

Additional unpredictability comes from the tactical complexity of the game: no matter how thoughtful the formation, a team's overall performance is vulnerable to a player's failure to keep her role even for just a few seconds. Thus, it is impossible to fully control our actions in the field—as in life.

b. *Player unpredictability.* Soccer is surely a peculiar sport where, unlike American football or ice hockey, it is quite common to find a great player who does not possess an extraordinary physical structure. A list of the greatest players of all times includes several possessing average or even deficient bodies. The great Garrincha had several birth deficiencies: his spine was deformed, while his right leg was bent inward, and his tremendous dribbling was due—partially—to his left leg being six centimeters shorter and curved outwards. Rather than preventing him from being a fine player, these features arguably contributed to make him one of the greatest of all times. Lionel Messi, *blaugrana* forward, at the age of eleven had been diagnosed with a growth hormone deficiency, and he stands now at only 1.69 meters. Nevertheless he scored a headed goal in the Champions League Final on May 27th, 2009. On a soccer field—as in life—everyone has possibilities that are not fully determinable by looking at the initial conditions. As Solon taught Croesus, initial conditions do not determine what we do and who we become (the story is narrated by Herodotus in *The Histories*, Book I, sections 29–33).

c. *The unpredictability of fortune.* Luck is an ingredient that everyone involved in soccer quickly—and often bitterly—comes to learn. Even a first-rate team, playing a great game, could lose because of a series of unlucky events. Netherlanders may have no difficulty grasping this point, remembering the match against Italy in the semi-final of Euro 2000. In life the same thing happens: often an unlucky event can produce disastrous consequences.

2. Soccer Means Winning or Losing

Every player knows the bitter taste of a loss—even an undeserved, unfair, or maybe unjust loss. Even the greatest players of all times such as Pelé, Maradona, Garrincha, Cristiano Ronaldo, Van Basten, Best, or Messi have seen astonishing victories in their careers, but also heartbreaking defeats. Along the same lines, an undeniable dialectic between winning and losing characterizes everyone's life.

3. Soccer Gives the Ref Undisputed Authority

The theme of the unfair or unjust loss introduces a feature that helps make sports (soccer as well as other sports) a good metaphor for life: the referee. The authority of the referee (and of the other officials) is almost undisputable. The need for accepting and respecting authority—beyond personal interest and opinion—is considered one of the most valuable pedagogical features of soccer. However, peculiar to soccer is the fact that referees always have to be in the middle of the action, so much so that not only can they touch the ball, but sometimes even unintentionally score a goal. (On September 22, 2001, referee Brian Savill even scored a goal intentionally during the match between Wimpol 2000 and Earls Coine Reserves; however, he was suspended for seven weeks and, refusing to accept the decision, retired from refereeing.)

But what is it that makes one activity a metaphor for another activity, or for life in general? Roughly, it is an appropriate transfer of meaning from one to the other. We'll call some area which can be used in a metaphor a *sphere of discourse.* For example, music, fashion, or the wine-making business are all portions of reality with a particular corresponding sphere of discourse.

Sometimes, two different spheres are juxtaposed. In a metaphor, one or more expressions belonging to one sphere are employed to transfer part of their meaning to expressions belonging to another sphere. Typically, this operation is performed by an identity claim, such as "Buffon *is* a wall" or "Maradona *is* a god." These statements don't claim that Buffon is *literally* a wall or that Maradona is *really* a god—both of these statements are obviously false—they simply draw parallels between the two.

No one would find such claims nonsensical. Yet it's extremely difficult (if not impossible) to spell out exactly in what respects Buffon is like a wall and Maradona is like a god. A sentence may be used to convey different meanings as uttered in different contexts and, moreover, the respects of similarity are potentially infinite.

For our purposes, the two juxtaposed spheres of discourse are *the sphere of soccer* and *the sphere of daily life*. Three major players within the sphere of soccer can be identified—the *team*, the *supporters*, and the *patronage* (which includes the owner, and the president with all its collaborators)—all of which are part of a *club*. The sphere of life includes all sorts of things, especially those that may influence or be influenced by soccer. Nevertheless there is one entity within this domain, which calls for some introduction—the '*bare individual*'. With this expression (which we borrow from contemporary metaphysics), we intend nothing more than the bare existence of a person stripped of any quality (think of it just as a proper name, for example 'John Smith'), which functions as a placeholder for any quality whatsoever.

The bare individual corresponding to the owner plays a key role in the mirroring process. Spelling out this role is pivotal to uncovering the logic of the metaphor embedded in contemporary soccer. Here is the illustration of a typical case of metaphorical transfer between a soccer patron and his public *persona*:

i. **the name 'John Smith', which picks out a bare individual in the sphere of life, is correlated to The Owner of the club in the soccer sphere;**

ii. **within the soccer sphere, The Owner is then linked to the other parts of the club, which enrich its image;**

iii. **such image is then projected onto the *persona* of John Smith, an individual of the sphere of life with all the qualities that are transferred to him, in multiple ways, via the different parts of the club.**

Thus, what initially was a mere name within the sphere of daily life becomes at the end of a mirroring process a full-fledged persona, which crucially passes through the soccer sphere.

Naturally, most everyday cases of patronage involve individuals that are *a little more* than bare individuals (when Roman Abramovich acquired Chelsea FC he was already somewhat renowned, although not in soccer circles or in the major mass media); moreover, mirroring processes from other spheres often play a relevant role.

Today clubs typically offer a peculiarly powerful mirror because of two emerging processes. First there is the increased media coverage of soccer events and the advent of pay-per-view. These have transformed the relationship between supporters and their clubs, whose popularity—in its social, economical, and political dimensions—has reached an unprecedented level. Secondly, there is the progressive decline of traditional forms of structured aggregation for young people—such as politically oriented groups or religious communities. This has transfigured the role and the nature of organized groups of supporters, both in their self-understanding and in the way in which societies at large deal with them.

Thus in today's culture, the persona of the patron is created by a reflection of properties of the soccer club. This metaphorical mirroring can produce very different personas, not only because clubs vary in character, but also in the way in which patrons hold themselves to their clubs. It is not just the character of the club but the mirroring relation itself that shapes and determines the persona of the patron. To see this, compare the Agnelli family, owners of Juventus FC, Silvio Berlusconi of AC Milan, and the owner of U.S. Città di Palermo, Maurizio Zamparini.

The Orpheus of Soccer

> There is an elegance which is not deliberated, but it is owned or interpreted once that wonderful shirt is put on.
>
> —Giampiero Boniperti

They call it *La (vecchia) signora*, the (old) lady. The nickname is a pun on its Latin name, which means "youth." With its fifty-one trophies, Juventus FC is not only the most successful Italian club, but it also boasts the largest basin of supporters: around twelve million in Italy, and one hundred and seventy-three million worldwide. The "Lady" sets the standards of Italian soccer in many other respects as well; *style* is what interests us here.

The so-called *stile Juve* functions exactly like a brand, instantly transforming the understanding of whatever falls under its scope. Being *juventino* is to endorse a certain ideal: a mix of natural elegance (described by Boniperti in the quotation above) and serene poise. As Darwin Pastorin once said, "To be *juventino* is just this: to live with serenity in any transitional phase" (*Juventus: 110 anni di storia*, Morandotti Editore, 2007, p. 305). This attitude developed under the guidance of the Agnelli family, who took control of the club in 1923, and whose distinctive public behavior became a model for the club members and its supporters.

The elder Giovanni Agnelli—whose *persona* was associated with the image of Juventus for decades—probably molded that style more than anyone else. Over the decades, he set peculiar standards for a soccer patron, never losing his detached and calm look in spite of the team's performance.

Among other behaviors, he was known for leaving the stadium at the end of the first half, no matter the result or the importance of the game. He used to give nicknames to the team's stars borrowed from *highbrow* spheres, such as art history or literature. Thus, Alessandro del Piero was "Pinturicchio" at the peak of his career, and "Waiting for Godot" when his performances became less brilliant. This *haute bourgoise* attitude was expressed by a member of one of the most wealthy and prestigious Italian families (who controlled, among others, the car-making company FIAT).

Unlike contemporary protagonists of the soccer patronage sphere, for the Agnelli family the process of construction of a well-rounded and renowned soccer brand had to grow slowly over decades. This was the time, indeed, when the soccer sphere was not dramatically overexposed to the public attention by mass-media.

It would be too simple, however, to associate the *stile Juve* with the Agnelli family alone: nearly all the foremost figures that contributed to the image of the club embodied it. Here, you may list players that distinguished themselves for their elegance and serenity inside and outside of the field, such as Giampiero Boniperti, Omar Sivori, Dino Zoff, Michelle Platini, Gaetano Scirea, Roberto Baggio, and Alessandro del Piero—just to name a few. And you may list team presidents and managers, such as (once more) Giampiero Boniperti, Vittorio Caissotti di Chiusano, Giovanni Cobolli Gigli, and coaches such as Giovanni Trapattoni and Carlo Ancelotti.

Through the models provided by its patrons and its most distinguished representatives, the *stile Juve* secured for itself a powerful, well-rounded, and long-lasting metaphor, which instantly transforms the image of the person or group associated with the club. Within the sphere of daily life, the domain of applicability of the Juventus's metaphor has basically no boundaries: for this reason, we can think of the *Signora* as one of the most wide-ranging and classic club metaphors in contemporary soccer. As Orpheus enchanted his audience with his lyre, Juventus charms any fan (and often opponents too) with its style. The benefits of this transformation have been felt—or simply sought, with different results—by key figures in the world of politics and business; but ordinary supporters can often appeal to (and at times even draw benefits from) such a distinctive style. However, the *stile* originally reflects upon the Agnelli family, who contributed so much to create it.

Hence, from the mere name of the '*Agnelli family*,' the image of a stylish team and patron was created. This image was powerfully reflected over the members of the family, giving a decisive contribution to create its myth outside of soccer, well into the business world (especially the car-making industry) and public life; but, the image also ethically shaped the *personae* of the players off the field, of the supporters when not talking about soccer, and, perhaps, of Italian soccer as well.

In recent year, however, the club has gone through some difficult times. It all started in July 2006, when Luciano Moggi—at the time the club's general manager—was sent off from FIGC (the Italian soccer federation) for bribing the referees and orchestrating a system aimed at favoring Juventus's team and some of its players. The accusation was backed up by an impressive amount of phone conversations, involving Moggi and a number of other high profile managers and administrators of Serie A clubs and the refereeing ranks. As we are writing, *La Signora* is struggling to promptly reaffirm the old metaphor, which contributed much to the development of Italian soccer. Meanwhile, Italian soccer acquired some new protagonists; one in particular was able to turn the soccer metaphor, with the aid of the new media, to create a different mythology within a very short time-span.

The Gods of War: Berlusconi and Mars

Silvio Berlusconi is the paradigmatic case of patronage for our study, if not the origin itself of the contemporary way of understanding the property of a soccer club and the image that can derive from it. To recall just some of his many titles, he is the main shareholder of Fininvest, one of the country's ten largest privately owned companies that operates in media and finance; the founder, with Ennio Doris, of Mediolanum bank; the main shareholder of Mediaset; and, last but not least, he is the leader of the political party PdL (*Freedom people*). Berlusconi's group has controlled three of the six Italian national television channels for almost three decades, several magazines and newspapers, and, as we are writing, he is the acting Italian Prime Minister.

Berlusconi acquired AC Milan on the 20th of February 1986. Just a few weeks later, on the 24th of March, he became president of the team and set about to change the world of soccer. Since the earliest years of his management, Berlusconi grasped the potential alchemy between mass-media and soccer. Especially through television, he reconstructed the sport's visibility, its relation with supporters, and the image that patrons were gaining through these things. The culmination of this revolutionary process was the broadcasting of live matches of the regular season, starting with Lazio–Foggia on the 31st of August 1993. The channel was *Tele+*, the first European pay-for-view TV, then controlled by Berlusconi, Vittorio Cecchi Gori (the president of AC Fiorentina from 1993 to 2002), Leo Kirch, and other smaller business partners.

Even though Berlusconi achieved wide notoriety since his acquiring of the club and his taking it "to the pinnacle of the world game" (see, "History" on AC Milan official website), it was with his debut into Italian political life that the significance of his patronage and his *public persona* were transfigured. On January 26, 1994, the Cavaliere officially *entered the political field*, proclaiming:

> Italy is the country I love. Here I have my roots, my hopes, my horizons. Here I have learned, from my father and from life, how to be an entrepreneur. Here I have also acquired the passion for liberty. I have chosen *to enter the field* and become a public servant because I do not want to live in an illiberal country, ruled by immature forces and by people who are well and truly bound to a past that proved both a political and economic failure.

During this famous speech—the first of his political career—Berlusconi chose to employ jargon of soccer in order to secure a metaphorical link between his extraordinary success as patron of AC Milan and his political activity, being sure that most Italians would have been able to understand it immediately (albeit unintentionally). That soccer played a very special role for Berlusconi is confirmed also by other interviews released shortly after that first speech. The day after the foundation of Forza Italia (his first political party), the PdL's leader declared,

"If I enter into the political life, I will resign from every other role but the presidency of AC Milan" (January 19th, 1994). More noteworthy words came just a few months later, on June 6th, after his party's victory in the elections: while greeting the Italian National team about to leave to compete for the 1994 World Cup, Berlusconi declared: "My political mission is like building a soccer team." Finally, during the celebration for the third consecutive *scudetto*—again, just a few weeks after his party's electoral victory—Berlusconi addressed a selected audience of AC Milan players and supporters with the following questions:

> "Are we tired of winning?"
> "Nooo!" they answered.
> "Will we win again?"
> "Yeees!"
> "Everywhere and anyway? Under our guidance, will Italy become like [AC] Milan?"
> "Yees!"
> "Then, we shall cut the cake, being assured that there are going to be lots of cakes for everyone!" (Taken from Alberto Costa, "Noi del Milan, mai stanchi di vincere," *Corriere della Sera*, April 19th, 1994, p. 41)

When compared to the construction of the *stile Juve*, Berlusconi's case is striking in its brevity. Within a few years, he succeeded in creating a new image for himself and for Italian soccer. The new media were a crucial component of this process, and Berlusconi had a long-standing frequentation with them. He was indeed the first to explore and understand the commercial potentials of private television in Italy: in 1978 he bought a small local television—Telemilano—and just few years later his business was controlling several channels, spread all over the country, thus able to broadcast nationwide. This was a formidable achievement, especially when considering that national television was at that time a State monopoly.

It is not an accident that the first major event Berlusconi decided to broadcast on his network was the 1980–81 Mundialito, a soccer tournament played in Uruguay during Christmas time. The teams involved were former world champions, Italy being among those. He had thus foreseen the novel alchemy—in terms of profit—between television and soccer: within less than ten years, Fininvest (nowadays Mediaset) became the only competitor of RAI in the Italian television market.

Berlusconi's connection with soccer, however, is not limited to the commercial aspects. On April 18 1994, the Cavaliere himself marvelously expressed how that sphere is related—and in the specific a patron—to his public *persona*:

> Soccer is a metaphor of life: from Milan's success people realized that mine is a winning philosophy, that by working hard ambitious goals may be reached.

At first sight, the metaphorical link between AC Milan and Berlusconi's *persona* may look commonplace. But once you begin unpacking the logic behind it, you become aware yet again of a lengthy and continuous process of meaning transfer from one sphere to the other. The story, however, gets more interesting. Not only was Berlusconi a forerunner in the use of soccer as a metaphor through mass-media, but the connection he puts to work relies on the surgical removal of certain elements of the soccer sphere, so that—as it was for the Roman god Mars—any turn of bad fortune for Berlusconi disappears.

No mirror provides an *exact* copy of reality. Some mirrors, however, distort more than others. In the fairytale Snow White, the Queen in asking, "Who is the fairest one of all?" cannot content herself with any answer but the one she desired. Analogously, Berlusconi cunningly arranges to receive the answer he desires from his team: no defeat. This wish clashes with a very basic fact: as any team is bound to come across victories and defeats, its metaphorical correlate will be accordingly mirrored. It is hence remarkable how Berlusconi systematically tries to escape this logic by avoiding having his name linked with AC Milan's bad fortune. This is why we are saying that, in relating himself just with the wins of AC Milan, Berlusconi is doing something of peculiar: he is creating a "winning team" by *fiat*, which would suggest that he is a winner because—indeed—*his team* is a winning team. (AC Milan is indeed among the most successful clubs in the world; nonetheless it has suffered incredible defeats, like the memorable 2005 Champions League Final against Liverpool.)

The question, then, quickly arises: "How can Berlusconi remove the defeat as a constitutive element of the story of his team—and of soccer *sans phrase?*" Answer: "By removing unpredictability"—that is: "By denying that *like life, soccer is unpredictable.*" This is achieved through a surgical and deliberate selection of the episodes in which the metaphor should be put at work. The effect is to create the image of a president who is able to overcome the power of any adversary and any fortune (as the prince portrayed in Niccolò Machiavelli's masterpiece). Here are some excerpts from Berlusconi testifying this point:

> The problem of Milan is that I do not take care of the team in first person anymore. Because of politics I have had to abandon the team. I have to think

about the Country and not about Milan, you are ruining me. (*Sette*, March 2nd, 2001)

Milan is not winning anymore because, since he entered politics, his president is not taking care of it anymore. (*Ansa*, February 6th, 1998)

Milan at Berlusconi's fashion: Roma defeated. A goal by Leonardo and two goals by Shevchenko: but it is of the Cavaliere too, that he asked forever a four-man defense to Zaccheroni. (*Il Giornale*, January 22nd, 2002)

No one talks about Berlusconi's Milan, but Sacchi's, Zac's, Ancelotti's Milan. However, I am the one who decided line-ups for the last eighteen years. (*Corriere della Sera*, March 17th, 2004)

Berlusconi obviously cannot deny the fact that his team sometimes loses. What he does is subtler. He simply understands and explains Milan's defeats as caused by his absence or by some kind of failing in the fulfillment of his directions. In Berlusconi's terms, the failed observance of his "winning ideas," or the impossibility of producing and communicating them, is the reason AC Milan is defeated. He endorsed this philosophy even as Prime Minister of Italy and, thus, as a representative of the Italian national team. The day after the clamorous defeat of the *Azzurri* in the final of Euro 2000 by France, Berlusconi officially declared during a press conference:

For the love of my country, I wanted to stay silent. Instead, I have to say that we could and we had to win. Zoff made shameful decisions: Zidane was always free to move and play, it was impossible not to notice that. Even an amateur would have noticed that and we would have won. Someone like Gattuso could have been the right choice. [...] It would have been enough to win. (*Corriere della Sera* August 17, 2005, p. 48)

It's not just by attributing the responsibilities to coaches or lamenting his lack of involvement (because of more pressing duties) that Berlusconi can avoid being identified with the defeats of his team. AC Milan possesses a very weird set of managers. Paradoxically, Silvio Berlusconi is not the President of AC Milan, but no one else holds—or can hold—this position. Adriano Galliani is vice executive president and managing director, while Paolo Berlusconi (Silvio's brother) and Gianni Nardi are vice presidents. Thanks to this administrative arrangement, the Cavaliere can deny being the president who (sometimes) loses, while celebrating being the winningest president in the history of AC Milan (and maybe of soccer). Like Mars, the Roman god of war, every time he enters the battlefield, he cannot lose.

Finally, there is the intricate relationship between Berlusconi and AC Milan supporters. These have been unusually critical of the management (regretfully, in violent ways too), a striking fact when posed next to the impressive number of competitions recently won by the team. The reasons for the conflict may be at least partially found in that very same mirroring process that helps in the constitution of Berlusconi's public *persona*. A handy example is the recent transfer of Kakà to Real Madrid. Faced with vehement fans' protests, Berlusconi readily denied any involvement in the trade: "If it would depend on me, I would keep him" (Furio Fedele, "Berlusconi: *'Ronaldinho sarà il faro del Milan'*," *Corriere dello Sport*, June 9th, 2009). This suggested that the player and the executive management (Adriano Galliani) were responsible and that, once more, there was no defeat for Berlusconi. However, Galliani in turn blamed the global economic crises: "Transfers of this kind are going to be popular in the next few years" (*"La vita continua anche senza Kakà,"* *Televideo*, June 5th, 2009) suggesting also that the ultimate reason for the transfer is to be found in some special fiscal laws that would favor Spanish teams over Italian ones. Unfortunately, the supporters' distress was not relieved by these comments and, ultimately, Berlusconi's public image was hurt.

We are now in a position to summarize the logic of metaphor underlying Berlusconi's link to AC Milan. The *bare individual* 'Silvio Berlusconi' is connected with the 'President' of AC Milan. The peculiarity of this process of mirroring is that the 'President' is *connected directly* to the subset of the team—the *winning team*—and just indirectly to the *losing team*, through the mediation of 'Collaborators' (Galliani and Leonardo). Since the relationships are loaded with value, we can identify the first one (President-winning team) as a *positive relationship* (in the sense that favors the construction of the 'winning' public image of Berlusconi), the indirect relationship between him and the *losing team* (losing team-Galliani and Co.-President) as a *negative-relationship*. The supporters are directly related to the team, directly related to Galliani and Co. and indirectly related in a *negative-relationship* to the 'President.' Thus, the *public persona* of Silvio Berlusconi (who is the Prime Minister of Italy, the founder of Mediolanum bank, the major shareholder of Fininvest and Mediaset, and so on and on!) is—at least in part—shaped through the mirroring process originating in 'being-the-President-of-AC Milan.'

Leonidas Goes to Sicily

Next time you go to San Siro do not sit in the tribune but in the curve.

—MAURIZIO ZAMPARINI

In the last two decades, the sphere of Italian soccer has seen the rise of another patron who, like Berlusconi, in a short time-span secured a strong metaphorical link between his club and his public persona; but, this time the emphasis was on virtuous upkeep, rather than on a winning character. When, in 1980s, Maurizio Zamparini attempted to acquire Udinese Calcio, his name didn't ring a bell for most Italians. Nowadays, the owner of US Città di Palermo is one of the most visible and controversial figures on the scene. Like Berlusconi, Zamparini is a self-made man and a successful entrepreneur who gained a prominent role in Italian soccer in a short time. And also like Berlusconi, Zamparini primarily relied on the new media to develop his public persona. However, while the former is the correlate of Mars, the latter embodies Leonidas for his non-negotiable appeal to virtue and morality.

In a sense, Zamparini is the nemesis of Berlusconi. He has been seeking to build a new course for Italian soccer, calling for a dramatic change in a number of its contemporary aspects. First, while Berlusconi wishes to link his image to the one of a winning team, Zamparini has stressed multiple times that, in order to save Italian soccer, what matters is to set "democratic rules": "I idealize sport as an activity where we are all really on a par and the best of us is the winner" (Saverio Lodato, *L'Unità*, November 2nd, 2004, p. 11). In this regard, his greatest achievement was the introduction of an agreement that more equitably distributes profits coming from TV broadcasting rights of soccer games. His democratic zeal was supposedly also at the heart also of Zamparini's quarrel with Galliani (AC Milan's vice-president) for a more democratic management of the Lega Calcio Serie A, a public discussion which reached very harsh tones at times.

Zamparini's appeal to virtue and morality was seen in other contexts as well. He has repeatedly and energetically demanded more secure stadiums. On the tragic night of the Catania-Palermo match, when a local policeman was killed in a riot, he declared, "Nobody won tonight, but everybody lost" (*Il Messaggero*, February 3rd, 2007, p. 2), and remarked on the necessity of improving the security measures within and around the stadiums. The most recent changes in stadium management—for example, the stricter controls over ticket sales and the exclusion of police forces from the stadium—are in keeping with Zamparini's proposals and owe much to his zeal. Also of note were the open letters that the president of the *Rosaneri* wrote to the Cavaliere. In these unusual documents, Zamparini publicly discusses both what connects and what separates the two powerful businessmen (all appeared in *Libero* on February 20th, 2009, p. 13, November 3rd, 2004, p. 14, and August 26th, 2003, p. 1). The missives, clearly linking Zamparini's *persona* to Berlusconi's, argued quite clearly that what is at stake is not just soccer, but also politics— revealing how close in the present-time the link between the two spheres is. But, in the most recent one of the series, our Leonidas reprimands his nemesis: "Next time you go to San Siro do not sit in the tribune but in the curve. There you'll hear the true voice of the people," By means of this, Zamparini chides the overtly detached behavior of Berlusconi and while reinforcing the need for patrons and teams to close the cultural and behavioral gap severing them from the supporters.

On the other hand, over the past two decades, Zamparini's business has grown along with his visibility. After owning Pordenone Calcio for a few years, in July 1987 he purchased Società Sportiva Calcio Venezia, which was on the verge of bankruptcy (and which he immediately merged with its longstanding rival Calcio Mestre). But when, in July 2002, the occasion to acquire Palermo arouse, he took it, even if that meant "abandoning" his native region and taking away from it a precious financial support. In the meantime, he has made investments in Sicily of about one hundred million euro, creating approximately one thousand jobs (*Corriere della sera*, January 18th, 2007, p. 24). His name has also been associated with the Moggi affair in 2006 and to a corruption scandal for tax evasion in 2007 (*Il foglio*, May 19th, 2006, p. 1 and Luigi Ferrarella, *Corriere della sera*, January 18th, 2007, p. 24). So do we really have here a Leonidas of soccer? We shall not pursue this issue further. But the facts we have suggest that he partially succeeded in securing a moralized public image.

Summing up, what to most Italians was a bare particular, 'Maurizio Zamparini', came to be linked in due time (and within the soccer sphere) with the patron of two Serie A clubs (Società Sportiva Calcio Venezia and US Città di Palermo). Acting in this role, in a short time and with the aid of the new media, Zamparini created a public *persona* in the sphere of daily life, which acquired notoriety and success.

A Season Ahead?

We conclude our analysis here. Before leaving you, however, we shall make a few remarks. First of all, our analysis was limited to a few notable examples of patronage. There are other kinds of cases deserving close study.

1. *Shareholding clubs*, such as FC Barcelona and Real Madrid AD. The mirroring mechanism is here quite complex, because the legal and administrative structure of the club prevents the affirmation of a figure who could emerge as the ultimate keystone of the team.

2. *Supporter's owned clubs*, such as Spezia Calcio. In these cases, the image of the club directly reflects the spirit of a town, whose members decide to represent the team financially as well.

3. *International patrons*, such as Roman Abramovich (patron of Chelsea FC) and the Abu Dhabi United Group Investment and Development Limited (recent patron of Manchester City FC). The global market has recently seen the rise of wealthy individuals acquiring the property of high profile foreign teams. For quite obvious reasons, in these cases the link between the patron and the public *persona* is established through the construction of a team of superstars, more than through the recourse to the cultural and historical heritage of the club; and, as for AC Milan, more attention is devoted to cultivate (through the media) a relationship with the far-away supporters rather than with the most *historical* devotee.

4. *Multi-club patrons*, such as Luciano Gaucci, Franco Sensi, and Massimo Moratti. The soccer scene hosts patrons who own and manage more than one club at a time. Usually, the teams do not compete in the same league; they may, however, exchange players and staff. Such cases are relevant to our issue in that they usually muddy the image that their patrons are trying to establish through one of the clubs they own. For example, Franco Sensi's image as patron of AS Roma was negatively affected by the secondary relations he entrenched with other satellite clubs (Olympique Lyonnaise, US Città di Palermo).

This is just a first, quick look at the way soccer can be used as a metaphor for life in general. Plenty of other cases could be examined, such as the way soccer is often used to interpret life's good and bad fortune, ethical virtue, creativity, loyalty, and honor.

KICKS FROM THE MARK

It's Down to Penalties

25

Bad Luck or the Ref's Fault?

ROBERT NORTHCOTT

My son and I couldn't believe it. England out on penalties yet again. Months of anticipation ended by heartache and misery, another generation's World Cup dreams dashed forever in the cruelest way. Because a penalty shoot-out is just a lottery, a matter of who gets lucky on the day. We all know that, yes?

But luck is a slippery concept. When we look more closely, it's impossible to make good sense of it without engaging a whole range of philosophical issues surrounding probability and explanation. Is luck really something objective, or just a convenient scapegoat? Let's see.

What Is Luck?

I am English (couldn't you tell?). England has a particularly miserable record in penalty shoot-outs. For some time, we seriously argued that there was no point even in practicing them. In the face of that attitude, persistently losing shoot-outs starts to seem less like bad luck and more like simple negligence. Now even England practices them beforehand—but there is preparation, and there is preparation. These days, it's becoming common for goalkeepers to have all previous penalties by the opposition players on film, even viewing them on an iPod during the event (as Ben Foster did to help Manchester United top Tottenham in the 2009 Carling Cup). Researchers have pinpointed the optimal ordering of takers, as well as precisely what kind of penalty is most likely to succeed. (Since you asked, a shot into the top metre of the goal scores ninety-nine per cent of the time. This suggests that, if skillful enough, players should be perfecting that. And the optimal order is for your best penalty-taker to take the fifth penalty, the second best the fourth, and so on back to the first.)

If you don't take advantage of these methods, twenty years ago maybe you could shrug your shoulders and blame bad luck but these days that won't cut it. Imagine entering a penalty shoot-out fielding a goalkeeper who was blind. No one would then blame the presumably inevitable defeat on bad luck, as it is obvious that being able to see improves your odds greatly. But there is good evidence that these other methods of preparation also improve your odds. So why should going in without any practice be thought any less culpable than going in with a blind man?

At the root of the notion of luck is a second one, that of *probability*. 'Bad luck' implies that it isn't your fault. The probabilities were in your favor, nothing more could be done, the dice just happened to fall the wrong way. Perhaps you prepared for a shoot-out super-professionally but by chance your keeper happened to dive the wrong way each time and so you lost anyway.

How far can we push this? The key phrase here is 'by chance'. It implies that, assuming your keeper has prepared all he reasonably can, he can't then be blamed if still he guesses the wrong way. But is any event truly chancy, or is all uncertainty merely a result of our ignorance? Is it really true that the opposition's penalties couldn't have been predicted better? Maybe a super-advanced alien scientist, by minutely examining the kicker's brain, could have predicted successfully which side he would shoot. Or, similarly, which way a goalkeeper would dive. In which case, diving or shooting the wrong way is not bad luck rather it is merely incompetence. After all, the alien scientist would never get it wrong.

Presumably, no one considers it reasonable to expect quite *that* degree of preparation. But maybe in the future a keeper who dives the wrong way will seem no more acceptable than one who is blind. In other words, all talk of luck seems not to be absolutely objective after all. Standards of judgment change. What was bad luck twenty years ago may just be negligence today, even though the physical event is exactly the same. Rain delays at the Wimbledon tennis championships used to be blamed on bad luck with the weather. More recently though, the reaction became, "why don't they build a roof?" And so, they did. The point is that all depends on what we judge a normal or reasonable level of preparation to be.

This doesn't apply only to penalty shoot-outs, of course. Is hitting the post bad luck, or just inaccurate shooting? Is getting injured bad luck, or just inadequate conditioning or concentration? Again, it all depends on what is considered normal or reasonable.

Fate and Determinism

These difficulties tie into a deeper issue, that of *determinism*. Is it true that, if only we knew the exact micro-composition of a coin, the exact movements of the air molecules around it and the exact strength with which it had been flipped, we would then know whether it was going to come up heads or tails? Similarly, if only we knew the exact state of every neuron in a goalkeeper's brain, could we then calculate with certainty whether he would dive right or left? If yes, then saying that a coin flip is fifty-fifty, or that it's fifty-fifty which way a keeper will dive, is merely to express our ignorance of the relevant micro-details rather than to capture any deep physical fact about the world.

Under the influence of Newtonian physics, for centuries many scientists and philosophers thought that deep down everything in the universe really is determined in this way. If only we knew every detail, nothing would be uncertain to us. More recently though, quantum mechanics has been taken to imply that perhaps the universe is fundamentally chancy after all, and uncertainty is *not* always a symptom of our ignorance. The controversy continues today.

In the case of penalties, we are applying the idea of determinism to the human brain. After all, our brains are presumably part of the physical universe too. But if, alien-style, I was able to predict other humans' behavior, could I not also predict my *own* future actions? In fact, what would there be for me to *decide* about at all? That's fatalism. My future decisions, and all my opponents' too, would already be determined. I could know in advance exactly what would happen and who was going to win. Penalty shoot-outs would become rather boring. So would all of sport for that matter, and plenty else besides.

It is often complained that the World Cup's knockout format does not reliably identify the best team because it is too chancy. But, in light of determinism, what is the "best" team? One that would have won, say, sixty percent of tournaments but, as it happened, not this one? But perhaps if we knew the state of the world in enough detail we'd also know for sure who was going to win the tournament, no doubts or percentages required. Any sixty percent figure would then be just a reflection of our ignorance, as would any "best" team claim—that team would merely have *seemed* best to us, not actually *been* the best.

A hypothetical omniscient creature to whom nothing is uncertain is sometimes called "Laplace's demon", named for the French philosopher and mathematician Pierre Laplace who put forward this metaphor for determinism almost two hundred years ago. Such a demon would have no truck with sixty percent chances of winning. To its all-knowing eye, everything would be either a one hundred percent chance or zero.

Can Luck Be Objective?

So is there nothing objective to luck or probabilities after all, rather just ignorance? That conclusion would be too hasty; we mustn't throw out the baby with the bathwater. It is true that all depends on whatever level of knowledge or preparation we consider reasonable. And, in turn, what we consider reasonable may be partly arbitrary—but also partly not. Let's focus on the glass half-full. Perhaps talk of luck can be rehabilitated as objectively respectable. Sure, it has to be relativized to a particular understanding of reasonableness but if everyone shares that understanding, where's the problem?

This approach has promise. The details of defining this relativized variety of objective probability turn out to be tricky, but all we need here is the rough idea. When we can agree on what's reasonable and what isn't, things start looking good again for objective judgments of luck. And often we *are* able to agree plenty enough. Consider a single penalty. Everyone accepts that, in the absence of bizarre alien technology, it is not reasonable to expect fantastic mind-reading skills. For that reason, assuming no other effective method is available either, all would agree that it is indeed a matter of luck whether the kicker guesses correctly which way the keeper will dive.

Here's another example: "penalty shoot-outs are more of a lottery than a regular game." The best way to examine this is to think about the chances of a good team beating a bad one. If that chance is 75–25, say, then outcomes are likely to reflect merit rather than mere luck; if only 52–48, then we are clearly in lottery territory. So the million-dollar question becomes: what are the numbers for a regular game and for a penalty shoot-out? It's only fair to castigate shoot-outs for being a lottery if it's their number that's closer to fifty-fifty.

Such numbers only make sense once we understand what 'good' and 'bad' mean. In the shoot-out case, perhaps a good team corresponds to one that makes all the specialized preparations mentioned earlier, plus maybe having a goalkeeper especially good at saving penalties. And perhaps even—a factor beloved of amateur psychologists everywhere—the confidence that comes from a good history in such shoot-outs. Define a bad team as one lacking all these attributes. What are the odds then of the good team winning the shoot-out? It's hard to estimate precisely without further research but it seems plausible that although the good shoot-out team would be favored, a good regular team would be favored in a regular game even more. In that case, we can say—objectively—that shoot-outs are indeed more of a lottery than regular games. (So perhaps England can pin some of the blame on bad luck after all.)

Notice a few further points here: first, this doesn't mean that shoot-outs are a *total* lottery. They're not fifty-fifty shots; just closer to fifty-fifty than are the regular games. (So it's probably not *just* bad luck that England have lost so many.) Second, it's perfectly possible for the same team to be rather bad at the regular game but pretty good at shoot-outs. They may therefore often win a shoot-out even after having been poor otherwise. But that's not necessarily luck—that's just being good at an especially vital aspect of World Cups. Blame the rules committee, not the winners. Third, maybe you disagree with some of my values for these numbers? Okay, but the real point is to nail down exactly which numbers are relevant. How you then fill in their values is a separate matter.

All this also raises a separate question: What figures should we *want*? Presumably fifty-fifty would make a sport pretty boring because it would be totally fluky, akin to a World Cup of coin-tossing. But equally, in the eyes of many, 100–0 would be pretty dull too—there should always be some room for an upset. Perhaps how best to strike the balance is ultimately just a matter of taste. Different sports offer different answers. The best player wins the tournament frequently in tennis, but only rarely in golf. Baseball is nearer the chancy end, as in a regular game a good team will beat a bad team at best 55 or 60 per cent of the time. Rugby and American football are rather more predictable. Football seems to be somewhere in the middle.

Whose Fault Is It?

So we see that we can't always blame everything on bad luck. What (or who) else can we blame a defeat on, then? It turns out to be tricky to pin everything on anything. Playing the blame game is easy to do but irritatingly difficult to justify.

There are few things more fun than whining about referees, for instance. But does it ever really make sense to pin the blame for defeat on one refereeing decision? After all, any defeat has myriad causes, such as the other goals, missed chances, injuries to star players, and so forth. Aren't these other causes equally as important? Claims of bad luck can be judged objectively if—but only if—we agree on standards of reasonableness. Something similar now turns out to apply when assigning blame too.

A recent strand in the philosophical literature defines a *cause* in terms of deviations from a default state. For example, physically speaking a stationary football's default state is to remain stationary and undisturbed, like a sleeping dog. A cause is then any deviation from this default state, in other words a disturbance that makes the ball move, such as being kicked. That may just sound like a roundabout way of saying that kicking the ball caused it to move, but the real point is how things are relativized to what we take to be the 'natural' default state. After all, strictly the ball's physical robustness was also a cause of its moving—otherwise, upon being kicked the ball would merely have shattered rather than moved. But we take this robustness for granted and thus it is disregarded as a cause. Because virtually all of us share this judgment of what's default and what's not, so we also all share the thought that being kicked—rather than its own robustness—is what caused the ball to move. If, in contrast, we had thought that a ball's robustness naturally fades over time, then the deviation from the default would have been the ball's *sustained* robustness and that *would* now have been fingered as a cause, just as we are happy to give causal credit to a marathon runner's unusual stamina.

So, alas for family values, deviance is where it's at—no deviation, no causation. Let's bring this back to referees. If our default expectation is that a referee gets easy decisions correct, then it's certainly a deviation from that if he refuses our team an obvious last-minute penalty. Such a critical mistake is endorsed as indeed a cause of our defeat. But many other candidates are not. For instance, the forty-yard shot that didn't go into the top corner, or the routine save that wasn't fumbled—in such cases, the actual outcome was exactly the default expectation, and no deviation means no cause. The same applies to 'causes' such as the presence of oxygen in the atmosphere. Sure, there's a sense in which the oxygen is a cause of our losing the game as without it the game presumably would have been abandoned as impossible. But unless the tournament is being held in outer space, happy levels of oxygen are clearly assumed by all so again there's no deviation here. Once given our shared default expectations, that is, it is perfectly objective to single out the referee's bad decision as the cause of defeat and to ignore the oxygen and the missed forty-yarders. In the same way, to explain a shoot-out defeat we usually pick out the missed penalties not the ones that were scored.

Exploring this point more widely, we can now appreciate better all those pundit clichés that concern credit and blame. Take the favorite mantra of the smarter-than-thou, namely that, "defense wins championships." What, if anything, might this claim amount to? After all, obviously many things win championships, not just defense. Sometimes, no doubt, the comment just is half-baked. But here are a couple of more charitable readings:

1. The difference between a good and bad defense matters more than that between, say, a good and bad attack, or good and bad tactics. (I'll assume sufficiently shared understandings of 'good' and 'bad' here.) Imagine someone saying it's important to know the rules of the game. Well, sure, but even relatively ignorant players know the rules well enough to play, so in practice it's not a big factor. The claim here is that in a similar way having a good rather than bad attack is not a big factor, or at least not as big as having a good rather than bad defense.

2. Alternatively, perhaps attack and defense matter equally. But whereas anyone can appreciate dazzling forward play, good defense tends to go unnoticed because it is less eye-catching. Emphasizing the latter, therefore, is a useful corrective to this common bias. Parroting "defense wins championships" serves to highlight that defense *also* wins championships, not that it does so *more* than other factors.

My own feeling is that there may be some of both 1 and 2 going on. Ultimately though, claim 2 concerns our psychology, so I won't pursue it here. But claim 1 is about picking out some causes rather than others, which is precisely what we've been talking about. Because the necessary understandings of 'good' and 'bad' are widely shared, I think we can adjudicate claim 1 objectively. An initial crude check, for instance, would be to see whether winning a league correlates more with having the best goals-against rather than goals-for record.

Regrettably, pundits are rarely explicit about what they do mean exactly, or even aware that they ought to be. Nevertheless, that doesn't mean that *we* can't spell it out for them. Here's another common pearl of wisdom: "the game will be decided in midfield." What could be meant by picking out the midfield (or wherever) in particular? One answer is that the difference between a good and bad outcome was especially great there. To put this another way, whereas the match-ups elsewhere were unlikely to be particularly one-sided, in midfield there was a realistic chance of one team dominating the other. Assuming that the default expectation is for rough parity in all areas, the biggest deviation—and so the most important cause—would therefore be in midfield. This claim is, in principle at least, objective. Moreover it may be true of some matches more than others, in which case it would actually be informative too—assuming it was right.

The same applies to much else emanating from blogs and TV studios: "at the highest level, you need quality," "England will never win, because of their tactical naivety," "you need a good squad these days, not just a first eleven," "forwards are match-winners," and so on. With effort, it may really be that all of these can be translated from mere hot air into something objectively testable.

Choosing the Scapegoat

Alas, often several different causes all qualify as deviations. As well as the referee's blunder, our striker also missed an open goal and our best player got injured. The default expectation, of course, is that an open goal will not be missed—that's why missing one is so memorable—and that, unless he's made of balsa wood, a player will not be injured. Accordingly, both of these other causes are endorsed by the default-deviation criterion and so there is no objective justification for singling out the referee's decision alone.

Then we are back to our original question—how can we justify picking out some causes over others? In terms of objective causation, it seems that we can't. John Stuart Mill, a nineteenth-century English philosopher, termed this, "the problem of causal selection." But often, as Mill himself noted, it's really other factors that do the work. Blaming the referee, for instance, is a well known way to divert attention from the equally blameworthy poor tactics or goalkeeping blunder. Indeed, so convenient is this tactic that you often hear it even when the referee hasn't really made a mistake at all.

Frequently though, it's *moral* feelings that direct us towards one cause rather than another, as when we blame an accident on a driver's drunkenness rather than on the bad weather. Likewise in football, if a coach or player is especially irritating, of course we'll seize gleefully on their mistakes rather than on those of others. And in a mirror image, if a player is one we especially like we tend to credit his contributions in particular. Perhaps it's because rule-enforcers are inherently irritating anyway that we are especially likely to pick out referees.

Really, much the same was true of luck as well. Does a reasonable level of preparation for penalty shoot-outs include proper practice? Maybe it's *because* I have long been irritated by the English players' lump-headedness that I am more inclined to say 'Yes'. So next time you're cursing bad luck or singling out someone to blame, ask yourself whether you aren't just dressing up your own prejudice. It's a very common human tendency.

As often, then, overall the truth is nuanced. Philosophy tells us that sometimes we really are objectively entitled to blame bad luck or the referee (or both). But only sometimes.

26

Kierkegaard at the Penalty Spot

ANDRE KRNAC

The summer of 2000 provided a license to those Dutch who sought a therapist at the bottom of a beer bottle. A fruitless exercise that only offers words of silence, but with each appointment the cruelty of sobriety for fans of *De Oranje* could be further washed away in a groggy undertow, hopefully taking with it the memories of Holland's unfathomable exit in that summer's Euro tournament. That Holland lost to Italy in the semi-final can simply be excused as one of the conditions of sport. That Holland largely authored its own demise escapes such a simple explanation.

And yet the unthinkable came to pass during that ill-fated semi-final. Over two hours of football would unfurl a tragic shipwreck tale, as penalty misses by Frank de Boer, twice, Patrick Kluivert, Jaap Staam, and Paul Bosvelt consigned Holland's chances of advancement to the briny deep. The debris that littered the score sheet explains Holland's demise rather crudely; five penalties out of six missed, two of which occurred before the end of stoppage time. On that summer day partisans of the *Azurri* were excused from pondering what transpired, as victory doesn't lend itself too often to excursions down the corridors of introspection. But for others, questions must have been raised after witnessing the unfathomable; the simplest of which must have been, "How can the penalty spot become such a source of tragedy?"

In the postmortem to the match, David Winner's *Brilliant Orange* (Bloomsbury, 2000) offered up two different explanations as to why five penalty attempts failed to acquaint the ball with the back of the net. One was represented by Johan Cruyff—Rinus Michel's greatest apostle of Ajax's Total Football ethos and esteemed denizen of football's pantheon—while the other was that of Gyuri Vergouw—a passionate Holland fan and something of a penalty theorist. The more established position was the one held by Cruyff, who essentially argued that penalty kicks are largely governed by the rather indifferent rules of chance (p. 246). This belief, often shared by many players, was one of placating fans by largely absolving responsibility from the players because if penalty kicks lie within the realm of chance, and luck plays a large role in determining the outcome, then fate was having a rather insatiable taste for misfortune that day, at least for the Dutch. On the other hand, Vergouw chalked up the position that penalty kicks as a game of chance is slightly nonsensical and skirts the larger issue. Vergouw placed the blame for failure squarely on the shoulders of the players and coaching staff, suggesting that they were ill prepared to succeed at the penalty spot. Vergouw essentially believes that penalty kicks can be approached with a measure of science, viewing penalty kicks as a learnable discipline that can minimize any dalliance with failure (p. 247). On one point Vergouw nods in agreement with Cruyff: penalties aren't really a part of football.

The Illegitimacy of Penalty Kicks

A reason why the concept of the penalty seems out of place is that the penalty itself is a kind of a palimpsest, as the teamwork that authored the fouled opportunity is erased to make way for a static two-person narrative, pensive penalty kick taker versus the nervously awaiting goalkeeper. At its heart, a penalty kick is a moment of abstraction from what a football match essentially is, a moment granted by the outstretched referee's arm that points to the dot of white paint twelve yards in front of the goal. The penalty shoot-out is an even greater abstraction, as the decision for penalties bypasses the referee's judgment entirely and is given by regulatory mandate. Regulations currently dictate that the only way to break the impasse of a draw is through a series of gun-averse duels, trading in a set of pistols for a series of penalty kicks, the last team standing wins. Regardless of match context, during or after, a penalty kick remains a static abstraction of a team game.

A further reason to support the idea that penalty kicks are seemingly out of place is that on many occasions they don't acquire any sense of legitimacy. The penalty kick as a way of dispensing justice may seem less than legitimate because a penalty kick is largely based on the judgment of a future that may have been, an approximation of the future. The implication a penalty kick carries with it is that it is based on the judgment that the player fouled in the eighteen-yard box would have generated a chance on goal and that the chance on goal likely would have resulted in a goal. In short, a penalty kick is an extrapolation about a future that was never allowed to happen, of which it can never be certain if the chance on goal would have even resulted in a goal. Can it be known for certain that a player fouled just inside the eighteen-yard box would have scored? Would a player fouled immediately in front of the goalkeeper actually have a clear opportunity to score even though geometry and a particular player's skill may suggest otherwise? The curiosity about the penalty kick is that it translates a hypothetical chance on goal into a circumstance where the opportunity to score is under ideal conditions. No defender is there to badger and obstruct the player with the ball and the mere centrality of the penalty spot provides the most usable angles, leaving the penalty kick taker with nothing but the need to make a simple choice. Still, a penalty kick remains difficult to take. (If you disagree, just ask Kluivert, Staam, Bosvelt and de Boer, twice). If it is indeed this act of choosing that makes penalties difficult, then what is it about making a choice that can prove so difficult?

Kierkegaard, the Self, and Choice

The thorny nature of a penalty kick was unlikely to impress itself upon the Danish philosopher and theologian Søren Kierkegaard. Kierkegaard died in 1855 in Copenhagen, at least a few decades before football began its global migration away from England's shores. The first club side established in Spain was *Recreativo Huelva* in 1889, with Danish clubs more than likely following suit at a later date. Despite football having evaded his experience, there is much Kierkegaard can offer to explain why the penalty spot can occasionally discredit the best of professionals. Kierkegaard's *The Concept of Anxiety* (Princeton, 1980) can shed some light as to why the prospect of the penalty kick can prime some for failure. A work driven in part by the issue of our relationship to freedom, it's mainly preoccupied with surveying the instances where a person's striving for freedom can run aground. Regardless of the various shades of unfreedom colored throughout the text, there are two interrelated aspects that can offer up a bit of clarity on why the penalty spot can be a menace: that the act of choosing requires something to guide the decision and that choice itself carries with it the potential to be saddled with a paradox.

What courses through the filament of our lightbulb of inspiration when deciding to do something? Why does a person choose as one does when making a choice? A simple answer is to view a choice simply as a means to obtain a desired state of affairs. A choice then becomes either correct or incorrect depending on if the desired outcome is met. An accomplished penalty taker such as David Villa would have chosen correctly if he scored, incorrectly if he failed to do so. But resting an evaluation of a choice simply on its success or lack thereof does not explain why a particular choice was made in favor of other available options. Couching the appraisal of choice on a matrix of success or failure fails to capture the full range of choices that can occur.

One reason why a choice cannot be simply evaluated on a crude success-fail matrix is because not all decisions carry the same weight of importance. Choices can range from the banal to the important largely on to what degree it reflects something meaningful to the individual. A penalty kick scored is much less important when a team is up by three goals than a penalty kick that is needed to either draw a match or take the lead. Circumstance can play an important role in determining the significance of a choice. But how does one determine what constitutes the banal choice and what constitutes the important one? For Kierkegaard, an answer can be had by assessing what part of and how much of the self is staked in making a choice. The Kierkegaardian conception of the self in *The Concept of Anxiety* is that the self is a tripartite construction, a synthesis of body and mind united in a third term, spirit (p. 43). To answer the question what provides a meaningful source for a choice is to determine what part of and just how much of the self is being engaged in the making of a decision.

Not all choices are purchased at the marketplace of rational ideas. Drives and desires, considerations driven by our own body, can and do make claims on our everyday lives. It is not so much that a desire is chosen but rather that the desire makes the choice on what one should do. To a starving person, the desire to obtain food will more than likely outweigh any other competing desire, such as a desire for friendship or a desire for some abstract notion of justice. One of the drawbacks concerning a desire or drive is that the consideration of any implications upon the external circumstances can be secondary to satisfying the desire itself. Francesco Totti's penchant for the Panenka chipped penalty may be his preferred method for taking a penalty, but any goalkeeper wise to his desire for the chip would be more likely to save his attempt if Totti were to attempt it all the time. One of the difficulties surrounding desires and drives is that they can, and by definition must be, narrow in scope, for their satisfaction can only be obtained by securing the object desired.

On the other hand, engaging the faculty of reason to consider choices reflects some awareness of universal ideas. Choosing to act in accordance with a universal, such as acting in agreement with a moral law for example, carries with it the recognition that the external, objective world is not just there for one individual's exploitation but rather exists for a community of people, thereby limiting what a person can do. An implication of acting in accordance with some universal notion is that it can hinder the possibility for individual expression. If everyone was obliged to act in the same way then the notion of a particular self begins to erode. But the compromise of self-expression seems to be of little concern for the penalty taker because the options for self-expression are severely limited; there are only a few ways a player can score a penalty kick. Nevertheless, a problem still remains: which of the options available should a penalty taker choose to realize? In trying to answer this question a penalty taker would certainly consider the objective concerns, that is to what side the goalkeeper will dive or what shot he feels more comfortable with to name just a few examples, in his deliberation on which way to send his penalty kick. Any rational deliberation focuses not on the expression of the kick but rather on what is the best means to obtain a desired outcome.

It's difficult to stitch together a compact definition of Kierkegaard's concept of Spirit. Spirit according to Kierkegaard is both "immediate" and "dreaming" in addition to being a power that is both hostile and friendly (p. 44). The immediacy and dreaming nature of spirit lies in its ability to occupy two tenses, it can abstract from the present to imagine a future. The hostile and friendly nature of spirit entails that spirit disrupts one's sense of self as a precondition of making a choice that will have some impact on the future. Difficult decisions in life, such as what career to pursue, always seem more difficult before they are made then afterwards because the various possibilities of that choice—will the choice prove successful or not—remain unknown. The unity Kierkegaard speaks of between body and mind united by the third term of spirit is that a person can only grasp their personhood in its entirety if both body and mind are marshaled together harmoniously in a decision that involves the future orienting nature of spirit. It is this difficulty in trying to invest oneself as mind and body towards a future choice where problems can begin to take hold.

Freedom and Choice, Anxiously Dispensed

Was it a matter of making a series of wrong choices that left the Dutch grasping for answers after the semi-final? Did some of the players simply doubt their choices, thereby making it difficult to execute their penalty kick? How much of the self should be invested in an action is one part of the problem with making a choice. But the greater difficulty is determining how a person will negotiate with the unknowns that are bundled up within the act of choosing. A person can buttress the 'what' of choice—"What will I do?"—with some kind of justification.

While they were both at Arsenal, Thierry Henry and Robert Pires could in some way explain their botched attempt at coordinating a penalty as a means of recreating Johan Cruyff and Jesper Olsen's infamous passed penalty first attempted at Ajax in 1982. The ability to underwrite the 'why' of a choice—"Why am I doing this?"—however remains elusive. For Kierkegaard, one part of the difficulty in trying to explain the 'why' of action lies in the nature of his conception of the individual as underdetermined. A part of the self always seems to lie outside of an individual's grasp. A person, barring oppression or illness, can lay claim to their body and be in possession of their thoughts, but their spirit, the force that impels them forward to invest their personhood into the future, is something that cannot be claimed as rightly their own. Kierkegaard regards the individual as not just a synthesis of body and mind but also of the temporal and eternal (p. 85). This facet of the Kierkegaardian self is that it is this elusive spiritual and eternal aspect that makes possible the capability to make future oriented actions.

Paradoxically, freedom itself further compounds matters regarding the negotiation of a choice. For Kierkegaard, freedom can be considered as the possibility to be able (p. 49). The possibility to be able has two sides, that one is free to think of different possibilities and also that one has the possibility to act on a selected choice. To be able requires both freedom of thought and the capability to act on that thought. The paradox of freedom is that since it is future bound, to choose to act out of a sense of freedom is in some sense to choose the unknown. Antonin Panenka's chipped penalty in the 1976 Euro final against West Germany is an expression of a free act. The chipped penalty towards the centre of the net was never attempted in competition before so there was no historical precedent to draw upon to determine its rate of success. Panenka based his decision strictly on the basis that the goalkeeper will most likely dive to the side, but he could never be entirely certain. The ambiguity of such a free act as the Panenka chip against West Germany is that the these types of free choices are difficult because they can never be justified with certainty, which makes the decision to choose to act somewhat ambiguous.

It's largely due to these unknown parameters—that a person is not entirely self determined and that the choice to act freely is in some way to choose an unknown future—that are embedded within the concept of freedom that can induce a sense of anxiety. Kierkegaard likens anxiety to a kind of dizziness that results from looking down into the abyss of the future, that anxiety is the dizziness of freedom (p. 61). The anxiety attending freedom results from a fear of making a choice due to the inability to accept the uncertainty of a choice's success. Anxiety manifests itself simply because the ability to make a free choice can provide no guarantee for pursuing that choice. Because of the weight of difficult choices and their uncertain outcome it can become easier to choose not to choose, or to settle for a lesser choice with a more certain outcome. Of course such is an evasion of one's freedom. One can argue that the easiest way to take a penalty is to simply not take one, which is why it is usually up to the coach and players to determine who will make the penalty attempts in a penalty shoot out and not up to the referee to randomly choose five players. Having the ability to not choose is a part of the very act of choosing, but in doing so, a lesser option is selected and a smaller, less future invested notion of the self is staked in that choice.

Double Dutch

Was it the anxiety of being unable to deal with the uncertainty of trying to obtain a desired outcome that undid the Dutch in the semi-final? Certainly the conditions were ripe for a sense of anxiety to pervade their attempts at the penalty spot. The Dutch required a victory to make the final so the margin for error offered was quite small. After the first penalty miss in the first half the pressure to make the right choices at the penalty spot must have mounted with each failure, ratcheting up the anxiety with each subsequent penalty miss. Any sense of uncertainty or lack of faith in our choice would effectively make it difficult to maximize our efforts. After the match Gyuri Vergouw rated De Boer's first half miss a five out of ten. For his shoot out miss, a lifeless zero, because his short run up generated negligible power and his body language and run up direction telegraphed shot placement, tipping all odds in the Italian goalkeeper Toldo's favor. De Boer's two failed attempts seem to suggest that anxiety played a hand in scuttling Holland's chances to advance, as his deterioration in competence speaks of a player struggling to negotiate with the uncertainties of trying to impose his choice at the penalty spot.

One of Vergouw's prescriptions for penalty kick success is that a player should have either two or three different penalty kicks from which to choose in order to pave the way for more goals. The ability to have options provides a sense of security and thereby a bit more confidence, at least on paper. But while having options may purchase a semblance of comfort, having a range of penalty kicks doesn't necessarily guarantee success. Reducing the penalty kick to a learnable skill may make the execution of a penalty kick easier, but it still doesn't make the matter of choosing which kick to execute any more certain. Take into account a pressure filled context such as a final or semi final and the opportunity for anxiety to rear its head becomes all the more great. "How will the player know which way the goalkeeper will dive?" is a question no amount of preparation can answer.

It might be argued that the simple task of a penalty kick is to score a somewhat charitable goal and not to realize a philosophical notion of how the matter of choice can remain inherently ambiguous, but the act of choosing itself, of having confidence in the choice despite its resting on an ambiguous ground can never be divorced from the act of taking a penalty. If anxiety's uncertainty can prove difficult when structured as a matter of choosing amongst a few options at the penalty spot and having the conviction to execute a selected choice, then when taken out of such a tightly structured environment the depth and possibility for anxiety becomes all the more apparent.

Existential choices, such as those revolving around a career choice for example, can carry more anxiety because the possible paths can be more numerous and the choices more broad and difficult. After all, a missed penalty can be papered over by scoring a goal in open play or getting another chance to succeed in a future match, season or tournament, but a bad decision regarding one's life may not have the possibility of being so easily erased.

27

"It's a Lottery!": Penalties and the Meaning of Winning

BEN SAUNDERS

"May the better team win," is something of a cliché in most sports, particularly football. We all know though that the best team—even the best team on the day—isn't always the one that actually wins, particularly when games are decided by penalty shoot-outs.

Many commentators and fans dislike shoot-outs, often branding them "lotteries" and suggesting that they aren't a proper way to settle a football match. If games are decided simply by luck, then there's no reason to suppose the best team will win. Penalties aren't lotteries, however, for they test skill rather than (or as well as) luck. Nor should we suppose the winners of a game always ought to be the better team anyway, for part of what makes football so exciting is its unpredictability. These considerations suggest that penalties are an appropriate way of deciding tied games.

Drawing a Blank

Since football's a fairly low scoring game (unlike, say, basketball or rugby), draws are relatively common. In league matches, this isn't a problem—each team can be awarded a share of the points. Sometimes, however, we need a winner. In knock-out tournaments only one team can progress or, if it's the final, win the trophy. A tied game's no good for deciding which team that should be. In these circumstances, it's often felt that 90 minutes isn't enough. If scores are level at what would ordinarily be the final whistle then teams usually either play extra time or stage a rematch at a later date. There are, however, limits to how long even two teams of professional athletes can play for or to how many extra fixtures can be packed into an already crowded schedule (particularly in international tournaments). We need some other way to decide the outcome of matches where the scores are level at the end of play.

Various mechanisms have been proposed or employed to resolve ties. Before the widespread introduction of shoot-outs, some matches were even decided by a genuine lottery: the toss of a coin. Nowadays, two-legged cup ties are sometimes decided by the "away goals" rule, while FIFA experimented with the "golden goal" rule, with the intention of ensuring that more matches were settled during extra time. Major League Soccer in the US uses the same sudden death overtime.

These measures increase the likelihood of the contest being decided without resorting to penalties, yet ultimately a penalty shoot-out remains the most enduring solution to the problem of separating two teams. Penalties can even decide who wins major titles. The World Cup Finals of 1994 (Brazil v Italy) and 2006 (Italy v France) both went to penalties, as did the European Champions League in 2005 (Liverpool v AC Milan) and 2008 (Manchester United v Chelsea).

Despite their widespread use, penalties have rarely been popular with players, fans or commentators. Perhaps, this is partly because some teams seem to have more success than others. The average German may well be more favourably disposed to shoot outs than your average Englishman—not for nothing did the former England striker turned sports presenter Gary Lineker once remark that "Football is a simple game—you play for 120 minutes and then the Germans win on penalties" (*The Daily Mirror*, 7th June 2008).

One can't help thinking that the unpopularity of penalties isn't simply sour grapes from the losers. Even the winners are often gracious enough to admit that a shoot-out isn't the best way to win a trophy. No doubt it's this widespread dissatisfaction with penalties that has led to so much experimentation with other ways of settling ties. It seems that no better solution has yet been found. Penalties, to paraphrase something Winston Churchill once said about democracy, are the worst solution apart from all those others that have been tried from time to time.

Libelling Lotteries

Why are penalties so unpopular? The common expression, wheeled out almost every time that a game is decided by spot kicks, is that shoot-outs are a lottery. But what's so bad about lotteries? Lotteries have enjoyed a mixed press over the years. Historically, the Church condemned gambling on games of chance, fearing that it made the undeserving rich and bred idleness. When the English clergyman Thomas Gataker first defended the use of lotteries for gambling, in his 1619 treatise *Of the Nature and Uses of Lots,* it caused quite a stir.

Popular suspicion of lotteries remains much in evidence, even in our less superstitious age. Proposals to distribute scarce goods, such as organs for transplant or school places, by lottery are routinely met by public outcry. Inequalities among local government provisions are criticized as, "postcode lotteries." When someone loses a competition, such as for a job, they're regularly consoled with the words, "it's a lottery."

Life, it's often said, isn't fair—all we can do is make the best of the hand we're dealt. The use of penalty shoot-outs is often seen as simply another case where winners and losers are decided by luck, rather than the appropriate standards of footballing merit. This public hostility towards lotteries seemingly rests on two confusions.

Firstly, many of the cases labelled as 'lotteries' aren't entirely matters of chance. Inequalities in regional provisions of healthcare aren't lotteries because, while where one is born may be a matter of chance, postcodes aren't simply assigned randomly—people can freely move houses and the danger of such inequalities is that the rich may buy access to better schools, healthcare and the like. In a just society, there may be no problem with allocating such goods according to willingness to pay, but the distribution of wealth in our society is not obviously just, even if being born rich is in some sense a matter of chance. One reason for using lotteries is to avoid the undue influence of wealth on one's access to other goods.

Similarly, penalties aren't strictly lotteries, because one can't influence one's chances of success or failure in a lottery. The paradigmatic example of a lottery is tossing a coin: whether you call heads or tails, you have a fifty percent chance of winning. Drawn football matches could be settled by tossing a coin. Indeed, this method has been used; for instance, a 1965 European Cup tie between Liverpool and Cologne was decided (after three drawn matches) by tossing a coin—and the teams were so hard to separate that even the coin had to be tossed twice after sticking in the mud! A penalty shoot-out, on the other hand, is not simply a matter of luck but a contest of skill, as well as nerves, and a more entertaining spectacle.

Secondly, lotteries are often employed to distribute goods because, where two parties have equal claims to some good that they can't both have, they're the fairest thing we can do. If two people need a kidney transplant, but we only have one kidney and no relevant way of choosing between them (each is equally needy, not responsible for their condition, and so on), then our only options are to give neither of them the kidney or to find some way of picking whom to give it to. An auction is one possibility, but obviously favours the rich. A lottery gives each an equal chance of receiving the good, which is the closest we can come to respecting their claims equally.

All's Fair in Love and Football

What exactly does fairness require? The notion of a "level playing field" is particularly apt in football, where it need not be understood purely metaphorically. As teams change ends at half-time though, a sloping pitch needn't be an impediment to an even contest, since it will favour each team for one half. Nor does a perfectly horizontal playing surface suffice to make the contest fair. If the referee's been bribed by one team, that's also unfair.

A cynical observer might question whether any match really involves a level playing field. The English FA Cup regularly pits the international superstars of clubs like Manchester United and Liverpool against the part-time players of non-league minnows. Similar mismatches occur at international level too, such as Mexico versus Belize in the CONCACAF World Cup qualifiers. Can any game really be a fair contest, when one team is so clearly superior to the other?

We all become familiar with the concept of fairness from an early age, as is evident from the frequency with which young children complain of unfairness. Nonetheless, specifying exactly what fairness requires is surprisingly difficult. Not playing by the rules, for example, is generally unfair. It doesn't follow that obeying the rules—whatever they happen to be—is fair though, because the rules themselves may be unfair. The rule, "no women are allowed to go to university," can be applied equally to everyone, but it's unfair because it arbitrarily discriminates against women, who have as much claim to a university education as men.

One thing that fairness doesn't mean is having an equal chance of winning. Earlier, I argued that a lottery may be the fairest way to distribute a good, such as a kidney, when we can't satisfy all of the competing claims. In that example, each patient stood an equal chance of winning, but only because each had an equal prior claim to it. We don't think *everyone* ought to stand an equal chance of receiving the kidney, because many people don't need it. To give the kidney to someone chosen totally at random from the whole society would be unfair. It's only fair to resort to a lottery once we've checked that the two claimants can't be separated on relevant grounds.

The fact that we can predict which team is more likely to win doesn't undermine the claim that the contest is a fair one, since we'd expect the better team to be more likely to win. Just because Liverpool's team is full of highly-paid international players, that doesn't mean that a match between them and, say, Grimsby Town is an unfair one. One can have a fair contest between unequal opponents.

Fairness may require us to give equal consideration to all parties, but this doesn't imply that they should have equal chances of winning the contest, because it means paying attention to relevant differences. When one person needs a kidney transplant and another doesn't, then giving equal consideration to the claims of each means giving the one kidney we have to the first rather than the second, instead of holding a lottery. Similarly, the better team should be more likely to win a football match, which is a test of footballing skill. Fairness does, however, exclude making the choice on irrelevant grounds, such as popularity, wealth, or shirt colour.

Not Moving the Goalposts

Giving proper weight to all relevant considerations means it's wrong to resort to a lottery too early. Suppose a prize is advertised for a violin contest. If the judges cannot decide between two contestants, it may be fair to award the prize by tossing a coin between them. It wouldn't be fair to simply hold a lottery before hearing the contestants play, as then we wouldn't have a violin contest at all—anyone would stand an equal chance of winning, regardless of their musical proficiency.

The same is true of football matches. If we simply tossed a coin to decide which team progresses, before playing the game, that might be fair but wouldn't be football. The point of the game is to identify the better team on the day, so we need to play it first to establish whether the two teams really do have an equal claim to progress. If scores are level at the end—be that after 90, 120, 180 or 210 minutes—then we take this to establish that the teams can't be differentiated on footballing grounds. Only then do we need some other way of separating them.

It's true that the better team—even the better team on the day—doesn't always win the match. We're all familiar with cases where our team (and it does always seem to be our team) batters the opposition, only to be frustrated by a combination of the woodwork, bad luck and bad officiating, before conceding—against the run of play—to a surprise counter-attack or set piece. Sometimes teams lose games they should've won. Conversely, sometimes they scrape lucky 1–0 wins when they didn't deserve to.

It's difficult to specify exactly what these claims mean. To presuppose standards independent of who scores the most goals may seem controversial, but goals need not result solely from footballing merit. Results can be affected by poor officiating decisions, such as wrongly given or disallowed goals. Moreover, although the common criticism of penalty shoot-outs is that they give too much place to luck, luck enters the regular game as well. Each team may be equally deserving of a goal, but one may score and the other not simply as a result of fortune, such as a lucky deflection. Thus, one team may deserve to score more goals than their opponents on the day yet fail to do so.

Better to Be Better on the Day

We may *say,* "may the best team win," but this is because we recognize that this isn't always the case. We may want the team that plays better on the day to win the contest, but part of what's so exciting about football is that anything can happen—fluke goals can come out of nowhere and allow giant-killings of David and Goliath proportions (or 'cupsets' as they are sometimes called).

What we usually mean isn't simply that the better team in general should win. We often know who that is anyway, from the league table or seedings. What we want is for the best team *on the day* to win. Even good teams can have off days, while even poor players and teams can produce flashes of brilliance. It isn't enough to simply turn up at the ground, compare teamsheets, and declare the winner. We want to know is who should win this contest, here and now, rather than who's best in general.

This is true of all sports contests. If we wanted to give the Olympic gold medal to the fastest sprinter, then we'd simply compare the personal career or season's bests of all the athletes involved. What we do is give it to the athlete who's fastest in one particular race—the final—rather than in general. We may want the fastest in general to be fastest in that race, just as we may want the better team to play better on the day, but they must establish their claim to superiority in that particular contest. It's not enough to be better on paper—that doesn't entitle one to anything. One must always prove one's claim to victory on the pitch. This is the sense in which football matches are fair contests. While the better team may be more likely to win, the scores start at 0–0. Both teams have equal opportunity to establish their claim to victory, and its rewards, in the game itself.

Since winning is defined as scoring more goals, whichever team has scored more goals at the end of the match can be said to deserve victory. This is so even if they don't—based on the balance of play—deserve to have scored more goals (it may be that their goals are simply fortuitous). In such a case, they deserve to win the match, and take whatever points or title is at stake, though they don't deserve to have deserved to win.

If the two teams finish level, then they're equally deserving of victory and have equal claims to whatever the match is supposed to establish—whether that's a trophy or simply progression to the next round. If they're equally-deserving of victory, then it's fair to give them equal chances—for instance by using a lottery.

May the Winners Be the Better Team . . .

We want the better team to win, but it doesn't always happen that the better team in general plays better on the day or even that the team that plays best on the day actually wins the match. Consequently, we can't infer from the fact that one team beats another, even by a considerable margin, that they're the better of the two teams.

If the winners were always the better team, then we'd face all kinds of puzzles. Sometimes, for example, Team A may beat Team B and Team B in turn beat Team C. Logically, if winning always established the better team, then this would establish that Team A was better than Team C; yet we see many examples where Team C beats Team A, creating a puzzling circularity. How can it be that A is better than B, B is better than C, but C is better than A?

In 2005, Chelsea won the English Premier League while Liverpool finished fifth. That May, however, Liverpool completed a remarkable comeback from 3–0 down at halftime against AC Milan to win the European Champions League in Istanbul. If that made them the best team in Europe, then we reach the surprising conclusion that Liverpool were the best team in Europe but not the best team in England! The winners of a football match aren't always the better team—and the game would be a lot less exciting if they were.

If the point of playing a game is to establish which team is the better side, then we must recognize that it's only a very imperfect test, since the winners aren't always the better side. The excitement of football is largely because of its consequent unpredictability, which means that the team who appear worse on paper are often able to snatch a win (or at least draw). This happens so often that we can't suppose the winners of a game are always the better team, which would lead to the paradoxical puzzles just mentioned.

The purpose of a game of football is simply to decide who wins, not who is better. The two teams each have eleven players and ninety minutes with which to out-score their opponents. If one team manages to do this, then they rightly win that contest and take the prize—whether than be a trophy, or merely progression in a tournament or three points. When we witness a giant-killing upset, it's obvious that the victorious underdogs aren't the better team in general, even if they were on the day. Nonetheless, we should say that they really did deserve to win, on the basis that they scored more goals than their opponents. This doesn't make them the better team in general, or even the better team on the day (since they may not have deserved to score more goals), but it does make them the rightful victors.

Winning the Battle versus Winning the War

We must resist the temptation to assume that the winners of a match are the better team—since it's sometimes obvious that this isn't so. This doesn't mean that match outcomes are meaningless; merely that they can't tell us anything in isolation. The outcome of a single game isn't a reliable indicator of the better team. This is particularly so in football because its low-scoring nature, compared to other sports (like American football, basketball, and rugby), makes upsets more likely. A single fortuitous goal can be enough to change who wins.

When we want to be sure of something, we usually double check our findings. This is true of anything, from scientists repeating their lab experiments to double checking that you've locked your door when you leave the house. Relying on a single test or result isn't always enough, especially if it's inherently unreliable. The same principle holds true in sports. In golf, players are tested not only over eighteen holes but also several rounds of the course. In tennis, they play best of three or five sets. In snooker, matches are decided over a number of frames—often more according to the importance of the match and how close the two players are likely to be. In each case, it's felt that a one-off test isn't reliable enough to indicate the better player.

Football follows a similar example in some cases, where matches are played over two legs. If we really wanted to be sure of the better team though, it would be more accurate to have two teams play each other many times over. If we really want to know whether Manchester United are better than Liverpool, for example, then one way to find out would be to have the two face each other thirty or forty times. The results of any individual match may depend heavily on luck, but the more results we have the more confident we can be of our findings. The aggregated results of enough games should show the better team, if the better team is defined as the one that wins more often.

We never have teams play each other so many times, but we have the next best thing. Rather than two teams playing each other repeatedly, they are tested not only against each other but a range of different opponents. League results reflect the performance of each team across a number of independent tests. The team that finishes top of the league is the one that's performed best across the whole range of tests, by beating many of the opponents faced, and thus should be regarded as the best team. Since what it is to be the better team is simply to win more often, this result stands firm even though the results of any individual game tell us nothing about the better team.

The more games that they've played, and the bigger their winning margin, the more confidence we can have in our judgement of the better team. People say, "the league table doesn't lie," but that's true only if it's taken to show who's won the most points, not who's the better team. We all know that the league table is a more reliable indicator of the best teams later in the season—after more games have been played—than earlier, as runs of good or bad form cancel out and teams rise (or fall) to their proper level. The final league standings may also have been overturned if the teams had gone on to play yet more games, but when the season comes to its designated end they're the best indicators we have of the quality of the respective teams.

The Ref's a Useless (Coin) Tosser

The purpose of an individual game is simply to decide the winner, rather than identify the better team. This is done by assessing their performance over ninety minutes, so when a game ends in a tie the two teams are equally-deserving. In such cases it's usually fairest for the teams to split the spoils, as happens when points are divided between them in a league match. The same principle could be followed when it comes to trophies and titles—theoretically they could be shared if two teams draw in the final.

Sometimes, however, a single winner is needed, as in the earlier rounds of a knockout tournament. Here we need some other way of settling ties. One possibility is to continue playing football until a winner is established, as in extra time or a replay. There are limits to how feasible this is given crowded footballing schedules, spectator patience and the physical endurance of even top athletes.

Penalty shoot-outs were introduced to provide a quick and exciting way of separating the teams. It's often alleged that such shoot-outs are a lottery, since they give either team a chance of winning, irrespective of their footballing quality. That's wrong, because penalties don't rest simply on chance but test skill, character and ball placement. Those in the game know there's a skill to taking penalties, which can be taught and practised. Even when they condemn penalties as "lotteries", commentators often contradict themselves and implicitly acknowledge that skill is involved by praising those who strike their kicks well.

Recall that, before the introduction of shoot-outs, some games were literally decided by lotteries. The 1965 European Cup tie between Liverpool and Cologne has already been mentioned, but this isn't unique. A coin-toss was used in the same competition in 1969, this time to decide between Celtic and Benfica.

If neither team can establish their claim to superiority over the preceding game then they are equally-deserving of victory. Consequently, a lottery giving each an equal chance is a fair way to decide between them.

Splitting Hairs

If we can't distinguish the teams on strictly footballing grounds, at least given our time limits, then it's acceptable to resort to some other basis to separate them. A lottery, such as a coin toss, is one possibility. We may prefer penalties because they test skill rather than simply being a matter of luck.

Rejecting lotteries doesn't uniquely favour penalties though. We could test the teams in all sorts of other ways, such as tests of ball control, or simply have them compete in other activities, such as sprinting. We could even have the opposing captains play each other at chess. This would be a test of skill, rather than a matter of chance, but one that's irrelevant to football.

In choosing between these possible procedures, we should bear in mind that football's an entertainment sport. One reason for favouring penalties is the tension and excitement that they provide. Moreover, penalties have the advantage over lotteries or other games, such as chess, of being part of the game of football. This makes them a more appropriate way of separating teams.

It's true that the skills that penalties test—calmness under pressure and ability to score from twelve yards (or to anticipate and save the shot, in the case of goalkeepers)—aren't the only ones relevant in the match itself. Thus, penalty shoot-outs provide somewhat different tests from the rest of the game. Nonetheless, since the abilities tested are part of the game of football, using them to decide the outcome isn't completely arbitrary, as a chess match would be.

If the advantages of penalties over a genuine lottery lie in their excitement and connection to the game, then it follows that the traditional shoot-out isn't our only option. If we're dissatisfied with penalties on these grounds, then we're free to experiment with alternatives. For instance, we could adopt the old North American Soccer League variant on the traditional shoot-out, in which strikers were able to run with the ball from the thirty-five-yard offside line and had five seconds to beat the 'keeper, or play sudden death overtime with fewer players. If these alternatives provide more exciting spectacles for the fans, then they may replace familiar penalty shoot-outs.

Our reasons for rejecting penalties shouldn't be that they rely on luck. Penalty shoot-outs involve both luck and skill, but this is true of the rest of the game too. The reason to prefer penalties to a lottery lies in the excitement and entertainment they provide, and their connection to the game. Thus we should reject penalties only if we have a better, more exciting, way to decide the match.

If one team really is superior, it's their responsibility to establish that by scoring more goals during the game. This reflects the sense in which the game really is a level playing field and explains why we say, "may the better team win." If neither team can demonstrate their superiority in the allotted time period, then there's no objection to treating them as equally deserving of progression and resolving the tie through a lottery or shoot-out. A match settled by penalties isn't, like one decided by an actual lottery, decided without any reference to the relevant standards of football. It may be that the better team didn't win, but that's true of any game.[1]

---

[1] Thanks to Robert Jubb, Patrick Tomlin, and the audience at the Corpus Christi MCR-SCR lunchtime seminar (Oxford, May 2009), particularly Christopher C.W. Taylor, Daniel Halliday, and Gerard Vong, for comments on earlier versions of this chapter.

28

The Loneliness of the Referee

JONATHAN CROWE

Football referees are a varied bunch, but there are several common types familiar to fans and players. There is the stickler, who always applies the letter of the laws. There is the ditherer, who avoids the hard decisions, often raising his whistle to his mouth, but rarely blowing for the foul. There is the frustrated player, who follows the game more closely than he applies the rules, and applauds good play like a fan. There is the poseur, who plays at being a referee: his stance is always a little too upright, his gestures too rehearsed. Finally, there is the postman, who issues yellow and red cards at the slightest opportunity, and the tough guy, who gets into players' faces and invites confrontation.

Fortunately, the ideas we need to understand these different styles of refereeing can all be found in the writings of the existentialist philosopher Jean-Paul Sartre. Sartre was an avid student of football, devoting a long and complex passage in the *Critique of Dialectical Reason* (Humanities Press, 1976) to the interactions between players. As he sagely remarks, "In a football match, everything is complicated by the presence of the other team" (p. 473). However, it is in Sartre's earlier works, *Being and Nothingness* and *Existentialism and Humanism*, that we find his theory of refereeing.

The Moment of Decision

The first lesson we can draw from Sartre's writings concerns the existentially challenging nature of the referee's role. The referee is constantly called upon to make choices that can fundamentally alter the course of a match. The stakes are often high: teams may be crowned champions or relegated from the league, players may win the golden boot or be suspended from the play-offs as a result of a single call.

The referee is free to choose what decision to make. The ball hits a player's arm in the penalty box: the ref is the only one with the power to raise the whistle to his mouth and stop the game. The assistant referee may raise his flag, the players may appeal and the crowd may roar, but ultimately everything depends on the referee. This is the moment of decision, when the fate of the game rests on the ref's shoulders.

The outcome of a whole season or tournament may turn on what happens in that moment. No Australian fan, for example, will forget the moment in the second round of the 2006 World Cup finals when, with the game drawn 0–0 in the ninety-second minute, Italian left-back Fabio Grosso fell over the outstretched legs of Australian defender Lucas Neill. The referee's decision to award Italy a penalty effectively ended the game: Italy went on to lift the World Cup, while Australia was on the next plane home.

The moment of decision plays a central role in Sartre's philosophy. Indeed, he presents it as the defining feature of human experience. In *Being and Nothingness* (Routledge, 1958), Sartre draws a distinction between two basic modes of existence: being-in-itself [*l'être-en-soi*] and being-for-itself [*l'être-pour-soi*]. The being-in-itself is a non-conscious object, which can be encapsulated by reference to a pre-determined essence or function. Inanimate objects, such as books and footballs, fall into this category.

The being-for-itself, by contrast, is a conscious agent or person able to perceive and reflect upon the world around her. Sartre suggests that, far from possessing a pre-determined essence, the being-for-itself is permanently haunted by the possibility of "nothingness" or negation. In other words, the being-for-itself is forced to continually confront the possibility that things might be otherwise than they are.

Freedom and Responsibility

In 1928, when Sartre sat the final exam for his *agrégation* (teaching licence) at the École Normale Supérieure in Paris, he chose to write his paper on the theme of contingency. Unfortunately, he failed miserably, ranking fiftieth in a class of fifty. (Sartre claimed he failed because he tried to be too original; others have suggested it was because he spent more time drinking and chasing women than studying. Georgie Best and Gazza had nothing on Sartre.) In 1929, Sartre took the exam again and topped the class. The theme of contingency would become central to his philosophy.

In our everyday lives, Sartre contends, we are constantly engaged in enquiries about the world around us: questions ranging from whether there is a God to where we put the car keys all place certain aspects of our existence into question. However, since any question we might pose raises the possibility of a negative response, it seems to us that our place in the world is not necessary, but contingent.

According to Sartre, this sense of contingency pervades the human experience of choice. However sure we may be that a particular decision was the right one to take, we are nonetheless aware that another course of action was possible. Since every course we follow is pregnant with alternative paths we might have taken, it seems that we cannot avoid accepting ultimate responsibility for our decisions. Sartre argues that this sense of inescapable responsibility tends to give rise to anguish.

Imagine you're walking along a narrow trail on the edge of a mountain. You are constantly aware of the importance of treading carefully, so as not to lose your footing. At the same time, however, you are also aware that, despite your present care and attention, you could just as easily throw yourself over the precipice (*Being and Nothingness*, pp. 29–32). Sartre points out that human existence is full of such potentially life-altering moments. The everyday actions of driving a car or having a conversation could be altered irrevocably by one decision: in the space of a moment, you could easily steer your car into incoming traffic or make a callous comment that would alienate a loved one forever.

For Sartre, then, human life involves an unavoidable double realisation. In the first place, the alternative possibilities present in my experience of choice reveal to me that I am free. At the same time, however, I am also aware that I am *responsible*, since I am confronted with the apparent absence of constraints on potential, significant exercises of my freedom. Whether I walk calmly along the ledge or throw myself head along into the abyss, the decision rests with me alone.

The Anguish of the Referee

Let's return to the moment of decision. The ball strikes a player's arm in the penalty area. The referee must decide whether or not to call the foul. In this moment, the referee is both free and responsible: nobody can tell her what decision to make and responsibility for the outcome rests with her alone. This position of power naturally gives rise to anguish, in precisely Sartre's sense of the term.

Many referees have lain awake at night running through the details of what unfolded on the field, wondering if they made the right decision.

Sometimes, the answer will be clear enough. Often, however, no amount of effort in trying to recall the events of the game will show definitively what the outcome should have been. This type of situation underlines the contingency of the referee's role: often, there is no reference point that can reveal a particular call as definitively right or wrong.

Even top international refs sometimes find the pressure of their role too much to bear. There is the case of the respected Swedish referee Anders Frisk, who retired from refereeing after receiving death threats from Chelsea fans due to his handling of a 2005 Champions League match against Barcelona. Or Swiss whistleblower Urs Meier, who had to be given police protection against disgruntled English supporters after disallowing a Sol Campbell goal against Portugal in Euro 2004.

Not to mention Norwegian referee Henning Ovrebo, whom Chelsea striker Didier Drogba labelled a "f**king disgrace" on international television for turning down a series of penalty appeals during the 2009 Champions League semi-final, again featuring Barca. It's a brave referee who can stand up in such circumstances and acknowledge that he alone bears ultimate responsibility for his decisions.

On a more prosaic level, hundreds of amateur referees give up the role each season due to the pressures of officiating local club games. It's not just the danger of an unhappy supporter trying to punch you in the parking lot after the match. (Or, indeed, throwing a packet of french fries in your face, as happened to me on one occasion. "Hey, ref, would you like fries with that?") More fundamentally, it is the existential anguish of being the only one who can answer for the many crucial decisions made during the course of a game. It's lonely out there in the middle. No matter how much unsolicited advice a ref may get from the sidelines, in the moment of decision he is on his own.

Authenticity and Bad Faith

Sartre argues that, in order to live an authentic existence, humans must embrace the simultaneous sense of freedom and responsibility that lies at the heart of their lives. They must acknowledge that the type of person they become, far from being dictated by external forces, is an outcome of the life they decide to lead. For the being-for-itself, as Sartre famously puts it in *Existentialism and Humanism* (Methuen, 1948, p. 26), "existence precedes essence." Our personal characteristics are not necessary or fixed, but contingent upon our choices.

A person, unlike an object such as a chair or a beer glass, is not brought into existence with a preordained set of defining features. We are not born honest, cowardly, loyal, or untrustworthy. These types of character traits are, and can only be, a function of the way a person chooses to live. An authentic life involves taking responsibility for our character and recognising our ability to change who we have become. It is only when we die that this project of self-creation is over.

The task of living an authentic life is a challenging one. It's tempting to shirk the responsibility for our choices, attributing them instead to hardwired aspects of our character or overwhelming external forces. However, Sartre depicts such attitudes as forms of bad faith [*mauvaise foi*]. Our existential freedom confronts us in literally every aspect of our existence. Any attempt to deny our capacity to shape our lives through our choices is therefore a form of self-deception, "a lie to oneself" (*Being and Nothingness*, p. 48).

The different refereeing personae introduced at the start of this chapter—the stickler, the ditherer, the frustrated player, the poseur, the postman and the tough guy—can all be understood as attempts to deal with the existential pressure of the referee's role. We have seen that the responsibility for deciding whether to blow the whistle rests with the referee alone. No wonder it becomes tempting for referees to shirk some of the responsibility for making difficult calls, by either postponing the decision as long as possible or seeking an external authority to justify their choices.

The Letter of the Law

The stickler, for example, seeks to reduce her personal accountability for her decisions by sticking strictly to the laws of the game, regardless of the context. Shirts must be tucked in and socks pulled up. Throw-ins must be taken from the exact spot where the ball went out. And minor infringements such as jostling and shirt pulling always draw a free kick, regardless of the impact on the flow of the game.

This approach to refereeing brings to mind Sartre's criticisms of conceptions of morality that equate virtuous action with sticking to a rigid moral code. The problem with this type of moral outlook is that it encourages people to avoid taking personal responsibility for their actions. People rely on the code to tell them what to do, instead of confronting each situation and making their own choices.

In *Existentialism and Humanism,* for example, Sartre illustrates this problem through the story of a student who approached him for advice (pp. 35–38). The student was trying to choose between joining the Free French Forces in England and staying in France to care for his aging mother. He found each option morally attractive, but for different reasons.

Leaving for England would enable him to defend his country and his ideals, but looking after his mother was important to him on a more personal level.

After considering the student's situation, Sartre responded with what must have seemed a very unhelpful suggestion: "You are free, so choose." His point was not that there can never be a right answer to a moral question, but rather that in this case the student could not resolve his dilemma by reference to some abstract formula. Rather, he faced a competition between two dearly held ideals: the only way to confront the situation was to make a choice and accept responsibility for the outcome.

Sartre observes that when people ask for advice on a difficult moral decision, they have often already made up their minds on what to do. He suspects the student had already made his choice, but he wanted to lessen his personal guilt by getting his professor's endorsement. If the student had wanted to stay with his mother, Sartre remarks, he would have sought advice from someone like a conservative priest.

A similar point applies to the stickler. The fact that the stickler applies the laws of the game does not excuse her from making a decision. The laws are vague: they need someone to interpret and apply them. According to Law 12, for instance, acts such as pushing are to be penalised if the referee considers them "careless, reckless or using excessive force". This sort of standard is inherently open to interpretation. The stickler exercises as much discretion as any other referee, but tries to disguise it by citing the rules.

Of course, it is not only referees who hide behind the rules when making a difficult or unpopular decision. Other decision makers, from bosses and bureaucrats to police officers and judges, often do the same thing. According to Sartre, however, this refusal to accept responsibility for one's decisions is a form of bad faith. Rules and policies may set out guidelines for our actions, but they do not and cannot determine what choices we ultimately make. Only we, as free and responsible agents, can do that.

Postponing Responsibility

At least the stickler is decisive. There's another type of referee even more reviled by fans and players. This is the ditherer, who regularly raises his whistle to his mouth, but rarely blows for the free kick. The ditherer's response to the pressure of his role is to avoid making a call. If he does not blow the whistle, he thinks, perhaps nobody will notice the foul. That way, he can avoid being criticised for taking a stand.

The ditherer's strategy, in other words, is to defer the moment of decision for as long as possible. Sartre discusses a similar example of bad faith in *Being and Nothingness* (pp. 55–56). The example concerns a woman on a first date. The woman's date flirts with her all evening, making racy comments like, "I find you so attractive!" (No doubt this was one of Sartre's favourite pick up lines.) However, the woman chooses to take these remarks as compliments to her personality, rather than her physical attributes.

Finally, the woman's date places his hand on hers. Surely, this is the moment of decision, where she must decide whether to return his advances. However, the woman does not want to respond, as she would have to either hurt her date's feelings or admit to returning his attraction. So she simply leaves her hand there—like a "thing", as Sartre puts it—while pretending not to notice. Like the ditherer, the woman has a decision to make, but she does not want to face the consequences. Her reaction is therefore to ignore the situation and hope it will go away. According to Sartre, she is in bad faith, caught in a lie to herself.

Playing the Part

The frustrated player seeks to escape the demands of his role in a slightly different way, by affecting the demeanour of a fan or player. He follows the play like a spectator, never missing an opportunity to applaud a good save or congratulate a striker on a well-taken goal. This type of referee wants to be one of the players; he tries to convince them he is on their side. Like a high school teacher trying to be cool, however, his efforts often fall flat. The players do not want a referee who pretends to be their friend. They want someone who takes responsibility for his part in the game.

A similar strategy is used by the poseur, who pays a little too much attention to getting his gestures exactly right. At even the most innocuous foul, the poseur will race up to the player involved, blow his whistle dramatically and throw out his hand smartly in the direction of the free kick. He rehearses his signals before every match, spending more time in front of the mirror than Cristiano Ronaldo. When running the line, nothing satisfies him more than the sharp "Crack!" of his flag as he whips it up to signal offside.

In *Being and Nothingness*, Sartre gives a famous example of a waiter in a café who tries a little too hard to inhabit his role. As Sartre puts it, "his movement is quick and forward, a little too precise, a little too rapid." He approaches the patrons a little too quickly, bends forward too eagerly and shows a little too much interest in their orders. Finally, he returns to the kitchen, walking with an artificially stiff and formal gait, "while carrying his tray with the recklessness of a tightrope walker" (p. 59).

The waiter in Sartre's example aspires to carry out his role in such a way that every part of it seems necessary and inevitable. He wishes to *be* a waiter, in the same way as a table is a table or a glass is a glass. Similarly, the frustrated player and the poseur both seek to lighten the burden of their duties by creating artificial roles. The former plays at being a player or supporter, in order to postpone the moment when he must face up to his duties. The latter, by contrast, plays at being a referee. He seeks to avoid confronting the contingency of his position by reducing it to playing a part. Every action is done because he is playing the role of a ref, rather than because he has taken stock of his responsibilities and decided what response best suits the case at hand.

Again, it is not only referees who adopt this sort of façade. Lawyers, bosses, judges and police officers all often cite the demands of their role as a way of justifying actions that sit poorly with their personal values. A lot of the literature on lawyers' ethics, for example (and, yes, such a thing does exist), is preoccupied with why lawyers can legitimately defend their clients' interests when they personally find them distasteful or repugnant. The most common type of answer emphasises the special nature of the lawyer's role: as if lawyers become different people when they step into the courtroom.

The Champion of Sincerity

Finally, we have the postman, who gives out yellow and red cards at the slightest misdemeanour, and the tough guy, who squares up to the players and deliberately invites confrontation. These referees fancy themselves as Clint Eastwood in *Dirty Harry*: "Do you feel lucky, punk?" (Of course, a yellow card is not quite as impressive as a .44 Magnum.)

The postman and the tough guy are well aware of the contingency of their decisions. They seek to compensate for it by emphasising their power over the players. Rather than behaving indecisively, like the ditherer, or insincerely, like the frustrated player or the poseur, these referees are belligerent. Their attitude says: this is my call, and you'd better learn to like it. They spend the game hoping for a penalty shout or an ugly challenge, so they can show the players they mean business.

The underlying hypocrisy of this attitude is captured in another of Sartre's examples from *Being and Nothingness* (pp. 65–66). Suppose a person who has behaved badly says, "Sorry, I'm just an evil person." Is this confession to be applauded? Sartre does not think so. This self-styled "champion of sincerity" appears to be owning up to his shortcomings, but really he is seeking to avoid liability for his behavior. His comment that he is "an evil person" treats his character as fixed, as though he were born evil and there is nothing he can do about it. At the same time, he seeks to gain merit in the eyes of others by being sincere about his flaws. He effectively turns his poor conduct into a badge of honour.

In a similar way, the postman and the tough guy tell the players, "This is the type of referee I am, and you'd better remember that before you mess with me." Rather than taking responsibility for each decision, they behave as though their reactions are predetermined by their character. As their reputation for strictness becomes known, it turns into a badge of honour: they become more and more concerned to live up to the part. This, in turn, gives them an additional excuse for their harsh decisions: the players know their reputation, so it is their own fault for provoking a response.

Confronting Contingency

What, then, is the ideal style of refereeing, which avoids the various existential traps that Sartre describes? It's often said that the best referees are the ones who do their job without interrupting the natural flow of the game. This suggests an ideal of the authentic referee, who accepts responsibility for her decisions, without exaggerating her authority or denying the contingent nature of her position.

The authentic referee does her best to make the right call, but does not pretend the situation is so certain that there can be no possible argument. She is confident enough to admit that there is often more than one possible view of an incident and others may have reached a different outcome. In the end, though, it is her responsibility to control the match; she confronts this squarely when a decision is required.

An incident involving Pierluigi Collina, arguably the greatest ref of all time, shows what I have in mind. In 1997, when controlling a Serie A match between Inter Milan and Juventus at the San Siro, Collina awarded a goal to Inter. Although the goalscorer had seemed to be offside, the assistant referee did not raise his flag. When the Juve players ran over to the linesman to protest, he explained that although the scorer had been in an offside position, the ball had been played through to him by a defender.

Collina overheard the assistant's explanation. He thought it was wrong: from where he was standing, it seemed clear that the scorer had been played in by another attacker. By this time, however, the Inter players had finished celebrating and were back in their half waiting for the kick off. Collina faced a difficult choice: he could continue with the game, although he thought the decision was wrong, or he could reverse his call and disallow the goal, in which case the stadium would erupt with protests.

It seems clear what some other referees would do. The ditherer would take the path of least resistance, getting on with the game and hoping nobody noticed. The stickler would reverse the decision, brooking no argument and citing the letter of the law. The tough guy would relish the confrontation, squaring up to the Inter players and daring them to overreact. Like the stickler, the tough guy would present his call as if it were the only possible outcome, ignoring the ambiguity of the situation.

Collina knew what he had seen. He also knew the linesman had reached a different conclusion. Yet, in the end, it was his responsibility to make the call. He decided to disallow the goal, but it is what he did next that shows his quality as a referee. He took the Inter captain aside and explained the reasons for his decision. Then he ran over and explained his decision again to the Inter bench. He was not looking for a confrontation, but he wanted the players and officials to understand why he had made the call. In the end, Roy Hodgson, the Inter manager, shook Collina's hand and said, "That's all right." He could see that Collina was doing his best in a tough situation.

Refereeing in the World

Sartre notes in *Being and Nothingness* that lovers often portray their love as necessary, rather than contingent: they talk about being soulmates, "meant for each other," "brought together by fate" and so on. The reality, as Sartre sees it, is both more ambiguous and, in the end, far more romantic: each of us has many potential partners, and if we end up staying with one person, it is because we *choose* them over the rest. Sartre describes love that embraces, rather than seeking to overcome, its contingent nature as "love in the world" (p. 370). Confronting the idea of love in the world requires us to take responsibility for our relationships, rather than simply presenting them as preordained or fated.

Similarly, the authentic referee practices "refereeing in the world," neither shirking accountability, nor pretending to be something he is not. He is decisive, but he does not pretend that his decision is set in stone and no other perspectives are possible. Rather, he calls it as he sees it, doing his best to make the correct decision and taking the time, if necessary, to explain his reasons to those affected by it.

He knows he won't always get it right, and others will invariably take a different view. Nonetheless, he takes responsibility for his call, saying: This is what I have chosen.

29

God Is Not a Referee

MOHAMMED MAJEED

During the Africa Cup of Nations held in early 2008 in Ghana, the host team, the Black Stars, won their first four matches but lost the fifth to the Indomitable Lions of Cameroon at the semi-final stage. The blame for this defeat was laid by many fans on the supernatural activities of "a true fan" of the Black Stars. He was in some sense special because he would neither shout nor sing, but would keep a feather in his mouth or hold a live bird throughout the match. He was fat, always bare-chested, and known among football fans and television viewers as "the Fowl Man." His real name, as I got to know later, was Hakeem. The fans argued that Ghana failed to win the Cup because God, to whom they had prayed for victory in each match, was annoyed with the Ghanaians for undeservedly expressing gratitude to the Fowl Man for the earlier victories of the Black Stars.

The Fowl Man was, or at least carried himself about as, a traditional spiritualist—someone who has supernatural powers and special knowledge of the spiritual realm. He claimed on Ghana Television's *Soccer Africa* show (hosted by Fiifi Banson, on February 7th, 2008) to have the ability to foresee and, with the help of some spirits, influence the outcome of matches. He gave the impression that he had a hand in the earlier victories of the team. He had won the acceptance of many fans because anytime he was seen in his spiritualist posture at the match, the team won.

Interestingly, he was relatively unknown prior to the tournament. He was not an employee of the Ghana Football Association, nor was he sponsored by them. Neither was he working under the specific instructions of any Black Stars player or any supporters' group. He said on TV that he loved the game and was using his "privileged" position to contribute to the advancement of the Ghanaian game. The cultural impact he had is partially explained by Asare Opoku's observation (*West African Traditional Religion,* 1978) that "An important aspect of the religious heritage of Africa is the recognition of the existence of mystical forces in the universe. Some of these forces, according to traditional belief, can be tapped by men who have the knowledge and ability to do so." Having been associated with the performance of the team and having become the focus of media attention, it is perhaps not surprising that he was blamed after the loss to the Cameroonians.

Since the Cameroonian defeat, the Fowl Man has disappeared. I have not set eyes on him again at matches involving Black Stars that I've attended; neither have I heard or seen him on any media. The lack of attention given to him by the media is not surprising though, because that is how deities, their representatives and all spiritualists are traditionally treated when they fail to meet the expectations of people. But he is certainly not going to be the last to appear in Ghana football. In fact, I expect more of his caliber at future tournaments when the stakes are that high. Because, when all is said and done, the Fowl Man is quintessentially Ghanaian.

One-Part Football, One-Part Religion, Stir Well . . .

The mixture of sports, particularly football, with religion in the Ghanaian context is not a recent development. This orientation to the game may be linked with the worldview, as found in the traditional belief system, that the world is both physical and spiritual. Ghanaian society is primarily religious, and solutions to human problems—health, familial, and general matters of human endeavour—are sought using natural, and very often supernatural, methods. This attitude extends to several areas of Ghanaian popular culture, including football.

I remember dislocating my left shoulder in the course of a match that I played when I was a member of a colts team. The team, called Pele Stars, was based at my home town, Tepa in the Ashanti region. Even at that tender age, eleven or twelve, we approached matches quite competitively. When the injury occurred, as was a common practice among colts clubs in my locality, the club did not bear the cost of my treatment. So, my guardians sent me to a traditional healer (a herbalist) in town for treatment. This choice, they managed to convince me, was made because they had as much confidence in traditional therapeutics as in orthodox medicine which, although available at the time, they regarded as slow. This attitude, I must admit, is still prevalent in Ghanaian society and common among many footballers. But, traditional medicine, as I know now, is shrouded in secrecy and mysticism to the extent that initiates are sometimes made to swear oaths of secrecy regarding the knowledge gained from both their masters and some (alleged) spirit beings.

Given the belief in the duality of the world and the tendency for our people to seek solutions in both realms, it's only natural (although not necessarily justified) that spiritual methods be conceived or entertained by some as applicable to football. In fact, this has always been the case. To gain some psychological advantage over an opposing team, a team may portray that it has the support of a spiritualist, a deity or some other traditionally-recognized spirit being. In the late 1980s there were two Division Three clubs in Tepa: Black Arrows and Iron Breakers. The former was from my neighbourhood, and it was my dream to play for them. In one derby match, with the Iron Breakers on the field awaiting the start of the match, the Black Arrows suddenly emerged from the Catholic cemetery that abutted the Catholic park which was the home ground of the Iron Breakers. Appearing out of the cemetery, rather than the dressing rooms, everyone assumed that the Black Arrows had dressed with the dead. (Years later I learned that the coach had the players prepare on the team bus, arrived early, and hid in the cemetery to deceive the opposing teams and spectators into thinking that they had dressed in the cemetery.) Such an action implied (at worst) that the Black Arrows had asked for the help of the dead and they had agreed, or (at least) had not deigned to interfere, implicitly blessing the Black Arrows. Our team won 2–0, and we were proud of our coach's comprehensive approach to the match.

Ghanaian Christians and Muslims do the same; they seek the assistance of God to achieve their desires in football, sometimes resulting in direct competition with the traditional ideology. For example, in a sports programme on a leading private radio station in Accra *Joy FM* (aired on June 5th, 2009), Osei Kofi—a celebrated ex-player of the Black Stars, but now a Reverend—revealed that when he substituted Christian prayer for traditional spiritual methods of preparation for matches at a Division Two club he once coached, he was sacked. Ghana's biggest newspaper, the *Daily Graphic,* reported on June 1st, 2009 that, amongst other suspected unlawful requisitions, the Sports Minister had paid for the services of a *mallam* (a Muslim Mystic) at the cost of GHC1,000 (about $900) per match played by the Black Stars during his three months on the job. (The Minister, who has been asked to step aside, denies the allegations and might not even be found guilty after the on-going investigations.)

This spiritual approach to winning matches is popularly called "ways and means" in Ghanaian football circles, and is seen as a significant complement by some to the athletic training of teams. *Joy FM* have bemoaned the resources some Ghanaian clubs allegedly channel into "ways and means." Another expression widely understood in Ghanaian football circles is "*mallam* goal." It refers to a goal suspected to have been the handiwork of usually a *mallam*, or any spiritualist. Such are goals perceived not to have resulted from any planned moves or intelligent kicks.

In this mixture of religion and football, the Fowl Man's belief that he can affect the outcome of a match is not out of place—as is the backlash against him after the team's loss.

Fairing the Foul and Fouling the Fair

Although referees are supposed to be fair in officiating, sometimes they are not. In this way, they can determine match winners by *fairing the foul and fouling the fair*. In a similar fashion, some believe that God, or other supernatural beings, can force victories to their side no matter what.

Throughout the 2008 CAF tournament, some Ghanaian football officials, fans, and players called for prayer when there was a match to be played. The call for God's intervention came from Christians and Muslims whose religion, at least for some believers, portray God as jealous and protective of His lordship. They also believe that God—in an anthropomorphic sense—is rational, free, all-good, all-knowing, compassionate, just and prayer-answering. From all indications, they put a mistaken football interpretation on these appellations; for, if God is foreknowing, rational and prayer-answering, then He has always known the sort of prayers He would answer or, rather, that He has always known the sort that His very nature would permit Him to answer. For instance, a God who is good cannot without contradiction be asked or made to *choose* or *promote* evil. This is because doing so will be contrary to His nature. Similarly, a just God cannot be asked, not even through prayer, to cheat a hardworking team out of its victory.

Following this line of reasoning, the ire towards the Fowl Man at the loss to Cameroon is misplaced. God could not, on the principle of fairness, have punished the majority of Ghanaians for the activities of the Fowl Man and his supporters. It is also questionable how this jealous God could have granted the wishes of those who prayed to Him up to the semi-final stage. Could it be that He did not answer their prayers even though they thought otherwise? Since they wouldn't deny that God knew of the Fowl Man's activities at the earlier matches, I strongly suspect, although the fans were unaware of this, that God had no interest or hand in the victories of the Black Stars.

Ignorance about the fruitlessness of intercessory prayer was not limited to the fans but was also shown by some players. Nor is this behavior confined to Ghana. The act of crossing oneself upon entering the field of play is too familiar internationally to need specific examples. But pointing to the sky after scoring, *à la* Kaká or Ronaldinho, to acknowledge the contribution or blessing of God is becoming more prevalent worldwide. This is most odd because the players are in the best position to know that their prayers before and during matches do not ensure divine victory. This must be because, first, there are numerous occasions in a player's career in which they prayed for a win or draw, but lost; secondly, it is highly improbable for there to be an accomplished football player who can claim that every time he prays before or in the course of a match, he wins; and finally, God should not, and cannot, have any logical basis to prefer a football team in a match, because His very nature prevents Him from being as arbitrary as any such preference undoubtedly entails. The gathering of players for post-match thanks-giving prayer, therefore, is unwarranted; and, it is most probably absurd if prayer is said after a defeat. The absurdity lies in the tendency to say to God: "God, we never thought for a single moment that You too can misunderstand prayer," or that, "We thank You for replacing our requested victory with a defeat," or that, "We are so happy for inflicting pain on us."

There is the objection that the football God is a fair minded being who only allows teams with good preparation and approach to matches to be victorious. But such an understanding of God takes him out of the match-winning equation. If God only rewards well-prepared and well-performing teams, and these are the qualities which would lead a team to win without God, then it is extraneous to consider the role of God. One only needs to consider how to prepare a team well. Since there's no evidence, either practical or conceptual, to suggest that a refusal to recognize God as a match winner will lead to the losing of a match, things will continue to happen the way they do, even in the absence of any football God. The advantage in excluding God is that one is able to minimize the number of uncertainties anytime one wants to tell how matches are won.

Failing to understand this, anyone who attempts to assign a result-determining role to God will find it extremely difficult to offer cogent explanations for why tactically-superior and well-prepared teams do lose matches. In situations like this, wrong reasons such as the Fowl Man are employed to explain away the failures of the football God. And, since God cannot be part of the match-winning equation, prayer to Him is inconsequential and ineffectual. God cannot play the role of a referee, and I believe He will be happier if football fans, players and officials do not involve him in any football confusion. The prayer of Ghanaians, therefore, could not have drawn God into a purely human game like the Africa Cup of Nations. There were no divinely prepared victories for the Black Stars, and the Fowl Man prevented none.

The idea of a football God might still be useful for two reasons: first, it can be a source of encouragement, a psychological motivation and a good mental tonic for both fans and players in the performance of their football duties. Second, it can also be a source of consolation for both players and fans in a time of grief or defeat, when they convince themselves that God has good reasons for denying them the victory or that God will make up for the loss in future. This notwithstanding, it cannot be said that God actually performs any match-winning roles. Thoughts about God's performance of such roles can only be imaginary. Indeed, the same can be said of the belief I used to have that the spirits of the dead at the Catholic cemetery helped our team—the Black Arrows— defeat its opponents on their own ground.

The Way Forward

To my mind, the game should not be polluted with supernatural considerations, since such patterns of thought will most likely divert attention from practically relevant methods that count toward the growth of the sport. To a critical mind, the inconsistencies in the outcome of intercessory prayers that are offered by football enthusiasts suggest that serious attention need only be paid to the methods or issues over which we, as humans, have some control. These include such issues as strategizing, player fitness, sourcing for funds, discipline, and fairness on the part of the referee. Of all these, discipline is the most fundamental. With it, players would adhere to well rehearsed strategies, submit to recommended training drills (or avoid practices that reduce their fitness levels) and engage in sound financial management practices that would eventually contribute to their psychological and emotional stability. Also, hardly would the need arise for us to talk about unfair officiating if the referee involved is disciplined.

Indiscipline has serious consequences on the growth of the game generally, as any club whose players and fans engage in it becomes unattractive to potential investors and face possible home bans. Aside from making difficult the future selection of culprits, on-field player indiscipline weakens a team, especially, when it results in the sending off of key players whose continuous play could have brought the team great fortune and history. A typical example was the sending off of Zinedine Zidane in the 2006 FIFA World Cup for head-butting Marco Materazzi (an Italian opponent) in the final. Zidane, a player I always admired for his mesmerizing skills and calmness, was by then a former FIFA Best Player and captain of the France national team. The headbut was in retaliation for some unkind words supposedly said to him by Materazzi. His leadership and individual brilliance, in my own assessment, was what brought France to the finals, only to lose the match and the Cup after he was sent off.

Although all the prescribed elements discussed in the two preceding paragraphs are significant, a necessary connection does not exist between them and match victory. A team can still lose even when those elements are observed. But unlike resorting to intercessory prayer for which there cannot be either logical or empirical basis, the practical issues outlined above have, first, an empirical nature similar to that of the game; secondly, they are part of what the game entails; and, finally, they allow for the consideration of human deficiencies and capacities. Unlike the supernatural approach that allow people to fail to take responsibility for the outcome of matches, recognizing football as a completely human affair commits them more to the game; and with such commitment comes the passion that will make them promote the game.

In this proper, empirical context of the game therefore, given a normal match condition—that is, with the presence of the practical elements mentioned above, including fair officiating—what is next needed to win a match is luck. Judging by the attitude of the worried fans of the Black Stars, chance is often the most under-rated or under-emphasized factor in the match-winning equation. To show how inadequate the good efforts of players, coaches, fans and sponsors are, let's consider 'strategizing' and 'playing to strategy' which, respectively, are part of the functions of coaches and players. It is not true to say that play is planned or strategized if by 'play' is meant every kick, catch, throw or header of the ball in a match. I learned from my play and study of the game that while the general orientation of a team can be pre-planned, the spontaneous reflexes of a pressured goalkeeper, or the instant decision of a striker to head instead of kicking the ball into the net, or the unplanned drifting of a midfielder to a position on the field that precludes him from placing the ball on the favourite foot of his striker (as a result of which the latter is unable to shoot into the net) can hardly be said to be part of any team's strategy. Strategizing, therefore, has a limitation; and the greater the number of spontaneous incidences, the greater the probability that pre-match strategies might fail. These spontaneous actions could affect a team positively or negatively, depending on how luck seems to function in a match. The good efforts of players and coaches do not make it easier for their team to be favoured by luck. It is tempting, I admit, to believe that "heaven helps those who help themselves," but ultimately it is wrongheaded.

This means that luck does not come to top up the efforts of teams. Otherwise, the question will arise again why stronger or better-prepared teams do lose to supposedly weaker ones? To avoid this circularity, then, the 'topping-up' argument must be abandoned. When teams are well-prepared they play with a lot of elegance and purpose. So when we award these features to teams, we may be admiring generally their style of play and not suggesting for a moment that their preparations would deliver victory on match day. That this cannot be done is as result of the element of luck in football. Luck makes uncertain all arguments made in support of any prediction of match results. Depending on the strength of the competing teams, the proportion of luck that could be said to have influenced the result of a competitive match may differ. For example, the amount of luck likely to be envisaged when any of the four top teams in the English Premier League (EPL) beat the other—since they are almost of equal strength—would not be as great as that needed by the last team on the league table to actually defeat any of the "Big Four." The amount would be far greater if the local team of my home town in Ghana is to beat any of them. But, the beauty of chance is that it makes victories by the underdogs possible. Additionally, the element of chance, from a sheer position of strength, renders unworkable an important law that all rational beings are expected to accept. This law—which philosophers call *Hypothetical Syllogism*—works as follows: if something *a* has more of a feature than another *b* and the latter more than some other thing *c*, it should be taken for granted that *a* possesses more of the feature than *c*. In other words, if we assume the first and last teams on the EPL league table are Manchester United and Stoke City respectively, and Manchester United beats Stoke City who in turn beats Sheffield United, we should take it for granted that Manchester United will beat Sheffield United. But, this law breaks down in football, since on a lucky day for Sheffield it can defeat Manchester United.

Luck is an enigma. It is real, yet we cannot tell how and where it will appear in a match. It is exactly as a result of our inability to tell what chance will bring or which team luck will favour that some football enthusiasts ignorantly appeal to some supposedly superior agencies to grant them a win or force the unknown element of the game to their side. Indeed, there is nothing in the way chance plays its role that has the semblance of logic. It seems rather to swing at will in any direction and in varied proportions.

The swing of luck, however, is not necessarily dreaded by soccer enthusiasts, including myself. Understood vaguely as an unknown part by the superstitious among us, they do not only recognize but sometimes agitate for that which brings them luck. I found an example in the 2006 Africa Cup of Nations football competition that was played in Egypt. In that competition, the Black Stars, who were four-time past winners and noted for their fine play over the years, did not only lose their last group match, resulting in their elimination from the tournament, but the team also played very poorly. As if that was not enough, they were eliminated by Zimbabwe, minnows in the sea of international football. Amidst the resultant frustration and disappointment, many fans attributed the loss to the colour of the jersey worn by the Black Stars in the match. To them, the team had gotten used to—and was identifiable with—bright colours such as yellow and, more recently, white and thus had no business inviting gloom upon itself by wearing black that day. As if in response to the agitation of those fans, the Black Stars have not worn black since. In 2008 the team lost to the Indomitable Lions although it wore white. The sequel to this is as follows:

There can never be, in the strict sense, an absolute match-winning formula in football that emanates from the perceived strengths and practical preparations of competing teams. Otherwise, we should always be able to assess teams and be certain of the outcome of matches before they are played. If certainty is guaranteed in football, it would be very bad for a game that thrives so much on excitement. In addition, certainty might serve as basis for a team, especially, the team assessed to be the loser, to not strive for success. This way, the competitive spirit of that team is killed, making the potential result of the match to not be contested. Competition is what drives football, but it does so only because it rides on the back of the unknown: chance. Chance or, at least, the expectation of its favours, is what makes each team so daring in a match, makes fans gather courage to see a match in which the opposing team appears far stronger, and was what made a first-time participant in the World Cup Final, Senegal, give their best to eventually beat France, the defending champions, 1–0 in 2002.

I'm not suggesting that the aesthetic value of football is not an incentive for some fans to want to see a match. Neither am I implying that practical efforts do not put teams in a proper position to compete. Rather, the aesthetic value contributes in some measure toward entertainment but very little toward the achievement of match result. I recognize, though, that there is a broader sense in which the term 'beauty' would encompass fair play, friendship, the act of accepting or learning to accept defeat, modesty, and discipline. In a deeper sense, these are the very things that constitute the playing of the game. If one does not have them, then s/he probably is not playing football at all, or s/he does not understand the nature of the game. They are the very things I, as do many, love about the game. They are the reason why in spite of the injury I sustained in my colts playing days, I never stopped playing and loving the game. Will I ever? Playing, maybe "yes"; but loving, I do not think so.

The beauty of the game can also be explained by football's expression of our common humanity. By virtue of our being human, we see the Other in our individual selves, and ourselves in the Other. When we feel compelled to act in a certain manner in response to our expectations, fears, happiness, commitments, support and grief relative to our team and its future, we at once appreciate the Other's right, capability or possession of similar sentiments toward their team. Therefore, in the game of football where players, fans and officials cut across neighbourhoods, towns, tribes, races, professions and cultures we are offered the opportunity to recognize our differences but promote our collective humanity. Hence, the African maxim—mentioned by Kwame Gyekye in his *African Cultural Values* (Sankofa Publishing, 1996)—that "humanity has no boundary" finds great expression in football.

The game of football is indeed beautiful, but I downplay our ability to determine match results on the basis of beauty because given that teams possess varied degrees of the components of beauty, I doubt whether there can be a standard or formula that would indicate how much of a component or how many components would be enough for a team to win or lose or draw a match. Can we say that whichever team has a certain amount of the components *will* win a match? It is due to these difficulties that the chapter drifts from practical efforts, including the components of beauty, to chance. Chance is the only thing that teams have no control over, and cannot make preparations toward having. It is the only thing whose beautiful surprises are eagerly awaited in the game of football. Without the element of chance, football not only loses its excitement but ceases to be a game altogether.

Football and Religion Don't Mix

Football, like any game, is full of uncertainties. And, when the worried fans of the Black Stars complained about the activities of the Fowl Man, they did not, I believe, think that this was false. However, the philosophical problems in their thinking have arisen mainly because of what they make of the uncertainties (that is, the aspects of football that are beyond human control). The obvious tendency on the part of religious-minded fans to attribute such occurrences to God—who ironically is believed to have a nature inconsistent with the sometimes precarious nature of match results—and their conception of a God who is just but at the same time is described by them in ways that portray Him as unfair, have been found not to be philosophically germane.

Chance is what brings excitement and meaning to the game. Those fans who attributed the loss of the Black Stars to the activities of the Fowl Man, while crediting previous victories to God, missed out on a substantial portion of the excitement that football offered at that tournament. I must hasten to add that the Fowl Man who thought he had a hand in the victories of the Black Stars was as wrong as the fans in not appreciating the non-supernaturality of the game.

This notwithstanding, if there are any roles for us as players, fans and officials to perform, then they are those that relate to such things as technical direction, organization, patronage, motivation and playing: together, I called them "the human efforts" or "the human element." And, since the game is human anyway, we would be doing no justice to ourselves and no good to the game if we fail to perform to our best these human roles. It's no fault of ours that we have fallen in love with a game. The only price paid is that we have tacitly agreed to subject ourselves, our individual and collective efforts, to the sovereignty of chance. We are, on this count, supposed to perform our roles well with the expectation that luck may smile on us. Chance can neither be set aside, nor wished away, nor prayed away because of what football essentially is: a game!

30

The Player Prophet
and the Phenomenology
of Reading the Ref

SETH VANNATTA

The soccer official is a despot. His whistle is law. A French ref might as
well say, "*L'état, c'est moi*," at least for ninety minutes. As a player, I was
sent off twice for not realizing this. But as a coach, I told my players what
my coaches told me: "Play to the whistle." As a player, this meant virtually nothing to me. As a coach, this meant almost nil to my players. The
ability to read the ref, play to the whistle, and not get sent off is what
drives my inquiry.

As philosophers, we reflect on the concept of law. What is law?
Where does law come from? What is the function of law? Legal philosophers often refer to the rules of games to illustrate their favorite answers
to these questions. But I want to know what the rules of soccer are, not
what rules are in general or what law is in general. Perhaps, you're thinking *that is an easy question, a simple matter of fact.* Just get on the FIFA
website, and order the latest official publication of the laws of the game.
Then read it. Problem solved.

But I don't want to know what the rules of soccer are as some sort
of disengaged outsider. I want to know what they are as a player and
a coach—as someone who needs to perform at the optimum level
within the ref's dictatorial realm without being exiled by being shown
a red card. Would reading these rules help me? The question stops
being empirical, (a search for facts), and starts being philosophical (a
theoretical reflection), when we realize how the general rules in print
fail to map-on to the specific conduct in each match. That there are
general rules in print which prohibit misconduct is straightforward
enough: tripping an opposing player results in a direct kick for the
team of the tripped player. Deciding which specific collision between
players constitutes a trip is where the boot meets the pitch, so to speak,

369

and this is what matters to the players and coaches, not to mention the fans.

Is there a legal framework that can help us answer this question? And if so, can it help us as players and coaches? I think so. So let's take a look at some of the proposals for answering the questions above about the concept of law and then determine if these suit our purposes concerning the rules of soccer. We want to be able to define the rules of soccer generally, we want to know about their origin and their function, and we're searching for all of this with a practical purpose in mind. We want to understand better the ref's behavior and our relationship and response to it as players and coaches, so as to describe and prescribe more effective and competitive playing.

The Ref's Right Reason in Accord with Nature?

Our first candidate for a legal framework applicable to the rules of soccer is natural law theory. Natural law theory gives us a look at the intersection between rules and morality. Proponents of natural law invoke nature as a norm which guides conduct and prohibits misconduct. They say things like, *it's not right because it's unnatural.* And for most natural law theorists, the laws of nature are immutable and unchanging—they're downright divine.

Opponents of this type of theory often wonder how we have access to the immutable laws of nature. How do mere humans, soccer players in constant flux and referees regularly making mistakes, tap into these unchanging laws? Natural law theorists appeal to reason (if not revelation) as the faculty which bridges the shifting world of becoming to the incontrovertible realm of being, which is eternally true and objectively fixed. That is, some human faculty, such as reason, gains access to the eternal and objective truths of the law for the purpose of our temporal and subjective participation within their jurisdiction. So if we believe we are dealing with natural law, but it fails to be internally consistent or leads to contradiction, then we are probably mistaken, if reason is indeed the operative faculty. Opponents of natural law might concede that having eleven per side is consistent while having uneven teams is unreasonable and unfair, but they might wonder whether the ref's decisions are a function of almighty reason or of ever-changing and fallible perception. If they are the latter, then natural law theory does not suit our purposes. Additionally, we might ask if it is more accurate to say that having eleven players per side is *natural* as rational, or merely *customary* as socially practical.

Natural law theory bridges mere rules with morals. Having an equal number of players on each team is fair and natural. Having rules which limit the chance of serious injury seems natural and morally sound. Even the structural parameters of the game might be looked at this way. The length of the game should be natural and age-appropriate as should the size of the field and ball. These mundane examples might help us consider the function of the rules as tending towards fairness, safety, and as governed by the dictates of what is natural.

A Soccer Contract?

But when we look at the origin of the rules of soccer, this model does not seem to help us much. Many of the natural law theorists were concerned with the origin of rule-making bodies themselves: they wanted to distinguish legitimate government from "the advantage of the stronger." They conceived of an original state of nature in which each of us had natural rights to life and liberty, and in which each of us could adjudicate our own disputes. This state often led to war, which Thomas Hobbes described as, "solitary, poor, nasty, brutish, and short." Without naturally free men giving up their right to be their own judges (and forming a social contract of civil society and government), or without players giving up their right to call their own penalties (and form some sort of soccer contract), soccer would be a game only of "nasty brutes, wearing shorts."

Perhaps the decision to stop calling one's own penalties cleaned up the game a bit, but surely Hobbes's description overstates the natural origin of the rules the ref enforces. At issue is whether the rules of the game could be conceived prior to our playing of the game. One famous political philosopher, John Rawls, proposed that we imaginatively put ourselves behind a veil of ignorance in order to suppose that we occupied an original position, not unlike the state of nature. In this original position, we are devoid of all particularities, skills, personality traits, intelligence, athletic ability, and propensity to risk-taking. Only here could we agree in a neutral and unselfish way what types of rules would be fair.

How far would this conception get us? In this original position we could rationally give rise to the rules of fair play in general. We might be able to originate an equal number of players per team or the principle that both teams follow the same scoring rules, but it would not apply much to the game of soccer. But I want to know about the rules of soccer from the perspective of a player and coach. Even the length of the game could not be conceived in this highly rational and theoretical way. We need to play to figure that out.

The FIFA Sovereign?

Another candidate to answer our question is the school of legal positivism. These folks tend to separate laws and morals. As they argue, law only exists as enacted by humans from some objectively valid source. One legal positivist, John Austin, described the law as a command by a political superior to an inferior, which imposed duties or obligations, enforced by the threat of sanctions or punishments (*The Province of Jurisprudence Determined*, p. 1).

Here we see that the politically superior governing body, FIFA, commands the laws of the game, and these stated dictates are the rules. The governing bodies under the political umbrella of FIFA are bound by duty to abide by its commands. Ultimately, the players are the inferior subjects of the FIFA sovereign and are obliged to follow the rules or suffer imposed sanctions. Testing the merits of this legal theory entails asking a few more questions. First, are players bound by duties not to foul? Second, are the rules really this top-down in origin? I think the answer to both questions is no, and I will tell you why a little later.

First, I should do more justice to the positivists by telling you about a more nuanced version of that theory. Herbert Hart conceived of laws as types of social rules, similar to the rules in games. He divided up rules into primary and secondary rules. Primary rules are those which prescribe and proscribe actions. *A player other than the goalkeeper cannot touch the ball with his hands within the field of play* is an example of a primary rule. The secondary rules govern how primary rules are to be changed, adjudicated, and recognized. For instance, a secondary rule in soccer, given by FIFA, allows for the size of the ball and field to change. FIFA also has procedural rules for changing primary rules such as the offside offence rules.

Hart also looks at rules from the perspective of those who experience them, and this seems to get us closer to the answer we're after. Hart's analysis of primary rules is both external, as examined by a disengaged outsider, and internal, as examined by a player of the game, for instance. An internal perspective on the rules of soccer is what we have been looking for, and here we might ask whether or not I have a duty as a player to abide by the rules. I think not.

The Player Prophet

When I play soccer, am I bound by a duty not to trip, push, and use my hands? A legal way of asking this question is when I sign a contract, am I bound by duty to abide by its conditions? Does a tariff impose a duty on me not to import my goods? To all of these questions I must answer no. I have an option to break the contract at a cost, which may or may not outweigh the expense of upholding the conditions of the contract. I may freely import goods into a country imposing high tariffs at a cost of paying those high import taxes. And I may freely shove an opposing player at the cost of giving his team a direct free kick, getting booked, or at worst, getting sent off. But as most experienced players understand, sometimes the costs of grabbing a player, getting called and even yellow-carded, do not outweigh the benefits of stopping a counter-attack, especially when the violation is in the opposing team's defensive half.

The most relevant question is one of cost-benefit analysis. Will the penalty of the transgression be worse than the consequence of self-control and a failure to foul? Such an analysis takes place by way of prediction. And here we see that Oliver Wendell Holmes, Jr.'s definition of the law suits the game of soccer: the law is the "hypostasis of a prophecy" (by the lawyer of the bad man) of what the courts will in fact do ("The Path of the Law," in *Collected Works*, Volume 3, p. 391). The player turns the prediction of the behavior of the ref into a thing, and that thing is the rule.

The full analogy runs like this. The positivist conception of law overemphasizes FIFA as the legislative body, by conceiving of law as posited in a top-down way. Instead the ref, as judge, uses FIFA's posited law as a mere motive among others for his behavior in calling the game. What matters is how he calls the game, and this is predicted by the player as bad man and his coach as virtually-powerless lawyer. Granted, the coach does not have the right to argue for his players, but the ref generally grants him more of a voice than the players. And doesn't the savvy host coach provide some refreshments and some good-hearted cajoling to the officials? At higher levels, we could consider the team captain a potential attorney as well. This picture of the law speaks to the importance of reading the ref. The good player must play just as physical as the ref allows. He must incorporate the ref's behavior into his own predictions about his future calls. Failure to do so may give the opposing team a physical advantage or penalty kicks, depending on the valence of his failed prediction.

The school of legal theory Holmes initiated was legal pragmatism, and its features help us understand the rules of soccer in many other ways.

Holmes showed how the law in its mature form was expressed by external standards, those available to the senses, such as a player grasping an opposing player's jersey, as opposed to internal standards, such as intent. This is why, despite the insistence of uninformed coaches and fans, there is no mention of intent in the description of a tripping penalty. What the player meant to do (gain possession of the ball) is not relevant, easily accessible, or legally material to the ref. Only what he did do (trip the opposing player) is evident, and the ref rules on that observation.

What the legal pragmatist admits, and that these other theorists are uncomfortable with, is the indeterminacy of the law. Any experienced soccer player, coach, or fan, is thoroughly schooled in the broad swath of indeterminacy in a ref's calls. The formalist judge feigns that the law is an internally consistent chain of logical decisions and that his decision simply finds the relevant general principle and applies it to the specific case. It would take a profoundly naïve ref to think that he simply finds and applies the rules of the game to the particular events of a match, without reference to the context, including the level of play, the weather conditions, the propensity for injury, and the need to control hot tempers. The legal case and the game of soccer are always specific, never universal, and so applying general rules to particular, highly contextualized games is radically indeterminate. Admitting and understanding this will help us read the ref and play to his whistle.

When we consider the origin of the rules of soccer, the pragmatists provide the best analysis for our purposes. Where the natural law theorists gave us rules of fairness and natural needs of the game at a high level of abstraction perhaps applying to any game at all, the positivists gave us statutory rules, put forth by FIFA as a legislative body. The former analysis does not help the player on the field understand how to read the ref because appeals to theories of justice and fairness will not help him play. The latter theory only pushes the question of origin back one step further. Why does FIFA legislate as it does? The answer to this question is the one we're looking for.

The origin of the law is in custom and social practice, and so the origin of the rules of soccer emerged organically just as the game did. Another pragmatist, John Dewey, emphasized this. The social activities, such as playing soccer, should be conceived as interactions and ongoing processes. Its rules both intervene in the game and are themselves in ongoing transition. The rules must be viewed within the conditions of the game and cannot be viewed apart from them as if standing above and outside of them. Dewey articulated a consequentialist and pragmatic standard for determining what the rules are. What we think of as the ref applying the rule is not an act that happens after the rule is stated, but instead, his blowing of the whistle is a necessary part of the rule. It is so necessary a part that we can often figure out what the rule is by reading the ref's behavior and judging the effects of his whistle on the game ("My Philosophy of Law," in *Later Works*, Volume 14, pp. 117–18). It is an empty prospect to discuss what the rule is apart from what the rule does.

Playing Phenomenology

This description of the rules of soccer according to a model of legal pragmatism has a practical upshot. The analysis above, which reveals a certain malleability of the rules by contextual or even the personal externalities of the ref, leads to the forthcoming analysis, which gives descriptive clarity to what so many coaches demand—that we play to the ref's whistle. Categorizing the rules of soccer as pragmatic and giving a phenomenological description of the experience of playing to the whistle will clarify both the importance of reading the ref and a description of how we can do it.

Phenomenology is a fancy word for the study, not of *what* is given to us experientially, but *how* it is given to us. Although Georg Hegel used this word earlier, the modern father of this school of philosophy was Edmund Husserl. Husserl's purpose was very different from ours, but his method will be helpful. He spent years just outlining a method of describing objects of perception with such clarity that he could achieve an objective certainty worthy of grounding science itself. He began by describing objects statically, without reference to movement or time. But later, he described the movement of the lived body and the way time is presented to us in and through our movements. He called this genetic phenomenology, but he might well have called it kinetic or dynamic phenomenology.

Where other philosophers of sport have described the essential structures of playing, Husserl described the movement of the body in time in such a way as to give an explanation of how we play at all. And given that the ref is part of our playing of the game of soccer, we can extend our phenomenological account of playing to our description of our interactions with the ref in order to show what it means to play to his whistle.

Husserl described our experience of time as a synthesis of retentions and protentions. We retain our just-past as we move across the field. Although I am not conscious of it, I keep with me the space of the field behind me as I make a run. This is not memory. In remembering, I need to present actively something to my mind that happened in my past.

Retention operates without this active remembering. This dragging my past with me as a comet's tail is half of the story. I also protend or anticipate my near future. Once again, this is not an active hoping or an active prognostication. Instead it is a tacit anticipation. I anticipate my near future in a way that conforms to my experience. I passively associate previous retentions together to constitute my anticipation, and I act, as a matter of habit, in a way which accords with those predictions. As a center midfielder I position myself twenty yards outside the eighteen-yard box, awaiting a clearing of a cross or shot by a defender, such that I can be there ready to trap it, and put it back into a scoring position. But I do not actively think through my positioning. What composes the thickness of my present activity in the soccer game is the synthesis or combination of the retention of my past and the tacit prediction of my future.

This analysis accounts for our ability to play the game if, by playing, we mean not thinking through our every actions. Much has been written about the peak experience in sports or about the athlete in the zone. Sports commentators often refer to these athletes as *out of their head* or *unconscious*. But even in the habituated activity of every soccer game and in each skill in soccer, there is an element of unconsciousness. We may think of the beginner in soccer as one who actively thinks through her movements: "Keep your head still," "Point your plant foot at your target." But the experienced player recruits certain retentions and uses them as protentions in what Husserl called passive synthesis.

The experienced soccer player spontaneously makes use of retained experience in shooting the ball, for instance, without an active presentation of those experiences. It is not the case that these active presentations just happen really fast. Rather, even decisions which take time can be the products of passive syntheses. Knowing where the ball will carom and being there before it does is an example. Husserl's concept of passive synthesis is an improved description of the impoverished concept of "muscle memory" in the habituation of specific soccer skills. This concept also explains the way we actively play passively. "Active passivity" is a strange phrase, but it speaks to those of us who reflect on our playing and know that over-thinking and trying to be too precise can result in mistakes on the field.

A Phenomenology of Reading the Ref

Have we ventured too far from the dictatorial ref with whom we began our quest? I don't think so. I propose to players and coaches that we attend to the ref as another very relevant feature of the game. The skilled coach points out that the opposing player has a weak left foot and tells his players to try to shepherd him to that side. The skilled player has habituated this perceptual aspect of the game himself. Is the tendency of the referee any different from the tendencies of the opposing players? Are they not equally relevant? Additionally, the conscientious and observant player and coach attend to the physical conditions of the game. How low is the grass cut? And thus how fast will the pitch play? Where is the wind coming from? And thus when do we need to keep the ball on the turf as opposed to in the air? Both teams have to play on the same pitch, whether in a world class facility or a recently converted skeet-shooting range (as my first soccer complex was).

An important insight follows. Both teams have the same ref, whose behavior is indeterminate and imprecise although susceptible to improved predictions throughout the course of a game. The ref's tendencies are equally important as those of the opposing players, and his indeterminacy is as relevant as the physical conditions of the playing field. So we need to proceed in three stages.

First, we need to understand that the ref is in fact the despot, whose will is law for the ninety-minute match. He operates amid a radical indeterminacy, which is a function of context, weather-conditions, the incongruity of general rules and specific penalties, and human fallibility and finitude. Perhaps the description of soccer rules should go beyond the realization of indeterminacy in legal pragmatism. Perhaps we should treat soccer rules as legal realists and include among the factors which inform the ref's decisions such things as what he ate for breakfast and the blandishments of his spouse. If we did this, perhaps we could be more attuned to the diplomatic element in hosting officials or chatting with them before kick-off.

Second, we need to coach our players to attend to the dynamics of the official's decisions early in the game. Generally, how much physical play is he allowing? Specifically, when I step in front of a player with the ball, making no attempt to play the ball, but effectively shield the ball from the player in position, does the ref consider this a legal shield or an illegal obstruction? This is similar to the adjustments we make to the changing physical conditions of the game. Rain might result in lightly damp grass and cause through-balls to skip and outrun the intended recipient. Or rain might result in sitting water and cause through-balls to hold up significantly. Conditions such as these are indeterminate, and that imprecise and unpredictable quality demands our flexibility and steep learning curve. So it goes with our need to read the ref.

Last, we need to play to the whistle, which is where we began. This meant nothing to me as a player. I was sent off in two varsity games because of the way I *reacted* to the whistle. And my highlighting this word *reaction* gets at the heart of the way the concept of passive synthesis helps us understand playing in general and playing to the whistle specifically. Explaining our ability to play as a function of reactions and muscle stimuli results in an awkward form of behaviorism which fails to determine why some soccer players master this skill and others do not. Passive synthesis accounts for the lack of determinism in the game and for the ability to act passively and predict accurately yet unconsciously our near futures. The ref is an immanent part of the game, and so playing to the whistle means predicting his behavior and habituating our behavior both before the whistle and after. Before the whistle we need to read the ref and adjust our game accordingly. After the whistle we need to habituate a fast defensive reaction if the call goes against us and a fast offensive posture if the call goes for us. As coaches we can actively develop these skills. We can make the goal of reading the ref transparent both before the game and at half time. We can make explicit the objective of playing to the whistle in practice just as we do with so many other goals and objectives.

What counts is how well we play the game. Reflecting on the rules of soccer benefits us only if we can employ the insights of such speculations, those which return us to the ref's whistle. Rambling on about the disparity between the perfectly called game and the way the match was actually officiated is a wasteful theorizing. Let others worry that the ideals of sportsmanship fall outside our pragmatic analysis. We must return to our experience in the match, where the ref is a true tyrant. The sooner we realize this, the better.

The rules of soccer are the embodiments of the players' predictions of the ref's behavior. Knowing this, we can strive to treat refs more humanely and with greater sportsmanship, recognizing the radical indeterminacy of their behavior, part of which is arises from human fallibility. And with the descriptive insights of Husserl in mind, we can offer to our players the additional skill of reading the ref and playing to the whistle, a skill I never mastered as a young player. If only I had read philosophy when I was younger!

31

The Boy Done Good?
Football's Clichés

TOM GRIMWOOD and PAUL K. MILLER

Football is often celebrated as a global language. No less global, though considerably less celebrated, is the plethora of football-specific clichés which make up the language of commentary, post-match interview and expert analysis. Often mocked, but rarely seriously analysed, the very ubiquity and persistence of these clichés suggests that their use is rather more than simple linguistic "laziness" on the part of pundits and players.

In order to explore the ordinary world of clichés in football, we will draw on the expertise of two philosophical pundits of our own: Hans-Georg Gadamer (1900–2002) and (the later[1]) Ludwig Wittgenstein (1889–1951). Prior to any actual analysis, however, we must first cast a glance at the field of play itself and ask: 'What exactly *is* a footballing cliché?'

When It Comes to Definitions, Cliché
Literally Gives 110 Percent

Early doors; our problem, philosophically speaking, is that the very notion of cliché itself seems to resist both "serious" analysis and straightforward definition. For a start, outside of football, cliché is often considered as simply a case of bad, lazy, or unimaginative expression, and hence written off before it can be taken seriously in terms of what

---

[1] Wittgenstein, the Brian Clough of twentieth-century philosophy, is treated by philosophers as being two different people. The "early" Wittgenstein produced a rigid "picture theory" of language that the "later" Wittgenstein rejected more or less wholesale in favour of the approach described in this chapter. From here on, then, "Wittgenstein" means his latter incarnation.

it actually, constructively does for speakers and listeners. Moreover, there is a widespread, commonsense assumption that any cliché is instantly, recognisably "what it is." After all, is a cliché not largely defined by its extraordinary familiarity?

But! If we look closer at the issue, we have a very real problem in defining a *bona fide* cliché *at all*. For example, one broad definition of cliché would be to say that it is more or less synonymous with a "stereotype" (the French verb *clicher* literally means "to stereotype"). When we hear World Cup commentators describing the "silky skills of the Brazilians," the "ruthless efficiency" of the Germans, or the "tactical naivety" of more or less any team from the African continent (regardless of what is actually happening on-field), we may well feel that there is more cliché than actual insight going on here. But at the same time, this definition seems *too* broad: if cliché is a stereotype, what makes it different from any other stereotyping? Why are we not more upset by such categorising of players on the grounds of race?

Bearing this in mind, we might adjust our definition and instead term cliché a predictable or unoriginal turn of phrase or action (indeed, this would be closer to the *Oxford English Dictionary*'s account of the word). But again this might cover too much: consider the time that Gordan Strachan was asked in a post-match interview about, "in what area the team played badly?" Strachan responded, "the large rectangular green area." An obvious answer—and given Strachan's renowned interview technique, very predictable—but certainly not as clichéd as the question.

Perhaps, then, predictability is not so much the issue, as repetition. We could argue that a cliché is a phrase that has been repeated so much that it loses any real meaning. But simple repetition doesn't quite seem to capture the essence of cliché. After all, "It's a goal!" is an oft-repeated phrase in football commentary, but isn't considered a cliché. "The ball was still moving when it hit the back of the net," as Kevin Keegan once astutely noticed (as opposed to those balls that hit the net whilst stationary), seems to capture something more of the *style* of cliché, despite the fact that, thankfully, it hasn't become a widely circulated statement.

Leaving simple repetition aside, then, we might go further and note that this 'style' of cliché involves non-sense of some kind or other. There certainly seems to be a way in which cliché limits or adjusts the literal sense that a phrase might have were it not a cliché. For example, the assertion that, "there are no easy games in this competition," might well flag-up the prestige of a particular tournament were it not for the fact that footballing pundits and professionals alike are inclined to make it, and are *known* to make it, when speaking of games in pretty much every competition—which rather negates the force of the claim in any given circumstance.

Think also of that (frankly ungrammatical) bastion of post-match praise, "the boy done good." Nonsense it may be, with all the predictability of a Cristiano Ronaldo step-over, but the fact remains that a footballing cliché such as this *is* nonetheless meaningful and totemic— not least because its forms a discursive backbone to the expert analysis of football pundits on TV and radio the world over. In other words, there is a difference between an individual such as Alan Shearer, in his capacity as expert analyst on *Match of the Day*, declaring that in order to win, a team needs to "score more goals than the other side," and the same sentiment echoed by Mr. A. Random-Fan in a pub discussion. In the hands of a known expert, cliché is (at least partially) lifted above the banality of repetition: it endows its user with an overriding authority for describing the game, and, in turn, the same clichéd words can become meaningful as expertise. This complicates the matter of what actually constitutes a footballing cliché further still: if the identity of the speaker functions as a modifier on whether a potentially clichéd phrase is hearable as a cliché at all as opposed to, say, "expert knowledge," then we are forced to ask whether "cliché" is really a property of the actual words spoken, the speaker who speaks them, the context of their invocation, or the interaction between all of these.

Thus perhaps the question, "What is a football cliché?"—while strong on paper—is likely to supply us with more problems than solutions. A better line of inquiry, and one which enables us to consider both Gadamer and Wittgenstein's views on meaning, would instead be, "What *makes* a football cliché hearably so? What differentiates 'meaningful' or 'authoritative' use of language from mere lazy or banal cliché?"

Gadamer's Game of Two Halves

Any attempt to explain the off-side rule to the uninitiated will rapidly reveal that understanding does not take place in a vacuum. Much in a similar way, the approach to language taken by our first expert philosophy pundit, Hans-Georg Gadamer, suggests that we cannot understand the world without a ready-made "horizon" of meaning. For Gadamer, we do not simply arrive at an object of interpretation—be it a text, person, delightfully executed through-ball, or whatever—from nowhere. Rather, we are bound to a tradition of understanding which enables interpretation to begin. Such a situated-ness provides us with an "horizon" for understanding. This horizon is a constantly changing frame of reference, shaped and moved by our own situation in the world—our experiences, for example, or our place in history.

This means that the act of understanding is to approach a situation with a set of pre-conceived notions, or as Gadamer calls them, "prejudices." He is keen to point out that the term "prejudice" is used here in the good sense, rather than the more popular bad sense of the word. For example, a good prejudice would be that I know West Ham wear claret and blue, I see you in those colours, and so I begin our conversation with the prejudicial idea already in place that you may well support West Ham; whatever you say I will likely understand on those terms.

A less informative prejudice would be that I see you in West Ham colours, I presume your intelligence to be lacking and your taste nonexistent, and I promptly give up on all hope of conversing in anything other than grunts and impolite hand gestures. The latter is "bad" because it closes, rather than enables, our open-ness to other horizons of meaning. The key point is that, in the act of understanding a phrase, text, or event, we are able to adapt and develop our prejudices in terms of the object of understanding. Our interpretation of the world is, for Gadamer, much like the structure of a dialogue which runs back and forth between the interpreter, situated within the horizon of their contemporary culture, and the event, situated within the horizon of its occurrence. We understand, not by absorbing the event into our horizon (so it means whatever we want it to mean), or surrendering our own to its (so we deny our own situatedness), but rather by "fusing" the two horizons, and in doing so, enlarging them. There is no meaning outside of this fusion of horizons: the cohesion of the dialogue (or "good will"—the assumption that there is understanding to be had between the two) creates the conditions on which we accept certain terms and meaningful and others as meaningless.

How would this account of meaning explain football clichés? Clearly, if our knowledge of what a cliché is comes from stereotyping or repetition, then it would form part of our interpretative horizon. This means that it is not the case that cliché gets in the way of meaning, or confounds our understanding of the game. Rather, along with other aspects of our interpretative horizons such as knowing the rules of the game, recognising player's movements as well-played, and so on, cliché forms the very grounds on which we understand the game. It's not that cliché will tell us anything new about the on-field action, but rather that it enables any such new knowledge, by marking out the old. As an example, consider Ian Holloway's brave attempt to answer a post-match question about an "ugly" win against Chesterfield in 2004 without resorting to cliché, and instead utilising metaphor:

To put it in gentleman's terms if you've been out for a night and you're look-ing for a young lady and you pull one, some weeks they're good looking and some weeks they're not the best. Our performance today would have been not the best looking bird but at least we got her in the taxi. She weren't the best looking lady we ended up taking home but she was very pleasant and very nice, so thanks very much, let's have a coffee.

The result was a rather amused bafflement on behalf of everybody, and, whatever other reasons there were for this, at least one was the fact that Holloway had clearly acted so far outside of the horizon of expectation, the cohesion of our understanding was disrupted.

Setting Gadamer's Stall Out: Cynical Challenges

Take, for example, Paul Scholes being red-carded for a characteristically physical two-footed challenge at Old Trafford. Certain home fans (tired from their long journey up the M1) would perhaps see it as "not a foul at all." They would, of course, be remaining firmly within the boundaries of their own horizon, seeing the world as they wish to see it, and thus not really "understanding," certainly not in Gadamer's sense. The "under-standing" fans, instead, engage with the event dialogically: fusing their horizon (which includes certain presuppositions over the superiority of their team) with that of the event (where this is challenged), they may well conclude that the tackle was simply "mistimed," the red card itself as "harsh," and its application as evidence of the referee's anti-United leanings.

The same applies when, later that night on *Match of the Day*, pundit and former Liverpool defender Alan Hansen describes the challenge as "cynical." A watching Manchester United supporter may well be more inclined to dismiss this as the tatty cliché of a career Liverpool fan than a piece of objective expert analysis. The accuracy of the description—if it can ever be accurate to attribute "cynicism" to a movement of one's legs in any statement other than a cliché—is determined in part by the standpoint from which one interprets. There is nothing outside of inter-pretation to appeal to. Were Hansen to describe the same event as, "a touch of typical over-exuberance," however, the same viewer may both interpret this as surprisingly unbiased analysis and adjust the standing of Hansen within their interpretative horizon accordingly.

In this sense, our idea of what a cliché is will be already in place, based on our prior experiences and fluctuating horizons, before we encounter it. It forms part of our tradition, which constitutes us as understanding subjects. The "good will" of the dialogue explains the 'non-serious' affirmation of the meaningless cliché as meaningful. Gadamer's use of "horizon" and "prejudice" turns away from the rather simplistic and more traditional notion that we understand every event in and by itself, and as such prejudice is something to be gotten rid of. In its place, Gadamer offers us a way of understanding how cliché not only affirms our knowledge of the game, but enables us to build on such an understanding. Cliché, at first, appears to constitute just such a horizon, which enables us to understand the game through the same necessary familiarity within any act of understanding.

But That Wittgenstein, He's Tough to Defend Against . . .

This approach, however, does have limits. Rather than express the meaningfulness of cliché to understanding football, it would seem rather that Gadamer's philosophy aligns cliché with the banal. In other words, there's a hole in the defence—it does not account for the specific purpose of the footballer's cliché.

Threading an incisive through ball through this is Ludwig Wittgenstein's assertion that, at the end of the day, the actual words we say (and what we intend them to mean) do not really matter so much as the differences those words make in the social world we inhabit. In short, the significance of a word, or phrase—or any other form of linguistic or physical action for that matter—is *only* definable in terms of what it does. To this extent, a phrase cannot be regarded a cliché until it does the job of a cliché in the practical context of its speaking any more than a firmly-uttered sentence is functionally a 'command' until someone actually obeys it.

Think of our example of the red card at Old Trafford. Once the tackle has been made, and the red card shown, no amount of expert rumination in the commentary box on whether it was "actually" a foul or not will alter the trajectory of that game. Nor will the specific intentions of the offending player as the challenge is made. The manner in which the referee interprets the action and intent, however, makes all the difference; if the challenge is taken by the referee to be a red card offence, then one team will then have to see out the remainder of the game without a full complement of players regardless of what pundits, fans or managers think. In short, the meaning of any such action is determined by what it does *in the game*.

Wittgenstein himself argues that when one learns a language, one learns to play a "language-game". A language-game is a "form of life"—

a way of being—and, like any other game (even football), is governed by rules. These rules are highly flexible, and relate to the functions that words can perform (asking, accusing, commanding, and the like) and also the activities with which linguistic actions are "interwoven" (answering, admitting-denying, obeying, and so on).

None of this is in any way innate; in order for people to make mutual sense, and therefore for social life to work at all, people require practical, first-hand training in the game. The rules in turn rest on upon shared, unspoken presumptions that people hold in common. These are not opinions, or matters of choice. They are the truths known, and held to be immutable by players of the game, and on the bedrock of which opinions and discussions are built. That Bobby Moore was "a great player" remains an opinion, no matter how easy it is to agree with. That Bobby Moore was "a footballer," meanwhile, is a foundational truth necessarily shared by all those acculturated in the language-game of English football. Failure to recognize this truth would inevitably disrupt any claim to broader footballing competence in a discussion where Bobby Moore himself became relevant.

Forms of life are, thus, learned in the doing. The language of football is learned through talking and reading about football, and listening to others talk about football. Common truths are peculiar to (fan) groups, given words can have a variety of meanings in different contexts and there are also countless, fluid types of phrase which serve as vehicles for interaction. This is why it's virtually impossible to seem expert in a second-language by simply learning the grammars and vocabulary from a book, and very difficult to sustain a convincing pub conversation on the current English Premiership season by simply knowing facts and figures.

Particular meaning in any language-game is always bound-up in such cultural, regional and contextual complexities as "manners," "irony," "common knowledge," and so forth. Meaning in the everyday language of football is no different, always being achieved through particular, and sometimes specialised, idioms. You may well favor the assertion that football is "a symmetrically dichotomised competitive physical practice," when making your point, but your friends in the Dog and Duck might better understand, "a game of two halves." Then again they might not. You won't really know until you try.

Wittgenstein: Taking It One Game at a Time

So, we would ask, how does this help understand the place and significance of football's clichés? A good place to start might well be

Wittgenstein's critique of James George Frazer's *The Golden Bough*, a famous anthropological study of ritualistic ceremonies in "primitive" tribes. Frazer argues the rationalistic line that since many such rituals (fundamentally) project an impossible cause-effect (for example, that a rain dance will make it rain), the thinking behind them can be regarded as neither logical nor comprehensible but is instead simply the mechanical outcome of false beliefs and pseudo-science. To this extent, Frazer essentially claims that a ritual such as a rain dance is itself a kind of cliché, an action that is unthinkingly and recurrently reproduced, and imbued with a unified (and largely nonsensical) meaning to practitioner and audience alike—"let's make it rain."

Wittgenstein savaged this perspective with some vigor, claiming that it completely missed the expressive-symbolic point of such human activity. Practitioners of rain dances are not generally inclined to perform them in isolation, or outside of the rainy season. Equally, to take a potentially 'clichéd' action from the world of football, we would venture that today's footballers rarely kiss the badges on their shirts without an audience, outside of the context of a goal celebration (or other equally positive moment), or in the genuine expectation of a definable impact on the scoreline.

Badge-kissing, like rain-dancing, can and should be understood as part of a form of life, fully intelligible to others who share it. But, from a Wittgensteinian perspective, we can take this point a little further still. Kissing a badge can both foreground the importance of the symbol itself as an object of collective esteem, and also signal one's own allegiance to it. Moreover, the gesture would likely have rather greater contextual significance to fans were it known that the player's future at the club is uncertain, though not mechanically so. What might be interpreted as a sincere expression of loyalty can also be read as a cheap and clichéd attempt by the player to win the fans' favour while concurrently trying to find a different club with a more personally profitable wage-structure—the exact opposite of loyalty.

From a Wittgensteinian perspective, no action has, in itself, a predefinable essence. It is what it does on the day, as part of a broader web of similarly meaningful actions. For example, is the player who kisses his badge cheered or booed, or even ignored? The ultimate, contextual meaning of the act—be that "an expression of loyalty" or "a self-serving cliché"—only ossifies in the ways that it alters that context. This is the way that, for Wittgenstein, meaning works in "real life"; people (other than philosophers of language, perhaps) are not really concerned, in the course of their everyday routines, with trying to find idealised and universal meanings. They want to know what the materials in front of them—words, phrases and gestures—are specifically about, which of the range of possible interpretations works best in-that-case. This requires that they take things one game, one context, at a time. This renders problematic a Gadamerian understanding of any action—such as Alan Hansen claiming that a Paul Scholes challenge was "cynical"—as predeterminably clichéd *or* banal. For Wittgenstein, specific meaning is located in practices of talking, writing and gesturing themselves, not in a 'horizon'.

A Funny Old Game

While we've mentioned the differences between Gadamer and Wittgenstein, there are also many convergences between the philosophical approaches of the two (there are, after all no easy games at this level). Foremost of these is that both treat language as a chiefly *expressive* medium—something in and through which meaning is actively created and modified—rather than a *designative* one, from which point of view we might be currently more concerned with analysing the truth of a football cliché against the real world situation to which it has been applied.

Designatively speaking, football is indeed a game of two halves. No contest. Unless, of course, the match is abandoned at half time. Or there's extra time. And then the analysis kind of swings on whether we are using "half" to describe a literal fifty percent of the game, or a forty-five-minute period of play. And a particular game of football, or football in general. All of which are interesting matters, but none of which help us get any closer to understanding the core issues pertaining to football clichés themselves.

Both Gadamer and Wittgenstein are relatively relaxed about the rules of understanding, insofar as they correspond to their general models of meaning: for Gadamer, the dialogical fusion of horizons, for Wittgenstein the moves in the language game. When Alan Shearer declares that the trailing team "needs to score more goals," neither approach fixes the meaning of cliché rigidly to, for example, Shearer's intention, or to the audience's reception. How one reaches the meaning of expression, for both, is based on an interactive sense of play, within the broad confines of either dialogical fusion or language game.

Core to Gadamer's whole analysis is the idea of horizon as a prejudice which informs any interpretation of the world: a historical, cultural, cognitive frame of reference (albeit a flexible one) that an individual carries like a constantly-revised encyclopaedia. If the "Recognised Football Clichés" page contains the expressions, "a game of two halves," and, "The boy done good," then these phrases can be understood as being clichés when uttered in the context of all things football.

This notion, that that an expression has the status of "a cliché" prior to its actual, practical utterance, is the key point at which the philosophies of Gadamer and Wittgenstein begin to diverge. For Gadamer, the meaning of cliché is effectively pre-established. When we hear claims such as "They gave 110%," or "He literally drove a bus through the defence," we do not immediately question our understanding of mathematics or how one fits a double-decker through the player's tunnel. Rather, the nonsense of each phrase establishes a certain commonality which enables understanding to happen. If we were to take "110%" as a genuine mathematical puzzle, rather than an expression of footballing effort, we would clearly not be partaking in the same dialogue as the football pundit, and a fusion of horizons would be unlikely to emerge.

For Wittgenstein, meanwhile, the self-same phrases may be heard and understood in a range of different ways, depending on their contextual uses: as jokes, perhaps (if deployed with a smirk, and invoking a laugh, it is difficult to uphold an interpretation of the familiar expression as simple lazy language-use), as universal tools for description or, indeed, as banalities or clichés. What a phrase means is what it does, and what it does is only evident in the differences it makes after the fact. Indeed, and to these ends, we may well wish to look at the function of labelling the very phrase, "they gave 110%," as banal or clichéd at all; these words are themselves parts of a language-game, largely used as accusations—to diminish the value of what has been said or the authority of the person who said it.

So who describes a familiar football phrase as a cliché? And when? And to what ends? You'll rarely see the term "cliché" used in an academic paper outside of a narrative on declining standards of language. If you're looking for an explanation of why clichés are clichés, this approach probably isn't very satisfactory. But as Wittgenstein himself said, people often get hung up on the need for an all-encompassing explanation of why things are, when the real solution is a description of how they work. It seems that, in this sense, the philosophy of language can indeed be a "funny old game."

The First Team

1 *Andrea Baldini* (ITA) Goalkeeper

Andrea is a PhD student at Temple University and at the Università degli Studi di Siena (Siena, Italy), where he also earned his BA in Philosophy in 2006. His areas of competence are Philosophy of Arts and Aesthetics, with a specialization in the Philosophy of Music. Born in Tuscany, he grew up here and there in North-Central Italy. When he is not busy cursing for a terrible game played by the four-time World Champion team, you can hear him screaming: *Milan, Milan, solo con teee*!

3 *Andrea Borghini* (ITA) Forward

Andrea, who holds a PhD from Columbia University (2007) and a BA from Università di Firenze, Italy (2000), is currently an Assistant Professor in the Philosophy Department at the College of the Holy Cross. His main research areas are Metaphysics, Philosophy of Science, Early Modern Philosophy, and philosophical issues related to food. Born and raised in central Tuscany, he is known to support nearly all the teams in the area: from ACF Fiorentina, Empoli FC, and AS Livorno to AC Pisa, FC Esperia Viareggio and Cuoiovaldarno Romaiano FC— which most Tuscans regard as a downright inconsistency.

14 *Steffen Borge* (NOR) Forward

Steffen plays striker for and is a co-owner of TPWB Fuzzball. TPWB Fuzzball is renowned for their possession-oriented football where the emphasis is on breakdowns and direct play, and strikers are known as first defenders. He is a product of IL Skrim with whom he has won Heddal Cup and been runners-up in Kretsmesterskapet i Buskerud. Borge is a card carrying member of Liverpool FC Supporters Club Scandinavian Branch, he also supports Vålerenga Fotball in Norway and Club León in Mexico. Borge's football-philosophical views have been shaped by the hard-nosed no-nonsense school of TPWB Fuzzball and that motley crew of internationals that played football with Borge in the quad every Friday afternoon at Syracuse University. Borge currently works at the Department of Philosophy at the University of Tromsø, Norway.

5 *Danielle Sarver Coombs* (USA) Midfielder

Danielle, assistant professor in the School of Journalism and Mass Communi-cation at Kent State University, has spent a lifetime suffering as a fan of the Cleveland Browns. Blind loyalty to the team led her to follow owner Randy Lerner on his new adventure as a Barclays Premier League owner. In about a year, Danielle traveled to England over fourteen times to cheer on the successes of the mighty claret and blue of the Aston Villa Football Club. She now spends her time recruiting other Americans to the fold.

26 *Tony Coumoundouros* (CYP) Defender

Tony is Assistant Professor of Philosophy at Adrian College in Michigan. He was born in Cyprus where soccer is the only sport and he could kick a ball before he could do anything else. His students know he is an Arsenal fan and avoid wearing Manchester United jerseys during class. He is interested in ancient philosophy, ethics, and political philosophy. When he's not philosophizing, teaching, or spending time with family, he either watches, plays, or dreams about playing soccer. He likes to believe that he is an average soccer player although his wife tells him that he is a spectacular one.

12 *Jonathan Crowe* (AUS) Forward

Jonathan is a Senior Lecturer in the T.C. Beirne School of Law at the University of Queensland in Brisbane, Australia. He is the author of *Legal Theory* (2009) and has published widely on the relationship between law and ethics. His chapter draws on ten years of experience as a referee of amateur football, which afforded ample opportunity to reflect upon the human condition. He wrote his contribution with a badly sprained ankle, sustained while playing in a seven-a-side competition against a bunch of his students. He's getting too old for that sort of thing.

16 *Víctor Durà-Vilà* (ESP) Forward

Víctor was born in Valencia but had the good sense to side with his mum's family (from Barcelona) when it came to football loyalties. He was an FC Barcelona supporter from a very early age in an environment that was rather adverse, to put it very mildly indeed, to FC Barcelona supporters. That was long before he knew about aesthetics and also before, through Johan Cruyff's leadership, FC Barcelona became the modern paradigmatic repository of the aesthetic values that are so in tune with Víctor's own, football-independent views. Apart from football, he developed his interests in science through reading and a degree in chemistry (MSci, Imperial College London), but later in life turned to philosophical matters by way of an MA and a PhD in philosophy (King's College London). His research is devoted these days in a tri-partite manner to philosophy of science (quantum mechanics), metaphysics (personal identity and persistence of objects through time) and aesthetics (performing arts, art and morality, creativity). It is the latter subject that gives him the opportunity to marry his philosophical interests with his own life-long devotion to music, dance, literature, and the arts in general.

19 *Tim Elcombe* (CAN) Midfielder

Tim's soccer career peaked in the mid-1980s as a midfielder for the Cambridge (Ontario) soccer club. After five consecutive championship seasons, countless uphill conditioning sprints, and repeated chants of "When in doubt, put it out!",

Tim retired in his prime at age fourteen. In a truly Canadian soccer moment, he once faked an injury to make it to hockey practice on time. Now Tim's involvement in soccer focuses on watching matches on television (or in beer gardens in Europe during the 2006 World Cup), critiquing soccer practices taking place behind his house, and sharpening his Manchester United pencil with his Manchester United pencil sharpener in honor of his grandmother. He currently serves as an assistant professor of Kinesiology and Physical Education at Wilfrid Laurier University (Waterloo, Canada). Tim's research focuses on philosophical issues related to sport and the connections between human movement and culture at-large.

25 *Yuval Eylon* (ISR) Midfielder

Yuval's long-lasting affair with football began on the very day his chosen team, Hapoel Jerusalem, yielded (4–1) its status as Jerusalem's leading club to local rivals Beitar, and began its descent to lower-division obscurity. The following year marked Eylon's initial introduction to Philosophy. On the eve of the 1974 World Cup final between Germany and The Netherlands, Israeli Television interviewed fans who were asked two questions: "Who would you like to win?" and "Who do you believe will win?" One fan stood out, wishing that The Netherlands would win, but predicting (alas correctly) that Germany would prevail. The possibility of thus separating wish from prediction perplexed the young Eylon. From here it was a mere thirty years to a PhD in Philosophy. A founding shareholder of fan-owned Hapoel Katamon Jerusalem (the "real" Hapoel Jerusalem), Eylon's research, confined to the brief intermissions between Champions League matches, focuses on Ethics and Analytic Philosophy. Eylon is currently a senior lecturer at The Open University of Israel in the Department of History, Philosophy, and Judaic Studies.

17 *John Foster* (ENG) Midfielder

An eleven-year old John Foster watched Fulham nick a draw against Exeter on Boxing Day 1996. He has been an irregular presence at Craven Cottage ever since. He received his BA in Philosophy and Modern History from Queen's University, Belfast, and in 2010 will begin an MA in Cultural and Intellectual History at the Warburg Institute in London. He has written for the Football Italia and Back of the Net websites, and for the *Journal of the Philosophy of History*. His day job is in the uncluttered field of philosophy-themed Mediterranean cruising. John's on-pitch career as a dainty pivote has been on hiatus since he unaccountably attempted to control a lofted pass with his crotch.

4 *Tom Grimwood* (ENG) Forward

Tom teaches Philosophy and Religious Studies at Lancaster University, England. His research deals with the philosophy of interpretation, in particular the productive value of ambiguity, and he has written articles concerning this on subjects as diverse as medieval anorexia, Simone de Beauvoir, Friedrich Nietzsche, and *The Hobbit*. He grew up in Southampton watching the Saints, and is thus at a loss as to why his argument that the existence of God is proved by Matt Le Tissier is yet to be academically accepted.

31 *Todd Hester* (USA) Defender

Todd is a PhD student in the Department of Computer Science at the University of Texas at Austin. His research focuses on robot soccer and reinforcement learning. He received his BS in Computer Engineering at Northeastern University in 2005 and has worked for the Air Force Research Laboratory, Sun Microsystems, Motorola, and Spaulding Rehabilitation Hospital. He also currently teaches robotics to elementary school students at a local school in Austin.

28 *Amir Horowitz* (ISR) Forward

"Amir Horowitz, the ten-year-old mighty center-forward of Maccabi Netanya's (Israel) children's team, scored a hat-trick in his team's 13–0 trouncing of Hapoel Ra'anana." Unfortunately, nobody bothered to publish this sensational bit of sporting news. Disillusioned, Horowitz switched to track and field, and specialized in the high jump. But again, nobody published this exciting move, let alone took notice of his soaring achievements. Horowitz got the hint, and switched again, this time to the less physically demanding field of Philosophy. His research focuses on philosophy of mind and philosophy of language. Horowitz is currently an associate professor at The Open University of Israel, a non-footballing organization located in Ra'anana (a.k.a. "city of 0–13").

2 *Paul Hoyningen-Huene* (GER) Defender

From 1997, Paul Hoyningen-Huene has been Professor of Ethics of Science and the founding director of the Center for Philosophy and Ethics of Science at the Leibniz University of Hannover, Germany. Although he is not a genuine football fan, his son dragged him into watching many matches with him during the 2002 World Cup. An alienation effect at one of the matches made him think about what the origin of the fascination of football might be.

33 *Jesús M. Ilundáin-Agurruza* (ESP) Goalkeeper

Born in Pamplona, Spain, Jesús M. Ilundáin-Agurruza's early years were spent in different cities as the family moved following his father's exploits in the Spanish *Liga* before returning to the city famous for the running of the bulls. Recess games at school soon made patent his footballing limitations regardless of position—but he gained an appreciation for what it takes to play beautifully. The desire to learn Shakespeare's tongue brought him to the US for his undergraduate and graduate education, which culminated with his PhD from the University of Illinois at Urbana-Champaign. He's currently Assistant Professor of Philosophy at Linfield

College. Areas of philosophic interest cover both sides of the pitch and transcend its boundaries with interests in: philosophy of sport, aesthetics, comparative philosophy (mainly Taoism and Zen Buddhism), philosophy in literature, and metaphysics. He has published chapters in edited books and articles in journals on sports and risk, the running of the bulls, football (soccer), sport and childhood, among others. Still a klutz with the ball, he prefers to watch beautiful football and race bicycles (which requires much less coordination).

21 *Rob Imre* (HUN) Midfielder

Rob is a political philosopher who was regaled with tales of the great soccer players of the 1950s from his parents' generation. Having witnessed the establishment of a deep loyalty to Canada from the Hungarian émigré community, Rob was always acutely aware of the politics of sport. The beautiful game was not just that, but it was also a contest for truth and goodness much more so than mere victories. When that failed or succeeded, people rewarded virtue with loyalty. These days he lives and works in Australia, at the University of Newcastle and has been accused of considering himself more of a Hungarian than Canadian despite the fact that his 'soil' is Canada.

20 *Matthew A. Kent* (USA) Defender

Matthew fell in love with kicking a ball even before he learned to walk. He became a soccer fan soon afterward, following the Detroit Express of the NASL. West Germany's tragic defeat in the 1982 World Cup final brought him to tears. Matthew played two years at Bishop Foley High School (Madison Heights, Michigan) and three years at Christendom College (Front Royal, Virginia). He hasn't played soccer formally since entering graduate school. But at least he received a PhD in philosophy from Fordham University in 2006. In 2003 Matthew began teaching at the University of St. Thomas (St. Paul, Minnesota). His wife Kristen is the best woman in the world. They live in central Minnesota with their precious baby girl, Mary. Above all, Matthew considers himself very blessed to be a Traditional Catholic.

10 *David Kilpatrick* (USA) Forward

David is Associate Professor in the Humanities Department at Mercy College. He is Commisioner of AYSO Region 324, President of ADFH United, serves on the boards of Arsenal America and the Nietzche Circle, and sings in support of the New York Red Bulls.

35 *Andre Krnac* (CAN) Midfielder

Andre is currently a graduate student at University of Louvain in Belgium at the HIW, focusing on Kierkegaard and Hegel. When not buried by a mound of texts he follows Valencia CF in Spain.

22 *Andrew Lambert* (ENG) Midfielder

Andrew is a philosophy instructor, football fan and journalist, with interests in ethics and Everton football club. Currently completing his doctorate in philosophy at the University of Hawaii, Andrew has been involved with media coverage of professional football since 2002. Working with FIFA and other sports organisations, he has covered football events such as the FIFA World Cup and the football competitions of the Olympic and Asian Games. His work has also appeared on various football websites.

11 *Nelson Lammoglia* (COL) Forward

Nelson developed enthusiastic feelings to anything that comes in red colors. This is why he is a diehard fan of both America de Cali Football Club and Manchester United. (Both teams are well-known as the "Red Devils.") But Nelson is also a philosophy hooligan. His principal interests in this area are related to ethics and aesthetics. For instance he took the notion of autopoiesis of Luhmann and linked it with ethics discussions posed by Wittgenstein and Foucault in order to propose a new way for observing systems called Autoethospoiesis. Nelson is a professor in the Department of Industrial Engineering at Universidad de los Andes, Colombia.

23 *Mohammed Majeed* (GHA) Forward

Mohammed is a lecturer in Philosophy at the University of Ghana with a very wide teaching experience at the undergraduate level. He has taught courses such as African Philosophy, Rationalism, and Logic and Critical Thinking. In spite of a busy life as an academic, he has always followed football with passion. He played for colts clubs and was part of his school football teams with the exception of the advanced levels of his education where academic pursuit got the better of his playing life. He was a very fast and intelligent striker, and his neighbourhood peers later likened him to Jurgen Klinsmann, the former prolific striker of Germany. He is an ardent supporter of the Ghanaian Premiership club Ashgold, the national team of Ghana (the Black Stars) and AC Milan of Italy.

7 *Kirk McDermid* (CAN) Defender

Kirk is a product of Canadian youth soccer and Arsenal broadcasts. He used to play center-half in partnership with his twin brother to confuse attackers; today he has no fixed position, playing the beer league version of Total Football. His research is in the philosophy of science, with articles in diverse journals such as *Physics Letters* and *Religious Studies*. He is currently an assistant professor of philosophy at Montclair State University in New Jersey.

42 *Paul Miller* (ENG) Goalkeeper

Paul isn't a philosopher at all. He's a social psychologist. His specialist areas of Conversation Analysis and Discursive Psychology do, however, bring him into regular contact with ordinary language philosophy, and he has a long-standing interest in the work of Wittgenstein. He works as a senior lecturer at the University of Cumbria, England, and his two substantive fields of research interest are sports on the one hand, and clinical depression on the other. As a lifelong supporter of West Ham United FC, he is currently considering a study of his fellow Irons fans. This, he believes, should provide an opportunity to combine the two concerns quite neatly.

15 *Stephen Minister* (USA) Midfielder

Stephen is an assistant professor of philosophy at Augustana College in Sioux Falls, South Dakota. His areas of expertise are nineteenth- and twentieth-century European thought, philosophy of religion, and ethics. Stephen gets a run-out each week in the Sioux Falls Adult Soccer League. He recently moved to Team SoccerWorld on a Bosman free transfer after FC Flying Monkeys deemed him surplus to requirements. In his younger days, Minister fancied himself in the mold of Thierry Henry, but as he has gotten older and defenders have gotten faster, he has reshaped his game along the lines of a Cesc Fàbregas.

34 *A. Minh Nguyen* (VIE) Defender

Minh is Associate Professor of Philosophy at Eastern Kentucky University. As a child, he played soccer barefoot on many a dirt road in Vietnam. Despite receiving a lot of playing time, he was rubbish then and is rubbish now at soccer. Still playing at forty-two, he has many scars but no trophies. He's grateful to Chelsea Amburgey and Charles Davis for including him in the EKU Honors Program Intramural Soccer Team, and to Thomas Hall and Charles Marz for allowing him to practice with his sixth-grade daughter's soccer team at Saint Mark's Catholic School in Richmond, Kentucky. An ardent fan of FC Barcelona and the Brazil National Team, he needs a compendium of superlatives to describe Ronaldinho Gaúcho, a legendary playmaker for both.

8 *Robert Northcott* (ENG) Midfielder

Robert is an assistant professor of philosophy at the University of Missouri-St Louis. He has published widely on philosophy of science and causal explanation. He has also played and watched far too much football. These days, he's given up dreaming of being a top player, but each time he watches on TV he dreams he could be a top pundit.

80 *Camilo Olaya* (COL) Midfielder

Camilo has been a soccer fan since he was a six-year-old, when his father took him for the first time to a soccer match of *Millonarios Football Club*—which became his beloved soccer team. Like almost any Colombian, soccer runs through his veins. In addition, he finds in philosophy the way to have a joyful life. He also finds in computer simulation the way to understand the complex world. As a natural result, he is developing a line of research on what can be called the "philosophy of computer simulation." He has also published various works on epistemology. Camilo is Assistant Professor in the Department of Industrial Engineering at Universidad de los Andes, Colombia.

18 *Anne C. Osborne* (USA) Defender

Anne, an associate professor and Associate Dean in Mass Communication at Louisiana State University, owns a complete set of Aston Villa winter wear, including hat, scarf, gloves and fleece. As winter rarely appears in Louisiana, these items go unused except during trips to Birmingham, England, to watch the Villa. While following her team, she enjoys pondering the intersections of philosophy, culture. and commerce.

54 *Michael Quinlan* (AUS) Midfielder

Michael is a Postdoctoral Fellow in the Department of Computer Science at the University of Texas at Austin with a research focus on machine learning techniques applied to robots. He was rewarded his PhD in 2006 from the University of Newcastle (Australia) where he continued working as a Postdoc before moving to Texas. He has competed in eight RoboCup events including using legged robots and has enjoyed playing competitive basketball, hockey, and soccer since early childhood.

36 *David Edward Rose* (ENG) Midfielder

David is a lifelong supporter of Aston Villa and once a season ticket holder for the non-league side Gloucester City FC when they played in the esoteric and not exotic Beazer Homes Premier League. That was his dad's fault who still goes along most Saturdays. Now, David lives in Newcastle (and works in Philosophy at Newcastle University) so he often sits amongst the geordies at St James's Park wisely keeping his own counsel most of the time. None of his academic friends are able to discuss football intelligently or articulately. They just don't like it. His children are half-Italian and, when they all play footie in the garden, David has noticed that the kids are innately predisposed to dive, defend deep, and they often beat him one-nil with a late, controversial goal. In his spare time, David writes on ethics, Hegel, action, and free will.

30 *Ben Saunders* (ENG) Defender

Ben is a Departmental Lecturer in Philosophy at the University of Oxford, where he completed his doctorate on the possible use of lotteries in democratic politics. He supports Liverpool FC and plays football (badly) with a bunch of other philosophers—it's just like Monty Python. . . .

13 *Peter Stone* (USA) Midfielder

Peter is an Alfred P. Sloan Research Fellow, Guggenheim Fellow, Fulbright Scholar, and Associate Professor in the Department of Computer Science at the University of Texas at Austin. He received his PhD in Computer Science in 1998 from Carnegie Mellon University. From 1999 to 2002 he was a Senior Technical Staff Member in the Artificial Intelligence Principles Research Department at AT&T Labs-Research. Peter's research interests include machine learning, multiagent systems, robotics, and e-commerce. In 2003, he won a CAREER award from the National Science Foundation for his research on learning agents in dynamic, collaborative, and adversarial multiagent environments. In 2004, he was named an ONR Young Investigator for his research on machine learning on physical robots. In 2007, he was awarded the prestigious IJCAI 2007 Computers and Thought award, given every two years to the top AI researcher under the age of thirty-five. Peter has played amateur soccer all of his life and has tried out for some professional teams. Even at the age of thirty-eight, he continues to delay his move to the over-thirty league, playing midfield on "Austin Villa" in the open premier league of the Austin Men's Soccer Association. He has been a leading member of the RoboCup initiative since its inception in the mid-1990s.

9 *Cesar R. Torres* (ARG) Forward

Cesar is Associate Professor in the Department of Kinesiology, Sport Studies and Physical Education at The College at Brockport, State University of New York. He received his early professional training in Argentina and obtained his Ph.D. from Penn State. A philosopher and historian of sport, he has published over thirty pieces in peer-reviewed journals and edited collections. Interested in the diffusion of sport philosophy in the Spanish-speaking world, he has edited *Niñez, deporte y actividad física: reflexiones filosóficas sobre una relación compleja* (2008) and co-edited *¿La pelota no dobla? Ensayos filosóficos en torno al fútbol* (2006). Since 2007, he has been on the *Journal of the Philosophy of Sport*'s editorial board. He is the reviews editor of *Soccer and Society* and a former member of the *International Journal of the History of Sport*'s international editorial board (1998–2004). Although a knee injury forced him to seriously ponder whether life without playing football is possible, he has recently enjoyed a glorious, if more sedate, comeback with his beloved childhood teammates.

38 *Kristof K. P. Vanhoutte* (BEL) Midfielder

Kristof holds a BA and MA in Philosophy from the Catholic University of Leuven, Belgium. He studied Spiritual Theology at the Pontifical University Gregoriana, Rome, obtained his PhD in Philosophy at the Pontifical University Antonianum, Rome, and recently was a Postdoctoral Research Fellow at the Institute for Advanced Studies in the Humanities (IASH) of the University of Edinburgh. While in Rome he developed an interest in Italian football and became a fan of Lazio Roma. Later, he had the good fortune to marry into an AS Roma family, so every derby he's the most hated person in the family; even more so when Lazio wins. For the rest of the year he's accepted as a Lazio fan, but just because he's a foreigner and thus not a true Lazio fan (because if he was one of "those" that could be grounds for a separation).

37 *Seth Vannatta* (USA) Defender

Seth is a doctoral candidate at Southern Illinois University Carbondale. His academic interests include legal, political, and moral philosophy in the American pragmatist tradition and phenomenology in the Continental tradition. He has also published and presented papers in the area of philosophy of sport. Seth played youth recreational soccer, competitive club soccer, high school varsity soccer, and adult league soccer. Summer soccer camps, watching the Oklahoma City Slickers professional team at Taft Stadium, and watching the 1982 World Cup on TV were formative elements in his soccer upbringing. Seth has also coached soccer at the recreational, junior high, junior varsity, and varsity levels for eleven years. He has never been and will never be a soccer ref.

24 *Luca Vargiu* (ITA) Midfielder

Luca teaches philosophy and history in the Italian secondary schools and collaborates with the Chair of Aesthetics at the University of Cagliari. At the same University he has taught various courses, including Aesthetics, Phenomenology of Styles, and History of Art Criticism. He has written papers and essays on aesthetics and art history, and won the Nuova Estetica 2009 prize given by the *Società Italiana d'Estetica*. He was born in Cagliari in 1970, the year in which the Cagliari Calcio won the Italian soccer championship (who remembers Gigi Riva?). The coach of that team, Manlio Scopigno, was nicknamed "the philosopher."

32 *David Wall* (ENG) Defender

David is a Lecturer in Philosophy at the University of Northampton, England. His research is focused in philosophy of mind, epistemology, and moral psychology, with special interests in desire, motivation, self-knowledge, and self-deception, and he has published scholarly articles in these fields. These research interests are uncannily reflective of his (long-finished) playing career in school and youth-league elevens. David remembers himself as a marauding full-back in the mould of Roberto Carlos, playing with passion and always demanding the ball on the overlap. His former team-mates, on the other-hand explain this desire in terms of their reluctance to pass to him and insist that he is deceiving himself if he thinks he wasn't put at the back to minimise the damage he could do to his own side.

27 *Edward Winters* (ENG) Midfielder

Edward studied Painting at Portsmouth Polytechnic and subsequently at The Slade School before attending Birkbeck College London to read Philosophy. He completed his doctoral thesis, "Appreciating the Visual Arts," in the Department of Philosophy at University College London. For several years he was a senior lecturer in the School of Architecture at the University of Westminster. Widely published in aesthetics, he is a regular contributor to international conferences on the philosophy of art; and has written on the visual arts for a number of art and architectural periodicals. He co-edited, with Caroline van Eck, *Dealing With the Visual* (2005); and his latest book is *Aesthetics and Architecture* (2007). Edward is currently writing a book on painting as a contemporary art; and another on aesthetics and everyday life. His research interests are in Aesthetics, Philosophy of Mind, Wittgenstein, Architecture, Painting and Contemporary Art. He played wide on the right for the Old Kingsburians, The Slade All Stars and Tufnell Park Rangers. His most memorable goal was a thirty-yard chip over stranded goalkeeper Patrick Buckley. Alas, both were playing for Tufnell Park Rangers at the time.

29 *Roberto Zarama* (COL) Forward

Roberto is an expert in games. He is particularly fond of Wittgensteinian language games and von Foerster's second-order cybernetics. In addition, he has developed models for enhancing learning in human beings through playing. For him soccer is "just" a game. Roberto is an Associate Professor in the Department of Industrial Engineering at Universidad de los Andes, Colombia.

Ted Richards (USA) Coach

Ted has spent most of his life with his head in philosophy and his feet on the soccer pitch. He has a BS in Physics and a BA in Philosophy from Southern Methodist University, an MA in the History and Philosophy of Science from the University of Pittsburgh, and both an MA and a PhD in Philosophy from Boston University. Ted had a brief semi-pro career as a midfielder before returning to amateur ball, has refereed professional and collegiate games, and, at various times, has coached youth, ODP, high-school, and college teams. He is currently a Lecturer in Philosophy and trains with the Men's Soccer Club at the University of Tennessee.

Index